The Best of Hard Times

Gender, Culture, and Politics in the Middle East
miriam cooke, Simona Sharoni, and Suad Joseph, *Series Editors*

Select Titles in Gender, Culture, and Politics in the Middle East

For a full list of titles in this series,
visit https://press.syr.edu/supressbook-series
/gender-culture-and-politics-in-the-middle-east/.

The Best of Hard Times

Palestinian Refugee Masculinities in Lebanon

Gustavo Barbosa

Syracuse University Press

∞ The paper used in this publication meets the minimum requirements
of the American National Standard for Information Sciences—Permanence
of Paper for Printed Library Materials, ANSI Z39.48-1992.

For a listing of books published and distributed by Syracuse University Press,
visit https://press.syr.edu.

ISBN: 978-0-8156-3737-0 (hardcover)
          978-0-8156-3723-3 (paperback)
          978-0-8156-5524-4 (e-book)

Library of Congress Cataloging-in-Publication Data

Names: Barbosa, Gustavo (Associate researcher), author.
Title: The best of hard times : Palestinian refugee masculinities in Lebanon / Gustavo Barbosa.
Description: First edition. | Syracuse, New York : Syracuse University Press, [2022] | Series: Gender,
     culture, and politics in the Middle East | Includes bibliographical references and index. | Summary:
     "*The Best of Hard Times* asks how today's lads (*shabab*) from the Shatila Palestinian Refugee
     Camp in Beirut, come of age and display gender belonging, especially in comparison to the 'heroic
     trajectories' of an older generation"— Provided by publisher.
Identifiers: LCCN 2021000132 (print) | LCCN 2021000133 (ebook) | ISBN 9780815637370 (hardcover) |
     ISBN 9780815637233 (paperback) | ISBN 9780815655244 (ebook)
Subjects: LCSH: Refugees, Palestinian Arab—Lebanon—Social conditions. | Masculinity—Lebanon. |
     Shātīlā (Refugee camp)
Classification: LCC HV640.5.P36 B36 2021 (print) | LCC HV640.5.P36 (ebook) | DDC
     305.38/89274056925—dc23
LC record available at https://lccn.loc.gov/2021000132
LC ebook record available at https://lccn.loc.gov/2021000133

Manufactured in the United States of America

To Shatilans,
including Rosemary

It was the best of times, it was the worst of times, it was the age of wisdom, it was the age of foolishness, it was the epoch of belief, it was the epoch of incredulity, it was the season of Light, it was the season of Darkness, it was the spring of hope, it was the winter of despair, we had everything before us, we had nothing before us.

—Charles Dickens, *A Tale of Two Cities*

Contents

Illustrations

Figures

Tables

Charts

Acknowledgments

As I put the final touches to this manuscript, the world has come to a virtual halt, deaccelerated by the agency of a mindless body (and the reader will soon become acquainted with my reservations about "bodies," an elusive concept that has become somewhat hypertrophied in the recent anthropological and feminist literature): the new coronavirus. To my mind, what the current pandemic has exposed, above all, is just how much we all are deeply and inescapably connected. Many in the developed world may go on thinking that the conflicts in Africa and the Middle East, through which raw material is provided for their latest high-tech smartphones and petrol is produced for their splashy four-wheel-drive cars, have nothing to do with them. But beware: they do. Like the virus that concerns and affects us all, those conflicts will also eventually reach us and may turn our life upside down. Even before the current sanitary dystopia, those conflicts in Africa and the Middle East were already about us, too, on an ethical and political level even when we preferred to turn a blind eye to them.

Turning a blind eye has ceased to be an option, though, and the time has come to concentrate instead on what connects us all, for that should not be limited to the deathly virus only. This book argues for patterns that connect and for metonymic relations: between the author and the *shabāb*, lads, from the Shatila Palestinian refugee camp, between the *shabāb* and pigeons, between refugees and water, and the list could go on to include you as well, dear reader, and the *shabāb* or you and those Africans and Middle Easterners whose lives are so often engulfed by conflict and precarity.

As patterns inevitably connect us, any intellectual endeavor is necessarily a collective project—hence, a collaboration, illusions of authorship notwithstanding. Accordingly, I wish to name a number of people without whose help the research I undertook would simply not have been possible. Prominent among them are the Shatila *shabāb* and their fathers, the *fidā'iyyīn* (fighters), whose biographies populate the following pages. In the case of the *shabāb*, they began by giving me "a hard time." "A hard time" is the special treatment they reserve for researchers and others in an effort to make them realize that the refugee camp is not there just to fulfill their academic ambitions or other interests. After a while, however, they spared no effort to make me belong, as is duly discussed in one of the chapters. So if this research "is happening"—to make their vocabulary yet again mine—I owe it to them and their fathers. I thank them dearly, this time extending back to them a word that exists only in my native Portuguese and admits no easy translation into other languages: *saudades*.

During the earlier work that led to this book, Martha Mundy and Rosemary Sayigh also gave me "a hard time," but I know that ultimately this was for my own interest and out of intellectual respect and the belief that I could effectively respond to the challenges they made to my lines of reasoning. They guided me through the sometimes mysterious and hazardous waters of academia and managed to rid the coming pages of several inconsistencies and mistakes. The ones that may remain are my entire responsibility, of course.

Marcia Inhorn has also been a constant lodestar, helping me traverse those troubled waters. If this book has come to see the light, it is surely because of her unrelenting support for the project from its outset. Marcia's way of combining work and humanistic ethics, academic rigor and a genuine interest in the other—be they research participants or still maladroit younger colleagues like me—constitutes a model I hope to replicate.

The merits of the chapters here must also be shared with numerous other colleagues. Throughout my stay in Lebanon, I counted on the help of four research assistants, *shabāb* in different moments of their lives, who generously provided me with always enlightening commentary on whatever we observed together: Ibrahim Maarouf, Alladin Helou, Majid Belkiss, and Rabie Zaroura. My professors, colleagues, and friends at the London School of Economics and Political Science, the American University of Beirut, the Universidade Federal Fluminense, the Museu Nacional, the Brazilian consulate in Beirut, the Brazilian embassy in Damascus, and beyond helped in many ways: reading different versions of my chapters, checking information and making articles and books available to me, continuously engaging in critical exchange, and providing me with support on many levels. Although there are too many to name here (I have always struggled with the word count, my Latin-inspired loquaciousness often being something of a hindrance), I prefer to run the risk of committing injustices and mention some of them in no specific order: Tom Boylston, Monika Halkort, Samar Kanafani, Denis Regnier, Aristóteles Neto, Daniela Kraemer, Sally Shalabi, Tania Lima, Gabriel Banaggia, Marcio Goldman, Sylvain Perdigon, Andrey Petrichtche, Thaera Badran, Elizabeth Saleh, Rana Bashir, Elizabeth Frantz, Aziza Khalidi, Salah Salah, Cathrine Moe Thorleifsson, Gustavo Pacheco, Alessandra Vinhas, Agnes Hann, Nayana Subasinghe, Miranda Johansson, Alanna Cant, EJ Fang, Philip "Ejer Fakkhoura," Sisira Jinendra, Ghassan Abdallah, Ana Paola Gutierrez-Garza, Dina Makram Ebeid, Laleh Khalili, Michelle Obeid, Nefissa Naguib, Giovanni Bochi, Kimberly Chong, Helena Nassif, Francisco Souza, Indira Arumugan, Richard Saumarez Smith, Matt Wilde, Michael Hoffman, Sittna Quiroz, Roger Saghbini, Heather Dawson, Rola Badran, Michael Lambek, Hollis Moore, Yanina Hinrichsen, Martyn Wemyss, Xandra Lorenzo, Rose Nakad, Laura Bear, Guy Summers, Nadia Dropkin, Stephan Feuchtwang, Charles Stafford, Ana Maria Azevedo, Rayaar Farhat, Mateus Moraes, Simone Duarte, Mathjis Pelkmans, Rima Afifi, Awad Joumaa, Maria D'Ajuda de Oliveira, Bruce Miller, Jihad Makhoul, Dave Robinson, Jihane Sfeir, Benjamin Humphries, Jaber Abu Hawash, Diana Allan, Hala Abu Zaki, Leonardo Schiocchet, Zorana Milicevic, Marten Boekelo, Judy Shuttleworth, Sa'ed Atshan, Amanda Dias, Sari Hanafi, Nisrine Mansour, Tara Mahfoud, Ankur Datta, Suheil El-Natour, Daniel Meier, Nayla Homsi, Moisés Silva, Renato Sztutman, Paulo Gabriel Pinto, Luiz Eduardo Pedroso, Elisabeth Engebretsen, Sara Escata, Gisele Fonseca, Sergio Bianchi, Ali Kadri, Mari Norbakk, Julieta Falavina, Sarah Grosso, Nicolas Puig, Miriam Stock, Sarah Parkinson, Muzna Al-Masri, and Zina Sawaf (who corrected my English and, together with Antoine Badaoui, braved my eclectic transliteration of Arabic, making it conform to the *International Journal of Middle East Studies* system). David Rodgers copyedited the manuscript before it went to the press: also a Portuguese speaker, he managed to make my English readable without taming my rather iconoclastic use of the language. Annie Barva conducted the final review, sensitively and brilliantly so.

Peggy Solic, Kelly Balenske, Kay Steinmetz, Lisa Kuerbis, Meghan Cafarelli, and the whole team at Syracuse University Press made the process of reviewing and preparing this manuscript for publication a pleasure. The two anonymous reviewers provided me with several suggestions on how to enhance the manuscript, so any merits this book may have are theirs too.

To Maher Shehadeh, a talented graphic designer from Shatila, I give my thanks for the inspiring ideas and graphics that found their way onto the book cover, captured fantastically well by Syracuse's Fred Wellner for the final version. I am grateful as well to Hisham Ghuzlan, a photographer from the camp who was my partner in an ethnographic photography laboratory in Shatila (as explained in the introduction): his sensitive eye and talent are revealed in several of the photos illustrating this book. Laura Boushnak granted me authorization to use on the book cover and in chapter 4 her photograph of the Palestinian rap band Katibe 5 from Burj al-Barajneh camp, close to Shatila. Katibe 5, for their part, agreed that I could include the lyrics of a few of their very provoking songs. Another rap band, Hawiyya Zarqā, also allowed me to use the lyrics of its song that goes by the same name. To the singer and composer Samih Shokair, I express my thanks for authorizing me to include the lyrics of his beautiful song "Romana" in this book.

Nada Sehnaoui, whose artwork has always inspired my reflections, granted permission for me to use a photo of her work, for which I (and also my reader, I bet) am grateful. The poster that illustrates chapter 3 is from the amazing Palestine Poster Project Archives (PPPA) (https://www.palestineposterproject.org): I thank PPPA and Dan Walsh for giving me the right to reproduce it here.

For authorizations to reprint the charts and tables in chapter 2, I thank the following scholars and institutions: Dalal Yassine, Åge Tiltnes, the Consultation and Research Institute, and the Fafo Foundation.

Abridged, simplified, and modified versions of chapters 2, 3, and 5 have been or are about to be included in the following volumes: *Un-settling Middle Eastern Refugees*, edited by Marcia Inhorn and Lucia Volk (New York: Berghahn, 2021); *Reconceiving Muslim Men: Love and Marriage, Family and Care in Precarious Times*, edited by Marcia Inhorn and Nefissa Naguib (New York: Berghahn, 2018); and *Arab Masculinities: Anthropological Reconceptions in Precarious Times*, edited by Marcia Inhorn and Konstantina Isidoros (Bloomington: Indiana University Press, in press). The publishers, Berghahn and Indiana University Press, have allowed me to reuse here parts of the published or forthcoming texts.

The Conselho Nacional de Desenvolvimento Científico e Tecnológico of the Brazilian Ministry of Science and Technology generously provided me with a grant for the first four years of my research. I subsequently counted on funds graciously made available to me by the Department of Anthropology at the London School of Economics and Political Science (LSE), and I received two scholarships: the Rosemary and Raymond Firth Scholarship from the Department of Anthropology at LSE and the Emirates PhD Support for Middle East Studies from the Middle East Center at LSE. The Center for Arab and Middle East Studies of the American University of Beirut hosted me as an associate researcher, ultimately enabling me to obtain a residence permit in Lebanon.

Obviously, the views expressed in this book do not necessarily reflect the perspectives of the institutions for whom I work or with which I am associated.

Finally, my family members have always been supportive and respectful, even when my options and ways of leading my life have made no sense to them. Together with me, they know simply all too well that it is genuine affection that creates the most enduring bonds: Roberto, Therezinha, Beta, Antoine, Gabriel, Chris, Juanito, Aude, Raji, Leila, and my little niece and nephew, Samar and Taha.

To all of you, I reserve my sincere gratitude.

And to the *shabāb*: *Yalla, it is happening!*

Lone Tree, Nairobi, July 2020

Acronyms

IJMES	*International Journal of Middle East Studies*
NGO	nongovernmental organization
NSSF	National Social Security Fund (Lebanon)
PFLP	Popular Front for the Liberation of Palestine
PHRO	Palestinian Human Rights Organization
PLO	Palestinian Liberation Organization
UN	United Nations
UNLU	Unified Leadership of the Uprising
UNRWA	United Nations Relief and Works Agency for Palestine Refugees in the Near East

Timeline

History of the Palestinian Diaspora in Lebanon

	Abroad	In Lebanon	In the Palestinian Camps	In Shatila
1948	Arab countries are defeated in the First Arab–Israeli War. The Nakba (Catastrophe): Palestinians are expelled from Palestine.			
1949				The Shatila camp is established.
1951		Ministry of Labor decides to make work permits mandatory for refugees.		
1962		Law is passed not to recognize refugee status to Palestinians.		
1963		Law is passed establishing that only foreigners with work permits can benefit from the National Social Security Fund, based on reciprocity.		

	Abroad	In Lebanon	In the Palestinian Camps	In Shatila
1964		Decree 17661 is approved, curtailing Palestinian refugees' access to the labor market.		
1967	Arabs are defeated in the Six-Day War, and more Palestinians are expelled from Palestine.		'Ayyām al-thawra (the days of the revolution) begin: the heyday of Palestinian political-military strength.	
1969		The Cairo Agreement gives Palestinians autonomy to administer the camps and launch attacks against Israel from Lebanon and recognizes their right to work.		
1970	"Black September" ushers in conflict in Jordan.	The Palestinian leadership and guerrillas are expelled from Amman, Jordan, and relocate to Lebanon.		
1975		The Lebanese Civil War begins.		
1976			The Tal al-Zaatar camp is destroyed.	
1978		Israel invades Lebanon.		
1982		Israel invades and submits West Beirut to a siege. Ministry of Labor decides to reserve seventy-plus professions for the Lebanese.	'Ayyām al-thawra ("days of the revolution") come to an end. The PLO, Arafat, and several fidā'iyyīn are forced to leave Lebanon.	The Sabra and Shatila massacres take place.

	Abroad	In Lebanon	In the Palestinian Camps	In Shatila
1985			War of the Camps starts.	Shatila is put under siege by Amal, the Shia militia.
1987		The Cairo Agreement is repealed.		Internal conflict occurs in Shatila opposing Palestinian factions.
1990	The First Gulf War starts.	After the signing of the Taef Agreement in 1989, the Lebanese Civil War comes to an end.	The "NGO era" in the camps begins.	Shatila comes under Syrian control.
1991	Palestinians are expelled from Kuwait.			
1993	Oslo Accord I is signed.			
1995	Oslo Accord II is signed.			
2000		The Israeli Defense Forces withdraw from South Lebanon.		
2001		Amendment 296 denies Palestinians the right to own property in Lebanon.		
2004				Shatila goes without electricity for seven months.
2005		"Cedar Revolution": the Syrian army leaves Lebanon. Decree partially allows Palestinians access to seventy-plus professions.		Shatilans elect a popular committee for the first time.

	Abroad	In Lebanon	In the Palestinian Camps	In Shatila
2006		July War: Israel bombards Lebanese infrastructure.		
2007			Nahr al-Barid camp is destroyed in the fight between the Lebanese army and Fatah al-Islam.	
2008		Opposing parties Mustaqbal and Hezbollah clash in Beirut.		

Gray shading indicates the duration of events that lasted for longer than one year.

The Best of Hard Times

Introduction

Thinking through Water

From the Ethnographer's Fieldnotes: The Disorder of Things

Shatila Refugee Camp, September 21, 2009

"You know, Gustavo, things shouldn't be like this."

For a change, the anger in Firas's voice was evident.[1] One of my closest friends in Shatila, Firas, twenty-eight, always managed to keep his calm. Only after being properly initiated was it possible to sense the almost imperceptible signs of inner turmoil in him: he started to stutter, his gaze became lost in the infinite, and he smoked, one cigarette after the other. Having become a passive chain-smoker, I knew that at such moments it was better to remain silent and let Firas speak.

This time, even more strongly than before, I shared Firas's anger. As it was Eid al-Adha, when Muslims commemorate the willingness of Abraham to sacrifice his son to God, I tried to pop in for a visit. I thought then

---

1. I have given the people in this book fictitious names in the hope of preserving the anonymity of my interlocutors and friends from Shatila and thus respecting their right to privacy. I have usually identified public figures, such as local leaders, by their real names unless there was reason for me to believe it was unwise to do so. Whenever people shared sensitive information with me, I have opted to change not only their names but also some of the details that might enable their identification. In a few extreme cases, I have gone one step further, "splitting" some of the research participants into two persons, using two different names but always taking care not to falsify data.

1

1. A micro desalination plant in Shatila: a glimpse at the neatly organized functioning of the nonstate. Photograph by Hisham Ghuzlan and Gustavo Barbosa.

and still think it is my duty as an ethnographer to observe local patterns of interaction in the vain hope of overcoming my difference in terms of class and cultural belonging, otherwise piercingly obvious. Shatilans visit friends on Eid al-Adha, so there I was, trying to get to Firas's place.

But I didn't succeed. It had poured with rain the night before, and as always happens whenever it rains heavily, Shatila flooded. Firas's place—the one-room apartment he occupied under his family's household where he kept his most precious belongings, his philosophy books—was completely flooded with water. Firas had a diploma in business administration and deeply regretted having been forced to quit his undergraduate studies in psychology because of a lack of money to pay the tuition. Unemployed for a couple of years, he cherished the time he spent away from the hustle and bustle of camp life, in his cramped room, where the dim light that poured in from the one tiny window did not dishearten him from engaging in his favorite pastime: reading. He had his preferred authors: Foucault and Deleuze and Guattari. There was a chance that under the water now lay *Al-Murāqaba wa al-muʿāqaba*[2] (Foucault 1990), the Arabic translation of Foucault's classic work *Discipline and Punish* ([1977] 1995), the reading of which Firas, oblivious to my limited understanding of classical Arabic, had encouraged me to embark on with him. We stopped at page sixty-two, with Firas depressed by Foucault's rendition of Damien's torture and me by my poor reading abilities in literary Arabic.

We remained silent, looking at the water as if by magic it might quickly drain away into a ditch. We were woken from our trance by the noise of the gate leading to Firas's family house. His neighbors appeared at the door, carrying his grandfather in their arms. The old man was unable to walk: normally, he was carried down to the street whenever he needed to leave home. This time, though, the neighbors were carrying Firas's grandfather in their arms with half of their own bodies submerged in the water. Firas's brother came after them, holding the old man's wheelchair over his head. The grandfather was being taken to a doctor's appointment. Firas looked at me and repeated: "And today is Eid, Gustavo, a day for celebration. . . . Things should definitely not be like this."[3]

London, June 22, 2010

I was happy when Nadine's email message showed up in my inbox from distant Australia. For a short while, Nadine and I had lived in the same guesthouse run by the nongovernmental organization (NGO) Children and Youth Center in Shatila. An anthropologist, too, Nadine was conducting fascinating research using disputes around access to water and

2. Save for names of places and people, which I have simplified to facilitate reading, I have adopted the *International Journal of Middle East Studies* (*IJMES*) system for the transliteration of words in Arabic, even for those expressed in the colloquial dialect ("*IJMES* Transliteration System for Arabic, Persian, and Turkish," n.d., at https://www.cambridge.org/core/services/aop-file-manager/file/57d83390f6ea5a022234b400/Trans Chart.pdf).

3. In quotations from the people I interviewed, interacted with, and observed in workshops, ellipses without square brackets around them indicate pauses in speech, and ellipses with square brackets around them indicate omission of parts of statements.

electricity in the camp as a gateway to understanding conflict between the different Palestinian factions. I sometimes felt envious of the inescapably material basis of her study, which made the highly discursive nature of my own object of interest—"gender"—look diaphanous. Nadine's message today brought back pleasant memories of our evenings in Shatila, when the heavy rain forced us to stay indoors and discuss our "findings" of the day.

Aware of how captivated I had become by her line of reasoning, Nadine, in a display of generosity increasingly rare among scholars, promptly replied to my request to receive some of her data on how access to water has been historically managed in Shatila. I reconstitute Shatila's "water story" here using her data.

Situated in a topographic depression, Shatila has always been subject to floods. Access to water has been less of an issue throughout its existence, though securing potable water has posed more of a challenge. The conditions of the drainage system in the camp and the lack of ready access to drinking water mirror the vicissitudes shaping the history of the Palestinian diaspora in Lebanon. Lebanon is a country of some four million inhabitants, belonging to eighteen different officially recognized religious communities, the main confessions being Maronite Christian, Sunni, Shia, and Druze. Often finding itself at the intersection of different local, regional, and international interests, Lebanon has been historically prone to conflicts. To safeguard their sectarian interests, the different Lebanese confessions seek out the support of powerful foreign allies. In this way, both Israel and Syria in the immediate neighborhood as well as the United States, Saudi Arabia, Iran, and Europe farther afield have been drawn into the Lebanese conundrum. Since 1948, Palestinians, the majority of whom are Sunni, have also played a significant role in Lebanese sectarian politics.

Initially, there was general sympathy for the Palestinians' plight after their expulsion from their territories in 1948 (Sfeir 2008). The local cultural obligation to extend hospitality to guests was adopted as an idiom to frame the way in which these newcomers were treated, at least in the beginning. As early as 1949, the United Nations Relief and Works Agency for Palestine Refugees in the Near East (UNRWA) was established by United Nations (UN) General Assembly Resolution 302 (IV) to assist those dislocated by the conflict of 1948 in Palestine. At the outset, UNRWA was intended to contribute to major infrastructural works in those countries with refugee populations and seek to employ Palestinians in these enterprises. The ongoing political crisis in the region, combined with constant cuts in UNRWA's budget and weariness on the part of host countries, led to the deferment of such works to a never realized future.

It soon became evident that the refugees' stay in Lebanon would be longer than initially anticipated. The idiom of hospitality was quickly replaced by one of security concerns, and the country's military intelligence, the Deuxième Bureau, was to extend its infamous controlling hand over the Palestinian community, whose activities and movements became closely scrutinized and severely curtailed. For a country like Lebanon, which had gained its independence from France only in 1943 and had been coping ever since with unresolved issues of self-identity, Palestinians became useful "enemies within" (Sfeir 2008), providing a handy "meeting point" through which the various Lebanese factions could set aside their differences in their shared opposition to the naturalization, *tawṭīn*, of the refugees.

It was thus an already politically burdened environment that the Palestinian leadership encountered in Lebanon following its relocation from Jordan in the aftermath of the Black September conflict in 1970. Although the Lebanese Civil War (1975–90) was the result of historic divisions within the country and rooted to some extent in class struggle, Palestinians did have a hand in it, serving as catalyzers for its explosion (Picard 1996; Trabulsi 2007). The years between 1967 and 1982 were the heyday of the Palestinian military resistance in Lebanon, a period that older refugees refer to as the golden era of the *'ayyām al-thawra*, the days of the revolution. This was the peak moment of strength of the Palestinian Liberation Organization (PLO) in the country as well as of its leader, Yasser Arafat, and of the Palestinian fighters, the *fidā'iyyīn*, a term that *The Hans Wehr Dictionary of Modern Written Arabic* translates as "freedom fighters," combatants willing to sacrifice themselves for their country. The year 1982 marks the turning point in this history. That year, the Israeli army invaded Lebanon, forcing the PLO leadership, including Arafat, to leave the country along with the *fidā'iyyīn*. A series of difficult years was to follow. Between 1985 and 1987, Amal, a Shia militia backed by the Syrians, triggered what came to be known as the War of the Camps.

With the end of the Lebanese Civil War in 1990, legislation depriving Palestinians of civil, social, and economic rights, including the right to work, began to be enforced more consistently. The Taef Agreement of 1989, brokered by Saudi Arabia and Syria, signaled the official end to the Civil War and sanctioned the exclusion and scapegoating of Palestinians, who were blamed for the conflict. Since 2001, Palestinians have also been denied the right to own real estate in Lebanon. Some Lebanese blame Palestinians for the Civil War and justify the denial of their rights as a means to protect Lebanon's fragile confessional equilibrium. The refugee community in the country has become increasingly dependent on financial and emergency aid as well as on services provided by UNRWA and local and international NGOs. Indeed, a period that might be called the "NGO era" started in the 1990s.

Prior to the arrival of refugees fleeing from the current civil war in Syria, Shatila was home to an estimated 13,000 people, many of them not Palestinians. Today a sprawling and increasingly vertical shantytown, Shatila is obviously not immune to the country's political realities. The camp's establishment dates back to 1949, when UNRWA leased the area for the first refugees, almost all originating from the same village, Majd al-Krum in northern Galilee (R. Sayigh 1979). Its bare two square kilometers (three-quarters of a square mile) have been the stage for several of the episodes marking the history of Lebanese–Palestinian relations, the most infamous being the massacre in 1982 during which a Maronite militia, the Lebanese Forces, together with other militias and supported by the Israeli army, killed some 3,000 residents of the camp and surrounding area, Palestinians and non-Palestinians alike (Nuwayhed al-Hout 2004). In 1985, Amal, the Shia militia, kept Shatila under siege for two years. In 1987, conflict broke out in the camp, opposing Palestinian factions backed by Damascus and their anti-Syria enemies (R. Sayigh 1993). Understandably, this episode is seldom talked about because it exposes the myths surrounding the idea of unity around the national cause.

In the aftermath of the Lebanese Civil War in 1990, Shatila fell under Syrian control. This status was to last until 2005, when, following the events of what came to be known as the Cedar Revolution, the Syrian army and intelligence were forced to leave Lebanon. In the explosion of violence that erupted while I was in the field in 2008, pitting the Sunni party Mustaqbal against the Shia Hezbollah, Shatilans feared that the camp might again be drawn into the disputes. This apprehension was exacerbated by the location of the camp, situated between the Sunni district al-Tariq al-Jadida and the Shia district Dahiya. It is indeed revealing that in 2008 the decision was taken to close off Shatila. With memories still fresh of the War of the Camps opposing Palestinians and Shia militias, Shatilans wanted to prevent the local *shabāb* (lads) from taking part in the events happening beyond the camp because this might attract acts of revenge toward the community. This brief historic sketch indicates how the fate and daily lives of Shatila inhabitants have been and continue to be shaped by circumstances well beyond their control.

The "water histories" collected by Nadine closely reflect this eventful trajectory of Palestinians in Lebanon. Throughout the 1960s, drinkable water had been supplied to Shatila by a pipeline connecting the camp to the Beirut network. This pipeline was the result of negotiations between UNRWA and the Lebanese government, when Palestinians and Lebanese were still on speaking terms and the refugees had not yet been identified as a favorite scapegoat, as would happen during the Civil War. UNRWA covered the costs for the supply of drinking water. This pipeline was severely damaged during the Civil War, however, and so the PLO/Fatah stepped in and commissioned the digging of three artesian wells. In fact, much of the remaining water infrastructure of Shatila was built by the PLO/ Fatah during the *'ayyām al-thawra*, the days of the revolution. One of the wells dug then was located at the top of a hill near the Sports Stadium, in the surroundings of Shatila, and provided water well beyond the camp's perimeter. But the area belonged to the Lebanese government. As a consequence, with the demise of the *'ayyām al-thawra* and the weakening of the PLO and Palestinians in Lebanon, the state took over the well during Rafik Hariri's premiership.

With the Palestinian leadership gone in 1982 and the specter of Damascus's increasing control over life (and death) in Lebanon having extended to Shatila, the camp popular committee[4] linked to the Syrians and known as the Taḥāluf (Alliance)—an umbrella coalition joining several anti-Arafat factions, including Saiqa, the Popular Front for the Liberation of Palestine General Command, and Fatah al-Intifada—dug two wells. The departure of the PLO effectively left Shatila without clear sources of authority: on various occasions, in fact, different popular committees linked to the various Palestinian factions were simultaneously at work in the camp (Suleiman 1999). This multiplicity of sources of authority[5]—with the mutual exchange of accusations of corruption among them—rendered the administration of daily matters of importance to the population, such as access to water, highly complex. Sari Hanafi (2008a, 2008b, 2010) describes this state of affairs as "the problem of governance" in the camps, providing a new paradigm for the analysis of refugee life in Lebanon. I take a completely different stance on the issue, however, and propose that Shatila residents have learned how to live without counting on protection or aid provided by statelike institutions. There is governance in Shatila: it is simply not of the state type.

The fate of the two wells dug by the Taḥāluf popular committee is telling of this state of affairs, in which no undisputed source of authority over the community has become consolidated. By 1999, the Taḥāluf had outsourced the administration of the wells to two men in charge of running the water supply on a daily basis against payment by individual

4. The popular committees provide some services, including security, to the camp.

5. I was made acutely aware of the competition over resources and unnecessary duplication of efforts caused by the existence of multiple sources of authority in the camp when one of the political factions invited me to volunteer as an English teacher for Shatila children. By then, I had already been working for several months as a voluntary English teacher for children at a local NGO. Wishing to avoid being identified with any political force in particular, I eagerly agreed to discuss the matter with the political faction in question and meet my prospective students. When I showed up for the meeting, the children waiting for me were the same ones I had already been teaching at the local NGO. I made this point to one of the political faction's leaders: "But the children here are the same ones I'm already teaching." "Yes, Gustavo," the leader replied, "but the organization you'll be volunteering with is not the same."

households. Several of the residents were willing to pay the monthly fee of 10,000 Lebanese pounds (less than US$7.00)[6] to guarantee reliable access to water. The private administrators had a larger portion of the clientele than the wells administered by the PLO popular committee, even though the latter charged only 3,000 Lebanese pounds ($2.00) for water per month. The PLO popular committee does not have the means to enforce payment and as a result could not maintain the wells properly. There was also a widespread suspicion among users that the money collected was never invested in maintenance of the wells. The private administrators linked to the Taḥāluf could keep their wells in proper order and enforce payment by simply cutting the supply of water to those who did not pay. Nonetheless, the two administrators fell out of grace with the Taḥāluf and to safeguard their trading interests had to seek the protection of the PLO popular committee.

With the different popular committees failing to reach an accord, there was room for NGOs to step in to ensure the provision of basic services.[7] In Shatila, NGOs financed the construction of two cisterns to store water pumped from the wells. Such facilities are especially important in light of the constant blackouts to which Shatila is prone: with no electricity, there is no power to pump water from the wells. In 2004–5, for example, when the camp went without electricity for seven months, residents faced water shortages, too. Having learned how risky it is to depend on the popular committees or UNRWA or the Lebanese government or NGOs alone for access to essential services, Shatilans have secured potable water by purchasing it directly from "micro desalination plants." These small shops are found throughout the camp and filter water through a system that is well hidden behind curtains, protecting it from the scrutinizing gaze of the ethnographer (figure 1).

6. Throughout this book, I use the exchange rate operating at the time of my fieldwork (2007–9) when US$1.00 was worth 1,500 Lebanese pounds. Recently, the Lebanese pound has been dramatically devalued. All dollar figures are US dollars, so from this point I have left off "US" in identifying those figures.

7. For a history of NGOs working with Palestinian refugees in Lebanon, see Bianchi 2011 and Suleiman 1997.

An ambitious project to sort out Shatila's issues relating to potable water and drainage illustrates this recent absence of any clear source of consolidated authority over the camp. Several stakeholders and powers-that-be claim control over Shatila, and the result, more often than not, is paralysis that threatens the continued provision of basic services. Counting on financing from an Italian NGO, UNRWA set in motion a twofold project: the construction of a deep well to ensure access to drinkable water for Shatila residents and the rebuilding of the camp's sewage and water-drainage system. It took a number of years for the latter intervention to move beyond the planning phase. As for the former, at the time of my fieldwork (2007–9) there was still no sign of its implementation. Despite funds having been made available to UNRWA in 2007, both projects had become mired in polemics. UNRWA held meetings with both the PLO and the Taḥāluf popular committees, but none of the committees approved of the deep well being located near their offices or the homes of party officials. It is no easy task to find a clear area in which to dig the well in Shatila, given its high population density and network of narrow alleys between crowded buildings. An obvious choice was in one of the few open squares in the area, terrain situated outside the camp but belonging to the PLO. This plot contains three apartment blocks built by UNRWA to shelter refugees who, originally from the Tal al-Zaatar camp destroyed in 1976, had been illegally occupying abandoned buildings in Ras Beirut, bordering the Mediterranean Sea, for a couple of years. Opposition to the construction of the well in this plot arose from the perception that were the project to move ahead, the building of a massive structure would render the area just as congested as any other in the camp and thus deprive its residents of natural light and breezes.

The large-scale rehabilitation of the sewage and water-drainage system was not spared controversy either. With no mechanism for draining storm water, the more low-lying roads and homes of the camp often flooded with rainwater mixed with sewage. The problem was reported by a member of the elected committee to a commission made up of UNRWA and Lebanese government officials during the commission's visit to the camp in 2006. In 2005, increasingly disillusioned with the internecine conflicts between the different Palestinian factions and in a pioneering if short-lived initiative, Shatilans elected their own popular committee (Allan 2007, 2014b; Kortam 2010; Palestinian Human Rights Organization 2005). One of its affiliates approached Richard Cooke, then UNRWA director for Lebanon, during the visit in 2006 and reported on the flooding of the camp every rainy season. A later meeting at UNRWA headquarters triggered the announcement of a $2.5 million project for the rehabilitation of Shatila's sewage and water-drainage system. But the project was to remain undone for years to come.

Because Shatila is a favorite target for rogue contractors who simply pocket the bulk of the funds designated for a project while implementing an inferior version of the original project on the ground, the camp's engineers' club, in an example of self-government and autonomy, demanded and gained access to the rehabilitation plans and the terms of the contract, with a view to monitoring the project's execution. The engineers identified two major flaws in the feasibility study for renewal of the pipeline: the diameter of the recovery pipeline was too narrow and the angle of its slope too slight to enable an adequate flow of water away from the camp. They voiced their concerns to the popular committees, expecting the latter to request a new feasibility study from UNRWA. Instead, the popular committees felt cornered. One of the *shabāb* (lads) interviewed by Nadine stated that popular committees are required to show the political factions to which they are subject that they maintain complete authority over the camp. For this reason, they wanted to keep the pipeline renovation plan going despite the engineers' public outcry. Caught in this political impasse, the implementation of the new plan was delayed by months.

It was only after Nadine returned to Australia that the reconstruction of the sewage and drainage system actually started. Throughout the summer of 2009, comprehensive earthworks took place in the main roads of the camp. Shadi was one of the construction workers hired for the project.

Shatila, October 13, 2009

Shadi was recovering from his work shift when I showed up for the interview we had arranged previously. He lay on a bed located in an open area connecting the various households belonging to his extended family in

Shatila. He was aware of what my research was about because by then I had gained a certain unwanted notoriety as the "foreign researcher" living in the camp. He knew I wanted to "collect" his life history: his work biography, the state of relations within his family, perceptions of Palestinian nationalism, and so on. Because one of the themes of my research is the limits of representation in ethnography, I will let Shadi, who is Syrian, speak freely, only minimally editing his words when strictly unavoidable and sometimes providing explanations in brackets. It is in a deliberately provocative spirit that I begin this study about the Shatila *shabāb* with the story of a *shāb* (lad) who, strictly speaking, is *not* Palestinian, being the son of a Syrian father. My intention is to begin to render all of these apparently solid materials, such as a "unified national identity," more complex and nuanced and thus, I hope, melt them into air.

ME: So, what can you tell me about your life?

SHADI: I'm twenty-six. I have a Syrian father and a Palestinian mother. [Silence.] In the future, after I finish my two-year military service, I want to build a house and have a wife. I've learned construction as a job. My father is Syrian, but he has been living here for forty-five years. He married my mother here. All of my brothers and sisters were born in Lebanon. My father used to be a *fidā'ī* [freedom fighter] and fought in the Camp Wars. One of my brothers, who died in that war, was a *shahīd* [martyr]. My father was a *fidā'ī* because Israel doesn't forget anyone and doesn't distinguish between Palestinians, Lebanese, Syrians, or even Brazilians. It hits us all. He had every right to defend himself and his land ['arḍ] and honor ['arḍ]. We were five siblings in the family; one died, so now we're four. [. . .] My father met my mother because he knew her brothers. My mother wasn't a *fidā'iyya* [female freedom fighter], but there were a lot of *fidā'iyyāt* during the *thawra* [revolution]. My father worked in construction, like myself. My mother is *bil-bayt* ["in the house," a housewife). [Silence.] I never saw Palestine, not even from the border. [Silence.] I studied until the seventh grade. I stopped because of family problems, even though I was a very good student and wanted to continue my education. Education is a good thing, and Mohammed—ṣallā Allāhu 'alayhi wa-sallam [may God honor him and grant him peace][8]—said, "'Uṭlub al-'ilm" [Seek knowledge]. I was twelve when I dropped out of school. My older brother stopped at the brevet level [ninth grade]. Even he stopped because of the same situation. The girls in my family didn't continue with their education. They studied until the sixth grade and stopped. When my father married my mother, he paid 5,000 Lebanese pounds as *muqaddam* [first part of the bride price, *mahr*]. Today, that's the price of two packs of cigarettes [around $3.50]! In the cases of my married sisters and brothers, the *muqaddam* was a golden lira. They all married Palestinians.[. . .] My second sister is divorced. Her husband was Palestinian. My father asked for her divorce, so there was no *mu'akhkhar* [second part of the bride price, negotiated prior to the wedding and paid in case the husband asks for a divorce]. [Silence.]

ME: And how's your work life?

SHADI: My work history? I started working while I was still at school. My first job was at a shop because I was still a *ṭifl* [little boy]. Human beings are *ṭammā'īn* [greedy]. And it was because of money that I stopped school, and I wish I hadn't. Money isn't everything. My family didn't prevent me [from dropping out of school]. I studied at the UNRWA school. For three years, I was studying and working at the same time. Then I stopped school and started working selling movies and CDs in several places. After that, I started working with my father in construction. Sometimes I work with my *khāl* [mother's brother]. Sometimes we have no work. And there was this project at the camp [for the recovery of the water pipeline]. My brother was a boss on the construction team for this project, so I started working with him. When I started working, I thought it was just construction, but it is also sewage. This project is financed by—Who's our president? Abbas Zaki?[9]—and UNRWA. They hired this company, [firm name omitted]. The situation and conditions of this project aren't much better than those of others in the past. The project has two parts: sewage and drinking water. The part about

8. Muslims often say this to praise Prophet Mohammed whenever his name is mentioned.

9. Abbas Zaki was in fact the Palestinian ambassador to Lebanon at the time of my fieldwork.

drinking water still needs to be done; nothing has happened about it yet. And as for the sewage, the project isn't succeeding. There are lots of mistakes in the project, and sometimes there are broken pipes inside the ground, and they haven't been replaced. In other words, the work wasn't professional. The work was *bazziq wa lazziq* ["glued with saliva," thus not properly done]. Lots of mistakes took place. As far as our salaries are concerned, payments were always delayed. As an example, today is my payday. They'll say, "Come tomorrow." And then tomorrow they'll say, "Come the day after tomorrow." And this goes on and on. That's why the project began to go astray. The workers started hating their work.[. . .] The lack of care shown by the managers and bosses is the reason for the project's failure. There was no management, no direction, and no follow-up. I was working pushing a trolley, and I fell. My hand was injured. I received treatment; they did pay for that. But they didn't pay for the days I couldn't work. There was a lot of stealing in this project. There was no contract between us and the company. Half of the money has been stolen. There was insurance, but the problem is that they say, "Go and get care. Pay and bring us the bill." The problem began when they started to delay our payments. No one had money to pay for medical treatment. So what can we do in such a situation? After my work on this project was over, I went back to working in construction with my father and brothers. All of my brothers work in the same field, but the girls in my house don't work. They aren't allowed to. But there are girls who work to help themselves and their families. This is excellent.[. . .] [Silence.] I'm here in Shatila because I was born here. And *min al-dākhil* [deep inside], I'm Palestinian. All of my friends are Palestinian. [Short silence.] For now, I'm living with my family, but I think of building a home for myself. If the camp stays the way it is now, I prefer to leave it. Because I want my children to live peacefully, *bi-hudū'* [quietly], with *al-dīn* [religion] and *al-'ilm* [education, although literally "science"]. I want to keep them away from harm. A person wishes his son to be better than him. [Short silence.] I have been in prison twice because I made trouble.[. . .] Both times, I only stayed in prison for a couple of days. [Silence.]

ME: What can you tell me about your friends?

SHADI: I have Palestinian and Lebanese friends. I don't distinguish between Sunni and Shia, Christians and Muslims. If a Christian is better than the Muslim, then I prefer the Christian. The reason why I have lots of *ma'ārif* [acquaintances] is that I don't ask about *jinsiyyāt* [sects, although literally meaning "nationalities"] or religions. [Silence.] Palestinians are rulers here in the camp, and nobody else. All the problems here are due to the *faṣā'il* [factions]. Me, my brothers, my family, we live in *ru'b* [terror] because of these problems and shootings all over. Even if a man is big as a mountain, another one comes with a gun and shoots him in the head. The problem is Fatah Abu-Ammar [PLO], which follows Tayyar al-Mustaqbal [former prime minister Saad Hariri's party of mainly Sunni composition, which sides with Saudi Arabia, the United States, and Europe, has a Westernizing view of Lebanon, and defends the implementation of neoliberal policies], which follows Saudi Arabia. And Saudi Arabia follows Israel. This is on the one hand. On the other hand, we have Fatah Abu Moussa [Fatah al-Intifada]. They follow Syria, which follows Iran. All of them on both sides, Abu Ammar and Abu Moussa, reflect the interests of their partners outside. [Realizing that I am scrutinizing the green ribbon wrapped around his fist] I know, this is a symbol of Harakat Amal [a Shia party]. But I don't use this ribbon because of them. I wear it because I want to. Sometimes I wear a blue one, the color of the Mustaqbal, sometimes a yellow one, the color of Hezbollah [a Shia party cum militia]. I don't think this is an issue. I hate all this *'inshiqāq* [division]. As an example, if I go up to al-Tariq al-Jadida [an area neighboring Shatila of mainly Sunni composition], and I tell them there that I'm Syrian, they'll say that I'm a Jew [because Syria is controlled by the Alawites, akin to the Shia]. If I go to Dahiya [another area neighboring Shatila, mainly of Shia composition] and say that I'm a Sunni, they'll say that I'm a Jew. So what do I do? When I go to al-Tariq al-Jadida, I say that I'm a Sunni and won't mention my nationality, that I'm Syrian. And they'll love me there. [On the other hand,] if I tell the Shia [at Dahiya] that I'm Syrian without mentioning that I'm Sunni, they'll love me there [because Hezbollah, which controls Dahiya, has strong links with Syria]. [Looking at me] *Yā 'akhī* [My bro], who in this country hasn't killed us? The Syrians destroyed Tal al-Zaatar [a Palestinian camp razed in 1976], and that happened because Palestinians had bombed a Syrian tank in Saida [a city thirty-seven kilometers (twenty-three miles) south of Beirut]. *Yā 'akhī*, in Syria, Palestinians have the right to become employers, to become ministers of the interior. Palestinians also take part in the national sports teams in Syria. This shows how Palestinians in Syria are *muqaddarīn* [appreciated].[. . .] I'm Syrian. If I was in Syria and talking about politics and a Palestinian came along and saw me, he could admonish me. He has that right even if I'm an *'ibn al-balad* [literally "son of the country," meaning a national], [and he isn't]. There, Palestinians have the right to do whatever they want, provided they stay away from politics.[. . .] [Silence.]

ME: How do you see the future?

SHADI: I think about marriage. I'd like to have a Palestinian wife. Now, I have a Palestinian girlfriend. But the situation is hard, and I can't marry right now. It's not possible to marry unless you are totally *mū'amman* [secure] for at least one year. There are the expenses of marriage and then children and paying for childbirth and so on. To marry, I need approximately $4,000 to buy a roof and then another $4,000 for construction and $2,000 for furniture and $3,000 for the *khuṭūba* [engagement, which normally requires that the groom buy an engagement ring and pay the first part of the bride price, the *muqaddam*], the *'alāma* [trousseau, normally consisting of clothes, makeup, and perfume for the bride], and the wedding party. Getting married in the past was easier. First of all, people were very close, and they used to love each other. If you knocked at someone's door, he wouldn't say, "No." Today, it's different. There are problems, few job opportunities; all of these make life harder. Times have changed. [Silence.]

ME: Have you got family outside Lebanon?

SHADI: I have relatives outside Lebanon. I'm from [location name omitted] in Syria. All my relatives are there, from my father's side. The family of my mother is here in Lebanon and also in Sweden. I only visited Syria once. Even in Palestine I have relatives, from my mother's side. The brother of my grandmother is there. [Silence.] I don't think of *safar* [migrating] because *al-ghurba* [homesickness][10] is not easy. I went to Syria and felt homesick. In Lebanon, there are two things that

---

10. *Al-ghurba* is a complex term in Arabic and admits several translations. It evokes ideas of nostalgia, homesickness, and longing for a place left behind. Some Shatilans who have managed to migrate to Europe and come back to visit, even though normally emphasizing how their present quality of life is incomparably better than the one they had in Lebanon, eventually report experiencing *al-ghurba* abroad.

make you live as a king. The first is money; the second is the fact that people don't interfere with what is going on around them. Money in Lebanon goes to those who have money already.[. . .] [Long silence.] [. . .] The *thawra* [revolution] is gone, and the reason is that there are no *fidā'iyyīn* as there used to be. If we fight against each other, we're like *al-wuḥūsh* [monsters]; if we fight against a *gharīb* [stranger], no one will join to help. Palestine is *'arḍ ṭāhira* [a pure land]. It's from the God of us all. We have Mecca in Saudi Arabia, also holy. If there was true feeling for Islam and Arabhood in Saudi Arabia, the Saudis would be the first ones to appeal for Palestine. [Very long silence.]

ME: How's your daily life?

SHADI: Everyday it's the same thing. From work to the house; I have a shower, and then I go to a coffee shop, and I play cards. Then I come back home to sleep. When I have free time, I go for a walk in Ain Mreise [an area near the sea in Beirut to which the *shabāb* like to walk as leisure] with my friends and with *ḥabībatī* [my girlfriend]. I do sports; I play football. [Short silence.]

ME: Do you pray?

SHADI: I used to pray; I used to fast, but not anymore. The reason why I don't fast is my work. It is very hard work, and we need to drink water while working. But every Friday I go to the mosque. [Silence.]

ME: What would you say are the phases in a person's life?

SHADI: It depends on the person. Every person lives his life as he wants. Some think about work and about *'illī jāyī* [what will come]. Others spend their lives with problems and fooling around. Others think about knives and pistols. When I was young, I was a *mashkaljī* [troublemaker]. This is the first year that I see myself as having *'aql* [the capacity to reason][11] and *māshī ṣaḥ* [walking the right line]. My family will not last forever for me. So I have to think about myself and my future. [Silence and then getting back to my question] If a girl is destined for marriage, she'll indeed get married. Marriage itself is considered to be half of the Islamic religion. [Silence.]

ME: What is your relation like with members of your family?

11. The term *'aql* refers to the eminently social "faculty of understanding, rationality, judiciousness, prudence and wisdom" (Altorki 1986, 51). It is an indication of coming-of-age. I come back to the concept in chapters 3 and 4.

SHADI: I have a normal relation with my mother. I keep no secrets from my family. That's because they'll be the first to help if something happens to me. With my sisters, I also have a normal relation. But everyone has problems in their lives and with their families. I also have my problems with my family. In general, I don't spend a lot of time at home. My mother and sisters are my *mas'ūliyya* [responsibility]. The way they dress is very important to me because they're my *sharaf* [honor]. A girl should be *muḥtashima* [modest]. My relation to my father sometimes is one of total friendship. When he starts acting toward me as a father, that's when our problems start. He doesn't like me to try new things, and he doesn't let me do what I want. Smoking, for example. He always tells me to stop, and I don't. I also used to drink, and he kept telling me to stop. I stopped. And as for me and my brothers, we're very close. They help me, telling me everything that's good for me. I feel responsible for my father, mother, and everyone in the house. And vice versa. If someone in my family gets sick, I take care of him, and he'd do the same for me. My sister takes care of me and helps me. She *takhdimnī* [serves me]. I do that for her, too.[. . .] The way my brothers and fathers dress does not concern me. My father, he's the one who tries to *yataḥakkam* [control]. He's Syrian. His way of thinking is Arab. For example, my sisters only learned how to write and then left school. [Silence.]

ME: How does life today compare to life in the past?

SHADI: Life in the past was better. But, at the same time, now there are things that are better. Freedom now is all over and for everyone. Fathers in the past used to tell their sons: "Don't go out." Sons would listen to their fathers. But now no one listens. [Silence.] [. . .]

ME: What do you think about the future?

SHADI: I think of the future. I want it to be better than the past. I have hope in the future. My dreams are like those of any of Adam's children [any human being]: to get married to the girl I love, to have a happy married life, and to build a *'usra jayyida* [nice family].

Water runs throughout these vignettes. As does precarity. The precarity of Shatila's infrastructure, which forces Firas's neighbors to mount a dramatic operation so that his grandfather can get to a doctor's appointment and which drowns his most precious belongings, his books. The precarity of

Shatila's polity, swamped by factional fights, compromising the emergence of a monopolist source of political authority and the functioning of statelike forces in the camp. And the precarity of Shadi's hopes and dreams, engulfed by his hazardous employment situation and future prospects, defying his plans to marry the girl he loves, have a happily married life, and build a *'usra jayyida*—all traditional indicators of adequate gender belonging and accomplished coming-of-age for Palestinian refugee men. Together, these three vignettes suggest several of the threads we will follow over the coming pages, such as the differences between the *fidā'iyyīn*'s "revolutionary and heroic masculinities" and the less spectacular "quotidian masculinities" of their sons; the consequences for Shatila refugees and the *shabāb* in particular of the demise of the *fidā'iyyīn* and the *'ayyām al-thawra*, the days of the revolution; and the characterization of water as a pattern that connects or as what, after Mary Catherine Bateson (1987), I call a "meta for" that enables reasonings through analogy lending intelligibility to the functioning of the "antistate" in Shatila. The challenge confronting me, therefore, is to try to understand what "gender," "power," "patterns that connect," and the "antistate" mean—or, rather, how they function (and sometimes do not)—in a place such as Shatila. Inspired by these three vignettes, I have before me a program of work: to attempt to bring order, unfortunately at the analytical level only, back to things that, in Firas's words, "shouldn't be like this." But then the relevant question is: What kind of order?

From the Anthropologist's Desktop: Framing the Field Is Not Taming the Field

"What's a Meta For?" Gender and Power

The specter of *Naven* ([1958] 2003), Gregory Bateson's "survey of the problems suggested by a composite picture of the culture of a New Guinea tribe," haunts me.[12] I find Bateson's classic simultaneously inspiring and

---

12. I have taken the question "What's a meta for?" in this and other sections' subheads from Mary Catherine Bateson (1987).

profoundly disturbing. The uneasiness with which he faces the daunting task of rendering a comprehensive ethnographic account of the totality of Iatmul culture—the "accomplishment" expected from classic, functionalist ethnographic monographs—is a feeling with which I sympathize intensely. Indeed, Bateson sensed the artificiality of the enterprise, and because "words must necessarily be arranged in lines" (3), his discomfort is patent when he is attempting to present, through this all-too-insufficient medium, the "elaborate reticulum of interlocking cause and effect" (3) that he believes defines a culture. Acutely aware of the issues raised by the predicament of representation at the moment of writing, Bateson ends up entrapped by what George Marcus calls a "hermeneutic-empiricist bind" (1985, 75): a loyal heir of the best of the British empirical tradition, Bateson is outspoken about his doubts concerning the ability of nonfiction writing to capture the "wholeness" of another form of life. In a sense, the strength of *Naven* comes precisely from the fact that it is a failed experiment.

A first aspect of Bateson's classic that informs the following line of argument is the way he portrays "gender" in *Naven*, even though the word itself is conspicuously absent from the text—for the good reason that in its contemporary sense it simply did not exist in the late 1950s, its widespread adoption coinciding only with the burgeoning of feminist struggles in the 1970s. In its exploration of the relations between the sexes, *Naven* depicts a feature that has been lost since this interaction became framed as "gender" by the civil rights movements beginning in the 1960s and found its way into academia from the 1970s on. "Gender" is not necessarily about power relations between men and women, and if meaningful at all, as *Naven* seems to suggest, it gains meaning in relation to several significant others as well, sometimes people of the same sex: a religious or political leader, an ancestor, and, placing "gender" right at the heart of kinship, a *wau*—the mother's brother among the Iatmul studied by Bateson—or a father, as among the Shatila *shabāb* who occupy us here.

Second, Bateson does not lose sight of the fact that his consecutive presentations of the *naven* ritual among the Iatmul—from a structural, sociological, and ethological point of view—are merely perspectives. They belong to what Bateson calls the world of "Creatura," the explanations about "reality." For "reality" itself, he reserves the name "Pleroma."

The distinction between Creatura and Pleroma comes with a warning, explained by his daughter, Mary Catherine Bateson, in "So What's a Meta For?" (1987): "If it is true that there are *things* in Pleroma, then nouns (which are not things) are a useful invention for talking about things—but with nouns we have invented the capacity for false reification. There are no things in Creatura—only ideas, images, clusters of abstract relations—but the vast convenience of talking about things leads us to treat any available idea—truth, God, charisma—as if it were thing-like" (188, original emphasis). Hence, treating the structure, sociology, and ethos of Iatmul culture as "reality" rather than as analytical tools for explaining and categorizing "reality" is to commit what Gregory Bateson identifies as the fallacy of misplaced concreteness, a major epistemological flaw. Such a mistake also characterizes analyses that fail to identify "gender" as belonging to the order of categorizations about "reality" and of discourse. *Gender*, I propose, is also a noun, thus belonging to the world of Creatura rather than to Pleroma.

In Pleroma, the world of "things," events are caused by strengths and impacts, whereas in Creatura, the world of discourse about "things," effects are caused by difference, like the marks on a map. A map is necessarily a representation of the territory, and it never captures the territory completely: it contains nothing but appearances (G. Bateson [1972] 1980b). Similarly, "gender"—being of the order of Creatura and the map—is an appearance. It registers differences. Differences, however, do not immediately and necessarily imply differential access to power and a hierarchy. It is in specific cultural-political settings such as those organized by state structures that differences tend to be framed as hierarchies. As a consequence, "gender" as discourse, when defined within the limits of such a cultural-political setting, may lose the capacity to reflect the ways in which difference is conceptualized where the state is not omnipresent, as in Shatila. I come back to this point at various junctures throughout this study.

In yet a third vein, Bateson's work supplies a point of reference—methodological this time—for what is to ensue. In the 1950s, while teaching a group of art students, many of them beatniks, Bateson placed a dead crab on the classroom table (G. Bateson [1979] 1980a). He provoked his students to identify the reasons why the remains of a living being were lying on the table. The aesthetic bias of the class conspired in favor of the experience: prompted to spot vestiges of life in the corpse lying on the table, the students immediately searched for the patterns connecting them to the creature. Their verdict: the claws of the crab suggest symmetry, precisely like our own limbs. In both cases, there are similar relations—a homology rather than an identity—approximating our members and those of the crab. At the level of logic, which could be termed metaphorical, we find the pattern that connects the crab to us. These syllogisms of metaphor, which Bateson calls "abduction," provide him with a new heuristic tool: "the search for insight through analogy" (M. Bateson 1987, 192), a search that will also guide our efforts in chapter 1. That is what *metas* are for: by the identification of the pattern that connects beatniks to crabs, the latter's claws may offer new intelligibility to our own limbs.

Likewise, it is my contention throughout this book that the search for what connects the *shabāb* (lads) of Shatila and me—the limited access to power that, however differently, we share—offers new intelligibility not only to the (non)functioning of the state in marginal places such as Shatila, an endeavor already undertaken in a number of ethnographic studies (e.g., Agier 1999, 2010; Das and Poole 2008), but also more originally about the functioning of the antistate in our own societies. Moreover, the pattern that connects also engenders a deep empathy that through my repositioning in the field has freed me from the "state blinkers" obsessed with power and enabled other views of "gender," as stated in chapter 1. This empathy created through the pattern that connects is actually the condition of possibility for a meaningful and critical anthropology: a study not only of how the social is but also of how it should and indeed could be (Sykes 2003). "Empathy is a discipline" (M. Bateson 1987, 195), a point to which I return later in this introduction.

"What's a Meta For?": The Shatila Shabāb,
the Ethnographer, and the Pattern That Connects

Because academic dialogue thrives not only by encouraging agreements but also by making defiant divergences, *Naven* is also disturbing in one specific facet. Although painfully aware of the inadequacy of academic writing to represent social reality and his depiction of it, Bateson does not extend his epistemological concerns to the moment of the constitution of data (Marcus 1985). Occasional moments of doubt notwithstanding,[13] he normally considers that it is part of his task as an ethnographer to register the behavior of the Iatmul. It is precisely in this sense that Bateson never ceases to be a good heir of the British empiricist tradition: his writings betray his anxiety about his activity as an interpreting analyst, but the concerns of the Iatmul, who are also interpreting subjects, do not trouble Bateson.

Being, at most, a bastard son of British empiricism, having been trained in a Marxist tradition at the London School of Economics but nevertheless initiated into anthropology in the much less secure waters of Brazilian academia, I did not find in Shatila a reassuring shelter to "set down surrounded by all . . . [my] gear, alone . . . close to a native village, while the launch or dinghy which . . . [had] brought . . . [me] there sail[ed] away out of sight" (Malinowski 1992, 4).[14] The *service*, a shared taxi very common in Beirut, that dropped me at the entrance to the bustling market of Sabra, which leads to the refugee camp, brought me to a place that utterly failed to feed into my neo-Orientalist expectations of what a Palestinian refugee camp should look like: dotted by tents and inhabited by intrepid *fidā'iyyīn* wearing Palestinian black-and-white square kerchiefs, the *kuffiyyāt*. While the adrenaline suddenly pumped into my blood as I walked through Sabra, anticipating the dangers I had been taught to expect in a refugee camp (Hanafi 2008a, 2008b, 2010; International Crisis Group 2009; Rougier 2007), what I actually encountered in Shatila was an anticlimax: a shantytown with children playing in the alleys, women seated on white plastic chairs chitchatting in front of their little stores, and men waiting for their turn to have a haircut at Suleiman's salon, where I

---

13. David Lipset (1980) reports that shortly after arriving to conduct fieldwork among the Baining, Bateson started measuring their skulls. At one point, a Baining asked him what he was doing. The question deeply troubled Bateson, who was unable to provide any convincing answer, especially in his rather limited pidgin.

14. Ellipses in quotations from secondary sources are in all cases my insertions to indicate omission of text.

would become a regular customer. The camp was thus not completely dissimilar from the favelas of my native Rio de Janeiro.[15] Moreover, contrary to my academically trained reverie that after an initial and short-lived resistance against their objectification (which I thought it was my duty to pursue) Shatilans would finally succumb to my research efforts, my informants from the camp, increasingly my friends, instead constantly objectified and represented *me* and my science back to me. My objects were not simply intractable: they were defiant.

Shatila, October 29, 2008

I popped in to Akram's office at a local NGO in the hope of getting an appointment with his boss, the president of the institution. Akram initially pushed against my request but ended up accepting it: "You know, Gustavo, I don't really like researchers, but there you go, I'll try to give you a hand."

Ali, a common non-Arab friend of ours who has been conducting academic research among the *shabāb* for a number of years now, made my discomfort even more pronounced: "You can understand, can't you? The reason why people here don't have a lot of respect for researchers. It isn't only that people from Shatila have been researched forever by now and nothing ever changes.[16] It is also because in your academic work you have to observe a certain format when presenting your results. The format ends up limiting what can be said. And what can be said within the limits of that format is not the best for us."

Stimulated by Bateson's work, how can I search for the pattern that connects me to the *shabāb* and yet avoid the risk of disciplining their difference, of forcing them to bow to sameness and share in our common

---

15. In her doctoral work, Amanda Dias (2009) compares, somewhat controversially, a favela in Rio de Janeiro and a Palestinian refugee camp in northern Lebanon.

16. Mayssoun Sukarieh and Stuart Tannock (2013) also make the same point in their article on supposedly overresearched communities, using Shatila as an example.

human nature, in my understanding of it? How can I frame my field and yet, taking full account of what I heard at Akram's office, not tame its difference? How can one still re-present (as in art, philosophy, or the social sciences) the social dynamics of a group without representing it (as in politics)? Accordingly, this book has no intention of speaking for the *shabāb* but rather attempts to depict their forms of self-expression—for instance, through rap (as in chapter 4) or through pigeon raising (as in chapter 5).

Here, a pattern that connects—which, following Karen Sykes (2003), I call "empathy"—needs to play a role in ethnography because it leads to a problematization of the normally taken-for-granted separation between subject (the ethnographer), forever thought of as sentient, and object (the *shabāb*), forever thought of as intractable, as a way out of the crisis of representation. Empathy conspires toward a certain "capture by an-other" to which some ethnographers, including me, capitulate in the field, as happened with Jean Genet (2004), who confesses to having become "a prisoner of love" in his period among the *fidā'iyyīn* in Jordan.[17]

In an ironical mode, I suggest my own way out of the crisis of representation by inviting in an additional crisis: a crisis of *political* representation. Indeed, the functioning of the antistate in Shatila—as illustrated by my earlier "history of water"—serves to defy the teleology of political liberalism that makes the state look analytically inescapable and has blinded scholars to the "antistate" effects at work even in their own societies. That teleology, since the Hobbesian attempt to justify the centralization of power in the hands of the king (Hobbes [1651] 2008), has reduced politics to a matter of alienation, completely obliterating the fact that earlier in the Roman res publica politics was a matter of delegation (Asad 2008). What is needed, then, is not simply an analysis of how the state looks when seen from the margins, as much of political anthropology has done (Abélès 2005; Agier 2010; Das and Poole 2008), but a true marginalization of the state—that is, a rendering of it as a margin to the citizen-body. Such an

---

17. The translation of Genet's title into English somewhat loses the sense of the author's desire to be captured, which is preserved in the French expression "*un captif amoureux.*"

exercise not only liquefies modernity (Bauman 2000) but also makes the apparently solidified state melt into water and turns bare not life (Agamben 1998)—Which ethnography could possibly have that as an aim?—but more appropriately the king and the queen.

All That Is Solid Melts into Water:
Taming Leviathan and the Bare King

The Antistate in Shatila

Prior to my studies in the United Kingdom, my initiation into anthropology in Brazil exposed me heavily to Gilles Deleuze and Félix Guattari's corpus of work. In *A Thousand Plateaus* ([1987] 2004), they describe states' proverbial discomfort with uncontrolled flows of water: "It is certain that the State itself needs a hydraulic science. . . . But it needs it in a very different form, because the State needs to subordinate hydraulic force to conduits, pipes, embankments, which prevent turbulence, which constrain movement to go from one point to another, and space itself to be striated and measured, which makes the fluid depend on the solid, and flows proceed by parallel, laminar layers" (400).

To this hydraulic science, the two authors oppose a hydraulic model of a different type: instead of making flows submit to the "royal science" of solids, this model treats fluids as fluids, accepts their movement, and takes proper note of heterogeneity as opposed to the constant, the identical, the eternal, and the stable. The sea is the hydraulic model par excellence, and it is precisely its flat character that Western powers spared no efforts in striating, making it dependent on the land with its fixed routes: "One of the reasons for the hegemony of the West was the power of its State apparatuses to striate the sea by combining the technologies of the North and the Mediterranean and by annexing [and attempting to submit] the Atlantic" (Deleuze and Guattari [1987] 2004, 427). Being from an Atlantic city, I would not allow myself or the previous anthropological tradition in which I was raised to be so readily submitted.

In my understanding, the hydraulic model offered by Deleuze and Guattari is the most analytically relevant for registering the functioning of antistate effects in a setting such as Shatila. The hydraulic model of the "nomad" or "minor science" that Deleuze and Guattari advocate, in contrast to the state and royal science, operates through the proposition of problems and not axioms: it is a "thought that appeals to a people instead of taking itself for a government ministry" ([1987] 2004, 417).

Although Shatila is not an antistate setting, the "antistate effects"—to rephrase James Scott's (1998, 2009) expression—are salient there and simply cannot be ignored. Indeed, my notes from the very first days in the field register my sense of "state strangeness" toward the camp. Having grown up in a country still coming to terms with dictatorship and military rule, I learned how to be acutely aware of the functioning of state forces with their capacity to silence dissenting voices and erupt in the middle of the night in the form of soldiers in plain clothes, invading one's household to abduct those who dare to think differently. Everything in Shatila—the idiosyncrasies of political life and local functioning of "power" (as developed in chapter 1); residents' economic strategies (as developed in chapter 2); sex roles (as discussed in chapters 3, 4, and 5)—eluded my "state logic" and the epistemological axioms (Marxism, feminism, and statistics) in which I was trained in the United Kingdom, compelling me to develop a fresh sensitivity toward and new lenses with which to look at the camp.

It is precisely the adoption of worn-out "state lenses" that has blinded many who write about Shatila to the antistate effects also at work in the camp. In a countervein to what is proposed by this literature, the prominence of antistate effects in Shatila does not mean chaos and a lack of order. The extreme discomfort that Shatilans, Palestinians, and refugees induce in Lebanon and states in general as well as in geographers, political scientists, and ethnographers wearing "state lenses" leads states and scholars alike to present as necessarily chaotic what simply functions differently. Having grown used to state effects, geographers, political scientists, and ethnographers experience nostalgia for them. Shatila's lack of a state apparatus or the weakness of that apparatus—as the literature thus produced suggests—has absolutely to be depicted as an issue: such is how the so-called problem of governance in the camps has acquired (undue, I believe) scholarly respect (Hanafi 2008a, 2008b, 2010; Hanafi and Long 2010; International Crisis Group 2009; Kortam 2010). In certain cases, echoing the aspirations of Palestinian nationalism, which was especially intense during the *'ayyām al-thawra*, scholars who conducted comprehensive fieldwork in the camps back then also seemed to long for a state (Peteet 1991, 2005, 2007; R. Sayigh 1993, 1995). Within such a theoretical framework, it becomes difficult to understand and accept that Shatilans have grown weary of states or statelike institutions, such as Lebanon and the Palestinian Authority, which have effectively done very little for them, and that they have learned how to live without them: there is governance beyond the state.

The fact that Shatilans' relation to Palestinian nationalism has changed is unsurprising when seen from the perspective of the camp residents (Allan 2007, 2014b). On two occasions, the residents have been utterly disregarded, to say the least, by their own leaders: in 1982, when Yasser Arafat left Beirut for Tunis, taking with him many of the *fidā'iyyīn* and leaving the camps vulnerable, and in 1993 with the Oslo Agreements, when the Palestinian leadership agreed to postpone discussion on the fate of refugees to a final round of negotiations with the Israelis in an unforeseeable future.

The prominence of antistate effects in Shatila does not mean that there are no state effects there—in precisely the same sense that the prominence of state effects in our own societies does not mean that there are no antistate effects in them (Barbosa 2004). It is the otherwise welcome empirical nature of ethnography that has led political anthropology to become more attuned to studying states as institutions rather than venturing into the apparently more diaphanous and nebulous domain of state or antistate "effects." As a result, political anthropology has multiplied typologies of political systems, African or otherwise, according to the strength, presence, or absence of the state as an institution or has plunged into a fruitless search for the origin, the very first moment of "eruption," of the state, inaugurating the "grand division," the ultimate severance between "us" and "them," which feeds easily enough into evolutionary classifications of political arrangements (Abélès 2005).

Of course, the antistate effects I witnessed in Shatila do not allow us to assert that we are in the presence of a group similar to the antistate Amerindians of Pierre Clastres's classic work *Society against the State* (1987). Obviously, Shatilans feel the state effects emanating from the Lebanese government, which, as demonstrated in chapter 2, issues legislation, such as laws barring free access to the Lebanese labor market for Palestinians, or from the Palestinian leadership, which has shown a pronounced unwillingness to respond adequately to the refugee issue.

Nevertheless, by paying attention to antistate effects produced by the political functioning of the camp, we discover how Shatilans have learned not to depend on—or to wait for—solutions from statelike figures (governmental and nongovernmental alike). They have developed a certain finesse in the art of *not* being governed (Scott 2009). The question we have to tackle is: In the context of a lack of state-consolidated and clearly established sources of political authority, how is it that life in Shatila is still orderly and that eventual and episodic eruptions of violence are kept under relative control? In a vein not dissimilar to the fission of Clastres's Amerindians, who, whenever menaced by the possibility of the consolidation of a sole source of authority over them, opted to split (Clastres 1987), or to the "divide that ye be not ruled" of Scott's (2009) Zomians, the various Palestinian factions, in constant rivalry, avoid the emergence and solidification of a sole source of power with the capacity to impose its will over the group. On the one hand, such a "strategy" is the source of various problems, including the very real issue of ensuring the functioning of sewage systems and adequate access to drinkable water in the camp. On the other hand, it keeps Leviathan at bay. Shatilans taught me that there is a social contract that does not necessarily lead to Leviathan and that one of the antistate effects can be, precisely and surprisingly enough, order. They liquefied the state for me.

"What's a Meta For?" Refugees and Water

There are several reasons why this study is organized around different movements of water, which I have used to name the various chapters. First, ethnographers working in diverse settings—for example, Jakarta (Kooy and Bakker 2008), Mumbai (Anand 2010), and Soweto (Von Schnitzler 2010)—have persuasively demonstrated that relations of rule are materialized through hydraulic networks, establishing who counts as citizens at both discursive and material levels. For Soweto, Antina Von Schnitzler argues that residents' opposition to the installation of prepaid water meters, framed as tools for technopolitical intervention, reflects all the ambiguities surrounding citizenship in postapartheid, neoliberal South Africa: a line of reasoning quite useful for the analytical need to liquefy the state and for the contemplation of other notions of citizenship also advocated here.

Second, the lads from Shatila, the *shabāb*, also liquefied anthropology for me. Anthropology has a pronounced if seldom acknowledged spatial bias and is haunted by a spatialized model of culture (Poole 2008), which is expected to "sit" in places (Escobar 2001): indeed, the spatialized "field" itself—the mandatory rite of passage for any anthropologist—does not let us suggest otherwise. Yet of all peoples, Shatilans—notwithstanding their understandably obsessive relation to a utopia, Palestine—have deterritorialized their relation to territory and have shown me just how interjected a place can be with diverse other "domains of meaning," such as "time," a theme to which we return in chapter 1. The Palestine for which several Shatilans yearn is situated in both an idealized past, with all its pastoral imagery, and a redemptive future that often assumes religious and eschatological overtones. The omnipresent olive tree and cactus (*ṣubbār*) exemplify the myth making and almost totemic thinking that inform the utopia of a place in which several Shatilans have never set foot and yet to which they wish to *return*. Because the word denoting "cactus" in Arabic, *ṣubbār*, shares the same root as the word denoting "patience," *ṣabir*, and because it is very difficult to eradicate the plant, which blossoms again and again despite every effort made to uproot it, *ṣubbār* has become a politicized term, evoked to symbolize Palestinian tenacity and their insistence on the return. This botanical imagery[18] sets into relief the fact that in the international order of states—informed by the sedentarizing images of "national soils" and "roots" (Malkki 1992)—refugees such as Shatilans

18. Christine Pirinolli (2009) reports a story that testifies to the force of plants as a means to justify claims to the soil. In 1906, in the Herzl reforestation project in Palestine, the agronomist in charge originally used Palestinians as a workforce. Jewish workers protested strongly, uprooted the trees, and then replanted *the same trees* afterward.

are "displaced" and "uprooted" people: thus, matter out of place (Douglas 1991), literally so. In Liisa Malkki's explanation,

> The danger of pollution posed by statelessness or refugeeness to the categorical order of nation-states corresponds quite neatly to the process studied by Mary Douglas in *Purity and Danger* (1991). Refugees are seen to hemorrhage or weaken national boundaries and to pose a threat to "national security" as is time and again asserted in the discourse of refugee policy. Here, symbolic and political danger cannot be kept entirely distinct. Refugees are constituted, in Douglas's sense, as a dangerous category because they blur national (read: natural) boundaries and challenge "time-honored distinctions between nationals and foreigners" (Arendt 1973). At this level, they represent an attack on the categorical order of nations which so often ends up being perceived as natural and, therefore, as inherently legitimate. (1995, 7–8)

It will come as little surprise, therefore, that in another myth making, this time the mythology informing the constitution and consolidation of nation-states, refugees are all too often depicted in water imageries: waves, flows, floods, inundations, and seas of people that need to be contained (Jayawardena 1995; Malkki 1995; Peteet 2007). In the case of the most recent war in Iraq, to take just one example, two strategists, Kenneth Pollack and Daniel Byman, as reported by Julie Peteet, proposed the establishment of "catch basins" to prevent the "spillover" of displaced people into neighboring countries. With "catch basins" being defined by *Webster's* as "sieve-like device[s] at the entrance of the intersection of a sewer, for retaining solid matter likely to clog the sewer," Peteet concludes that in this hydraulic image displaced persons not only become no longer human but are also transformed into the equivalent of a biological by-product of filth: sludge (2007).

If refugees are matter out of place in the international order of states, and if, as Malkki (1995) reminds us, "people categorize back," let us listen to what the people themselves have to say, as I did, for instance, with Shadi, the *shāb* working in the restoration of the pipeline in Shatila, and as I will do again and again throughout this study, or to what they have to sing, as I do in chapter 4. Let us see what they can teach us not only about the functioning of the state at the margins but also about the functioning of the antistate at the so-called center:[19] that is, about a true marginalization of the state (Asad 2008), which is not to be taken for granted.

At the margins of Beirut, there are other possible ways of making cities, or what Agier (2010) describes as "faire-ville," and these "other cities" are based on and lead to other notions of citizenship, exposing the deep ambiguities of subjectification, particularly within the Western political philosophical tradition. Indeed, for this tradition, a subject, even while being "subject to something" and thus a citizen, also has the capacity to act: the subject has obtained agency, yes, but in and through subjectification (*assujetissement*) (Foucault [1977] 1995). In Shatila, as chapter 5 shows, pigeons fly for other reasons and do not easily allow for "pigeonholing" in a national order of things. As Mariane Ferme convincingly argues, "In these ambiguous zones [of rights that all states produce,] there are also possibilities for flight, and it is here that the reconstitution of subjectivity beyond the categories of citizenship, refugees and migrants can unfold" (2008, 114).

In Shatila, I was also matter out of place, which is probably the condition of possibility for any meaningful ethnography. There was ground for the utmost empathy—which, as we have seen, is itself a discipline (M. Bateson 1987, 195)—with and toward the *shabāb*, who are also matter out of place on more than one level. Not only are they refugees and thus out of place in the national order of things, but as men destitute of power they also find no easy location in this other discipline that sometimes comes across as rather disciplinarian: "gender."

(En)gendering/Endangering Knowledge:
Impurity, Danger, and the "Gift" of Gender

From the standpoint of both the national order of things and the order of things established by much of the academic discourse on gender, the Shatila *shabāb* of today count as "pollution": impure, they are matter out of

---

19. In the topography of political liberalism, the center, as Deleuze and Guattari ([1987] 2004) show, is surprisingly not exactly at the center but rather above.

place. Not only are they stateless refugees, but they are also men with limited access to power and yet not emasculated. From Mary Douglas (1991) and Liisa Malkki (1995), we know that being out of place is dangerous, yet not just for those immediately concerned. Being out of place is also creative because it throws into relief the fact that there is nothing natural in the categories applied. Matter out of place produces noise in widely accepted categories and creatively clears the way for change: matter out of place endangers the world as we know it. At issue, then, is a politicization of one of the traditional themes of anthropology: the study of social classification.

Although obviously welcome, the feminist appeal to "en-gender" knowledge—to open it up for women's point of view, recognizing, therefore, that much of the scholarly production thus far had been biased by a male perspective—entails dangers. As a double-edged project, simultaneously academic and activist, feminism has provided fertile terrain for questions relevant to one domain invading (and sometimes hijacking) the other. In academia, such a demarche has been fundamental to a long-adjourned and nonetheless necessary (politicized) destabilization of well-established categories. This destabilization has been accompanied, however, by certain specific political agendas of Euro-American feminist activists infusing gender preoccupations as an academic discipline and thereby becoming exported into other ethnographic settings where political agendas can be quite different. By offering themselves as "gifts" to other settings, gender activism and studies may have unwittingly contributed to silencing the subaltern (Spivak 1988).

Before this analytical perspective elicits the criticism that I am anti-feminist, let me hasten to stress that this study not only is inspired by the feminist debate but also in a sense wishes to take that debate to its limits: it aims to submit feminist studies themselves to a feminist critique. Accordingly, it shows that there is a "gender bias" to "gender studies": actually, there is a "gender" to "gender." As Marilyn Strathern (1988) appropriately observes, one cannot be a half-hearted radical. In rightly insisting that "women's" perspectives be taken into account and forcing scholars to realize what a difference perspective makes, "gender studies" have sometimes, though, opted to turn a blind eye to the fact that "women's perspective" too was precisely a "perspective." Human problems are not the same every-where, Strathern reasons, and "women" may not be a universal issue. To support her argument, she brings in Donna Haraway, according to whom "gender might not be global identity after all" (Haraway 1985, quoted in Strathern 1988, 40), and remarks that the adoption of the "feminist view" leads to suppression of "internal differences" among women in terms of class, ethnicity, and sexuality. Many "other women" thus end up silenced by the "essentialized woman" of some gender discourses.

Reflecting on her own personal trajectory from social activist to aca-demic and on the increasing difficulties she encountered in attempting to combine these "discourses," Ellen Messer-Davidow (2002) shows how feminism, a venture launched with the objective of changing academic and social institutions, has itself been transformed and captured by these very same institutions. The issue is not only that feminism has become a discipline over the years but that it has also been disciplined along the way. Strathern remarks: "The field or context for feminist debate itself (women's oppression) entails the activation of conceptually conserva-tive constructs" (1988, 27). She points out that "domination"—whose denunciation some tendencies in "gender studies" assume as their pri-mary task—is deeply informed by how "property" is conceptualized in Western societies. According to Strathern, Westerners see themselves as proprietors—of themselves, their personal attributes, their genders, their cultures, and their societies. As property, a culture can be owned by some to the detriment of others. The reasoning offered in some trends in "gender studies" proposes that men normally own culture and mold it according to their perspective. As a result, women's experience of "cul-ture" may be at odds with their experience of themselves and their bod-ies. But what happens to this theoretical edifice if property is taken out of the equation? In Melanesia, where Strathern conducted fieldwork, local systems of knowledge are organized differently. Thus, "we must . . . stop thinking that an opposition between male and female must be about the control of men and women over each other. Realizing this ought to cre-ate fresh grounds for analyzing the nature of that opposition" (1988, 15). Indeed, other ethnographic settings may understand "gender" and "op-position" differently.

In Egypt, the participation of women in a Cairo revivalist movement offered Saba Mahmood (2001, 2005) the opportunity to discuss some of the feminist movement's liberal presuppositions. Her argument is that within the feminist framework "agency" has come to be defined somewhat narrowly as resistance to domination: in such a mindset, a prediscursive self has the "naturalized" will to be free from coercion and domination. Such an analytic framework, however, does not capture the experience of the women with whom Mahmood worked: these women actively participate in a movement through which they learned to accept subordination in their quest to attain a pious life. Their docile agency—the capacity for action within historically specific relations of subordination—exposes a liberal bias in much of what is written under the label of "gender studies," and it comes as no surprise that in various circles these pious women's situation elicits a call for a "diagnosis" and attempts at reform. In their own liberal vein, certain trends within feminism assume a prescriptive character at both analytical and political levels. Mahmood opts to parochialize some of the assumptions of liberal feminism, denaturalizing its normative subject and revealing its teleological certainties. It is feminism and feminists that may emerge transformed from the "clash" with the mosque-goers in Cairo: "Critique, I believe, is most powerful when it leaves open the possibility that we might also be remade in the process of engaging another's worldview, that we might come to learn things that we did not already know before we undertook the engagement. This requires that we occasionally turn the critical gaze upon ourselves, to leave open the possibility that we may be remade through an encounter with the other" (2005, 36–37).

Property and individual free will are two of the tenets of liberal and neoliberal ideology. Has feminism—or at least some of its trends—contributed, perhaps unwittingly and unconsciously, to the consolidation and solidification of the liberal and neoliberal project? Has it yielded to the latter's power? Is it part of the colonizing process, spreading its specific technologies of political order to other settings, along with new forms of personhood, means of manufacturing the experience of the real, and novel ontologies of representation (Timothy Mitchell 1991)? If so, are we still in a position to decolonize the methodologies we adopt (Smith 1999) in order to crystallize alternative futures (Messer-Davidow 2002), ones in which language, meaning, and political order have not been disciplined by the metaphysics of liberal representation (Timothy Mitchell 1991)? Can we "unlearn" (Spivak 1988) the precepts of liberal representation, so that the subaltern—Cairo mosque-goers, brown women (Spivak 1988), brown men, and Shatila pigeon raisers—can finally be heard?

"Les Enfants de l'Apatrie"

This study deals with what in the national order of things or what in the order of things of the academic discourse on gender is an oxymoron—or, as Foucault ([1970] 2010) would have put it, a heterotopia:[20] the Shatila *shabāb*, stateless men with very limited power.[21] For me, however, rather than being the representatives of the oxymoron of power discourses—academic or otherwise—the Shatila *shabāb* were friends.

Accordingly, this book investigates how acting as a "male provider" has increasingly become an avenue closed to the Shatila *shabāb*'s coming-of-age and display of sex belonging. The specialized literature on Palestinians before the Nakba, or Catastrophe, as refugees refer to their forced departure from Palestine in 1948, suggests that a man would come of age by marrying at the appropriate age and having a son (Granqvist 1931, 1947). In the saga of the Palestinian diaspora in Lebanon, acting as *fidā'iy-yīn* throughout the 1970s provided an alternative mechanism for the coming-of-age and display of sex belonging. The central question of this study is: How do the Shatila *shabāb* come of age today and display their sex belonging?

The answer to this question is far from obvious, particularly taking into account two factors. First, Lebanese legislation, through what I name "institutional violence," bars Palestinian refugees from free access to the

20. I see no reason why heterotopias should be limited to places and spaces.

21. Suggested by François Chatêlet to Jacques Meunier (2001), the expression "les enfants de l'apatrie" in this section's subhead plays with the phonetically similar line of the French national anthem—"Allons enfants de la patrie" (Let's go for it, children of the motherland)—and means something along the lines of "children of no motherland."

labor market, forcing the *shabāb* to postpone plans for getting married and starting an independent household. As a result, the economic avenue of acting as "male providers" for their families has ceased to be the straightforward track for the coming-of-age and display of sex belonging that it used to be before 1948—precisely in a place situated in the Middle East, considered by much of the feminist literature as a region where "patriarchy" acts as a structural axis for the very constitution of people, culture, and society (Ahmed 1992; Charrad 2001; Ghannam 2013; Gruenbaum 2000; Hatem 1986; Hoodfar 1997; Joseph 1993a, 1994, 1999a, 2000, 2004; Kandiyoti 1991, 1994, 1996; MacLeod 1993; Mernissi 1987, 1991; Moors 1996; Saadawi 1980; Sabbah 1984; Sedghi 2007; Singerman 1995; Wikan 2008). Second, the Palestinian Resistance Movement in its military version no longer exists in Lebanon. The political-military avenue for coming of age and displaying adequate sex belonging is thus not open to the *shabāb*, either, unlike how it was during the 1970s—precisely in Shatila, which much of the literature on nationalism often considers to be one of the bedrocks of Palestinian resistance (R. Sayigh 1979, 1993).

To explore this issue, I conducted my research using a plethora of investigative techniques: participant observation, questionnaires, focus groups, and open-ended interviews. During the fieldwork, which spanned from 2007 to 2009, I lived in Shatila for a year, conducted a household survey with thirty-nine families,[22] and held workshops using music as a prompt to trigger debates. I also interviewed sixteen sets of parents and children (first with each parent and child separately and then with the two together),[23] collected the life stories of twenty *shabāb* and three *banāt*

---

22. The thirty-nine families were distributed as follows: twenty-four were Palestinians living in Shatila; six were Palestinians living outside the camp (because I was interested in investigating whether residence made a difference to the stories I collected); and nine were non-Palestinians living in the camp (because I wanted to check to what extent being Palestinian made a difference). Some of the data gathered this way are explored in chapter 2.

23. Fourteen of the sixteen pairs were composed of fathers (the other two of mothers), all of them former freedom fighters, and their sons (in two cases, daughters). Chapter 4 provides more details on some of these interviews and draws on the results.

(young women), and talked to a number of local leaders, UNRWA and NGO staff, as well as scholars researching Palestinian refugees in Lebanon. My aim was to register the differences between the *fidā'iyyīn* and their offspring, the *shabāb*, with respect to their coming-of-age and display of sex belonging, in particular by comparing the "revolutionary masculinities" of the former to the "quotidian masculinities" of the latter.

Does examining the differences in the ways in which pre-1948 Palestinians, the *fidā'iyyīn*, and the *shabāb* "do" their gender allow the full historicity and changeability in time and space of "masculinity" to come to the fore? Furthermore, are the scholarly concepts "agency" and "gender" transformed and possibly undone in the process? In studies of the Middle East and arguably of other regions, "gender" tends to be strictly defined in terms of power and relations of domination. Does such a definition grasp the experience of those, such as the *shabāb* from Shatila, who possess very limited access to power? Rather than presenting them as emasculated for being unable to act as fighters and for facing difficulties in acting as "male providers," should the analyst instead take issue with the concepts "agency" and "gender" and propose that defining agency only as "resistance to domination" and gender only in terms of "relations of power" is highly restrictive? As the reader becomes aware of the "antistate effects" at play in Shatila, might this study also point to the (dangerous) liaisons between "gender" and "agency" as concepts and the canons of the royal, state science (Deleuze and Guattari [1987] 2004)? What happens to "gender" (and "agency") when the state effects are not taken for granted as part of the picture, organizing and solidifying a "sex-gender" system at the local level?

This is how I proceed in following the "trajectories" (Ghannam 2013) of the *fidā'iyyīn* and the *shabāb*. Chapter 1, "Submerging: Under Siege," shows how life in Shatila decolonized my methodological assumptions and canons (Smith 1999). Rather than arguing only for the power and heuristic value of local methodologies (Smith 1999), should scholars not also take issue with the idea that methodologies need to be informed by power? It was only when I realized how lacking in power I myself was in Shatila that a sense of deep empathy (M. Bateson 1987; Sykes 2003) with the *shabāb* was established and my research took off. Through this repositioning in my field, I was able to see what I had previously been blind to: the antistate effects in operation in the camp.

Chapter 2, "Drowning by Numbers and Legislation: Statistics and (Non)State Making in Shatila," asks what happens to the "economy" and "political life" when we look at them without the aid of "state lenses." Are two of the tasks traditionally associated with states, enumeration (Jeganathan 2008) and law making (Poole 2008), transformed as a result? Do statistics, as an essential tool for state making, falter in the presence of antistate effects? Are numbers feeding statistical tables on the economy of the camp of limited significance, and do they really capture the way Shatila's "economy" functions? Does Shatila allow for a different gaze into the mechanisms of "making the economy"? And does it also uncover new ways of "making a city" (Agier 1999, 2010), revealing along the way alternative visions of citizenship? Is it the case that alternative instruments for money circulation, social security, and savings—represented, respectively, by local dowry practices, "cooperatives" (*jam'iyyāt*),[24] and women's golden bracelets—operate in Shatila but are nevertheless completely ignored by the statistical surveys on living conditions in the camp?

The *shabāb* and their fathers, the *fidā'iyyīn*, speak in chapter 3, "Swirling and Twirling: The *Fidā'iyyīn*'s Heroism and the *Shabāb*'s Burden." Do their biographies, as narrated by themselves, show how coming-of-age and the display of sex belonging have changed from one generation to the next, providing an example of the pliability and full historicity of "masculinity"? Do they serve to illustrate the sense in which "gender," understood as different access to power by men and women, may work as an analytic tool to make sense of the fathers' trajectories but then loses much of its heuristic reach when applied to the life stories of the *shabāb*? Do these biographies also depict changes in the perceptions of Shatila through time:

---

24. *Jam'iyyāt* is the plural form of *jam'iyya*, a joint pooling of resources by different households. These resources can be used by those taking part in the arrangement if and when the need arises.

from the "cradle of the *fidā'iyyīn*" in the 1970s to the dreadful shantytown of today, which is to be left behind when an opportunity to move out or migrate arises?

The extreme conditions leading to utter poverty in the camps are reflected in the rap music produced by the *shabāb*. In chapter 4, "Pororoca, Thinking through Music: *Fidā'iyyīn* and *Shabāb* Talk (Sometimes) Past Each Other," *shabāb* and *fidā'iyyīn* go on talking—no longer to the ethnographer, but to each other and through music. Chapter 4 reports on workshops held in South Lebanon and Shatila with Palestinians from different generations, during which participants were invited to listen to and express their views on two songs: "Romana" (Pomegranate/Grenade),[25] a typical example of Palestinian nationalistic music from the 1970s and 1980s, popular among the *fidā'iyyīn*, and "Ahlān fīk bil-mukhayyamāt" (Welcome to the Camps), a recent rap song by the Palestinian band Katibe 5, which the *shabāb* never seem to tire of listening to. Does what emerged from the workshops show the different ways in which *fidā'iyyīn* and *shabāb* relate to Palestine? Do the former feed into the ideology of the return and the latter opt for a "contextualized engagement" (Puig 2007), where a much more nuanced relation to what counts as the "motherland" merges with another preoccupation: coping with the dire conditions of life in Lebanon? Through rap, do the *shabāb* find a medium to speak about what would otherwise be forced into silence: that the never-forgotten calls for the return have to be combined with more urgent demands in Lebanon, where refugees do not have the right to acquire real estate and where access to work is heavily curtailed? Are rap songs infrapolitical, therefore, as Nicolas Puig (2007) posits, or do they point instead to other ways of being political?

Based on pigeon raising by the *shabāb* as well as on another workshop—this time one on "gender" held at a local NGO's facility—chapter 5, "Reemerging: Noncockfights," interrogates the extent to which the activities of Shatila's young men can be framed as "gender performance." Rather

---

25. The proper transliteration for "Romana" should be "Rummāna," following the *IJMES* system. I have decided to use "Romana" instead throughout this book to facilitate the reading of the song title.

than portraying the *shabāb* as emasculated for not being in a position to perform a "gender," should scholars not take issue with "gender" itself? In its final pages, this study asks whether "gender" circulates in a semantic universe defined by the quest for political power. As such, is "gender" not problematic when applied to lives so deeply marked by antistate effects as those led by the Shatila *shabāb*? Does such a discussion have consequences for the way in which anthropologists and feminists frame yet another concept—"agency"—and thus expose some of its liberal underpinnings?

The final chapter, "Resurfacing: The Antilove of Empire," brings together the various threads and lines of reasoning presented throughout the study. It also takes us back to where we started: the (dis)order of things. Foucault ([1970] 2010) teaches us that the history of order imposed on things (whether by nationalistic or academic discourses, I would add) is the history of the Same. In such an order of things, are heterotopias—like the universes navigated by the stateless and powerless young men in Shatila—in any sense disturbing? Heterotopias, Foucault goes on to reason, undermine language, dissolve our myths, and destroy syntax because they make obvious how difficult it is to hold together disparate elements: words and things. As such, do they also question representation—including, as in the case here, political representation? Has not the time perhaps arrived, therefore, to venture into new skies?

Before we set off, I wish to reflect on the kind of language I use in this book as well as on the photographs I include in it. This book is written by a proud speaker of Portuguese and thus a *non*native speaker of English. What Talal Asad (1993) has identified as the inequality of languages—and the varying levels of power with which they are imbued—naturally finds its way into academia. I am therefore forced to express myself in a language that is not mine or the *shabāb*'s and that neither of us completely inhabits. But, then, as Deleuze and Guattari ([1987] 2004) argue, even English, its universalistic ambitions notwithstanding, is assaulted by "minor" uses, with Black English and other American ghetto dialects, for instance, corrupting and compromising its constants and supposed homogeneity. For a book advocating the need *not* to take power for granted—in the methods we use, in the way we conceptualize "gender"—it is logical that at the very level of expression and the language deployed, the presumedly inevitable "power" of English is also contested and problematized. Thus, I invite my reader not to give up on the book even when challenged with sentences that might have been written differently by a native speaker. What I offer, in a sense, is not only the *best* English I can afford but also the English I *want* to offer. Or, as the *shabāb* would put it, "the best English ever happened."

I am indebted to the talented eye of a Shatila photographer, Hisham Ghuzlan, for the disturbing beauty of several of the pictures in this book. Hisham, being who he is, will probably (and unfairly) insist on sharing that merit with me. When my field research was coming to an end and I was about to leave Lebanon, I realized that I had taken no pictures of the camp, very much because of my discomfort with the artificiality of freezing life—movements, attitudes, and people—in images. I shared my uneasiness with Hisham, who, having also doubled for a couple of months as my Arabic teacher, had by then become a friend. Hisham suggested we go around Shatila taking photos together. The end result of this "visual ethnographic lab" illustrates some of the following pages. But these pictures are also illustrative of something else: my relation to this Shatila *shāb*, Hisham. Today, Hisham and I can no longer identify which photos are his and which are mine. Our authorship of the material and our views of the camp became intertwined, entangled, confused. For a book advocating for patterns that connect, it seems simply right to select pictures that belong to a Shatila *shāb* and also to me and that in a very deep sense are *ours*, just as I hope (perhaps unduly) that this book, rather than being just *about* the *shabāb*, can also become *theirs*.

1

Submerging

Under Siege

Under Siege

I regretted having missed the installation by Lebanese artist Nada Sehnaoui in downtown Beirut in April 2008. The work—given the suggestive title *Haven't 15 Years of Hiding in Toilettes Been Enough?*—consisted of six hundred lavatories placed in one of the rare empty spaces not yet claimed by the rapid postwar reconstruction of the city center (figure 2). When I finally managed to find my way to the exhibition, the lavatories—symmetrically arranged over the area in an eerie evocation of a cemetery—were already being removed. Sehnaoui's objective was to provide a compelling memoir of the Lebanese Civil War (1975–90), during which Beirutis frequently took cover in their bathrooms, the internal corridors of their buildings, and underground parking lots. I could not have anticipated that weeks later I would find myself pondering whether to sleep in the bathroom.

"Please, Gustavo, open the gate downstairs for me!," Latif, twenty-nine, a Palestinian chemist from the surroundings of Shatila, shouted over the interphone in my building late in the afternoon of May 8, 2008. By then, the Lebanese political stalemate had escalated to a full-blown crisis, and the country seemed poised on the brink of a new civil war. Earlier that day, forces belonging to the opposition party Hezbollah had encircled Qreitam in the western part of Beirut, reacting against the government's decision to curb the party's parallel communication network and to dismiss one of its delegates from the strategic position of security coordinator at the

43

2. *Haven't 15 Years of Hiding in Toilettes Been Enough?* Nada Sehnaoui's installation in downtown Beirut, April 2008. Photograph reproduced by permission of Atelier Nada Sehnaoui.

International Airport. The palace resided in by Saad Hariri, inheritor of the Mustaqbal movement from his father, the late premier Rafik Hariri, is located in Qreitam. He was one of the leaders of the US-Saudi-supported alliance then governing the country, and his lavish headquarters was one of the targets of Hezbollah on that eventful May 8. Between Hezbollah and the Mustaqbal militiamen sat the dilapidated building where I kept a small pied-à-terre in the hope of securing a place to which I could retreat to take notes and recuperate from the harshness of daily life in the Shatila camp. Trapped in the exchange of fire taking place in the neighboring district of Hamra, Latif had decided to seek refuge in my apartment because the rapid multiplication of military and paramilitary checkpoints throughout the city made returning home impossible. In the following hours, Latif, a survivor of Shatila's various sieges during the Camp Wars of the 1980s, taught me how to stay alive in such situations. This experience marked my own coming-of-age as an ethnographer, and Latif and I emerged as brothers from the siege, evidence that, in addition to the oversexualized mores of blood relations (Schneider 1968), relatedness may also stem from pure dire necessity.

With the city brought to a standstill, I opened the door for Latif, and in the following hours he initiated me into how to survive a siege. "No, Gustavo, the situation is not bad enough yet for us to sleep in the bathroom. Let's just move the beds away from the windows so that we won't be hurt by shards of glass if there's an explosion outside." That was just one of the many pieces of good advice he gave me. He explained why bathrooms are the safest places in a house: the absence of large windows greatly reduces the risk of being lacerated by shattering glass. Furthermore, the compartment above the bathroom where water heaters are normally installed provides an extra layer of protection should the building be severely hit and collapse. Even though Latif had little empathy with the Mustaqbal, he taught me that pragmatic considerations outweigh ideology in certain circumstances: "We're both on Hariri's side at the moment, Gustavo, since it's his men who are protecting us right now." He also scolded me for still not having purchased a TV set: "How the hell are we going to know what's going on in the city?!" Throughout the night, we ate only sparsely, too: unprepared for a crisis of such magnitude, I had failed to stock up on provisions and had just a few vegetables and fruits in my fridge. The next day we rushed to one of the few neighborhood shops that remained opened to buy canned food. Aside from the vendors, Latif and I were the only men in the shop. I had read that during sieges women are more mobile than men because snipers will think twice before shooting at them. Such had been the case during the Camp Wars in Shatila in the 1980s,[1] and the same applied again in my own neighborhood on that early morning of May 9.

The lessons I learned from Latif that night were not limited to surviving a siege. He also taught me something fundamental about what

---

1. Evidently there is no guarantee that snipers will not shoot women as well, though, and, indeed, several women were killed while trying to bring food into the Shatila or Burj al-Barajneh camps during the sieges of the Camp Wars.

he had once disapprovingly described as "this anthropology of yours." I had always imagined the exercise of rapprochement with (and distancing from) the "other," the basic tool of ethnography, as simply an intellectual task. During that rainy night in May, under the Hezbollah-imposed siege, while Latif's and my own destinies seemed both interconnected and uncertain, and while we chatted about the fear of death and the importance of having children to leave grandchildren for our parents, my identification with Latif moved well beyond the limits of a mere intellectual exercise. I was finally able to fully understand Julie Peteet's remarks about her own days living under siege during the Israeli invasion of Beirut in 1982: "A strong overwhelming solidarity in face of invasion and siege bound together the residents of West Beirut. Muslim and Christian, Arab and foreigner. Facing the siege together forged the sense of sympathy that Kirschner (1987) describes as an essential component of the interaction between self and other. But to distance oneself, the other component of ethnographic interaction, was emotionally, as well as physically, impossible" (1991, 211).

On the morning of May 9, the Brazilian embassy contacted me to ask whether I wanted it to send a car to evacuate me from Qreitam to Baabda, a Christian suburb east of Beirut. I again asked for Latif's advice. He strongly recommended that I accept the offer. I told him that I would, provided he came along. He countered that it made no sense for him to go to Baabda, even farther away from his home, and added that should he need to escape, I would be a burden to him: "Besides, Gustavo, I will never forgive myself if you turn down the offer from the embassy and then something happens to you afterward. I just ask you to let me stay in your apartment until I manage to get back home."

I hugged him tightly in front of the Commodore Hotel, near my flat, where the embassy car was waiting for me. Latif returned to my place. On my way out of Qreitam, I saw several checkpoints, some with soldiers from the Lebanese army and some with nonuniformed men, probably from the Hezbollah militia. I had a glimpse of what it means to leave one's place, one's friends, and one's belongings behind, counting on coming back someday but not being entirely sure whether that would be possible.

When I finally returned to my Qreitam apartment a couple of days later, with the crisis over, I found a message in Arabic that Latif had left. It just said: "Thanks, brother." It was a sharp change from our first meeting a couple of months earlier when he thought I was a British researcher and refused when I asked for his mobile number—"because I don't actually know you, do I?" When he finally relented, he gave me the wrong number. The next time we met after the crisis, it was Latif who strongly embraced me and said, in English this time, "We're brothers, now, Gustavo, because we've suffered together." My own standing vis-à-vis the very suspicious *shabāb* (lads) from Shatila improved after the siege. Since news had gotten around that I had not panicked during it, one of them explained to me that I had been promoted to "hardcore Palestinian." Another commented: "Buddy, you're in the game now."

This chapter describes my education by Shatila research participants, which was simultaneously a "diseducation" in some of the tenets guiding the sciences that I have been trained in. Just as Latif taught me how to live through a siege and precisely when sleeping in the bathroom became a necessity, I learned from other Shatilans and Palestinians what space, time, violence, and history meant for them. I was also prompted to revisit some of my methodological assumptions about the power supposedly, inescapably, and (in)famously characterizing the ethnographic encounter. In Shatila, in fact, it was Shatilans who were in the know and had control, not I. Recognition of my fundamental vulnerability was essential for my field research to take off: it prompted my actual and existential engagement with Shatilans and forced a reelaboration of the central theme of my research, gender, compelling me to think of it beyond its mere definition as differential access to power by men and women. For this reason, this chapter is permeated by death, the ultimate vulnerability.

The Map Is Not the Territory

"So, you really like that map, Gustavo?" I sensed a speck of sarcasm in the voice of Dalal, a twenty-four-year-old Lebanese Palestinian woman and resident of al-Tariq al-Jadida, a district neighboring Shatila, who has a diploma in English literature. Indeed, after being admitted into "the game," I realized that to remain a "buddy," I would have to come to grips with the complex ways in which space, time, and their representations interacted for my Palestinian friends.

In a remarkable scene from the movie *Roundabout Shatila* (2005), directed by Maher Abi-Samra, a man reproaches his female neighbor for not sweeping the sidewalk in front of a dwelling belonging to another family in the refugee camp. The woman's adamant refusal is met by the man's insistence: "Think of the pavement as being Palestinian territory. It's 1948." She remains defiant: "It isn't 1948. It's 1967." In 1967, following the Arab defeat by Israel in the Six-Day War, new Palestinian refugees found their way to Lebanon and other neighboring countries. The pavement that the woman in the movie refuses to clean is in front of a house belonging to a refugee family who arrived in Lebanon in 1967, whereas her own family left Palestine in 1948. This scene, combined with Dalal's evaluation of my map, forced me to ask a series of questions: What happens in a place like modern Shatila, where the state is not present to produce and impose ostensibly indisputable representations of space and time? What does it mean to yearn for a return to a space, Palestine, where one has never set foot and to a time, the years prior to 1948, in which one has not lived? Moreover, what does such a longing feel like for a Palestinian such as Dalal, who has lived her entire life in a highly politicized, conflicted, and divided country such as Lebanon?

Until my chat with Dalal, I was very happy with the map I had purchased at the fashionable bookstore Antoine. I thought it provided a relatively sound illustration of the Lebanese sectarian patchwork. Dalal quashed my illusions pitilessly: "This map is a total lie, Gustavo." Dalal's point went beyond the fact that by selecting the brighter color red to represent the Christian Maronite communities but paler colors to depict other communities, the map gives the impression that the Christians are more numerous than is actually the case. In addition, the caption under the map states that it reflects data from 2004. No census has been carried out in Lebanon, though, since 1932. Because the statistical data collected way back then serves to freeze the distribution of political power among the various sects, Dalal rightly questioned the information on which the map was based. Further, she called my attention to the fact that the map was published by someone identified as "François Eid." "Most definitely, a Christian, Gustavo," she remarked, before adding her by now irrefutable conclusion: "This map serves as a political statement."

It is indeed telling that over time I have come to think that a poster caricaturing the Civil War that I bought at a rundown bookstore near the American University of Beirut is more revealing than François Eid's map. Rather than claiming to represent "reality" on the ground, the caricaturist aims simply to make a comment. The initial impression one gets from the caricature "Beirut, Have a Nice Day" is that the conflict-ravaged capital of Lebanon was a completely chaotic place: the poster shows a crowd of people, several cars, and buildings, and it takes a while for the viewer to discern what is happening. With closer inspection, the drawing reveals a city striving to maintain its everyday routine despite the war-related violence: businessmen on their way to work and students walking to school; housewives running errands; roads being repaired and construction work going on; dealers selling drugs; and lovers making love.

Indeed, the image functions as a compelling argument concerning the absolute impossibility—in the case of Lebanon and Beirut as well as probably elsewhere—of separating violence from nonviolence as though some kind of rule determines that conflict cannot take place on an everyday basis (Cushman 2004; Hermez 2017; Khayyat 2012, 2013). It works, too, as a post facto critique of what one of my instructors at the university in London where I did my PhD observed when I announced my intention to conduct research among Palestinian refugees in Lebanon: "But how are you going to pursue that objective? You'll be dragged in by the politics of it all."

In places such as the Middle East and Lebanon and presumably in the United Kingdom, too, conflict and politics are fully social matters and thus arguably invite sociological analysis. A brief detour to Iris Jean-Klein's (2001) and Tobias Kelly's (2008) depictions of the First and Second Intifadas (1987–92 and 2000–present, respectively) corroborates the point. Their representations of the two Palestinian uprisings in the Occupied Territories can hardly be further apart. Jean-Klein interprets Palestinian practices during the First Intifada as an outcome of the decision to suspend everyday life. Unable to manifest revolt through the usual political channels because of Israeli control, West Bank Palestinians infused their everyday activities (such as writing shopping lists, visiting, eating together, and celebrating marriages) with political meaning. They did so by suspending the customary ways in which such actions were performed.

Jean-Klein argues that Palestinians sought to preserve their own capacity to assign meaning to their suspended daily activities by presenting the effects of Israeli control as self-authored. Accordingly, if the traditional costs of marriage celebrations became prohibitive during the intifada, Palestinians presented the ensuing sobriety as originating from their own decision not to be joyful. In Jean-Klein's account, Palestinians did not succumb to passive victimization: they asserted a heroic agency, exemplified by the mother who protested against the description of her son's imprisonment as a case of him being taken away by the Israelis: "What do you mean, 'They took him?' He went!" (Jean-Klein 2001, 114).

In focusing on the Second Intifada, Kelly sheds a different light on the same West Bank Palestinians. He maintains that rather than being mesmerized by outbreaks of animosity, analysts should pay due attention to *non*violence and to their informants' persistence in maintaining their mundane routines. Second Intifada West Bankers, according to Kelly, strove not to let their lives be disrupted by the Israelis. One of his young informants, for instance, decided to continue his studies to become an accountant despite the conflict. Jean-Klein's combative First Intifada activists appear to have been pursuing somewhat more bourgeois goals only a couple of years later, considering Kelly's fieldwork.

Nevertheless, what Jean-Klein's and Kelly's explanations hold in common is more revealing than what sets them apart. Both Jean-Klein and Kelly emphasize that the ordinary is itself an inherently political category and that the social and political are inextricably linked. As a consequence, if in Palestine, as in other conflict-ridden areas, "more time is [still] spent watching television, waiting for buses or preparing dinner" (Kelly 2008, 371)—or coming of age and displaying adequate sex roles, to bring this debate closer to the one that occupies the following chapters—that does not mean that the ordinary is apolitical. The decision either to suspend the ordinary, like Jean-Klein's First Intifada activists, or maintain it, like Kelly's second Intifada accounting student, entails an intrinsically political process. The key question here is precisely what counts as "ordinary." As Kelly (2008) argues, this should not be left unexamined as a residual analytical category but rather needs to be probed.

Indeed, in some parts of the world—in the Middle East, with its active warzones, in particular—violence and conflict *are* ordinary. If a caricature seems too weak a basis for such a contention or for my assertion about the porosity between violence and nonviolence in Beirut, three photos from the Civil War period, two by Lebanese photographer Stavro Jabra, help support my case. The photos show a traffic jam in war-torn Beirut, a tank stuck right in the middle of the cars; a child casually reading a newspaper while leaning against another tank; and a Lebanese woman enjoying her day by the sea, wearing the latest beach fashion and a rather unexpected accessory: a machine gun.

True enough, these photos date from the Civil War period, and the situation today is not the same. Yet there is ground to assert that violence and conflict continue to inform daily life in Beirut. An illustrative example is the fast-food outlet Buns & Guns, which opened in the Hezbollah-controlled Shia district of Dahiya while I was in Lebanon. With the motto "a sandwich can kill you," the restaurant, an immediate if short-lived commercial success, adopted a military theme for its decor and its staff uniforms. The dishes served were given the names of weapons, and a leaflet celebrated the efficiency of the company's home-delivery service, claiming that the food arrived at its customers' homes faster than a bullet.

It makes sense, therefore, to ask whether our difficulties in thinking simultaneously about violence and nonviolence, conflict and the everyday, do not arise from a certain ethnocentric expectation of how societies should function. Indeed, such an expectation is far more revealing of our own anxiety about conflicts, which are often ignored, and my London university instructor's remark may ultimately have had much more to do with how conflict is (or is not) perceived in the United Kingdom than with the reality of the city where I conducted my fieldwork.

Although the everyday nature of conflict in Beirut and Lebanon, the impossibility of separating violence from nonviolence, and the intertwining of war and daily living should be insisted upon (Hermez 2017; Khayyat 2012, 2013), some caution needs to be taken not to banalize clashes and disputes, for they do have consequences: in the case of the incidents in May 2008, for instance, at least eighty fatalities. This is why the "structural violence" paradigm, as formulated by Nancy Scheper-Hughes (1992), proves insufficient to render intelligible the daily violence in Beirut. When the author asserts that mothers in Northeast Brazil display a malign neglect toward their children, sometimes contributing to their deaths, and that this negligence is owing to the "structural violence" of everyday life in the country, it remains unclear what precisely she means by this modality of violence. What does this "structural violence" comprise, and how does it affect the lives of these women or, in the case of this study, Palestinian refugees in Lebanon? Circumventing these insufficiencies, in my own field I prefer to think along the lines of a "legal and institutional violence." This concept enables me to concretely locate the sources of violence, such as the Lebanese legislation that bars Palestinian refugees from free access to the local labor market, as chapter 2 demonstrates.

My friends and informants, Lebanese and Palestinians alike, used the term 'ādī (normal) to describe the outbursts of violence that occurred throughout my time in Beirut. The Abu Tarek[2] family, for example, whom I interviewed in Shatila, proudly told me that they were not even woken up when Israeli jets destroyed the nearby airport flyover during the July War of 2006. "We have a military mindset," Abu Tarek explained to me. In February 2008, in addition to street fights in Beirut, the city was hit by a series of earthquakes of minor magnitude. A friend who called me to talk about the event could barely disguise her excitement about what she had seen on TV: a clairvoyant predicting that the Lebanese capital would be struck by a tsunami following the earthquakes. I had felt the tremors, too, but had attributed them to bombs exploding somewhere in the city, far away enough

---

2. It is a common feature throughout the Arab world that a man comes to be known by the name of his eldest son, as in "Abu Tarek," meaning "Father of Tarek." This patrilineal naming system works, further, as an indication of the respect due to older men. The fidā'iyyīn, the Palestinian fighters, have followed such a pattern when adopting their noms de guerre. In some instances, they have become known as "Father of So-and-So" even when they have not borne any sons. Such is precisely the case of Yasser Arafat, who bore only one daughter and yet is known in the camps by his nom de guerre "Abu Ammar."

not to be dangerous, and in Beiruti style I had simply kept on working on my notes: "Kul hadhā 'ādī" (all this is normal). Dalal would agree with this perception. She once remarked to me: "Don't let yourself be impressed by moments of peace here, Gustavo. What we live in Lebanon is a cold war."

History Is Not the Event

It was the first day of Eid al-Adha in November 2009. We—a group of young Shatila men and women, a British scholar friend, and I—met before dawn in front of a local NGO center in one of the few squares in the refugee camp. Following the Muslim tradition of commemorating the dead on the first day of Eid al-Adha, we were going to the cemeteries near Shatila, led by Abu Mujahed, a former fighter (*fidā'ī*) and presently the director of the NGO. In the soft breeze of the very early morning, he drew our attention to some of the graves. The group listened attentively while Abu Mujahed spoke about the destruction of the Tal al-Zattar camp in 1976, pointing to a grave that contained corpses from there. We stopped again at the spot where Ghassan Kanafani, a famous Palestinian novelist, painter, and militant, is buried. Kanafani and his niece were assassinated in a car-bomb attack in Beirut in 1972, allegedly by Mossad, the Israeli intelligence service, possibly in retaliation for his nationalistic literature. Later, Abu Mujahed pointed out an epitaph to me that, surprisingly enough, featured a cross. He explained that the corpses of some Palestinian Christians had been refused burial in the city's Christian cemeteries and were laid there instead.[3] Once the visit was over, we returned to Shatila, and after a brief stop in the modest mosque where the remains of the martyrs (*shuhadā'*) of the Camp Wars are kept, we rushed back to the NGO center for breakfast. By then, we all were very hungry.

In September 2009, I attended a commemoration of the Sabra and Shatila massacre of 1982, during which Lebanese Christian militiamen, with

3. Other friends explained to me that Christians considered to have died as martyrs (*shuhadā'*) tended to be automatically buried at the cemetery near the camp.

the support of the Israeli army, killed an estimated 3,000 inhabitants of the camp and its surroundings (Nuwayhed al-Hout 2004). Organized by an Italian NGO, the commemoration was conducted outside Shatila in an auditorium graciously made available by the administration of Ghobeiry municipality, where the camp is situated. The participants—mostly women and children from the camp, especially those with ties to NGOs, and foreign sympathizers—listened to a few speeches before making their way to the mass grave located near the camp, where the victims from the massacre are buried. The area is mainly Shia, and for quite some time, particularly during the Camp Wars, Shatilans had no access to the grave.

On an earlier visit, my Palestinian friend Rania had called my attention to the Shia character of several features of the mass grave. A placard in one corner displays the photos of a family massacred in 1982. "That was a Shia family, Gustavo, not a Palestinian one," Rania said. Next to the placard, a sequence of posters reminds the emotionally overloaded visitor of more recent attacks by the Israelis in Qana, Marawahin, and Chiah during the war in 2006: all against the Shia. The few centimeters separating the first placard from the posters glossed over the twenty-four years between 1982 and 2006, including the War of the Camps of the 1980s, which set Shia against Palestinians and Palestinians against Palestinians, a period many prefer not to talk about. If allowed to surface, this period would compromise the Shia political reappropriation of the grave and of the massacre as well as the myths surrounding Palestinian unity. "Even the gatekeeper here is Shia, Gustavo," Rania whispered to me as we were leaving the place.

◦ ◦ ◦

I was arriving home to the camp on an especially hot midafternoon in the summer of 2009 when I noticed that several plastic chairs had been arranged in the square in front of the local NGO center. I was not aware of any celebration taking place that evening. When a date important to Palestinians is remembered, some of the political factions hold events in the square, showing movies with Arafat in them or performances with traditional Palestinian songs and dances. The occasion for the gathering that day, however, was more somber. While walking in the camp's alleys, one of the residents, Samira, died when a brick fell from a building and struck her on the head. Because her house was too small to accommodate all those wishing to visit the mourning family, male relatives sat in the square receiving condolences from male acquaintances and friends, while the women did the same elsewhere.

Shatila is not a Palestinian community in any obvious sense. Perhaps some 50 percent of its inhabitants are not actually Palestinian, but Shia Lebanese, Syrian, Kurd, Dom,[4] Iraqi, and, more recently, Syrian refugees fleeing from the civil war ravaging the neighboring country. These "foreigners" are attracted by cheaper rents in a relatively central location with the extra advantages of such utilities as water sometimes being available for free and, for those with documentation irregularities, with the assurance of not being harassed by Lebanese officials because the latter normally do not enter the camps. Nevertheless, Shatila does occasionally and for limited periods crystallize as a Palestinian community—most strikingly when inhabitants gather to remember their dead, mourn, or celebrate the highly scarred events marking the refugee saga. Here, history—or, given the absence of any official history in Lebanon, historical events—play a role, and so do the fighters and the martyrs (*shuhadā'*), who upon death, strangely enough, acquire "agency," the capacity to act and make a Palestinian community out of Shatila. As a community, Shatila is also composed—and perhaps primarily so—of those who are no longer there.

When I went to pay a visit, Umm Yousef was busy trying to get her and her neighbor's sons to study.[5] The boys had a history exam in the coming days and, to Umm Yousef's despair, did not seem very worried.

---

4. The Dom—often referred to rather derogatorily as "Nawar" or "Gypsies"—are a nomadic population that lives between Syria and Lebanon. Those living close to the border between the two countries, often earning a living from making dental prostheses, have maintained their nomadic residence patterns. Those in Shatila have developed more sedentary habits and make a living by selling fake brand watches at traffic lights. Shatilans often criticize them for supposedly not sending their children to school. Very little has been written about the Dom—a thesis by Giovanni Bocchi (2007) and a study by the NGO Terre des Hommes (2011) being among the few texts that have come to my attention.

5. Some mothers were known in Shatila after the name of their first-born sons, as in "Umm Yousef," meaning "Mother of Yousef."

While they engaged in lively chatter with one another, the books, their pages celebrating the majestic history of ancient Egypt and Babylon, were forgotten. I asked Umm Yousef how Palestine and the history of Lebanon were presented at UNRWA schools. "They aren't Gustavo. *Mamnū', mamnū', mamnū'* [forbidden, forbidden, forbidden]." UNRWA follows the Lebanese academic curriculum, and at Lebanese schools the history of Lebanon after 1943 is left untaught—precisely the year when the country started to exist as an independent political entity. Lebanese history is highly controversial, and there are several versions of the same events, framed according to the readings of the interested parties. No textbook of Lebanese history exists that enjoys approval from all the various sects. For the earlier grades, UNRWA has given a green light for teachers to use a brochure with some general data on Palestinian history and geography, as I observed while sitting for *tarbiya madaniyya* (civil education) classes for the elementary cycle held at the Ariha school in the camp. More advanced students, such as Umm Yousef's children, do not learn any Palestinian history or geography at school.

It is through participation in activities such as the commemoration of the dead in the first days of both Eid al-Adha and, mostly, Eid al-Fitr that Shatila youth become acquainted with a Palestinian understanding of their history in Lebanon. Indeed, history is not simply a sequence of events: these events need to be glossed and commented on so as to enable a certain organic intelligibility. Shatila youth are not taught but end up learning anyway at varying depths that the idea of a permanent settlement for Palestinian refugees in Lebanon (*tawṭīn*, or "naturalization") has always been anathema to the government in Beirut, which has been legally constituted by the sectarianism endemic to Lebanese political life, one of the reasons for the murderous Civil War (Picard 1996; Trabulsi 2007). The prohibition of Palestinian *tawṭīn* has even been incorporated into the Lebanese postwar Constitution. The rhetorical excuse for this policy is to avoid weakening the cause of the refugees' right to return by recognizing their permanent status in the host country. The pragmatic reason, though, is that assigning full citizenship to Palestinians in Lebanon would dramatically unbalance Lebanon's fragile demographic politics (R. Sayigh 1995) because it would increase the number of Sunni voters.

Before and during the Civil War, Palestinians played an active role in Lebanese sectarian politics. The *ayyām al-thawra* (days of the revolution, 1967–82) constituted the heyday of the Palestinian Resistance Movement in Lebanon (Peteet 1991, 2005; R. Sayigh 1979, 1993; Yezid Sayigh 1997). Through the Cairo Agreement of 1969, some civil rights were ensured for the refugee population in the country. Palestinians also obtained official permission to launch attacks against Israel from Lebanese territory and gained virtual autonomy for the administration of the camps. Expelled from Amman, Jordan, in 1971, the Palestinian leadership and guerrillas found their way to Lebanon, which became the focus for Palestinian political and military activity until 1982. The invasion of Lebanon by Israel, the forced evacuation of the PLO, and the massacre of thousands of Palestinians in Sabra and Shatila, all in 1982, marked the demise of the *ayyām al-thawra*. In addition, the position of Palestinians in Lebanon was further eroded by their confrontation with the Shia Amal movement in the Camp Wars of 1985–87.

Since 1982, the Lebanese government has been trying to regain authority over Palestinians in the country. The Taef Agreement of 1989, which marked the official "end" to the Lebanese Civil War, sanctioned the exclusion and scapegoating of Palestinians. A law that had been passed in 1962, made more stringent in 1982, and partially lifted by a decree in 2005, albeit with little change in practice, forbade Palestinians from working in any of more than seventy professions and trades. Unemployment levels are consequently very high among the refugee population. In the crisis of May 2008, when Lebanese leaders gathered in Doha, Qatar, to discuss a solution to the country's stalemate, the Palestinian issue was not even on the agenda, an expression of the Palestinians' irrelevance to the political equation.

Events affecting the Palestinian refugee population elsewhere in Lebanon have immediate repercussions in Shatila, which in many ways has always been an iconic camp. Rosemary Sayigh's (1993) ethnohistory narrates Shatila's saga from the largely single village camp of 1948 to today's sprawling vertical shantytown. Peteet demonstrates how reminders of the camp's scarred history populate its landscape: "the armed guards . . . [monitoring] the camp . . . , the pervasiveness of the handicapped, extreme forms of poverty, the multitude of female-headed households" (2005, 170). The Israeli invasion in 1982 left the camp completely devastated. Shatila was again severely affected during the Camp Wars and barely survived three sieges during the late 1980s. Its modest mosque, sheltering the bodies of the fallen *fidā'iyyīn* that I visited with Abu Mujahed on that Eid al-Adha, remains a compelling aide-mémoire to Palestinian vulnerability in Lebanon.

In the eventful history of the Palestinian diaspora, the years 1982 and 1993 are benchmarks, as I came to learn when I listened to elders and leaders talking about the subject, just as Shatila youth do. "Everything changed in 1982," Abu Mujahed told me, "because it was then that the leadership accepted [the defeat and expulsion of] 1948 and gave up fighting to win the whole of our country back." Abu Maher, another elder from Shatila, is of a similar opinion: "Before the Palestinian Liberation Organization came to Lebanon, we had no problems getting jobs. The Lebanese didn't look down on us the way they do now. If no position was available here, it was relatively easy to travel abroad. And there was no competition from the Syrians. When the PLO left, everything changed, and we started to worry about how to get jobs." UNRWA's relief and social service officer for Beirut, Abu Rabieh, illustrated the point, citing his own work of providing assistance for refugee families classified as hardship cases by the organization: "Before 1982, there was no social relief program because it was simply not necessary. The PLO was here [. . .], and Palestinians [. . .] were then mobile and could work." The provision of relief services by UNRWA only began in 1983. Since then and especially after 1987 as a result of the Camp Wars, the number of families on UNRWA's list of hardship cases entitled to assistance has been increasing. At the time of my fieldwork, in the Beirut area alone the list included 2,200 families living below the poverty line, who received $10 per member and some provisions in relatively small quantities every three months.[6]

6. I collected these figures from the UNRWA officer responsible for delivering relief services to Palestinian refugees in Beirut. I also had a couple of meetings with the officers responsible for the same task in Shatila and the surrounding area. Finally, I interviewed a number of families who used to be or were still on UNRWA's list of hardship cases.

The situation is even more dismal in terms of health care. Before 1982, the PLO shared with UNRWA part of the costs for hospitalization. "Today, some corpses are held in hospitals because families can't afford the bills," the director of the Palestinian Human Rights Organization, Ghassan Abdallah, told me, again recalling the changes that Palestinians have faced in Lebanon with the fluctuation in the PLO's strength in the country. "Throughout the 1980s," Abdallah continued, "some funds kept arriving for refugee families from relatives who had managed to escape the Camp Wars and obtain asylum status in Germany and Scandinavia or who had migrated to the [Persian] Gulf." In Abdallah's evaluation, the most dramatic changes in the standing of refugees came after 1990 with the war in Kuwait, Arafat's support for Iraq, the closure of the Persian Gulf as a destination for migrant refugees, and Libya's decision to cease issuing work permits to Palestinians. Abu Rashid, an elderly resident of Shatila, concurred: "In 1993, after the Oslo Agreements, the PLO started focusing on the [Occupied] Territories and stopped helping people here. The economic problems of refugees became evident, and the era of the NGOs started." Indeed, twenty-eight-year-old Akram remarked to me once, jokingly, "Gustavo, we're born in NGOs."

From the perspective of Shatila's residents, the Palestinian leadership has turned its back on them at least twice. The first time was in 1982, when Arafat left Lebanon, taking with him several of the *fidā'iyyīn*; and the second was in 1993, when the PLO opted to direct its resources to Palestinians from the Occupied Territories and agreed to postpone discussion of the refugees' status to an unforeseeable final round of negotiations with the Israelis. Understandably, Shatilans today are extremely disillusioned with politicians, and it is my sense that they have learned how to live without having to rely on them.

Perhaps there is just one way in which Shatila resident Umm Ahmad's life story is atypical: her family owned farming plots in northern Galilee before 1948. Umm Ahmad, sixty-six, is from the *jīl al-Nakba*, the generation of the Catastrophe, as Palestinians refer to those who were children when forced out of Palestine in 1948 or were born just after that. She left Palestine when she was four and settled with her family, who had lost everything, in the Tal al-Zaatar refugee camp. Following the destruction of that camp in 1976, her life became one of constant displacements and new beginnings. She lived in Dekwene in eastern Beirut, then in the Beqaa Valley, in Syria, in Damour (to the south of Beirut), in al-Tariq al-Jadida, which neighbors the Shatila camp, and finally in Shatila itself. In Syria, she met former servants of her family. "We're all the same now. We're all refugees," she remarked to them. In the 1980s, one of her sons went missing in the Camp Wars, and the family, by then living in a house they had purchased in al-Tariq al-Jadida, decided to lock it up, leave it, and move into Shatila, where they felt safer. Once the war was over, they found out that the house had been occupied by a Shia family linked to the Amal movement, who refused to give it back.

Umm Ahmad started working as a cleaner at a relatively advanced age when her husband became severely ill, and she had to step in so that the family could make ends meet. Because she had unmarried adult sons at home, the family was not entitled to assistance from UNRWA, despite her children being unable to find work. Her son Ahmad, thirty-one, had the following to say about the Palestinian saga in Lebanon: "We don't have the rights to live here as human beings. We don't have the right to work; we don't have the right to register a house in our names. I don't know why they [the Lebanese] allow us to study for careers we can't work in—like law, for instance. We can buy a taxi license, but we can't work as taxi drivers. I don't know which situation is worse: when we were killed by guns or now when we're killed by hunger."

Ahmad believes in the return to Palestine, but just before the prophetical end of time. "It's written in the Qur'an," he told me. "When Jesus returns, we'll fight the Jews and win back our land." It was also a mythological version of the return that Shakir, twenty-six, an accounting student, shared with me one evening when we were talking about Palestine. We had visited the bars in Hamra popular with Palestinian activists and decided to stay at my place in Qreitam for the night instead of finding our way back to Shatila. We got home, and he immediately connected to the internet from my computer. That infuriated me because it was late and I wanted to sleep, but the computer was in my bedroom. Shakir started checking the Facebook profiles of several blond girls from Germany and Sweden. He used to do this frequently and assured me he was attracted to their physical features. I always suspected, though, that the fact that these women might be able to get him a visa out of Lebanon also played a role in the attraction. When he was done with Facebook and I thought he would finally make his way to the sitting-room couch, he received an email. To my complete despair, it included several photos of Palestine attached. Shakir opened every single one and kept calling me to check out the photos: "*Shūf* [Have a look], Gustavo, see what Palestine is like with all those olive trees. They're nice, aren't they? Palestine is like Europe." Such rural imagery, specifically the ubiquitous olive tree, was often evoked to lend consistency to the kind of mythology making I was witnessing. The olive tree gave some unity to Shakir's discourse. Although he wanted to migrate to Europe, where the blond girls who could provide him with a visa out of Lebanon lived, the Europe he envisioned was an idealized one: a Europe similar to Palestine, to which he wanted to return, and a Europe covered by olive trees.

Mourning Academic Power

"I'm not sure I'll get married, Gustavo." At first, Farid's remark seemed to me unsurprising. I had by then become used to remarks made by *shabāb* that revealed considerable anxiety about not having the means to get married and start an independent household. What was relatively unique in Farid's case, though, was that he *did* have the means. Age twenty-eight, Farid was a middle-class Palestinian living in the surroundings of Shatila and held a diploma in physics from a renowned Lebanese university. I thought it was my duty to probe him for a clearer explanation. Yet I was unprepared for the answer: "I'm a nonstraight guy, Gustavo."

In the long silence that followed, I perused on the notepad in front of me the set of questions I had formulated beforehand for my interview with Farid. They now looked somewhat pointless as investigative tools to unravel the complexity of his biography: "Do you plan to get married? Does your wife need to be a relative, Palestinian, or Sunni? Can she be Shia, Christian, or a foreigner?" I had already surrendered to Latif's obvious superior knowledge on how to tackle a siege and submitted to my Palestinian friends' readings of the space, the map, the territory, and events to remain a "buddy" and take part in the "game." Now, with Farid, my own understanding of what Latif once disdainfully named "this anthropology of yours" was being challenged and the respective limits—mine and my discipline's—painfully exposed. At the same time, however, unsuspected potentialities for both—my discipline and me—came to the fore.

I had read Vincent Crapanzano's book *Tuhami* (1980) and was aware of the difficulties and risks surrounding ethnopsychoanalysis: it can indeed go dreadfully wrong. Besides, I had never been trained as a counsellor. Yet my interaction with Farid did assume a therapeutic character from this point on and at his own initiative. Our initial interview unfolded into a set of four interviews and a total of around seven hours of recording. He shared with me the difficulties of being a "nonstraight guy" in a setting where homosexuality is highly taboo: his fears about not being a proper son to his very caring mother; his anxiety about not living up to the expectations placed on him and not adequately honoring his father's memory; his sense of melancholy from having opted for celibacy as a way out of his many dilemmas. Shatila was a late discovery in Farid's life. Constantly haunted by the feeling of not belonging—among his university peers as one of the few Palestinians around and among his male friends as a "nonstraight guy"—Farid found in Shatila a place where he felt at home and among his own people. The camp seems to have allowed Farid to start processing some of his unspoken emotions. The same happened to me.

I started collecting Umm Raad's life story while pursuing my usual very ambitious set of questions. When I first arrived at her home in Shatila, Umm Raad, a thirty-eight-year-old woman, did not stand up to greet me, contrary to what normally would happen. I saw a cane lying in one corner of her very modest sitting room and thought that she, like so many other Shatilans, had been partially disabled by one of the many wars experienced by the camp. Originally from Tal al-Zaatar, she had left that camp when it was destroyed in 1976 and moved to Shatila, where she witnessed the massacre in 1982. With a sad laugh, she remarked: "I move from massacre to massacre." In the razing of Tal al-Zaatar, she lost her father, a brother, and a sister. With my set of questions in front of me and interested in investigating visiting patterns among camp dwellers, I quizzed Umm Raad about whether she often received friends at her place and returned their visits. She told me she always received visitors but did not go to her friends' places often enough. My curiosity stirred, I pressed her for an explanation. She lowered her eyes and after a moment of hesitation lamented: "I'm very sick. I have cancer."

This word, *cancer*, is the last one I registered on my notepad that evening. My questions obviously did not offer an easy refuge from the situation in which I had placed myself and were meaningless, anyway, in the face of Umm Raad's very tragic biography. We remained silent for several minutes, during which she came very close to crying. I did too. For a short while, we both tried to make small talk, but that seemed completely artificial. I decided to tell her about my own experiences of loss. In sharing our experiences of loss, we managed to establish a bridge between one another and effectively communicate. There is more to anthropological fieldwork than collecting migration trajectories, work stories, and kinship charts, as I had been doing until then. If anthropology should be a two-way bridge, as Pierre Clastres (1968) proposes, then my ethnography of the Abu Raad family and Umm Raad's ethnography of me began once we established this human connection, notwithstanding our obvious differences of gender, class, and culture. On my way out of her house, Umm Raad insisted that I should come back. I never did. I met her only one more time in the surroundings of the camp, and we waved very shyly to each other. It was as if we had done something academically indecent by not observing certain canons that normally discipline the interaction between interviewer and interviewee. Nonetheless, she and Farid were essential for my coming-of-age as an ethnographer and my "Palestinian-becoming": they repositioned me in my field.

Renato Rosaldo (1989) also writes about being repositioned in his field. Highlighting the traditional vice of classic ethnography in which the ideal of detachment is taken too far and reaches the point of actual indifference, he shows how self-reflexivity does not necessarily mean being so completely absorbed by oneself that the culturally different "other" is abolished. He avows his initial difficulty in understanding headhunting. When the Filipino Ilongot tell him that they engage in headhunting raids to placate the anger they feel when bereaved, Rosaldo considers their explanation too opaque or too flimsy. It is only when he becomes repositioned in his field following the devastating loss of his wife that he begins to grasp what the Ilongot mean by anger in bereavement. He does not suggest that the Ilongot's feelings and his own are identical: there remain differences in tone, cultural form, and especially the consequences of the anger felt in each of their cases. Moreover, he insists that the analyst's attention when studying mourning should not be focused solely on the programmed unfolding of prescribed acts typical of ritual situations—as though bereavement were only about adequately following the rules of a book of etiquette rather than being an open-ended process, trying to cope, *à peine*, with death. Yet concentrating on prescribed acts is what ethnographers of mourning rituals so often do, safeguarding their "comfort zone" and keeping emotions at bay.

In different ways, Latif, Dalal, Farid, and Umm Raad submitted me to a "diseducation" and exposed the limits of the perhaps arrogant view I held of myself and "this anthropology of mine" before I found my way to Lebanon. I was previously convinced that in the field the researchers, never the locals, are in control and in the know. In a setting such as Shatila and probably elsewhere, too, this somewhat colonial presupposition simply does not apply. Indeed, this is precisely the source of the difficulties I have with some of the discipline's guidelines on ethics (American Anthropological Association 1998, 2009, 2012), which may invite a "tick-the-box" legalistic attitude toward the issue.[7] A purely legalistic approach to ethics serves more to protect anthropologists from juridical claims and to preserve their standing vis-à-vis their peers than to safeguard the safety and well-being of both respondents and ethnographer. Although ethnographers should certainly not discard wholesale the discipline's codes on ethics, they need to recognize that these codes were elaborated for ideal environments, where quietude, freedom from fear, and stability facilitate

---

7. Such an approach is probably informed more by the preoccupations of funders and administrators than by anthropologists. We should not lose sight of the fact that anthropology does not involve anthropologists alone.

data collection. In a minefield like Shatila, this ideal could not be further from reality. Thus, my humble acceptance of local definitions of ethics—what J. Christopher Kovats-Bernat (2002) names as a "localized" approach to the question (as well as to risks, maps, and events)—is nothing other than a pragmatic recognition of the dramatic shift in Shatila of the infamous "power relations" characterizing the ethnographic encounter. In Shatila, it is Shatilans who know and are in control, not I (even if they might be in control of little else other than, temporally, me).

An ethnographic vignette serves to illustrate the point. On my first trip to Lebanon and contact with Shatila, I wore a green ribbon around my wrist, a souvenir from Northeast Brazil, with a distant religious meaning and superstition surrounding it: the wearer needs to make three wishes while wrapping it, with three knots, around the wrist and then use the ribbon until it breaks; otherwise, the wishes will not come true. I was surprised to discover that in Shatila the political-religious meaning of green ribbons is not distant at all. It may be an indication that the person wearing it has visited the Shia Zeinab mosque near Damascus. Furthermore, during the Camp Wars, some of the Shia militiamen manning the checkpoints to Shatila wore a green strap across their shoulders. All these elements, combined with my rather Islamicized classical Arabic during my first days in Shatila, led several of my acquaintances to suspect that I was actually Shia and just hiding that fact. The memories of the Camp Wars are still painfully felt in Shatila, to the point of not normally being talked about, so their suspicion that I might be Shia was a hindrance that I refused to accept. At one point, the usually protective Shakir, a lad from the camp, winked at me and suggested: "You might very well cover that ribbon." I followed his advice and bought myself a watch.

"Palestinian-Becoming," "Gender," and Power

"I'm going to say it very slowly, so that you can repeat after me: 'Lā 'ilāha 'illā Allāh, wa Muḥammad rasūl Allāh' [There is no god but God, and Mohammed is his messenger]." Sheikh Habib was talking to me on the staircase leading to his apartment in Shatila. He was encouraging me to repeat the *shahāda* (testimony), a single but sincere enunciation of which is considered by several Islamic schools to be sufficient for the speaker to convert to Islam.

My friend Fawaz, in his early twenties and a militiaman with one of the Palestinian factions in the camp,[8] had taken me to see the sheikh. When our friendship started to deepen, Fawaz became increasingly perturbed by the fact that I was not Muslim. That afternoon, after checking whether I had five minutes to spare, he sat me on the back of his scooter and took me to Sheikh Habib's. The sheikh was not home. As we waited for him a while on the staircase, I was completely unaware who we were there to see and what was to follow. Just as we were about to leave, the sheikh showed up. There, on that humble Shatila staircase, the process of my "Palestinian-becoming" (Deleuze and Guattari [1987] 2004) reached its peak.[9]

The process had started several months earlier and had developed very smoothly. When I first arrived, the *shabāb* subjected me to the same kind of treatment so often reserved for the naive and rather uninformed foreigners who find their way to the camp: they gave me what they like to describe as a "hard time," using the expression in English. "But we decided to give you a chance," Akram, the social worker with a local NGO, told me. "Besides, you have a very genuine laugh," Shakir explained.

At a certain juncture, I too started questioning the validity and usefulness of my research. "In the end," I commented to Shakir, "nothing will change. I'll write yet another book on Palestinians, and everything will remain the same." He came to my rescue: "No, Gustavo, some things do change." I had grown increasingly suspicious by then. "What will change, Shakir?" "Well," he answered, "you'll get your PhD in the end, won't you?"

---

8. Some young men are employed by different Palestinian factions to provide security to the camp. Several research participants, especially those of an older generation, criticized the way these young men executed their tasks, supposedly thinking of them merely as a job rather than as a national duty, which—the same informants claimed—was the case with the *fidā'iyyīn*.

9. As inspired by Deleuze and Guattari ([1987] 2004), "Palestinian-becoming" is not the same as "becoming Palestinian." It also worked for me as a heuristic tool to overcome my own (state-oriented) foreignness.

It was only when I realized that the *shabāb* and I were not there just to fulfil my academic interests that my research took off. This happened when I abandoned any illusion of control and power I may have nurtured until then. I started letting the *shabāb* take the lead and very often to dictate the pace and content of our interactions. Akram triggered the process of my "Palestinian-becoming": "You need to have your hair cut in Suleiman's salon in the camp. You know, we need to contribute to the local economy." "But I don't have the specific vocabulary in Arabic to explain to Suleiman how I want my hair cut," I observed. "You don't need to, Gustavo." Akram explained. "He cuts the hair of all of us in the same way."

When I emerged from Suleiman's salon, I had the same short military-like haircut of the Shatila *shabāb*, a style I ended up being very fond of. In fact, going to Suleiman's became one of my favorite activities in Shatila, and the interaction in this all-male environment was sometimes very informative. I got into the habit of going to Suleiman's late in the evening, just before finding my way to my Shatila dwelling and going to bed: I suffer from chronic insomnia, and having my hair cut helped me unwind. Whenever I showed up, just before the salon closed, I checked whether Suleiman would still have the time for one more haircut. My question— "*Maftūḥ* [Open]?"—was invariably met by an explosion of laughter from the customers. It was only toward the end of my stay in Shatila that Suleiman decided to explain the sexual innuendo in my question, imperceptible to me until then: "It's almost as if you are asking if I, and not my shop, am open. . . ." I also came to understand, for instance, why beauty parlors for men in the camp and the surrounding area so often have a fish tank: for Palestinians, fish are so closely associated with men's sexual potency that I rarely came across a Shatila woman who liked fish.

My diet was the *shabāb*'s next target. Shakir was always very critical of my predilection for salads and fruits. Knowing of my particular taste for Arab proverbs, he once told me: "'Akl al-rijāl 'alā qad 'af'ālahā [A man eats what he does]."[10] Feeling at ease in my home, which he had helped reinvent

---

10. Based on fieldwork in Cairo, Nefissa Naguib (2015) investigates the links between food and masculinity, but much more from the perspective of men as nurturers.

as a Palestinian space by offering me several pieces of memorabilia to distribute around the house, Shakir would uninhibitedly open my fridge to check what he could grab for a snack: "Gustavo, all these vegetables, this isn't food. You should eat like an Arab man."

After a while, my "Palestinian-becoming" and "diseducation" started paying off. The *shabāb* barely concealed their pride when they witnessed me giving a recently arrived American scholar a "hard time." "Best hard time ever happened, Gustavo," Latif remarked, employing another broken-English expression, "best thing ever happened," for which the *shabāb* show a special predilection.

When they realized that I was already forty and unmarried, some of the *shabāb* started teasing me about the need to find a bride: "Let's go to Dbayeh, Gustavo, to get you a woman." Dbayeh is the only Palestinian camp in mostly Christian East Beirut, and its inhabitants are Palestinian Christians.[11] Although there was no question that my prospective bride should be Palestinian, the *shabāb* still thought that I, as a non-Muslim, was not a suitable partner for one of their sisters. When I observed Shakir making some timid advances toward a Brazilian friend of mine, I teased him: "This is not the practice in my country, Shakir. To have access to my women, you need to give me one of yours." His response would have pleased Gayle Rubin (1975): "So you traffic in women?" On yet another occasion, I remarked to Shakir that I did not think it fair that a Muslim man can marry a Christian woman, but a Muslim woman is out of reach for a Christian man. "This is what is written in the Qur'an, Gustavo," he explained. I decided to provoke him further: "But then the Christian man can always convert. Conversion to Islam is very easy." He put a stop to our conversation: "Yes, but for that one has to feel the need for the conversion deep in one's heart." My Shatila adoptive mother took a somewhat

11. Often overlooked by researchers, Dbayeh was the camp selected by Leonardo Schiocchet (2011) for the field research for his doctoral work, in which he compares senses of belonging in this predominantly Christian camp to those prevailing in a predominantly Muslim camp, al-Jalil, in eastern Lebanon.

more pragmatic approach toward conversion: "You say the *shahāda*, and we get you a wife from here." She even introduced me to a few candidates, normally Shatila widows around my age. Once, her conversation with a prospective bride, right in front of me, even had clearly sexual contours, to my complete embarrassment. "Have a look at him," she advised her. "He's good-looking, and you like good-looking men." Turning to me, she asked whether I understood what she was saying. I said no, even though my very red face gave me away. Both women laughed.

For quite some time, I thought that Shatilans' efforts at "Palestianizing" me, marrying me off, and converting me were attempts to exert "power" over me. They knew I was there to conduct research: by turning me into one of "them," they might be trying to ensure that I would propagate sympathetic images of the camp. Because the issue of conversion to Islam was strictly linked to partnering me, at the beginning I also framed it as a way of controlling my sexuality. It took me quite some time to realize that the endeavors at making me "belong" were not just about power: those most troubled by the fact that I was a Christian and most entrepreneurial in making me "fit" were the Shatilans who actually cared about me. One of my closest friends, Anis, once observed, "Gustavo, I want to go on thinking that my God is just. And you're a nice chap. But you won't be saved because you're Christian. I once even talked to a sheikh about it: Can't a Christian be saved if he's a nice person? The sheikh said 'no' and that that was the will of God."

Naturally, the easiest solution to Anis's dilemma was my conversion. My university training in London had made me very sensitive to and aware of instances of power. For that reason and for quite some time, I insisted on framing remarks such as Anis's as having the intention to establish power over me. Nonetheless, I finally came to appreciate that there were possibly other reasons informing the attitudes held by Anis, my adoptive mother, and the fighter Fawaz. As a result, not only did I reposition myself in my field, but the very object of my research, "gender," was also reconceptualized. As a concept, "gender" is deeply informed by political power struggles that have more to do with the politics of Euro-America than with the place where I conducted my fieldwork. What other ways might there be of conceptualizing the display of adequate sex belonging in a situation where both women *and men* have very limited access to power?

On a very early morning as I was leaving the camp, Fawaz stopped me. We had already chitchatted on a couple of occasions. At that time of day, Shatila's alleys are still very empty, and I worried when Fawaz, who was on duty and holding his machine gun, told me, "We need to talk." My worry almost approached panic levels when he asked, "Are you Christian?" His reaction to my affirmative answer finally allowed me to relax: "You should consider converting and come pray with us." I replied that I most definitely should but never gave it a second thought—until the day he asked me if I had some minutes to spare and put me on the back seat of his scooter.

At the beginning of my time in Shatila, some people named me "Mustapha." The sounds made by the letters *g*, as in the English word *garden*, and *v* are nonexistent phonemes in Arabic, and Shatilans of an older generation, with more limited exposure to formal schooling, found my name "Gustavo" particularly difficult to pronounce. Some of them started calling me "Gestapo" (with the *ge* similar to the French *je*). As I reacted against that pronunciation, they renamed me Mustapha. When I descended from Sheikh Habib's staircase that afternoon, I had officially been renamed "Mustapha."

Yet my "Palestinian-becoming," as is the case with all "becomings," is necessarily a frustrated process. In the end, I will never be completely a "local." Even when I went as far as partaking in some of the *shabāb's* feelings, my "becoming" was still partial. Once I got to know them close-up, several of my friends told me that they have *maraḍ nafsī*, which can be translated as a psychological condition or *mal d'âme*, soul sickness. UNRWA provides psychiatric assistance only for extreme cases, and only very recently had the NGO Doctors without Borders started a program of psychological support aimed especially at Palestinian refugees in the not-very-distant camp of Burj al-Barajneh. The majority of the *shabāb* are not victims of *maraḍ nafsī*: several indicated to me they had very troubled years during adolescence—when some experimented with drugs and reported being persecuted by *jinn*, or genies, magical creatures with free will mentioned in the Qur'an—a period followed nonetheless by recovery. Several kept dreaming that they would manage to migrate or find a foreigner willing to marry them and thus provide them with a visa out of Lebanon, to the point that I started asking myself about the role dreams play as a coping mechanism or in devising economic strategies.

Badr, in his late twenties, succeeded in finding a Palestinian with a German passport to marry. He was happy in Germany, but once his wife found out that he was sleeping around, she asked for a divorce, and he lost his residence rights, forcing him to return to Shatila. I met him in my prefield visit to Lebanon, when he still nurtured the hope of returning to Europe: "Here, it's so dirty and noisy. I miss Germany a lot. And German girls like me. If you know of one available. . . ." When I came back to Beirut, he had disappeared from the camp's alleys. A mutual friend told me what had happened to him: "He spends his days at home now. He has *maraḍ nafsī*, Gustavo."

Another case of *maraḍ nafsī* was my friend Firas, twenty-eight, whom we met in the introduction. The holder of an undergraduate diploma in business administration, Firas also studied psychology for three years but left the course prior to graduation because he couldn't pay the tuition. Unemployed for quite some time, he often spent his days in his very tiny room, reading. He once explained to me that it was simply logical to have no hope:[12] "Gustavo, our lives and destinies as refugees are determined by instances completely out of our control. We live on a day-to-day basis. There are no grounds for us to have any hope. The future is black." I had to agree entirely with Firas's remarks. The fact that I had difficulty seeing any hope for those I had grown so close to took its toll at the end: I also fell victim to *maraḍ nafsī*. This was precisely the reason I decided to move out of Shatila. Shakir had anticipated that this would happen. He once prognosticated: "You like Shatila, Gustavo, but actually you can't stand

12. This lack of hope contrasts with the hope that young northern Egyptian men invest in "grand schemes"—Islamic revivalism, consumerist capitalism, romantic love, migration planning, and revolutionary activism—despite and in a sense because of the frequent frustration brought on by these projects (Schielke 2015).

it. You like Shatila because you know you can leave. For me, Shatila is not a game I can easily escape." I thought of yet another Arab saying: "Illī byākul al-'iṣī mish mitil illī bi'iddā" (He who is being whipped is not like he who is counting the blows).

Counting is precisely the theme of the next chapter.

2

Drowning by Numbers and Legislation

Statistics and (Non)State Making in Shatila

"Watch out when you're collecting those figures, Gustavo," Abu Mujahed warned me. I went to see him at the outset of my field research, hoping to obtain some data on the size, composition, and income levels of Shatila households, thereby appeasing my scientifically trained obsession with numbers. Abu Mujahed knew very well what he was talking about: prior to becoming the president of a local NGO, he had studied social sciences during his exile in Cuba and wrote about the housing situation of Palestinians in Lebanon. He even published an article on the subject under the name he shares with the Palestinian politician Mahmoud Abbas (Abbas et al. 1997). He explained the reasons for his suspicion toward numbers: "You may find that, for instance, an average of 3.5 people live in each room in the camp. But that tells you nothing about the conditions of the real rooms or the kind of interaction among the residents." The way out was obvious: to visit the rooms and get to know the respective residents. I followed his advice, which marked the beginning of a household survey I conducted with thirty Palestinian families, registering their living conditions and collecting their work stories. At the end, I was left with a considerable quantity of data of an arithmetical nature but also with an acute unease about the numbers I had collected and a pronounced awareness of the limits of the history they revealed.[1]

1. Throughout this chapter, I use the statistical studies available at the time of my fieldwork (2007–9) or shortly thereafter. New statistical studies on the situation of

73

3. Electrical wires exposed in Shatila, an increasingly vertical shantytown. Photograph by Hisham Ghuzlan and Gustavo Barbosa.

4. No light exposure: an alley in Shatila. Photograph by Hisham Ghuzlan and Gustavo Barbosa.

5. Daily life in Shatila. Photograph by Hisham Ghuzlan and Gustavo Barbosa.

At first glance, the work stories of the four different families depicted in the following pages tell a similar tale: economic hardships, interrupted schooling, inadequate housing, and attempts to migrate in search of a better future. Yet there is something fundamentally different among the four families in question, as will soon become clear. Their "exceptional" situation—as revealed in a later section of this chapter by the analysis of social-economic indicators and relevant parts of the Lebanese legislation

---

Palestinians in Lebanon have been conducted and published since then (for two examples, see International Labor Organization, Committee for the Employment of Palestinian Refugees in Lebanon 2011, 2012). However, I have decided *not* to use the more updated versions because the older figures claim to reflect the situation at the time when I was effectively collecting information about Shatila. In any case, what I argue in this chapter seems to remain valid for the newer studies as well: these newer studies also reveal as much as they conceal because, similar to the older ones, they do not normally bring to the fore how similar the life conditions of Palestinian refugees may be to those of other people living in the country, including many Lebanese.

6. Shatilans' ironic take on realpolitik. Photograph by Hisham Ghuzlan and Gustavo Barbosa.

impinging upon some of those families—is not an exception at all. It appears so only when seen from the perspective of a state, an awkward point of view in a setting such as Shatila. Accordingly, I examine the links between "statistics" and state making and problematize the adequacy of a "numbers-only" and solely economistic or legalistic approach to the refugee issue in Lebanon. Furthermore, I interrogate the extent to which the work of Sari Hanafi (2008a, 2008b, 2010) and of Sari Hanafi and Taylor Long (2010), presenting the camps as "states of exception," is based on a narrow reading of recent developments in political philosophy (Agamben 1998, 2005; Foucault 1991). Moreover, as the coming pages also show, Hanafi's corpus of work may have contributed to a further unwelcome "othering" of Palestinian refugees, with potentially hazardous political consequences perhaps not completely anticipated and, in any case, hardly acknowledged by the paradigm established by him.

The More It Changes, the More
It Remains the Same (1): Work Stories

Ahmad's Family

"As the Arab saying goes, "Al-rijjāl mā biʿībū ʾillā jibū [Only his pocket shames a man]," thirty-one-year-old Ahmad told me, commenting on his own difficulties in making ends meet. We were sitting in his well-kept sitting room in Shatila with his sixty-six-year-old mother and his twenty-three-year-old wife, who had just put their eight-month-old daughter to bed. An unexpected item of decoration hung from one of the walls: Ahmad's diploma in accounting from one of the local institutes (*maʿhad*). Perceiving my surprise, Ahmad explained: "I've never managed to get a job as an accountant. So I framed my diploma and hung it there."

Actually, Ahmad holds two higher-degree diplomas: the first in accounting obtained in 1988 and the second in computer engineering in 2003. His mother supported him throughout his studies. Because he was unable to get a position compatible with his skills upon his first graduation, she suggested that he return to the institute and work toward a second diploma. With one brief exception—a one-month position as a computer engineer in a Lebanese company—Ahmad has never found work in either of his majors. The job at the Lebanese company, where he had no formal contract, did not end well: after enduring shifts of ten hours, with half-hour breaks for lunch and dinner, Ahmad was paid $200 at the end of the month. "And I spent half of that just on my meals," Ahmad complained. He also tried a couple of manual jobs: prior to his classes at the ma'had, he repaired air conditioners, and before getting his second diploma, he worked as a painter. He started repairing air conditioners at the age of seventeen, but this activity was cut short by a dreadful accident that severely burned parts of his body. His firm paid for the $12,000 billed for several surgical interventions, but he was not entitled to compensation.

Ahmad's mother, the very talkative Umm Ahmad, is from the jīl al-Nakba (generation of the Catastrophe) and left Palestine when she was four years old. We already met her in the previous chapter. She lived in the Tal al-Zaatar camp as a married woman, but her husband left to work in Qatar, where better job opportunities existed for construction workers like him. From Qatar, he sent remittances back to his family in the camp. He came back to Beirut after the destruction of Tal al-Zaatar in 1976. A couple of years later, cancer and heart disease prevented him from working. He passed away in 2005. Throughout her husband's long ailment, Umm Ahmad worked as an office cleaner to support her rather large family: five sons (one of whom went missing during the War of the Camps) and three daughters. Her family was always refused assistance from UNRWA under the justification that she should count on the young men she had at home. "But we could not find jobs," Ahmad lamented and added, "She was the man of the house."

Umm Ahmad's loquacity contrasted with her daughter-in-law's silence. Only after being prompted to speak did the latter tell me how she dropped out of the first year of training in business administration at the ma'had because her father could not afford the fees. Prior to her marriage in 2006, she worked at a nursery, a job she liked. Differently from her mother-in-law, Ahmad's wife thought it better for a married woman not to work outside her home in order "to preserve the harmony of the couple." Nevertheless, she planned to work as a hairdresser in the future if Ahmad were to save enough money for them to set up a salon for women in the camp.

Ahmad's family lived on the ground floor, just below Umm Ahmad. The house belonged to Umm Ahmad, bought from one of Ahmad's uncles, who was leaving for Germany and needed the money for the trip. "That is, my mother owns the walls, not the ground," Ahmad clarified. "For we, as Palestinians, aren't allowed to own property in Lebanon," he added, referring to a prohibition dating back to 2001, when Law 296 regulating ownership of real estate by foreigners, including Palestinians, was approved (al-Natour and Yassine 2007). Umm Ahmad used to rent out the ground floor for extra cash, but she agreed to cede it to her son when he married.

At the time of my fieldwork, Ahmad made his living in the cramped entrance room of his house by giving private classes to high school students. He made $300 per month, tutoring some thirty students from 9:00 a.m. to 9:00 p.m. The summer months normally witnessed a sharp decline in Ahmad's income owing to school holidays. In the summer of 2007, he earned some money by making deliveries. He considered himself too old and overqualified for this kind of work, but with a family to provide for he had no other option. He complained that it is easier for women to get jobs because they accept working for less. He once tried to migrate illegally but was caught when entering Greece and forced back to Lebanon. He would now consider migration only if accompanied by his mother and wife: there was no way he would leave them behind because he did not think Lebanon is a safe place for either old or young women.

I asked Ahmad how he had succeeded in putting the money together to get married. He told me that his father-in-law, "a wise man," decided that Ahmad would pay just one golden lira as the bride price (*muqaddam*). The father-in-law even helped the newly established family by buying some pieces of furniture for them. An NGO officer had already told me that it is becoming more and more common for the bride's family not to insist on an expensive *muqaddam*. "Otherwise," she added, "no one would get married since no one has the money." The situation is different, though, when it comes to the *mu'akhkhar*, the sum to be paid by the husband if he asks for a divorce. Families insist on marriage contracts making the appropriate provisions for the *mu'akhkhar* and inflate the respective values, a way of protecting their daughters should a divorce take place. For Ahmad, this would mean having to pay the unaffordable amount of $5,000. "So I'll never get divorced," he said and winked at me. When reflecting on his own situation, Ahmad talked about some of his dreams:

> To tell you the truth, without my mother's help, I wouldn't have completed my education. My mother's work wasn't nice because she was serving people. But it was honest work. We don't like to put women in that situation. We like women to stay in the house and be the lovely lady. That's how we think as Arabs. But these days we need the support of our ladies.[. . .] Now women are the men. Some of the men have no work, while their wives work outside the households. I have the dream of being able to keep my wife at home, of giving her a happy life. But sometimes our destiny doesn't allow us that.[. . .] I have a dream: I want to sleep one night, one night only, not having to worry about the next day, not having to worry about what will happen if the milk is finished, if my daughter or my mother gets sick. What if I can't even pay for my mother's medication? Then what did she raise me for?

The Abu Sahar Family

Umm Sahar, forty-one, struggled with the remote control of the newly acquired air conditioner. Oblivious to the fact that it was not yet summer, the thermometer was already exceeding 30°C (86°F). The device had been purchased with the money sent back to Lebanon by Abu Sahar,[2] forty-seven, who had relocated to Dubai only three months earlier. Unemployed for a while in his native Lebanon, Abu Sahar secured a position as a construction worker in the United Arab Emirates. The couple decided that he should travel alone: life being cheaper in Lebanon, it made sense for his wife to remain behind with their three children, ages sixteen, thirteen, and eight, so that some money could be saved. "But he calls all the time because he worries about us by ourselves here. You know, Lebanon isn't a

---

2. I have opted to identify Abu Sahar by his daughter's name so as to avoid the multiplication of different names in this study. Nevertheless, as commonly happens throughout the Arab East, Abu Sahar is known in the camp by the teknonym identifying him as his son's father.

safe country," Umm Sahar was telling me when the phone rang. It was her husband.

Umm Sahar has never worked outside her household. She performed well enough in the baccalaureate to study chemistry at university, as she would have liked. Originally from the Tal al-Zaatar camp, she left it when it was destroyed in 1976 and moved to Libya. While there, she met Abu Sahar and got married at the age of twenty. Soon thereafter, the birth of a mentally challenged daughter forced her to shelve her further education plans for good. The child died young, but other pregnancies followed, and Umm Sahar stayed at home to look after the children: "Having to take care of three children is enough of a workload!," she remarked, laughing. She thought it appropriate to add: "Mind you, I don't have issues with women working outside the home to help their families. I have no problems, for example, if my daughters find work outside Shatila. But it needs to be a respectable [muḥtaram] job, suitable for women."

The Abu Sahar family left Libya in 1994. It was getting increasingly difficult for Palestinians to find work there, so they thought it better to return to Lebanon and settle in Shatila. "I didn't expect the situation for refugees here to be even worse," Umm Sahar lamented. She was about to continue when we heard knocks on the door. It was her prospective son-in-law, Mahmud, nineteen, who had showed up with his mother for a visit.

In Mahmud, Sahar, sixteen, had met a supportive partner to pursue her academic and professional plans: once she graduated from high school in the next few months, Sahar wanted to enroll at an institute (ma'had), then find a job, and keep it after marriage. "Of course, women can work, if they want, to help their families," Mahmud affirmed. The wedding was to take place in some two or three years, the period Mahmud needed to set aside enough money for the bride price and to complete the house he was currently building.

"Our home is almost ready," he rejoiced, while placing the charcoal in the hubble-bubble, which filled Umm Sahar's modest sitting room with a pleasant apple aroma. "But I still need to buy the furniture," he clarified. To start earning money faster, Mahmud left his professional training in hotel management and worked double shifts as a delivery boy. He also counted on some money sent back home by his brother, who had migrated to Germany. Mahmud would like to follow the same path as his brother, but he knew that obtaining the appropriate visas is difficult. His mother applied three times but was not granted the visa that would allow her to see how her eldest son was living in his new country with his newly acquired German nationality. Despite his mother's negative experience, Mahmud had not lost hope: "I'll still apply because life in Germany is easier than here. And Europe is better as a destination than the Gulf. My two sisters will remain in Lebanon and can look after my mother. If we, Sahar and I, manage to migrate, life will be easier. If we stay here, we'll face poverty. But we'll cope."

Once the interview was over, Mahmud accompanied me as I made my way out of Abu Sahar's household. He confided: "Sahar and I, we aren't relatives, you know. We met during the relief efforts, in the 2006 war, and immediately fell for each other. We're marrying out of love."

The Abu Ubaida Family

The strong, sweetish smell of lamb meat was wafting from Umm Ubaida's kitchen. Yet again my interview with a Palestinian family was to turn into a feast, and my tentative plans to become a vegetarian would have to be postponed. More often than not, my Palestinian hosts opted to ignore my own predilection for the lower-status *mujaddara*, a tasty combination of rice, lentils, and caramelized onions. Guests are to be properly honored by serving an appropriate menu, with meat as the invariable pièce-de-resistance. I was in no position to decline the Abu Ubaida family's generous offer of hospitality: meat is a relatively expensive item, reaching 20,000 Lebanese pounds (around $14) per kilo at a butcher's in the popular Sabra market, and my hosts' household budget was tight.

"My monthly income varies a lot. Sometimes I make up to $600; at other times, I make nothing," fifty-six-year-old Abu Ubaida, a carpenter, told me. His career began quite early, when at nine years old he worked at a hairdresser's and a juice shop in the summer during the school holidays. He dropped out of school prematurely during the third grade, complaining that the teachers beat him. Already at fourteen, he was working full-time, following the path of one of his brothers, an accomplished carpenter.

The older sibling set a model for Abu Ubaida in another domain, too: his brother was a Palestinian fighter, a *fidāʾī*. "I also picked up arms because we were being attacked and had to defend ourselves," Abu Ubaida recalled. "And I went to Palestine," he added. My aroused expectations of a report filled with daring guerrilla activities conducted in the Palestinian territories were cut short by the more dramatic and no less heroic outcome of Abu Ubaida's military years: "I was incarcerated in an Israeli prison in Eilat for one and a half years. From there, I was sent to Algeria." Returning to Lebanon in 1984, Abu Ubaida felt the time had arrived to move out of Shatila.

His sister exerted a decisive influence on another of Abu Ubaida's decisions, one that would have lasting repercussions. She spotted Umm Ubaida, eighteen years younger than her future husband, and thought she would be a good match for her brother. Belonging to a family originally from Kfar Shuba in southern Lebanon, Umm Ubaida is Lebanese and was born in the Fakhani area, close to Shatila. She spent most of her youth in Fakhani, except when wars forced her family to relocate for brief periods. Umm and Abu Ubaida met only two or three times prior to getting married. "There was no love or anything of the kind," Umm Ubaida recollected and added: "It made no difference in the eyes of my family that my husband was Palestinian. My brother and sister married the same way. Lebanese, Palestinians, there isn't a lot of difference among us." By then, Abu Ubaida was making enough money to start a family and could afford the wedding costs. He paid the $800 required for the bride price from his own earnings.

Umm Ubaida only briefly stopped working after the marriage. Her career had also begun early, when she was fifteen. The young Umm Ubaida divided her time between work and school. She held a number of short-lived jobs: as a junior clerk in a company, a teacher in a nursery, a hairdresser, and a junior accountant. Her school career was more successful than her partner's: she studied until the tenth grade and stopped only because her family could no longer afford the fees.

Only three months before I conducted the interview and attended the lamb banquet that followed, Umm Ubaida had started working again in a Palestinian NGO, providing remedial classes for students with poor performances at the UNRWA schools. She had a lengthy experience with NGOs: she was trained as a coiffeuse and accountant on vocational courses offered by some and worked at a nursery belonging to an NGO. Her new job assured the family 400,000 Lebanese pounds (around $270) per month, a much-needed income at times when Abu Ubaida's earnings are so erratic.

With three children ages sixteen, thirteen, and five to provide for, Umm Ubaida was almost shocked when I asked whether women should work: "*Lāzim* [It's necessary]! You know, we don't exactly lead easy lives here." She further explained: "We need to pay for everything in Lebanon: for proper education or adequate health care." I interjected: "But what about the services available at the UNRWA clinic?" This time it was Abu Ubaida's turn to express astonishment: "At the clinic, no matter what the disease is, you're always medicated with Panadol. Palestinians have nothing here, no health care, no civil rights, no proper work." Umm Ubaida corrected her husband's remark: "The situation isn't much different for the Lebanese. To get work, to get medical assistance, one needs *wāsṭa* [connections]."[3] Abu Ubaida did not disagree: "Very true. All we can do is study and hope to get a position in the Gulf."

Despite having close relatives in Denmark, Canada, and Saudi Arabia, the Abu Ubaida family did not seriously consider migration, though they had given it some thought. Umm Ubaida was very realistic about their meagre chances of getting out of Lebanon: "To begin with, one needs to show the embassies bank statements with considerable amounts of money, and we have none. So what's the point of getting passports and applying for visas when you know beforehand that there's no chance? We've never even tried."

Abu Ubaida's evaluation of their perspectives was even gloomier: "We have no future here." However, the most striking commentary on their current situation came from a rather unexpected source, the young

---

3. Literally defined as "means," *wāsṭa* refers to the network of influence one deploys to speed up procedures or strengthen one's chances of success—when, for instance, renewing a passport, seeking a job or a promotion, or securing a bed in a hospital.

Ubaida, thirteen. Toward the end of the interview, I inquired about the existence of electronic devices in the Abu Ubaida household. The family had all the basic appliances, but no luxury ones, with the remarkable exception of a battered car and an obsolete computer. When I asked about the existence of air-conditioning or heating (*chauffage*), Ubaida expressed extreme surprise: "Chauffage? Shū chauffage?! [Heating? What is heating?!]," as if my question were somewhat absurd.

The Abu Walid Family

Abu Walid's children, ages eleven, nine, and seven, were smartly dressed, waiting for "the researcher." In what was most likely an exceedingly tedious experience for them, they remained amazingly quiet and well behaved throughout the two hours I spent chatting with their parents. My friend Ahmad had made the arrangements for me to visit the Abu Walid household. Their eldest daughter was a student of his: he helped her with the demanding homework from the private and relatively expensive school she attended. Abu Walid had already considered sending the children to study in Syria, where they could benefit from free education. At the same time, he was still trying to keep his family with him in Lebanon: "Sometimes, my boss pays for the school fees because if my salary lasts until the tenth day of the month, that's already an achievement!," Abu Walid, thirty-six, complained. As an aluminum worker, he did not make enough money to cover his family's expenses: in addition to the children's school fees, he had to pay $200 in rent for his two-bedroom apartment in Shatila. He moved there in 1997, shortly after his marriage to Umm Walid, now thirty-two.

Abu and Umm Walid are cousins, both from the same village, which facilitated the negotiations leading to the wedding. She studied up to baccalaureate level. For the time being—and with an eye to her husband's approval—she preferred not to work outside the household. "I'm not against women working, but, you know, we have three kids for her to look after," Abu Walid explained. Umm Walid nodded.

Umm Walid spoke with a Palestinian accent. Abu Walid shifted, speaking Lebanese to Lebanese, Palestinian to Palestinians, and Syrian to

Syrians as a result of his wider exposure to off-camp society. Despite the capacity to adapt revealed by his language skills, he confessed to me that he did not feel entirely comfortable in the camp: "I like this building where our apartment is. I've known my neighbors for quite some time[. . .]. They're all from the same extended family [*ā'ila*]. After all these years, they've come to think of us as part of the *ā'ila* as well. For instance, if something happens here to my family while I'm out at work, I can count on my neighbors for help. But it isn't like that all over the camp. Shatila has changed a lot over the years. Beforehand, it was a respectable [*muḥtaram*] place to live. Not anymore, with all these *shabāb faltānīn* [loose lads] out in the alleys, carrying guns."

Abu Walid had the opportunity to move away from the camp. He opted to stay, though, because of his neighbors and the relative short distance to his job. He had been working with the same aluminum company since 1997: "I used to carry my boss's son on my shoulders, and now the son has become my boss!" he said, laughing. Prior to this employment, Abu Walid was in military service for three years, from 1994 to 1997. In 1989, having failed the ninth grade, he dropped out of school and worked as a doorman until 1994.

He trusted his neighbors so much and vice versa that he had become a member of his building *jam'iyya*, a joint pooling of resources by different households to be used by those party to the arrangement if and when the need arises. That is precisely why he did not seriously consider moving out of Lebanon or Shatila: "I feel like a fish outside water when I travel, even for short trips," he told me.

By 10:00 p.m., the children's eyes showed obvious signs of tiredness, and I realized it was time to leave. It was quite chilly by then: I interviewed the family in winter, and there were no luxury items—computers, air conditioners, or *chauffage*—at Abu Walid's house.

○ ○ ○

Despite their similarities across socioeconomic indicators, the families whose work stories I have told in this section differ in one important way: of the four families, only Ahmad's and Abu Sahar's are Palestinian and live in Shatila. Abu Ubaida's family is Palestinian as well, though Umm

Ubaida is Lebanese, but they live in Sports City, in the vicinity of the camp. Abu Walid's family members, for their part, are Shatila residents but have Syrian nationality. These differences indicate the problematic nature of some of the abstractions—the "imagined populations," I call them—with which statisticians work. Accordingly, in the following sections of this chapter I ask: What do generalizing labels such as *Lebanon, Palestinians,* and *refugee camps,* which show up so habitually in studies of a statistical nature and within the "state-of-exception" literature (Hanafi 2008a, 2008b, 2010; Hanafi and Long 2010), effectively mean? In the process of manufacturing such generalizations, what is being left out and silenced?

As a matter of fact, researchers often portray lives like Ahmad's and Abu Sahar's families but very rarely visit families like Abu Ubaida's and Abu Walid's: my interviews were the first that the two families had undertaken with a researcher. Although there is no doubt that Palestinians face barriers against legal inclusion in Lebanon, a topic covered in the next section, I argue that, together with other sectors of the population, Lebanese or otherwise, they also face barriers to social and economic inclusion. In this sense, despite the efforts of Palestinian nationalism and of some of the scholars who do research on Palestinians to make Palestinians a single case and an exception, there appears to be more in common between Shatila and other poverty-stricken districts of Beirut than initially supposed. By accepting the terms of Palestinian nationalism and emphasizing the "Palestinianness" of Palestinians, researchers may have contributed to "othering" refugees in Lebanon, tending in the process to downplay other kinds of belonging, such as class.

The More It Changes, the More
It Remains the Same (2): A History of Work

All in all, it took less than five minutes. At 3:02 p.m. on August 17, 2010, the members of the Lebanese Parliament started deliberating on a bill prepared by the Justice and Administrative Committee that would grant Palestinian refugees some working rights (Lamb 2010). The version prepared by the committee was a watered-down rendition of the original draft proposed by the Druze leader of the Progressive Socialist Party, Walid Jumblatt, earlier that summer. Jumblatt's proposal had stipulated that refugees should have the right to work on equal footing with the Lebanese, should be covered by the National Social Security Fund, and should be allowed to buy real estate in the country. An outcry from some politicians and manifestations of support from others immediately followed. The Justice and Administrative Committee had managed to rid the draft of its most controversial aspects, and by 3:06 p.m. on August 17, only four minutes after deliberations began, the members of Parliament agreed to change Article 50 of the Labor Law of 1964. They did so by unanimous vote, which was quite surprising given the persistent deep divisions on the Lebanese political scene. The fact that little, if anything, was to change with the new piece of legislation enabled the members to reach unanimity on the issue and ensured the expediency with which the matter was dispatched.

In this section, after a brief examination of the economic conditions prevalent in Palestine just prior to the Nakba and in Lebanon immediately after the Palestinians' exodus and arrival in the country, I present a succinct history of the legal framework affecting refugees in the country, up to August 17, 2010, when the parliamentary deliberations on the bill to change Article 50 of the Labor Law took place.

In times of world conflict, such as the Second World War, peripheral economies may benefit from a certain upsurge in development, precisely owing to the loosening of the grip connecting them to the central powers. Palestine under the last years of British rule and postindependence Lebanon were no exceptions. With European ships facing mounting difficulties to reach the Levant, there was an increase in the demand for native products, accompanied by a boost in investment levels (al-Natour 1993). As a consequence, the Lebanese industrial sector saw a rapid expansion during the war years (Yusif Sayigh 1952). The Arab defeat to Israel in the war of 1948 and the large number of Palestinian refugees forced to migrate to neighboring countries would cut short these promising prospects.

Although the figures for the number of refugees expelled from Palestine are heavily disputed, it can be firmly stated that most of the some 130,000 who found their way to Lebanon were of rural origin. Prior to their eviction, they mainly cultivated their own small farms or worked as agricultural laborers. Insufficient income was supplemented by casual work in villages or urban centers. A significant number of middle-class urbanites also found their way to Lebanon, a country with which they were familiar as a business and educational hub or as a holiday destination. The work profile of this sizable population was very similar to the profile of the population in Lebanon, then still mainly an agricultural country but with a substantial community of skilled urban traders. Quite predictably, the host country's capacity to absorb the Palestinian labor force was limited.

With 10,400 square kilometers (6,462 square miles) of mainly mountainous terrain, Lebanon has little agricultural land and, already in 1951 could only barely support its 1,300,000 inhabitants, the highest-density population in the Arab world (Yusif Sayigh 1952). Under France's authority, Mandate Lebanon adopted an externally oriented liberal economic policy, which increasingly privileged trade at the expense of other labor-intensive sectors, leaving the country highly vulnerable to outside shocks (Picard 1996). Menaced with unemployment or underemployment, a considerable portion of the Lebanese population searched for better job opportunities in Africa, Australia, and the Americas. Whereas the bi- or trilingual and relatively highly educated Lebanese secured positions abroad and sent remittances back home amounting to a significant 20 percent of the Lebanese gross domestic product (*Daily Star* 2009), the local economy was manned by cheap foreign labor: at certain points Syrian, Egyptian, and, more recently, Southeast Asian but also continuously Palestinian. Because the integration of foreign workers, if it occurred at all, happened at the margins of Lebanese society, there were pernicious social consequences to such an economic policy.

To the structural weaknesses characterizing the Lebanese economy should be added the immediate effects of the war with Israel in 1948. On one hand, the Arab boycott of the newly created Jewish state boosted the role of Beirut's port and the Lebanese service economy. On the other hand, Lebanon also lost Palestine as a market, and many Lebanese with jobs on the other side of the border had to find their way back home. The main burden, nonetheless, remained the more than 100,000 refugees, who composed some 10 percent of the Lebanese population at the time and whose skills were already largely available locally.

The newly arrived refugees contributed to sectors where opportunities existed. In agriculture, Palestinian knowledge of specific crops and techniques contributed to the intensification and improvement of cultivation. In addition, the vigorous pace of the booming construction sector in Beirut took advantage of the readily available Palestinian labor. It remains true, however, that for the vast majority of the *fallāḥīn* (peasants) who crossed the northern border of Palestine, exile in Lebanon meant unemployment and utter poverty (Yusif Sayigh 1952).

In turn, with inadequate investment levels and insufficient job vacancies, the Lebanese economy was inescapably affected by the arrival of the newcomers, especially in terms of wages and property rent (Yusif Sayigh 1952). Counting on UNRWA aid and in desperate need of income to supplement their meagre rations, the refugees agreed to work for salaries that were not viable for the Lebanese. The refugees thus inadvertently strengthened the bargaining power of entrepreneurs, who were able to impose lower salaries on their employees, including the Lebanese. Notwithstanding the brisk pace of construction in Beirut, housing has always been in short supply. Even though a number of other factors intersect to explain the high price of accommodation in Lebanon's urban centers, the influx of thousands of Palestinians in need of shelter certainly exacerbated such a tendency.

Undoubtedly, though, economic conditions alone do not explain the varying treatment refugees have received throughout their history in Lebanon. The potential political effects of the arrival of mostly Sunni Palestinians on the complex Lebanese sectarian patchwork have generated the fear of *tawṭīn* (naturalization). Elsewhere as well, refugees tend to be an uncomfortable presence because they remind governments and citizens alike of just how fragile "national identities" are. For a young state such as Lebanon, recently emergent from the mandate period and with unresolved questions of self-identity, the problems caused by the arrival of a large number of refugees after the Nakba in 1948 soon reached the point of eruption. The politicization of the refugee issue in Lebanon quickly ensued, with Palestinians effectively exacerbating it, especially during the *'ayyām al-thawra*, days of the revolution.

Still, to achieve a more complete picture of Palestinians' history in Lebanon, we need to consider the economic dimension of the equation. In fact, the Lebanese reaction to Palestinians has varied not only throughout history and between/within sects but also according to class and access to the government in Beirut, particularly with respect to competition over the latter's limited resources. Moreover, Lebanon's economic history helps explain the puzzling alternation between harshness and laxity in the application of the Lebanese legislation limiting the refugees' access to the labor market. Although this alternation reflects the sectarian nature of the Lebanese state and the shifting political strength of Palestinians over different periods, it also mirrors the specific needs of the economy at certain times. Thus, although in 1951—and in spite of the public manifestations of sympathy for the Palestinians' plight, expressed during debates in the Lebanese Parliament—Minister of Labor Émile Lahoud approved a decision requiring refugees to obtain work permits (al-Natour 1993), in practice, attending to the needs of the economy, this decision had only limited immediate results: as one analyst put it at the time, "The practical effect of the official attitude has boiled down to a prohibition of refugee employment in government offices and concessionary companies, and to its [refugee employment's] toleration elsewhere until there is a public outcry or the clustering of refugees becomes notoriously evident" (Yusif Sayigh 1952, 64).

Nonetheless, the basis for the legal discrimination of Palestinians in the job market had been established. Public outcry eventually did follow, and toleration of Palestinian workers grew shorter over the years. Although Palestinians kept on working, the fact that they often lacked the permits needed to exercise certain trades left them vulnerable to exploitation, especially by small and medium-size firms.

Throughout the 1950s and 1960s, with expectations for a rapid solution to the Palestinian issue waning, the Lebanese government increasingly treated the refugees as a security issue. In 1962, a law was passed regulating the entry, exit, work, and residency of foreigners in Lebanon, which included Palestinian refugees in precisely this category of "foreigners." By placing Palestinians on an equal footing with other foreigners living in Lebanon, the legislators chose to ignore their refugee status, which would later conflict with obligations assumed by the Lebanese state under a number of international conventions, notably the International Covenant on Economic, Social, and Cultural Rights and the International Covenant on Civil and Political Rights, both passed by the UN General Assembly in 1966 (Aasheim 2000; al-Natour and Yassine 2007; Said 1999).

Decree 17661 of September 18, 1964, which regulated foreign labor in Lebanon, did not break with the legal orthodoxy of treating Palestinians as foreigners with supposedly the same status as others residing in the country. In due time, a few exceptions were made to this rule, facilitating Palestinians' access to work in construction and agriculture, thus meeting the needs of the Lebanese economy for cheap labor in these sectors, and allowing them to hold positions with UNRWA and Palestinian organizations. Generally, though, in order to work legally, Palestinians had then and still have to obtain work permits from the Ministry of Labor—permits that over the years and despite the growing numbers of refugees in the country are granted on an increasingly rare basis, as shown in table 1.[4]

The figures in table 1 are even more revealing when compared to the total number of work permits issued to nationals from other countries, whose communities in Lebanon are considerably smaller than the Palestinian community. According to one study, for instance, the number of

---

4. As an initial indication of the difficulties involved in analyzing numbers relating to Palestinian refugees, an issue further developed later in this chapter, the figures in table 1 should be considered with caution. Although effectively revealing the general decline in the number of work permits issued to Palestinian refugees over the years, they remain problematic. For different years, Souheil al-Natour and Dalal Yassine collect statistics from different sources (the Lebanese Ministry of Planning and Ministry of Labor and Social Affairs, *al-Nahar* newspaper, and the Central Administration of Statistics). This approach not only raises questions about the consistency of the data over the whole period but also explains the remarkable discrepancy between the figure for 1985 and those for previous and subsequent years. Moreover, nothing is indicated about the number of refugees applying for work permits, which may also have declined over the years because of the widespread expectation that obtaining a permit was difficult anyway. In an interview on the blog *Qifa Nabki*, the former director for the Center of Lebanese Studies at Oxford University, Nadim Shehadi, stated that only 261 work permits were issued for Palestinian refugees in 2007 because only 261 were applied for (*Qifa Nabki* 2010).

Table 1
Work Permits Granted to Palestinian Refugees [in Lebanon]

Year	No. of Permits	Year	No. of Permits
1966	9,887	1993	327
1967	1,244	1994	350
1968	2,448	1995	354
1969	2,362	1996	271
1970	1,826	1997	460
1971	1,990	1998	355
1972	1,866	1990	350
1973	1,850	2000	229
1977	307	2001	316
1978	312	2002	293
1979	284	2003	245
1982	319	2004	245
1985	2,362	2005	272
1992	193	2006	188

Source: Al-Natour and Yassine 2007, 72.

work permits granted to Palestinians from 1968 to 2005 amounts to the same as those given to Filipinos in 2004 alone (Consultation and Research Institute 2007).

While the legal orthodoxy has opted not to grant Palestinians any special status, remaining oblivious to their condition as refugees, the adoption across the board of a second legislative principle—the principle of reciprocity—at the same time excludes them from the category of foreigners on an equal footing with other foreigners living in the country. According to the principle of reciprocity, a state should return in kind any favors, benefits, and penalties accorded to its nationals by other countries. Because Palestinians cannot claim to belong to any recognized state, the application of the principle of reciprocity to them has placed them in a de facto situation of "stateless foreigners."

Until very recently, such a condition prevented refugees, even the rare holders of work permits, from benefiting from the National Social Security Fund (NSSF) and forbade them from practicing the so-called liberal professions as well. Dating back to 1963, the Lebanese legislation on social security determines that foreigners can benefit from NSSF funds only if

Table 2

Membership in Syndicated Professions [in Lebanon]

Name of Professional Association	Specific Conditions for Foreign Membership	Quota˙	Fees for Membership	Relevant Legislation
Order of Physicians	• Work permit • Principle of reciprocity	No	• Same as Lebanese • No benefit from NSSF	Law 1658 (1979)
Order of Engineers	• Work permit • Principle of reciprocity	10%	• Same as Lebanese • No benefit from NSSF	Law 636 (1997)
Lebanese Bar Association	• Work permit • Principle of reciprocity • Special intervention by the president	10%	Not applicable	Law 8 (1970) (and later amendments)
Pharmacists	• Work permit • Principle of reciprocity	N/A	N/A	Law 367 (1994)

˙[*Author's note*: Even though not mentioned in the original table from the Consultation and Research Institute, I believe the quotas refer to the percentage of non-Lebanese workers allowed to exercise these professions in comparison to the percentage of Lebanese workers.]

Sources: Consultation and Research Institute 2007, 37, combined with data in Hanafi 2007 and al-Natour and Yassine 2007, 76–81.

they hold the appropriate work permit and if their countries of origin apply the same principle to the Lebanese living there. For the few Palestinians who have obtained work permits, this effectively means that they are obliged to contribute to the fund without being entitled to its benefits in cases of disease, unemployment, and retirement.

As for the "liberal professions," their exercise in Lebanon is possible only through membership in the professions' syndicates. Unions may legally adopt sets of internal rules that, by applying the principle of reciprocity, bar the exercise of these professions by the stateless Palestinians. Table 2 summarizes the conditions foreigners must meet to become members of the unions of physicians, engineers, lawyers, and pharmacists in Lebanon.

The stringent legislation curtailing refugees' access to the labor market was lifted for a while after the PLO and the Lebanese government cosigned the Cairo Agreement in 1969. Following clashes between Palestinian factions and the Lebanese army, the Cairo Agreement not only allowed Palestinians to launch attacks against Israel from Lebanese territory and to administer the camps but also acknowledged the right to work for those refugees already residing in Lebanon. A period of strengthening of the Palestinian presence and institutions in Lebanon ensued, the "glorious days" of the *'ayyām al-thawra*, at least from the refugees' perspective. With funds flowing in from international donations, the Palestinian leadership erected the apparatus necessary for its functioning on Lebanese territory. Its offices had to be staffed; hospitals under the Palestinian Red Crescent Society required specialized personnel to provide care for the *fidā'iyyīn* (fighters) and their families; cooperatives and nurseries were established under the Palestinian organization Samed; publishing houses were founded. Jobs for Palestinians, including women, were then in no short supply. It was a service economy, though, created to attend to the demands generated by the presence of the Palestinian leadership in Lebanon. Accordingly, its foundations were highly vulnerable, and when the leadership was expelled from Beirut in 1982, that economy quickly collapsed.

The impact of events in 1982 should be evaluated against this background. The departure of the PLO for Tunis, the massacre at Sabra and Shatila, and the Israeli siege of Beirut set the tone for decades to come. For a while, some Palestinians were not fully aware of the economic dimensions of the difficulties because they continued to rely on remittances sent by those who had migrated to the Gulf states or to Germany and Scandinavia, where refugees obtained asylum status owing to the conditions prevailing in Lebanon during the War of the Camps. In 1991, in reaction to the PLO's support for Iraq in the first Gulf War, Palestinian refugees were expelled from Kuwait, and the doors of the oil-producing Arab states became increasingly closed to them. In Lebanon, in sharp contrast with the years before 1982, Palestinians' economic problems now acquired the contours of a true crisis.

Among the mounting difficulties faced by refugees, Minister of Labor Adnan Mroueh issued a decision in 1982 reserving some seventy professions for the Lebanese alone, barring access to Palestinians. His successors renewed the list of prohibited professions in 1993 and 1995. Although the Lebanese government made efforts to absorb members of the various militias when the latter were demobilized with the signing of the Taef Agreement in 1989 and the end of the Civil War, creating job opportunities for them, nothing of the kind was envisaged for Palestinians. No longer able to count on the structure set up by the PLO in the previous decade, lacking the remittances that for a while kept arriving from the Gulf, and hindered from free access to the local job market by a plethora of Lebanese laws, decrees, and decisions, refugees had no option but to accept work under exploitative conditions. They plunged into utter poverty.

In June 2005, in what was prematurely celebrated as a breakthrough, the departing minister of labor, Trad Hamade, issued ministerial memorandum 1/67, allowing refugees access to fifty professions in the banking, administrative, and clerical sectors, out of the seventy-odd professions formerly forbidden to them (Consultation and Research Institute 2007; al-Natour and Yassine 2007; UNRWA 2007). Table 3 lists the jobs that are now permitted to Palestinian refugees, provided that they were born in Lebanon and have registered at the Directorate General of Political and Refugee Affairs. In practice, though, very little has changed.

First, in effect the ministerial memorandum simply attempted to "legalize" professions that Palestinian refugees were already engaged in, albeit informally. It did not address the vigorous disincentives toward regularization of the working conditions of Palestinians, which remained intact. With the adoption of the memorandum and in the event refugees were to work legally, they would have to start paying taxes, and, together with their employers, to make the appropriate Social Security deductions. As has already been noted, even when contributing to the NSSF, Palestinians could not benefit from it because of the application of the principle of reciprocity. A rigorous implementation of Hamade's memorandum, therefore, would lead to a *decrease* in refugees' salary levels, without any corresponding benefit.

Table 3

List of Jobs Allowed by the [Lebanese] Ministry of Labor (2005)

Memorandum 1/67 of June 2005	
Employees	*Employers*
All administrative and mercantile work of whatever nature, in particular the work of director general, director, personnel manager, treasurer, secretary, archivist, file clerk, computer, commercial officer, marketing officer, trade consultant, foreman, warehouse officer, seller, money exchange, jeweller, laboratory, pharmacy, electric mains, electronic works, paint works, glass [installation], mechanics and maintenance, doorkeeper, concierge, guard, driver, cook, waiter, barber, elementary, intermediate and secondary schoolteacher	All commercial work of whatever nature; banking, accounting, assessors, engineering work of whatever kind, contracts and trade in building, jewellery, manufacturing of shoes and apparel, all furniture work of whatever kind and the industries that rely on it, sweets industry, printing, publication and distribution, haircutting and styling, clothing press and cleaners, car repair (metal work, mechanical, glass attachment, upholstery, car electric works)

Source: Consultation and Research Institute 2007, 13.

Second, the memorandum did not waive the requirement for Palestinians to obtain work permits in order to engage in the professions newly opened to them. Table 1 shows the insignificant number of work permits issued for Palestinians from 1966 to 2006, leading to a situation whereby relatively few refugees are willing to apply. It is unsurprising, therefore, that Hamade's legal change has failed to produce major shifts in the situation of the Palestinian workforce.

Finally, as jurists quickly pointed out, Hamade's memorandum, owing to its very nature, can easily be undermined. As a ministerial memorandum, it occupies the lowest rank in the statutory hierarchy and can be overridden by a presidential decree, which, in turn, can be overruled by a parliamentary law. In addition, it might be annulled at any time by another ministerial memorandum. Easily nullified, thus, it did not offer sufficient leverage for effective legal change in the long run.

The bill approved by the Lebanese Parliament on August 17, 2010, may have addressed the latter issue, the legal frailty of Hamade's measure, but not the first two. To begin with, the disincentives to regularization of the Palestinian workforce remain in place. Only in the case of retirement or end of service can Palestinians now benefit from NSSF coverage. For sickness benefit, maternity leave, and family allowances, a private fund must be set up to avoid "burden[ing] the Treasury or the National Social Security Fund," the bill states. Second, and probably more seriously, the new legislation does not waive the requirement for work permits: it simply exempts Palestinians from paying the required fees. The Ministry of Labor had already reduced the fees for Palestinian and Syrian workers, so that was not the sticking point. As the PHRO pointed out at the time the bill was passed, "The requirement to obtain a work permit opens the door for procrastination and administrative bureaucracy" (2010, 2), fomenting employer disinclination to hire or regularize Palestinian workers. Finally, the bill fails to address the highly politicized and thorny issue of the liberal professions, access to which remains forbidden to Palestinians. The PHRO classified the move by the Lebanese Parliament as simply "gestures" (2010, 1), not enough to produce major changes in practice. The *Financial Times* reported on refugees' reaction to the legal changes: "When asked what he is thinking of doing with his business studies degree, 23-year-old Mohammed Sheikh grins ruefully from the money transfer stand [where] he is working in Sabra refugee camp [*sic*]. 'I'm not thinking about anything. I'll graduate and then come back here'" (2010).

Given this legal-historical background, what do the figures on Palestinian labor in Lebanon tell us? Starting with the publication of Hani Mundus's groundbreaking study of the workforce in the Tal al-Zaatar camp in East Beirut (Mundus 1974), some trends and patterns are identifiable, such as persistently high levels of unemployment and the concentration of refugee workers in manual and menial jobs. These patterns suggest a tendency observed throughout the history of the Palestinian diaspora in Lebanon, with the refugee workforce reflecting the changes within the Lebanese economy and acting as a perennial reservoir of abundant and cheap labor. Other more recent features—such as the minor impact of higher education on career perspectives and the small but increasing participation of women in the labor force, clustering around the relatively higher-status positions in the education, health, and social work services with NGOs and UNRWA—are also telling.

Analysis of the situation of the Palestinian workforce in recent years encounters several difficulties, two paramount among them. The first is the caution needed when handling figures relating to refugees resident in Lebanon provided by different stakeholders. Presently, UNRWA indicates that there are more than 470,000 registered refugees in Lebanon, but shortly after my fieldwork ended, that figure was 425,000 (UNRWA n.d.). Scholars and policy makers, however, opt for figures ranging anywhere between 210,000 and 600,000, varying figures that often fuel differing political agendas. Such a discrepancy in the numbers affects the quantification of the Palestinian workforce. Nevertheless, the figure 210,000 seems more realistic because it takes into consideration two recent phenomena: the rapidly declining fertility rate among refugees and the widespread out-migration of young men, leading to a situation in which eight out of every ten families have close relatives living abroad (Tiltnes 2005). Based on the numbers of *registered* refugees, the Norwegian Fafo Foundation indicates that 37 percent of Palestinians are effectively in the workforce, as shown in table 4. Chart 1 breaks down these data by sex and age, revealing that 63 percent of men are in the labor force versus only 13 percent of women, with marriage tending to force the former into work outside the household

Table 4
Percentage Distribution of Palestinians in the Labor Force in Lebanon (2006)

Total Population 450,000	
Working-Age Population 69%	
Persons included in the labor force (economically "active") 37%	Below Working Age 31%
Adults not in the labor force 63%	

Source: Consultation and Research Institute 2007, 17, based on Tiltnes 2007.

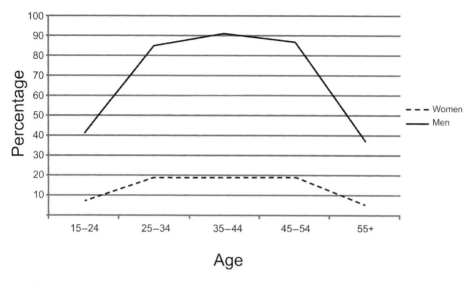

Chart 1. Palestinian labor-force participation by sex and age (2006). *Source*: Tiltnes 2007.

while keeping the latter away from it. Chart 1 also exposes the overall limited participation of women in the workforce. The Palestinian workforce, in reality, is very similar to that of the Lebanese, which is also young and dominated by men. The study of unemployment patterns in both populations, however, reveals some remarkable differences, as we shall soon see.

The second source of difficulty when it comes to studying the recent situation of the Palestinian workforce in Lebanon is the controversial definition of unemployment adopted by the International Labor Organization.[5] This is how employed and unemployed populations are defined within the organization's framework:

5. In an International Labor Organization document dating from 2019, a slightly different definition is given for employment and unemployment: "Persons in employment are defined as all those of working age who, during a short reference period, were engaged in any activity to produce goods or provide services for pay or profit. . . . Persons in unemployment are defined as all those of working age who were not in employment, carried out activities to seek employment during a specified recent period and were currently

The *employed population* is made up of persons above a specified age who furnish the supply of labor for the production of goods and services. When measured for a short reference period (of one week or one day), it refers to all persons who worked for pay, profit or family gain during that period. . . . The *unemployed population* is made up of persons above a specified age who are available to, but did not, furnish the supply of labor for the production of goods and services. When measured for a short reference period, it relates to all persons not in employment who would have accepted a suitable job or started an enterprise during the reference period if the opportunity arose, and who had actively looked for ways to obtain a job or start an enterprise in the near past. (2010, original emphasis)

Even though an international standard is important to allow for comparisons between different economies, the one-week or one-day rule is highly arbitrary and more applicable to liberal labor markets, where structural flaws do not hinder job seekers' chances to find employment, which is hardly the case in Lebanon. Besides, such a definition tends to conceal the occurrence of severe underemployment and does not address the situation of "discouraged workers," those who have given up looking for a job out of a lack of hope of finding one and who constitute a high proportion among refugees in Lebanon. According to the International Labor Organization framework, the unemployment rate of Palestinian refugees in Lebanon was 10 percent at the beginning of my fieldwork (2007), peaking to 25 percent if a "relaxed" definition is used instead to account for the "discouraged" (UNRWA 2007, 8). These figures are higher than those found among the Lebanese in the same year, whose unemployment rate ranged between 8 and 15 percent (Consultation and Research Institute 2007, 23), although strictly comparable data were not available at the time. Unemployment, as shown in chart 2, affects especially youths and women—precisely those not expected to be the main breadwinners in their households and normally the ones being provided for.

---

available to take up employment given a job opportunity" (2019, 6). The limitations of the older definition pointed to here seem to remain perfectly valid, nonetheless.

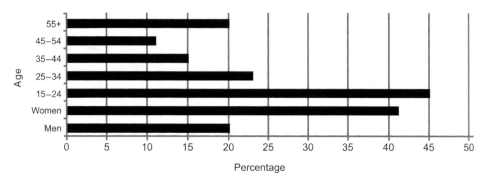

Chart 2. Palestinian unemployment levels by sex and age (2006). *Source*: Tiltnes 2007.

One of the most striking characteristics of the Palestinian workforce in Lebanon is the minor impact of higher education on the jobseeker's chances of securing employment (Consultation and Research Institute 2007). Analysis of chart 3 leads to the counterintuitive conclusion that pursuing higher education does not necessarily translate into higher employment rates. Such figures may reflect out-migration, with young skilled Palestinian men finding their way to better-paid positions elsewhere, especially in Europe and the Persian Gulf. Nevertheless, this alone does not account for the phenomenon, and it is likely that a sizable quantity of Palestinians with upper-level diplomas cannot find work in Lebanon matching their qualifications—not surprisingly, because the highly controlled access to the so-called professions in practice bars refugees from exercising them legally. One exception to this general rule, however, does exist: education has an impact on *women's* career perspectives, and women's participation in the workforce increases according to years spent in schooling (Egset 2003).

This particularity results from the very specific working conditions of refugee women. There is indeed a clear gender clustering around specific sectors of the economy. Whereas trade and agriculture count on a mixed workforce, the physically demanding, often hazardous, and highly "informal" construction sector employs almost solely men. Women, for their part, are overrepresented in the higher-status education, health, and social work sectors, where formal contracts, paid holidays, and sick leave are more

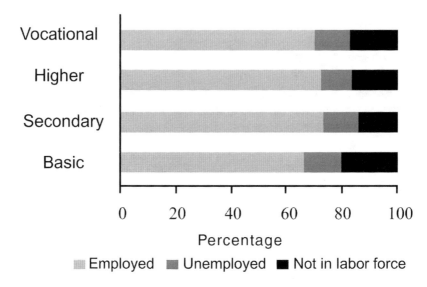

Chart 3. Palestinian educational levels in relation to employment (2003). *Source*: Consultation and Research Institute 2007, 22, adapted from Jacobsen 2003, 93–95.

common. It is true that among Palestinian refugees "formal" and "informal" economic activities do not function as a sharp dualism (UNRWA 2007): some workers may not have a formal contract yet still benefit from paid leave and health insurance. Nevertheless, the construction sector tends toward seasonal work and "informality," whereas formal contracts, especially with UNRWA and NGOs, are more frequent in education, health, and social work. One in every three working women is employed in the latter sectors, where higher education is often a prerequisite and incomes are considerably higher (Tiltnes 2007), to the point of rendering women's salary levels comparable to men's, as depicted in chart 4. Thus, although only a minority of Palestinian refugee women effectively take part in the workforce and secure positions in the labor market, female workers' social visibility well exceeds their numerical importance. It is no wonder that their husbands, fathers, and sons have been so sensitive to the eventual impact of such a trend on traditional gender hierarchies. In fact, one in two men disapprove of women working outside their homes, and among those women who are not part of the workforce, a considerable number report

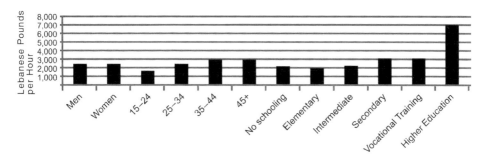

Chart 4. Salary levels among Palestinian refugees (2006). *Source*: Tiltnes 2007.

familial obligations, such as caregiving, and social restrictions among the main reasons for their nonparticipation (Jacobsen 2004). In practice, those familial obligations and social restrictions translate into a relatively low participation of women in the workforce and restricted mobility: among those with jobs, the majority work in the camps where they live.

Chart 4 also reveals the overall low salary levels for refugees in general, the mean hourly wage not exceeding 2,600 Lebanese pounds ($1.73). This low wage is even more problematic in a country that has known inflation in recent years and whose economy is faltering because of constant political turmoil. The volatility of the Lebanese political situation has deepened the economic recession: in the job market there has been a sharp decrease in the demand for labor since 1996 (Consultation and Research Institute 2007), with companies and institutions very wary about expanding their businesses. In addition to coping with a highly discriminatory set of laws hindering their access to the labor market, Palestinian refugees also strive to find jobs in a shrinking economy—one in which, moreover, they have faced competition from Syrian labor, especially in the construction sector, even before the current large rise in the numbers of Syrian refugees fleeing the civil war in their home country.

There is a lack of studies evaluating the true extent of the participation of Syrian labor in the Lebanese economy. The figure of 1.4 million workers advanced for 1994 is too alarming and appears to be politically motivated (Consultation and Research Institute 2007). After the assassination of Prime Minister Rafik Hariri in 2005 and the general hostility shown against Syrians, many of them left Lebanon. Even prior to the current war in their country, though, Syrians had already started returning to Lebanon. Leaving their families behind in their homeland, where prices are lower than in Lebanon, Syrian workers could afford to work for less and went after job vacancies similar to those targeted by Palestinians, thus representing a substantial source of competition to the latter.

The combined effects of this scenario—a shrinking economy and fierce competition from the Syrian labor force, only intensified by the current war—in addition to the plummeting decline in UNRWA aid, which affects Palestinians in Lebanon more than in other countries (R. Sayigh 1995), have kept a vast number of Palestinian refugees in utter poverty. This destitution can be seen in figures 3, 4, 5, and 6, photographs that provide a glimpse into the living conditions in Shatila. Despite the negative impact of the labor regulation, which hampers Palestinians' free access to the regular job market, income from employment, on average not exceeding $3,367 per year, still represents the major part of household revenues (Tiltnes 2005). The outcome is that poverty among the Palestinian population is considerably higher than the rate prevalent not only among the Lebanese but also among refugees living in Jordan and the West Bank. As far as poverty levels are concerned, only in Gaza is the situation worse than in Lebanon (table 5). Social support and remittances from relatives living abroad constitute a vital compensatory scheme for the lowest-income households but can only partially counterweigh the cumulative results of the structural situation, a state of affairs described by one author as a "negative spiral" (Tiltnes 2005, 9). Given the focus here, a brief analysis of three arenas—health, housing conditions, and education—will suffice for the portrayal of this "negative spiral."

War-related chronic illnesses, disabilities, and psychological distress affect the refugee community in Lebanon more than in neighboring countries,[6] and these matters are rendered worse by the lack of access to long-term and comprehensive care. Although child and mother health care has improved over the years, it remains worse than in other areas of UNRWA's operation. Child nutrition continues to be a problem, with 5

---

6. The data I am analyzing here predate the present-day conflict ravaging Syria.

Table 5

Percentage of Households That Are Poor (Less Than US$2 per Person) and Ultra-poor (Less Than US$1 per Person)

	Lebanon		Jordan		West Bank		Gaza Strip	
	Camps	Gatherings	Camps	All	Camps	All	Camps	All
Ultra-Poor	15.0	13.2	8.6		13.0	8.4	23.9	21.6
Poor	36.2	31.3	30.6	8.0	19.2	14.5	37.7	33.0

[*Author's note*: Although not indicated in the original table, the amounts $1.00 and $2.00 per person in the table title seem to refer to a day's pay.]
Source: Tiltnes 2005, 45.

percent of children malnourished and 4 percent vulnerable. These figures are high, particularly when compared with the 1 percent and 2 percent, respectively, registered for Jordan (Tiltnes 2005, 19, 20).

As far as housing conditions are concerned, war has left its marks: three-quarters of the infrastructure of the camps and "gatherings"[7] have been destroyed, and some 6 to 15 percent have not yet been restored, especially in the southern part of the country. Overall, connection to sewage systems and septic tanks, access to piped and drinking water, and refuse collections are deficient, and both camp and gathering dwellers complain of the lack of reliability of water and electricity supplies (Jacobsen and Khalidi 2003, 185; Tiltnes 2005, 29, 38; Ugland 2003, 270).

Notwithstanding improvements in the education status of Palestinians over time, education levels are lower, and grade repetition and dropout rates are higher than those found among Lebanese students and among Palestinian refugees in other UNRWA countries. Though not directly comparable, available data suggest that illiteracy is twice as high among refugees than among the Lebanese. Educational achievements are poor, with only 16 percent of the Palestinian refugees of working age holding a secondary diploma, ten percentage points lower than in Jordan and Syria. Pass rates at the end of the preparatory cycle for Palestinians in Lebanon

7. An important number of Palestinian refugees live in informal "gatherings," which UNRWA does not recognize as official refugee camps.

are also much lower than the pass rates for Palestinians in neighboring countries (Tiltnes 2005 15, 17; Tyldum and Bashour 2003, 115, 118, 119).

Bendik Sørvig (2001) characterizes migration to Europe or the Gulf as a mechanism for coping with such adverse conditions. Various studies advance differing estimates for Palestinian out-migration from Lebanon, ranging from more than a quarter of registered refugees living abroad to the alarming estimate of half (Consultation and Research Institute 2007). In spite of the controversy surrounding the figures, analysts concur on the favorite destinations—the Gulf countries and Europe—and on the general profile of typical migrants: unmarried men of working age, leaving the country on their own. This profile affects the population pyramid of refugees in Lebanon, which shows a disproportionately low number of working-age men.

Out-migration has varied through different periods. In the case of the Gulf, it preceded the oil boom of 1974 and considerably receded in the aftermath of the Gulf War of 1991. Europe became a particularly prominent destination during the Camp Wars in the mid-1980s, when young men managed to obtain asylum status in Germany, Sweden, and Denmark. It has declined in recent decades under the impact of more restrictive migratory laws. Highly educated Palestinians normally opt for the Gulf, where their qualifications can immediately be converted into economic gains. The majority, though, select Europe as the favorite destination, despite the fact that discrimination, language barriers, and different educational standards normally mean a devaluation of skills, at least during an initial phase (Sørvig 2001). One of the reasons Europe is preferred is that the stateless refugees may eventually obtain proper papers and a nationality there. In contrast, the temporary work contracts offered in the Gulf do not provide the stability sought out by potential migrants. In effect, migrant candidates identify the desire for "stability and normality," together with economic motivations and the longing to escape the "boredom" of refugee life,[8] as the main reason for wanting to leave Lebanon.

---

8. Samuli Schielke (2015) identifies the same feeling among the young men from northern Egypt with whom he worked.

With more and more barriers obstructing entry into the Gulf coun-tries and Europe alike, aspiring migrants resort to two main avenues to achieve their objectives, both of which require family connections and the pooling of resources. First, marriage to family members or acquaintances who have already succeeded in migrating may provide, through family reunification, the necessary visa out of Lebanon. The second route involves buying fake documents and visas, without which even boarding a flight is impossible. A "package" for Europe, including plane tickets and fake doc-uments, normally reaches the prohibitive amount of $4,000 (Sørvig 2001, 106),[9] more than the average yearly income of refugee households. For this reason, pooling resources from different family members, whether still in Lebanon or already abroad, is vital for migration attempts. If successful, the migrant will send remittances back home and thus maintain ties of mutual obligation linking him to his family, which has remained behind. Sørvig (2001) emphasizes the importance of the role played by families in the strategies adopted by refugees to handle the challenges faced in Leba-non. Household economic coping makes more sense than individual cop-ing, he maintains. Marwan Khawaja and Laurie Jacobsen's study, however, points to the limits of the culturalist argument about the "uniqueness of [the] Arab extended family in nurturing exchange" (2003, 599). Although exchange does effectively occur within families, it tends to take place between those able to reciprocate, thus excluding from the network the poorest members and those most in need. Given the highly skewed nature of the division of wealth in the camps, this selective exchange has huge implications in terms of how external aid should be distributed.

Åge Tiltnes sums up the three key conclusions of the Fafo Founda-tion's report on the living conditions of Palestinians in Lebanon that I have been describing:

> First, the current living conditions are certainly better than they were for the first generation of refugees. However, a closer look at outcomes compared to those found among Palestinian refugees in neighboring

---

9. As of 2013, according to my own findings, the cost of such a package had risen considerably, often reaching $8,000.

countries shows a faltering development in Lebanon. Whatever prog-
ress made during the first decades after 1948 is seriously stagnating and
even deteriorating. . . . Second . . . , it is primarily in Lebanon camp
and gathering households that we find that poor outcomes are directly
linked to the *location* in Lebanon. . . . Third, the exclusion of refugees
from the Lebanese labor market through a number of mechanisms,
puts households in general, but young refugee men in particular, in a
unique situation compared to refugees elsewhere. Those that can, leave
the country. Those that cannot are forming a large group of young men
who are leaving schools or performing poorly there and have little hope
or ambition for the future. Thus, both processes contribute to seriously
undermine the stock of human capital in the communities not only for
today, but perhaps more importantly, for the future. (Tiltnes 2005, 9–10,
original emphasis)

It is to these young men, the *shabāb*, that this book is dedicated.

Averting Drowning by Numbers and Legislation

Now, what stories does this history based on figures and legislation reveal,
and what stories does it conceal? To what degree do the numbers and
legal documents surveyed here speak of the "reality" and convey Shatilan experiences? What "realities" and alternative stories do they silence,
as suggested by Abu Mujahed's words of caution with which I opened this
chapter? What are the methodological and epistemological underpinnings of a history based on figures and pieces of legislation, and what are
the respective limitations?

Based on fieldwork on the Greek–Albanian border, Sarah Green
(2005) demonstrates that numbers make certain features noticeable and
others invisible. Numbers are ultimately the result of negotiations and of
the interweaving of statistical and nonstatistical information, thus revealing the social relations and power dynamics characteristic of the place
where research is conducted. The same probably happens everywhere, as
it most definitely does in my field.

For one brief moment only, the Fafo Foundation's authoritative and
largely statistical depiction of the living conditions of Palestinian refugees

(Tiltnes 2005) concedes to report on what *has not* been said: on page 27, one reads about a "general difficulty in data gathering . . . during field-work: some women may be wearing (precious) necklaces or rings, with-out considering them household savings. It is reasonable to assume that this resulted in at least some underreporting of savings of this kind." This observation should have been enough to put the surveyor in alert mode.

What if survey questions are being asked in such a way that the very framing of what counts as "the economy" becomes of limited purchase for understanding the camp economy? Instead of inquiring about salary levels, bank savings, access to formal social insurance, and work stories, as I did at the beginning of my fieldwork, what if the surveyor were to invite research participants to talk about bride prices (*muqaddam* and *mu'akhkhar*) as forms through which money is made to circulate in the camp? About golden bracelets and rings as savings instruments? Or about *jam'iyyāt*—the local pooling of resources for use by those taking part in the scheme if and when need arises—as local mechanisms for providing some kind of social protection? What if surveyors were to ask how research participants spend their days instead of probing for biographies of formal or informal employment? Would doing so bring us any closer to an eco-nomics that functions otherwise, in which women may not consider the hours they spend at the family's small shops as work, opening them when-ever domestic chores allow, bringing the children along, and operating all kinds of alternative credit mechanisms based on a complex negotiation of trust/suspicion toward their customers, who often are neighbors and kin? This chapter started with certainties informed by statistics and pieces of legislation and is about to end with heuristic doubts about the distance separating numbers from the world, figures from life. It further sets the tone for the coming two chapters, which are also about heuristic doubts and other distances: those between concepts ("gender" and "youth") and life, words and the world.

In addition, other factors may have informed the attitudes of respon-dents to some of the questions in the Fafo survey. In a country such as Leb-anon, where no census has been conducted since 1932—precisely because the data collected back then have served to freeze the division of politi-cal power among the different sects, completely ignoring the dramatic changes the Lebanese population has undergone in the near century since then—Palestinian refugees themselves have come to realize that there is power invested in numbers.

Yasser taught me that when it comes to understanding the numbers my own informants provided me, it is essential to realize that lying—an action condemned by local notions of morality—is different from holding back information, which is not particularly problematic, especially when one does not know how the figures collected are going to be used. We had only just left the household of a family I had interviewed in Shatila when Yasser whispered so as not to be overheard: "You know they haven't told us the whole truth over there, right?" He had facilitated the meeting and probably thought it was his obligation to call my attention to its shortcomings. Not wishing to show signs of my naivety, it was actually I who lied: "Of course, I know." He probably sensed my lack of sincerity: "When you asked if they receive money from their relatives abroad, they replied that they don't. Well, they don't, but when the relatives come to visit, they bring presents and money. They do the same when it's Eid." That was my first lesson that the numbers being reported in a setting such as Shatila are always the result of a negotiation: they may, at most, function as the starting point for an investigation rather than its end point.

If I have to come to terms with the nonexact standing of numbers in my fieldwork setting, then I have to do the same as far as the legislation is concerned. How can one understand the variation in the leniency or strictness with which the legislation has been applied throughout the history of the Palestinian saga in Lebanon? Is the leniency or strictness of application indicative of the standing that legislation itself occupies in a conflicted and socially and juridically complex country, whose legal corpus reflects differing traditions and where personal-status issues are governed by religious tribunals and non-personal-status issues by civil courts? Undoubtedly, the Palestinian issue in Lebanon is one of legal entitlement, but not only. Although NGOs working with refugees in Lebanon have secured resources by insisting on the latter's lack of legal entitlement— often because this argument provides a "facile" idiom, easy for donors to understand—the refugee question is also undeniably one of social and economic inclusion. Here there is more approximating refugees to the

Lebanese—or, at least, to *some* Lebanese—than there is separating them. Moreover, can I really derive my informants' multilayered subjectivities from their economic and legal standing? Roger Zetter (1991) focuses on the stereotyping often implied by labeling someone a "refugee," normally to meet a notion of bureaucratically defined "needs." Shakir, an accounting student from Shatila whom we met in the previous chapter, provided the most potent critique of my poor attempts at labeling.

Shakir and I decided to go to the cinema. The previous time we had watched a movie together, we did not do it the proper way: the medium, the seventeen-inch screen of my computer, and the film we selected, *Lila dit ça* (Ziad Doueiri, 2004), had not been the ideal options. *Lila* tells the story of a supposedly sexually liberated French woman living in an Arab neighborhood. At a certain juncture, the main male character of the movie, tempted by Lila, who wants to show him her vagina, says something like, "If I were given the choice of choosing between a cunt and liberating Palestine, I would opt for the cunt." Shakir laughed a lot and exclaimed: "Gustavo, this guy is a fucker." He criticized the French woman's behavior and repeated one of his favorite mottos: "I don't trust girls!" The movie prompted us to discuss women's sexual behavior, and the conversation—which eventually turned to topics such as a brother's relations to sisters and some German women's habit of not waxing their armpits, which annoyed Shakir—was marked by me frantically taking notes. When we chose to watch a movie again, we thought we should do it the proper way: in a cinema. We opted for an American blockbuster so that I would not have the excuse of turning a leisure activity into work. Our outing, though, did not go smoothly.

The movie we selected was being screened only in the upper-crust shopping mall ABC Ashrafiyeh, in the eastern, mostly Christian part of Beirut. To my astonishment, Shakir had no idea where the mall was, a sign of the persistence of profound sectarian and class divisions in Beirut. I panicked: having read the guidelines on ethics governing ethnographic research, I was only too aware of the class and power differences between Shakir and myself. I worried about spoiling him and about allowing him access to activities that would be completely out of reach once I left. I finally conceded, though, and we found our way to the shopping center.

To my despair, Shakir loved the mall, filled with the blond women he finds attractive. I reacted: "You shouldn't forget you're an 'ibn al-mukhayyam [son of the camp] and poor and a stateless refugee. This place and these girls aren't for you." I deserved Shakir's pitiless criticism of my "labeling effort": "So that's it, Gustavo. For you, I'm a refugee and nothing else. So because I'm an 'ibn al-mukhayyam, I can't come to places like this and enjoy it and fancy the girls around?"

The label refugee is obviously inadequate to capture Shakir's complex life and desires. The very labels I have extensively used in my statistical charts and analysis, Palestinians, camps, and Lebanon, are also grossly overgeneralizing. If Lebanon includes the likes of the Hariris, one of the richest families in the Arab East, with commercial links to the Saudi royal dynasty, then it comes as no surprise that Lebanon is sharply different from camps. Nonetheless, an analytical demarche along those lines not only glosses over the similarities between the immediate neighborhood of Shatila—which is also part of "Lebanon"—and the "camp" itself. It also overlooks the sense in which the lives of Umm Sahar and Umm Ubaida are alike, although the former is Palestinian and a camp resident, and the latter is a Lebanese national and non–camp dweller. Similar to the academic work in the "states of exception" vein that I examine in the next section, statistical studies lump together "camps" in an overarching unit, compressing social-economic realities that are both very similar and very different. Considered on its own, every camp tends to be very similar to its immediate surroundings while at the same time very different from other camps, reflecting its own specific history or integration into the surroundings or the origins of its residents or the sectarian composition of the neighborhood. By producing "imagined populations" such as "Palestinians," "camps," and "Lebanon," the overarching labels render both these differences and these similarities invisible. The biographies of the families presented in this chapter constitute counterevidence to such a discourse, however. Their exceptionalism—in that they live far below the levels of well-being and comfort to which human beings should be entitled—is in no way an exception.

Statistical labels, in spite of the fantasy-like nature of certain figures they produce, do contribute to making up a reality in the terrain and not only because the numbers they juggle inform interventions by relevant stakeholders and policy makers. In Lebanon, numbers concerning Palestinians have shaped the very perception that they are different from the Lebanese, thus serving statist nationalisms and the hardening of identity barriers, which are certainly more pronounced today than they were in 1948. Although labels such as *Lebanon* and *Palestinian* might not have meant much before or just after the Nakba, today they increasingly inform political agendas on all sides of the ideological spectrum.

Michel Foucault (1991) shows how "statistics" is the "science of the state" and tells the story of how the concept of "population" gradually emerged from the eighteenth century onward to increasingly become the object targeted by governments. Counting serves the functions of surveillance and control in state-making projects, as Palestinians, of all peoples, know all too well (Zureik 2001). Thus, it should not raise any eyebrows that in a setting with pronounced antistate effects such as Shatila, refugees are highly aware of the political implications of counting and have come to realize that withholding information makes perfect sense. One must concur with Jean Genet when he observes that "each Palestinian is true" (Genet, Barrada, and Wischenbart 1987, 74), even when—and through—withholding information. They are true to themselves, and, hence, having access to that truth is a privilege hard to obtain.

During a lecture at the Jerusalem Forum in Amman, Rochelle Davis (2011) used some British Mandate statistics to show that the Jewish population was in the majority in Jerusalem by 1946. The audience, Palestinians, many of whom had lived in Jerusalem as children or adults prior to 1948, promptly disputed the figures, which were completely at odds with their remembrances of an Arab Jerusalem. Several reasons were proposed as to why the British statistics were unreliable: women were probably undercounted because a male researcher would not be supposed to have access to their names; similarly, young men were probably undercounted because of leftover fears of conscription into the Ottoman army; and some Palestinian villages, even though geographically close enough to Jerusalem, were probably not considered because they did not lie within the official boundaries of the municipality. In any case, what is revealing in Davis's interaction with her audience is the latter's claim over and challenge to the knowledge produced about them. Knowledge, Ann Laura Stoler argues, bases its assertions of truth on "disqualifying some knowledges and valorizing others, . . . establishing a hierarchy of knowledges" (quoted in Davis 2011, 138). Nonetheless, sometimes this hierarchy is disputed.

When I asked Ahmad to explain to me the meaning of the numbers written on the external walls of some Shatila dwellings, he told me that they were the result of a project dating back some three years earlier to install electricity meters in every house: "The project involved UNRWA, the popular committees, and Électricité du Liban [Electric Company of Lebanon]. But it was only some months ago that they started to install some meters, so I don't think the project got very far. I volunteered in the project, but for two days only. The reality is that no one can register anything here, Gustavo. Houses here are uncountable because people keep building on top of each other. The situation changes all the time. Like birds flying in the sky."

Exceptionalism Is Not the Exception

The exceptionalism captured by the figures presented earlier, insofar as they illustrate the "negative spiral" Tiltnes (2005) writes about, is not at all exceptional, as indicated by the biographies of the families presented at the beginning of this chapter. Yet some analysts—paramount among them sociologist Sari Hanafi (2008a, 2008b, 2010)—go one step further and, oblivious to the marked differences between the refugee camps in Lebanon, characterize all of them as "states of exception." Hanafi draws heavily on a highly selective reading of Foucault's propositions concerning biopolitics as a technique of control, discipline, and surveillance as well as of Giorgio Agamben's concept of the *homo sacer*, who, reduced to "bare life," is seen only as a body to be fed, lacking social and historical attributes and an individual subjectivity and barred from the political domain. In Hanafi's publications, "exception" assumes more than one guise. It is used to characterize the camps as closed and confined, showing a marked spatial bias, as well as to describe them as devoid of a clear authority and mechanisms of control (for a sample, see Hanafi 2008a, 2008b and Hanafi and Long 2010).

In reality, Shatila is *not* "confined": it is certainly part of Beirut and has an impact on the city, just as the city has an impact on it. The failure to understand the extent to which Shatilans are also Beirutis, exposed to the same exclusionary mechanisms created by unrestrained liberalism and a very raucous laissez-faire economics, certainly compromises the kind of anthropology needed to understand a place like Shatila—located within the city, communicating with it, and yet situated at its margins. It is actually the nature of the links between Shatila and Beirut/Lebanon, therefore, that leads to exclusion: Shatila is at the margins precisely because it is *not* a confined space.

If class is considered, can other large and poor sections of Lebanese society also be seen as an "exception"? If so, we might then legitimately ask what is *not* an exception. In this sense, have scholars played a role in further "exoticizing" Palestinians, obscuring the features they have in common with other poverty-stricken sectors of Lebanese society?

Regarding Hanafi's definition of *exception* as a "void of authority," although it is true that there is no clear authority in Shatila, this does not mean—contrary to what the sociologist seems to imply—that the camp lacks mechanisms for social control and conflict management at the local level. Camps, Shatila in particular, are not lawless time bombs ticking away until the moment of explosion, where instability is nurtured and young unemployed men are easily seduced and enlisted by Salafists to engage in jihad (as depicted in International Crisis Group 2009 and Rougier 2007, respectively). In reality, some academics are so bound to a state-centered perspective that they remain blind to mechanisms of social control or conflict management beyond the state.

I once attended a presentation at the American University of Beirut where the imagery of camps as time bombs was evoked during the launch of a study by the International Crisis Group entitled precisely "Nurturing Instability" (see International Crisis Group 2009). I remember asking myself during the presentation how people can live in such places. Once the talk was over, I left the university's pleasant campus and found my way back home: to Shatila. As I arrived in the camp, the *shabāb* welcomed me and asked what I had been up to that afternoon. I lacked the courage to tell them about the images purporting to represent them to which I had been exposed: "Oh, not much," I lied once again.

**Governance beyond the State: The More
It Remains the Same, the More It Changes**

To my dismay, Shakir, the *shāb* with whom I went to the cinema, stopped talking to me. He was one of the first *shabāb* I got close to in Shatila. I complained to a common friend, Omar, twenty-eight, that Shakir had suddenly ceased replying to my calls and texts. Omar asked whether I wanted him to intervene. He asked Shakir what was wrong. He returned to report that the time was not yet ripe for resolving the differences between Shakir and me.

What Omar attempted is a simplified version of a *ṣulḥa* or *muṣālaḥa* (reconciliation), a traditional mechanism for dispute settlement in historical Palestine and other countries of the Arab East (Jabbour 1996; Pely 2008–9). In its more elaborate form, a *muṣālaḥa* is conducted by a *jaha* committee, composed of respected members within the community, almost invariably older men. Through the prominent role elders assume in *muṣālaḥa* processes, they often crystallize their political authority over the rest of the group. Julie Peteet (1987) demonstrates how the Palestinian leadership opted for a cautious campaign of legal transformation during the *'ayyām al-thawra*: instead of completely ignoring local mechanisms for dispute settlement, it chose whenever possible not to disrupt the authority of family heads, sheikhs, or elders but to build on their influence. Nevertheless, elders increasingly faced a challenge from the young educated men arriving from abroad, who constituted the core of the Palestinian leadership in Lebanon during the *'ayyām al-thawra*. The leadership also did not hesitate to intervene decisively and exert its authority forcefully whenever a legal breach deeply offended the community's notions of morality and justice or risked an escalation of intersectarian violence—intervention that ended up further eroding the elders' authority.

After the *'ayyām al-thawra*, the elders never entirely recovered their earlier prestige. Today in Shatila, the Rābiṭa ahl Majd al-Krum (Association of the People of Majd al-Krum) is still called upon to mediate in *muṣālaḥāt*, but increasingly rarely. The *rābiṭa* brings together older representatives of the families from Majd al-Krum, the Palestinian village to which the original settlers of Shatila belonged (R. Sayigh 1993). These families still benefit from a high standing in the community, yet this status has not been enough for the *rābiṭa* to keep its former role as a regular mediator in conflicts. One of the members admitted to me that the *rābiṭa* had been involved in more *muṣālaḥāt* in the past. Today, young people sometimes initiate processes of dispute settlement, and only at a later stage is the *rābiṭa* called upon to give its blessing to the outcome. There was a certain sorrow in the *rābiṭa* member's tone when he reported that "the new generation doesn't have much respect for the older one."

The case of a *muṣālaḥa* conducted by young men in Shatila some time ago shows that the *shabāb*'s participation in the episode has not led to a crystallization of statelike political power to their benefit. The dispute occurred between two friends, Asad and Bishr, both very close to Ahmad. It involved the always explosive terrain of *sharaf* (honor) and the standing of sisters in the community. Asad's brother was secretly dating Bishr's sister. The couple was spotted hand-in-hand in Sanaya, one of the few green parks in Beirut, and the news quickly reached Bishr. Bumping into Asad in one of the alleys of Shatila, Bishr shouted, for everyone to hear, "I'll fuck your sister." Asad went back home to try to cool down but could not resist the provocation. He grabbed a knife, returned to the spot where he had been insulted, and stabbed Bishr in the abdomen. Bishr survived the attack but spent several days in the hospital, and the bill reached an astronomical $5,000. Recovered and back in Shatila, Bishr received frequent visits from other *shabāb*, including Ahmad, who recommended that he forget the episode to prevent it from escalating. Bishr would not listen to anyone, though, and kept repeating the threat against Asad's sister. Ahmad lost his temper and yelled at Bishr before slamming the door at the latter's home, "Asad's sister is like a sister to me, too! And I would do the same Asad did and stab you for saying those things!" Bishr sent someone to Ahmad's place, inviting him to make a reconciliatory visit. During the visit, Ahmad spoke with Bishr's father as well, whose tone was more restrained than that of his son: "If someone says such things about your sister and you don't kill him, you deserve to die.[. . .] Let's close this whole affair. I propose Asad pays for the hospital bills and moves out of Shatila." Ahmad managed to renegotiate the request that Asad move out because that would compromise Asad's earning capacities and his chances of covering the costs of Bishr's hospitalization. Counting on his mother's and brother's help, Asad managed to collect $3,600 but pledged to continue paying over the following months. Bishr's father agreed: "You see, now Asad is asking me to give him credit. But *la 'uyūnak* [for your eyes]." The expression *la 'uyūnak*, which can be translated as "you're welcome," indicated the father's acceptance of Asad's proposal. Only at this juncture were the elders invited to witness the ceremony during which Asad gave the money to Bishr's family. The two *shabāb* met for the first time since the stabbing and stood one in front of the other, staring at each other with eyes full of anger. Two days later Bishr's father went to the police to drop the case against Asad. The officer said that Bishr's and Asad's families, as Palestinians, should resolve the situation by themselves, without involving the Lebanese police. With the problem sorted out, Bishr remarked to Ahmad that he actually respected Asad. According to Ahmad, Bishr said that Asad behaved the way a man should and that he would even give Asad his sister in marriage. It took Asad years to recover from the financial setback of the episode.

This story of a *muṣālaḥa* serves as counterevidence to academic texts that depict camps as lawless spaces of void and chaos. Camps appear to be places where law is temporarily suspended only to those who, captivated by a state-centered perspective, cannot see beyond the state and so continue to be amazed by the absence of clear sources of crystallized authority in places such as Shatila. In this vein, it is worth noting Ronald Jennings's (2011) word of caution about anthropology's current fetish with sovereignty. He sets out by describing the genealogy of Giorgio Agamben's critique of sovereignty, tracing it back to its Sorelian roots and passing through Schmitt and Benjamin, and then he investigates the crystallization of that critique in the pages of *Homo Sacer* (Agamben 1998). In addition to highlighting the critique, though, Jennings asks what is bracketed out in the current mesmerization with the Agamben effect. It is in Hannah Arendt's work (1963) that Jennings identifies what is being left out: the possibility of imagining local and nonsovereign political futures. Shatila enabled my gaze upon such futures, a point to which I return in the concluding paragraphs of this book.

Only after a couple of months did I find out why Shakir stopped talking to me. Shakir had asked for my help to pay for his university fees. As he was facilitating and translating some of my interviews, I agreed to advance the payments due to him, which covered part of what he owed to the Beirut Arab University. He was thankful and invited me for dinner at his place in Shatila. When I arrived, I was startled to discover that Shakir had begun constructing a house on the roof of his family's dwelling: because the costs of buying a house are prohibitive and Palestinians cannot acquire real estate in Lebanon, young men planning to get married, such as Shakir, often construct an apartment on the roof of their family's dwelling. In a moment of pronounced lack of ethnographic sensitivity, I blurted out to Shakir in front of the other guests: "You tell me you have no money to pay for your university fees, but you're building a new house!"

After several months, when we were on speaking terms again, Shakir remarked that my reaction during the dinner that day showed my limited knowledge of his predicament: "Gustavo, I'm already twenty-six. My life is very different from yours. I can't graduate and then get a job and then marry. I can't wait. I need to do it all at once."

He often scolded me for my misconceptions about camp life: "Gustavo, you need a hundred years to understand us." I still have ninety to go. The next chapters register precisely my first efforts at figuring out the plights and pride of a *shāb*.

3

Swirling and Twirling

The *Fidā'iyyīn*'s Heroism and the *Shabāb*'s Burden

Some Romance

Kabab-ji, Hamra, Beirut, April 17, 2009

Nawaf, twenty-eight, a clerical worker and aspiring painter, took a long puff of his cigarette. It was his fifth, but there was obviously no room for me to complain: by then, I had become a passive chain-smoker. Nawaf hesitated for several seconds and after gathering his thoughts finally continued.

We were sitting together for the second time to record his life story. On this opportunity, we had opted to eat a meal at Kabab-ji, a restaurant in bohemian Hamra belonging to a chain of eateries serving Arab food, away from the scrutinizing ears of Nawaf's mother, four sisters, and brother, with whom he shares a tiny two-piece dwelling in Shatila. Between dips of hummus and sips of oversweetened tea, Nawaf directed our conversation.

Nawaf is one of the children from his father's second marriage. All of Nawaf's four brothers from his father's first marriage were *fidā'iyyīn*. Nawaf barely disguises his pride when talking about the deeds of his brothers, one of whom was part of Arafat's personal entourage: "I remember it all quite clearly: how they carried their guns and defended the camp."

At the Hamra eatery, Nawaf decided to talk about his love life. After a couple of short-lived relationships, he first discovered the pleasures of sex with a European activist who had moved to Lebanon to develop her Arabic. The intense relationship lasted during her stay in the country.

7. Fatah poster for the battle of the town of Karāma, 1968. *Karāma* is also the Arabic word for dignity. The meaning of *karāma* seems to have changed from the *fidā'iyyīn* to the *shabāb*. Poster art by Natheer Nabaa. From and reproduced with permission by the Palestine Poster Project Archives.

Her departure forced the love story to come to an end, with Nawaf lacking the means and visa to follow her. Another European, also an activist, captured the attention of the still heartbroken Nawaf a short while later. She came from a family of Communists and moved to Lebanon out of the political conviction that she had to contribute to the Palestinian cause. Her affair with Nawaf ceased abruptly. This time, however, it was he who decided it should end: "You know, Gustavo, she loved the Palestine in me. What she liked most about me is the Palestinian hero that I know I can't afford to be."

Nawaf's gloomy love life and the relationships he could not afford to have established a dissonance to his own depiction of the heroic accomplishments of his *fidā'iyyīn* brothers. Back in the 1970s, the situation was indeed quite different. As noted earlier, some civil rights were ensured for the refugee population via the Cairo Agreement in 1969. With donations flowing from the Arab oil states, the Palestinian leadership began to assemble the military and bureaucratic apparatus needed for its operation from the camps, which underwent a period of nationalistic fervor. Shatila back then could legitimately be described as a "cradle" for the *fidā'iyyīn*.

The "feminine" is avoided in the *fidā'iyyīn*'s recollections of their heroic deeds during the glorious *'ayyām al-thawra* (days of the revolution). Samar Kanafani (2005, 2008) describes how the nationalistic discourse and the *fidā'iyyīn*'s narratives colluded to frame Palestinian men's passage from boyhood into manhood within a hegemonic notion of masculinity, which purges the emasculating effects of refugee lives in Lebanon and shuns feminine spatial and symbolic spheres. To be fit for the "consequential agency" (Kanafani 2008, 314) of fighting to reconquer the motherland, Palestine, depicted in Palestinian imagery as a female victim of a rape in 1948, the *fidā'iyyīn* had to detach themselves from another "mother-land": home. Acceptance into the homosocial environment of military life was contingent on the abandonment of the sphere of feminine domesticity, the perceived excess sentimentality of which might affect a *fidā'ī*'s resolve. The way in which Abu Fawzi, sixty-two, a former Fatah commando, talked about his biography is fairly typical: "I joined the *fidā'iyyīn* without my family knowing. When they found out, my mother cried a lot, and my father forced me into my first marriage, hoping I'd leave the *fidā'iyyīn*. But my marriage didn't last: I gave up my wife but not the *thawra* [revolution]."

A nonfighting man or a fighting woman does not find any comfortable space within the limits defined by the discourses of Palestinian nationalism and the *fidā'iyyīn*. The handful of women fighters who joined the *fidā'iyyīn*'s ranks, although highly respected by their comrades, paid a heavy cost for their acceptance. As Umm Latifah, forty-seven, a former woman fighter who joined the Popular Front for the Liberation of Palestine (PFLP) at the age of thirteen, told me, "When I speak of myself, I say that I'm a man [*zalamī*] because I've spent my life with the *fidā'iyyīn*. During the *thawra*, I didn't think of marriage. Before my parents finally forced me into marriage, I was engaged twice and split. And my life before marriage was more beautiful. Some people feel comfortable with marriage, but I never did.[. . .] I tell the *shabāb* that I don't feel like a woman. So that's why I started using eyeliner, so the *shabāb* realize I'm a woman. I'm used to being what I am. I don't feel my femininity ['*unūthatī*]."

In this chapter, I explore how Nawaf's biography and coming-of-age are profoundly different from Abu Fawzi's experience (and from Umm Latifah's). With the military dimension of the Palestinian Resistance Movement increasingly demobilized in Lebanon from the 1990s on, Abu Fawzi's extraordinary heroism cannot be reenacted by Nawaf, a fact that bespeaks the full historicity and pliability of masculinity over time. And yet Nawaf still needs to do what a "man's gotta do."

I begin this chapter with a consideration of the concept of "gender," demonstrating how it is deeply imbued with notions of power.[1] As such,

---

1. It would take us well beyond the scope of this study to engage in a full discussion of what "power" is. I admit to using the term rather loosely, and in the course of this chapter it may sometimes appear closer to the stricter Weberian (Weber 1978) understanding—as the capacity to direct someone else's behavior, even against that person's will—but at other times to the looser Foucauldian (Foucault [1977] 1995) depiction as actions dispersed throughout the social body that structure the field of other possible actions. Whether one prefers one definition or the other, I believe the case can be made that at least within certain feminist trends gender as a concept mandates differential access to power by men and women. Gender tends thus to be reduced to hegemony.

it perfectly captures the *fidā'iyyīn*'s masculine trajectories,[2] but not the *shabāb*'s. Next, I provide ethnographic depth to this argument through the life stories of four *fidā'iyyīn* and six *shabāb*, which allows me to arrive at the chapter's conclusion: that the *shabāb* do not experience any crisis of masculinity. Rather, it is a certain narrow definition of gender as characteristic of differential access to power among men and women that by heuristic fiat has forced into supposed crisis those men unable or unwilling to conform to the requirements of an ideal–typical hegemonic masculinity. Accordingly, the closing paragraphs of this chapter suggest an alternative take on the "sex/gender" complex that I believe to be contextually more adequate for the place where I conducted my fieldwork (and probably beyond it).

Gender Theories: A Gendered Anthropology (or Theorizing Power)

Mar Elias Camp, Beirut, July 19, 2007

It was an oppressively hot early evening in July 2007 during my prefieldwork trip to Lebanon. I was attending English lessons for adults at the Mar Elias camp in West Beirut. The teacher spoke in Arabic to cater to students with different levels of English. For a moment, she switched into English to say "gender equity" and immediately returned to Arabic. I decided to provoke her:

> ME: You don't actually have a word for "gender" in Arabic.
> TEACHER: Of course, we do: it's *jins*.
> ME: But *jins* is actually "sex," right? It isn't "gender."
> TEACHER: *Jins* is "sex"; *jins* is also "gender."

2. In contrast with the stiffer concept of "life cycle," dependent as it is on a fixed repetitive socialization of individuals into well-established and socially sanctioned roles, I consider Farha Ghannam's (2013) dynamic notion of "masculine trajectories" more compelling to depict *fidā'iyyīn* and *shabāb* biographies. Ghannam defines "masculine trajectories" as the "continuous quest for a sense of (illusive) coherence that has to be cultivated and sustained in different spatial and temporal contexts to garner the social recognition central to the verification of one's standing as a real man" (7).

To end our conversation and return to her class, she added: "There isn't a problem here, all right?"

Late twentieth-century gender theorists maintained that there *was* a problem and that "sex" should be differentiated from "gender." The vignette from Mar Elias looks less bewildering, though, if we consider that "gender" is an academically generated concept. Indeed, the academic debate in the 1970s and 1980s argued that "gender" should be differentiated from "sex." Anthropology has made a major contribution to this discussion (Moore 1999): as the cultural elaboration of the supposedly natural differences between men and women, "gender," according to some anthropologists, cannot be subsumed by "sex." Evidence of varying social elaborations for the men/women distinction taken from diverse ethnographic settings was provided to demonstrate this point. Separating "gender" from "sex" made sense at the time because it reflected the structuralist taste for binaries as well as the nature/culture divide, a central disciplinary parameter in anthropology. In analyzing sociocultural topics, anthropologists busied themselves with studies of "social gender." "Natural sex," in its turn, remained undertheorized.

Since the inception of the sex/gender debate, the term *gender* has allowed for political mobilization and change, unlike the term *sex*. Psychology with Sigmund Freud (1964, 1991), philosophy with Simone de Beauvoir ([2009] 2012), sociology with R. W. Connell (1985, 1987, 2002), and anthropology with Gayle Rubin (1975) share the insight that both masculinity and femininity are attainments and, as such, constructed. Although medical science and some schools of psychoanalysis may promote deference to the normative rules governing such constructions, philosophy, sociology, and anthropology have endeavored to demonstrate how such rules are constitutive of inequalities that need to be politically "denaturalized." The difference between the constructions of masculinity and femininity was largely taken to imply inequality (Leacock 1983), and inequality has served to establish a hierarchy in terms of the differential access to power among men and women (Ortner 1974; Rosaldo and Lamphere 1974; Strathern 1988). From this hierarchy has ensued an association of masculinity with power and of femininity with a lack thereof. Liberal ideology has perceived this different access to power between men and women as unfair and, in an attempt to correct it, has set a political agenda that mandates mobilization, a project with which scholars have been duly engaged. On the ground, however, ideals of masculinity have a complex relation to practice, varying from place to place and time to time. Unable to replicate the heroic personas of the *fidā'iyyīn*, the *shabāb* in Shatila, with less access to power, quietly try to live their lives, engaging in the relatively mundane routines of building a house and getting married and raising pigeons, as we shall soon see.

At this juncture, it is helpful to redeploy Judith/Jack Halberstam's (1998, 2002) analysis of female masculinity as masculinity without maleness. Inspired by queer studies and new gender politics, Halberstam explores enactments of masculinity. In Halberstam's view, the burgeoning field of masculinity studies has consistently ignored female forms of masculinity, thus reinforcing hegemonic norms of class, race, and sexuality as well as obscuring men's persisting roles in the maintenance of patriarchy. Halberstam disrupts accounts of masculinity centered on male embodiment and male privilege, refusing authentication of masculinity through maleness. Thus, there can be masculinity without male embodiment. Accordingly, I contend that one can also contemplate the possibility of maleness and male embodiment without hegemonic masculinity, which may precisely be the case for the *shabāb* in Shatila.

A movie directed by Gabriel Baur, *Venus Boyz* (2002) exemplifies Halberstam's discussion. The film invites the audience on a journey through the universe of the female masculinity of drag kings in London and New York. In one of the movie's scenes, a character announces: "Every time I put on a suit jacket, I feel a little bit more powerful." But what of someone, such as the Shatila *shabāb*, who cannot or has no reason to put on a suit jacket or military gear?

Men's studies display a similar "mesmerization by power" that occasionally blends into a "mesmerization by the spectacle" conducted in public, a tendency even more pronounced in research on Mediterranean and Middle Eastern societies (Caton 1985; Gilsenan 1996; Herzfeld 1985). Because of the persistence of the controversial notion that these societies are marked by a sharp distinction between public and private, domains conceived to be exclusive and gendered, scant attention has been paid to the way in which men act as "engendered and engendering subjects" (Gutmann 1997, 385) through their everyday chores and their (very) mundane anxieties: how to get married, start an independent household, fly pigeons, as happens with the Shatila *shabāb*.

Michael Herzfeld's book *The Poetics of Manhood* (1985) provides the consummate instance of such an "anthropology of the spectacle." According to him, in Glendi, Crete, a man not only has to be a good man but also has to be good at *being* a man. When playing cards, abducting women, dancing, or stealing animals, men have to display "performative excellence" by exceeding themselves and others. In order to gain *simasia* (meaning), deeds have to be narrated and displayed in public by their perpetrator, who shows off his latest daring goat theft, with the ethnographer providing the more than attentive audience. But what if some men are pursuing a quest of a moral nature, simply that of being good men according to a local ethics, rather than spectacularly bragging about their excellence at being men?

Following the example of the *shabāb* of Shatila, I refused to be part of an all-complying audience to the *fidā'iyyīn*'s narratives. Had I done so, I would simply have been contributing to the consolidation of certain discourses about hegemonic masculinity, which cost the *shabāb* dearly. When the *fidā'iyyīn* recollect their deeds, not just the feminine is shunned, as Kanafani (2005, 2008) points out, but the *shabāb*'s burden also disappears from view. The *fidā'iyyīn* were all power, all gender as precisely a discourse on power, all public, all spectacle. Their narratives amalgamate everything for which the heroic 1970s stand: territorial nationalism, Third Worldism, socialism, and, in the case of the rare women fighters, a feminism of power. Nonetheless, certain tropes of the 1970s have become an impossibility for those coming after that period, such as the Shatila *shabāb* and I.

"Bodies That Matter": The *Fidā'iyyīn*'s Heroism

At first, it is impossible not to be awestruck in the presence of a *fidā'ī* narrating his heroic deeds.[3]

---

3. This section is named after Judith Butler's book *Bodies That Matter* (1993).

● ● ●

Abu Fawzi—the sixty-two-year-old former Fatah commando we met earlier in this chapter—showed me the impressive scar on his leg, proof of his intrepid activities as a *fidā'ī*, which included several incursions deep into Palestine. He bragged to me: "I still have a very strong body. I did wrestling when I was younger.[. . .] In our *niḍāl* [struggle], we never stop; we don't retire. We fight until we die."

Massaging the tips of his long moustache, Abu Fawzi recalled how he tried to keep his mother and father in the dark about his adherence to the factions. His own father had been a fighter, but in Palestine. He was against carrying arms in Lebanon. The young Abu Fawzi, though, was too rebellious to follow his father's advice: "I always do what is in my mind."

All of his brothers were *fidā'iyyīn*, and one of his sisters was a nurse, "taking care of and healing the fighters." Only when I prompted him did he comment on women who acted as fighters: "Oh, yes, there were women with us. They worked the same as we used to work. They had military training and served us very well. In war, they did everything we did. If you're fighting and see your wife or sister with you, you fight like a lion. My sister, who worked as a nurse, was kidnapped by Fatah Abu Moussa [a faction opposed to Arafat's mainstream group Fatah Abu Ammar]. They were after me. Sometimes she still works as a nurse. She never got married."

Other Palestinian factions may not have caught Abu Fawzi, but the Syrians eventually did. He spent sixteen days in a Syrian prison and was tortured. Neither this nor his second wife's criticisms that the time he spent with the *fidā'iyyīn* meant that the family could not afford to buy a house outside the camp dampened Abu Fawzi's determination. Only in 1985 did Abu Fawzi finally relent and start accepting money from the *tanẓīm* (organization) he belonged to. It was not an easy decision: "Our *thawra* was corrupted by money. People started getting paid and thinking of their participation as work, not as a duty. They became spoiled. But, for me, it has never been like that."

Abu Fawzi still defined himself as a fighter: "I continue to think of myself as a *fidā'ī*. I never look back, only toward the future. And I never feel sorry for what I did. This made me the man I am today.[. . .] The future belongs to those who fight and don't accept defeat."

Throughout our conversation, a question kept crisscrossing my mind—"What's it like to kill someone?"—but I never came to verbalize it. Instead, having seen a carefully kept cigar box on one of the shelves in Abu Fawzi's sitting room, I made a mental note that I should offer him a Habano. A couple of months after our meeting, I did.

One occasion was not enough for me to familiarize myself with Abu Jalil's biography. In the roughly eight-hour period I spent with him over two days, I became fascinated by how the personal story of Abu Jalil, sixty-three, a former Fatah commando doubling as a cameraman at the time of the interview, intertwined with the eventful saga of the Palestinian refugees in Lebanon.

He picked his father's departure from Palestine as the starting point for his recollection:

> My father actually came to Lebanon even before the *hijra* [migration from Palestine in 1948].[4] He married my Lebanese mother and lived here for a couple of years. It was only in 1955 that we moved to Shatila.[. . .] In the beginning, Palestinians had hope they'd go back. But here they faced humiliation [*'idhlā*] and were not entitled to a decent life [*ḥayāt karīma*]. This is what gave origin to hatred [*ḥiqd*] in the heart of Palestinians.[. . .] This situation went on until there was a crisis in government in 1958 [when oppositionists staged a revolt against the then president of Lebanon, Camille Chamoun, who refused to break off relations with Britain and France following nationalization of the Suez Canal in Egypt][. . .].[5] And, after the coup d'état failed, the Deuxième

4. Abu Jalil used the word *hijra*, "migration," rather than the more common name "Nakba" (Catastrophe) to refer to the Palestinians' forced departure from Palestine in 1948.

5. In 1958, anti-Chamoun oppositionists revolted and applied pressure on Lebanon to associate itself with the United Arab Republic, recently formed between Egypt and

Bureau [military intelligence] became all too powerful.[6] If a Palestinian wanted to travel from the Beqaa to Beirut, he needed authorization. We were watched all the time.[. . .] It was at this time that I started to understand [*afham*][7] things and became a *shāb*. And I was watched even more closely.

To Abu Jalil, the pressure exerted by the intelligence apparatus helped trigger the Palestinian revolt: "All this pressure affected Palestinians inside. And then in the 1970s, the *thawra* entered the camps through the main gates. People were really happy in the beginning." Already back then, however, the *thawra* carried the seeds of internal conflict, according to Abu Jalil: "Palestinians said: '*Khalaṣ* [Over)]! We're done with the disgusting police [*qaraf al-darak*].' In those days, we had two kinds of people. Some of us understood and said: 'Our revolution isn't against the *darak*; it's for a bigger goal, which is to get back to Palestine.' But others thought that the *thawra* was against the police and the government [*al-ḥukūma*] and started acting too freely."

Yet again Abu Jalil linked the Palestinian political awakening with his own, claiming that the revolution brought him to the threshold of maturity: "During the time of the *thawra*, we lived a different life altogether. I started to understand [*afham*] things, and I knew I was with the *thawra* not because I loved to fight or wanted to die. I knew that my voice wouldn't

---

Syria and proclaimed as a triumph of pan-Arabism. The Lebanese army commander, General Fouad Shehab, refused to attack the insurgents, many of whom were Muslims, fearing that the military would split along sectarian lines. Having gained popularity by his actions during the crisis, Shehab was recognized as a compromise candidate to succeed Chamoun in office (Hirst 2010; Picard 1996; Salibi 2005; Trabulsi 2007).

6. Under General Shehab, the military intelligence, called the Deuxième Bureau, went through a process of hypertrophy and was used strategically by the president to bypass deadlocks caused by sectarian strife. The bureau exerted strict control over the Palestinian refugees (Hirst 2010; Picard 1996).

7. I later return to this concept (*afham* or *waʿī*), the importance of understanding and achieving '*aql* (the capacity for reasoning) in order for a person, especially a man, to be deemed to have reached maturity.

be heard if I only spoke and that the *bunduqiyya* [machine gun][8] was the only way that my voice could reach all the corners of the world."

Fathering six children, Abu Jalil found himself split between his duties toward his family and his commitment to the revolution: "Before the invasion [of Lebanon by Israel in 1978], I already had six children. And I wanted to terminate my work with the military organization [*tanẓīm*]. The *tanẓīm* accepted, but I didn't stop completely. I continued visiting them and fighting in my free time. But I had six children and needed to take care of them, to teach them."

Through educating his children, Abu Jalil found another way to continue his struggle: "The greatest gift Allah gives us is the *'aql* [capacity for reasoning],[9] and that's the most important weapon with which to fight the enemy.[. . .] Today, the *shabāb* get an education, become engineers, but where can they work?[. . .] The Israelis are betting on time. They think that the elders will die, and younger people will forget. But that's impossible; this will never happen.[. . .] If you keep squeezing something too hard, it bursts in your face."

For Abu Jalil, once one is Palestinian, one will always be Palestinian, despite all the difficulties:

> The Lebanese made the question of nationality and naturalization [*tawṭīn*] a strawman.[. . .] From inside, I'll always be Palestinian. Even after a hundred years, every Palestinian stays a Palestinian. Even if he's angry and pretends to ignore [*yiṭayyaz*, literally meaning "to show somebody one's ass") Palestine, his will be empty words. I have lived in five different houses as a result of wars. I don't remember me and my

8. Over time, the machine gun, or *bunduqiyya*, became iconicized together with the *fidā'iyyīn*. Both are celebrated in Mahmoud Darwish's famous poem "Rita and the Rifle" ("Rita wa al-bunduqiyya"), the musical version of which is sung by Marcel Khalife. In the poem, the poet-fighter is torn between his love for Rita and his love for the machine gun that stands in the middle of their relationship.

9. Soraya Altorki defines *'aql* as the "faculty of understanding, rationality, judiciousness, prudence and wisdom" (1986, 51). See note 7 in this chapter and note 11 in the introduction.

elder children ever having known tranquility [*hudū'*]. We lived all the wars.[. . .] In 1985, my family left the camp [because of the Camp Wars]. By then I had started my own business, working with wood for construction. And I had purchased a pickup. I lost everything in the war: pickup, wood, house—everything was gone. I left everything behind, and we moved out of the camp.

With the end of the Lebanese Civil War in 1990, the Abu Jalil family decided to return to Shatila: "But everything was on the ground. I rebuilt our house."

At the time I talked to him, Abu Jalil had not abandoned his hope of eventually returning to Palestine: "As a *fidā'ī*, I went to Palestine several times in military operations. Every time I went there, I became more attached to the idea of going back. I think it'll be hard in my lifetime to go back, but I think it'll happen in my children's lifetimes.[. . .] But it's true that the *shabāb* today are completely lost [*ḍā'i'a*].[. . .] The problem is with the system [*al-niẓām*] that brings emptiness [*farāgh*] to their lives.[. . .] The problem with the *shabāb* today is that they have been hit by politics, but not in the way we were. Their lives are empty. And because of that, the political parties [*al-'aḥzāb*] can easily take advantage of their sorrow and anger and use it the way they [the political parties] want."

Abu Jalil took care to keep his own children on the right track—significantly enough, no longer the one that prescribed joining the militias, a path that was at one time almost mandatory: "My eldest son went to the Mu'askar al-'Ashbāl [Cubs' Camp, a Boy Scout–like movement that trained young Palestinian men during the *thawra*].[10] But I wanted him to take proper care of his education, so I only allowed him to go to the 'Ashbāl on Fridays." Old habits, however, die hard: "When he grew up and

---

10. A whole generation of young Palestinian men (and some women) trained militarily with the 'Ashbāl. Young girls were sometimes sent to the Zahrāt (Flowers) gatherings, where they sang nationalistic songs or read and wrote nationalistic poetry. The Zahrāt did not provide military training, though, which would not have been considered culturally appropriate for young girls, according to several research participants.

acquired consciousness [*wa'ī*],[11] he decided that he wanted to be a *fidā'ī* full-time. As a result, he lost his education. So with my other children I was much more careful. I always told them: educate yourself, get cultured for the *thawra*. But my daughters always stayed out of the game."

Abu Jalil is ambiguous when it comes to appreciating the role of women in the military ranks of the *thawra*: "Women played a part. There was the Women's Union, which involved lots of activities. Some of them carried weapons, while others spread consciousness and educated others. Some sewed clothes and flags; others taught. Women were always supporting the *fidā'iyyīn* so that they could perform their role. The percentage of women fighters was very small. You know, men have a strong build [*bunya*]."

Mention of his health situation prompted Abu Jalil to share his memories of prison: "I was in prison three times. The first time was in '68 in a Lebanese prison, where I was accused of being a *fidā'ī*. I stayed for four days only and was released after committing myself to work for them as a *mukhābir* [intelligence agent], which of course I never did. Instead, I told my brothers-in-arms that we have to be more careful! The second time was in '83. The Syrians arrested me because of a similarity of names. I stayed in prison for two months, and they had no proof against me! But they tortured me anyway, and as a result [. . .] my spinal cord was injured. The third time was in '88 under the accusation that I was with Fatah."

Still, in Abu Jalil's view there is no room to falter: "The *fidāya* [fighters' movement] was a duty [*wājib*] and not work [*shughul*]. Through it, I told the world that we're the problem [*al-mushkila*] but also the solution [*al-ḥall*].[. . .] Today, there is no *fidāya*; there's *sulṭa* [sovereign power].[12] But who built the *sulṭa*? The PLO itself." And he went on to give his diagnosis of the state of the *thawra* today, which brought our conversation to an end: "It's possible that the struggle [*al-kifāḥ*] has been delayed, but now

11. See note 7 in this chapter.

12. *The Hans Wehr Dictionary of Modern Arabic* defines *sulṭa* as "power, might, strength; authority; sway, dominion; influence, sovereign power, jurisdiction." *Sulṭa* is also the word used to refer to the Palestinian Authority in the Occupied Territories. Abu Jalil's use of the word admits both meanings.

it isn't the time for fighting; it's the time for tactics.[. . .] The Palestinian Revolution exists to stay. The activities and strategies may differ, but the main goal remains: the liberation of Palestine.[. . .] Everyone tries to keep Palestinians in the same place, to kill the ambition [al-ṭumūḥ] that we once had.[. . .] Yet every generation is more active [ḥirik] than the previous one. We aren't dinosaurs: we won't become extinct."

Abu Naji, thirty-nine, who retired from his military position with Fatah when he got a job at UNRWA, claimed his heroic persona even before we properly started our interview. Barely one minute had lapsed after I entered the sitting room of his dwelling in Shatila when he volunteered, "Do you want to see my wounds?" I could only respond, "Err. . . ."

Ignoring my hesitation, Abu Naji raised his shirt and showed me several scars on his lower and middle back, a result of war-related injuries. He went on: "And, now, do you want to see my bunduqiyya [machine gun]?"

I showed no hesitation this time: "Yes . . . wow! It looks pretty new!"

Abu Naji winked at me: "I always keep it clean!"

Abu Naji's self-presentation of his heroic persona should come as no surprise. To begin with, he probably thought that I, like other researchers and journalists in Shatila, was seeking evidence of his heroism. In addition, Abu Naji had grown up among the fidā'iyyīn. Younger than the latter and with many siblings (his father, a womanizer, married seven times, bore several children with each wife, and was unable to give much attention to any of them), Abu Naji left school at a very early age and spent his time in the military ranks. He even employed military language to describe his family: "We're so many, we could probably start our own tanẓīm [military organization]!"

He claimed the battles fought by his comrades as his own, even though he was too young to have effectively taken part in them: "I spent my childhood with the thawra, fighting against the Kataeb [a right-wing party cum militia, also called Phalanges and supported mainly by Maronite Christians]. And then against the Lebanese army. And then against the Kataeb again. And after that against [Ariel] Sharon [a former Israeli prime minister, military commander, and minister of defense who was held personally responsible for the Sabra and Shatila massacre of 1982]. And, finally, I fought in the Camp Wars. And we survived the six-month siege, during which we even had to eat cats." He in fact had acted as a *fidāʾī* only in the last battle, as he finally conceded: "My beginning as a *fidāʾī* was against the Shia [during the Camp Wars]. I was young during the Sabra and Shatila massacre and also during the war against the Kataeb. At school, no one talked about the *thawra*, but we knew. Abu Ammar [Yasser Arafat's nom de guerre by which he is normally known in Shatila]—God bless him—used to come himself to see and kiss us."

Abu Naji was severely injured during the Camp Wars and almost died: "It was Doctor Giannou [a Canadian doctor who performed medical surgeries in besieged Shatila][13] who brought me back from the dead. He operated on me twice. And then I was sent to Italy for treatment." In Italy, Abu Naji befriended an Italian patient who was recovering on the bed next to his. After they were released from the hospital, the Italian man found Abu Naji a job and wanted to give him his own daughter in marriage. Abu Naji did not want to follow in his father's steps and decided to honor the family commitments he had left behind in Beirut: "I had just got married here one week before I was injured. So I returned to my wife." Umm Naji graduated as a pharmacist, but Abu Naji is not keen on the idea of her working: "I have nothing against women working. But not my wife. People here talk."

Even though his years as a *fidāʾī* are pivotal to Abu Naji's sense of self, he forbade his own son from becoming one: "In my opinion, no one should be a *fidāʾī* unless there is a war. If something happens in Shatila, I'll be the first to defend it." And in a comment that surprised me because it established a distance from his remarks at the beginning of our interview, he confessed: "You know, I actually don't like Kalashnikovs [Soviet-made machine guns often used by the *fidāʾiyyīn*]. This is not my life. I just need it to defend Palestine, to fight our enemy, but not the Lebanese. No, I've never seen Palestine. I only hear about it on TV. We hear about Ramallah,

13. Chris Giannou describes the twenty-seven months he spent in besieged Shatila in *Besieged: A Doctor's Story of Life and Death in Beirut* (1991).

Ariha. But I'll never forget Palestine. If I'm told that the border is now open, I'll leave my wife and children and go to Palestine."

Yet Abu Naji thought this wish was unlikely to be fulfilled in the near future: "No one actually thinks of the future. Everyone here thinks of tomorrow only and of how to provide food and clothing to one's family. [. . .] My hopes? Well, I hope to return to Palestine, but without all these differences and divisions.[. . .] And my dreams aren't good. Why does anyone want to dream? Since 1948, we dream of going back. Tomorrow, there'll be a new generation, and we're still saying that we'll return."

With Abu Majid—fifty-one, a former member of Fatah and the PFLP but now an independent; a writer cum journalist cum commerce graduate; the son of a baptized Palestinian Sunni who had been born to a Lebanese Shia father—my previous placid belief that a *fidāʾī* is always a *fidāʾī*, a patriarch and a hero in a virile, superhealthy, and heterosexual, even if scarred, body, began to wobble.

Abu Majid was born in Tyre, outside the camps in southern Lebanon. During the late Ottoman period, his Lebanese Shia grandfather left the south of Lebanon for Argentina, where he managed to amass considerable wealth. When he returned in 1923, Lebanon was under the French Mandate. Because the underdeveloped southern part of the country offered him limited opportunities for investment, he opted to move to Palestine and saw no point in registering with the French authorities in Lebanon. The family established itself in a border town on the Palestinian side of the region known as Naqura.

"You need to understand, Gustavo, that the borders made no sense back then," Abu Majid explained to me. "You see, that's Palestine. My grandpa lived in this border town, together with several other Lebanese, in this very Christian village, al-Bassa, where there were also a considerable number of Sunni. There were many intermarriages between Christians and Sunni, and my Shia grandfather was welcomed and accepted into the community. It was normal for children to be baptized, even Muslims. So my father, born to a Lebanese Shia, was baptized. And later he converted to become a Sunni."

The ill-fated decision to buy an orchard for 2,500 Palestinian pounds just before the Nakba caused Abu Majid's grandfather to lose all his liquidity, meaning that the family was cash strapped when forced out of Palestine. They set up in the grandfather's village in southern Lebanon, where they were looked down upon as Palestinians in spite of their Lebanese origins:

> In Palestine, my father used to be called *al-lubnānī* [the Lebanese man], but with no intention of ridicule. Here, my Lebanese neighbors used to mock me.[. . .] Even though we had some wealth because my father managed to secure a job as a teacher at an UNRWA school in Tyre, and even though we had Lebanese origins, we were looked down upon as Palestinians and treated as outsiders. But like other Palestinians, I feel dignity [*karāma*].[. . .] I like Lebanon, I'm of Lebanese origin, but I feel Palestinian. Palestinians planted most of the lemon orchards in Lebanon; a Palestinian from the Chammas family set up the best school in Tyre; the largest bank of this country [Lebanon], the Intra Bank, belonged to a Palestinian. We brought our money and experience to Lebanon. No, we weren't a *fallāḥ* [peasant] family. My grandfather was a *fallāḥ*, but not us. We lived in the city and didn't work in agriculture. We had a car; we bought the first TV set in the neighborhood; we had a magnetophone. We were upper-middle class and still thought of ourselves as Palestinians. Mind you, I've always been aware of our difference: back then, we didn't live in a camp, and even when we moved into a camp, it was al-Bass in Tyre, which is better than other camps in Lebanon. I know my life wasn't like that of other Palestinians, but I felt Palestinian and identified with my people.[. . .] You need to understand, Gustavo, that, for me, "Palestinian" isn't a race. My Palestinianness is an idea.

Because Abu Majid himself had brought the issue of class into our conversation, I decided to probe him further along this line. "OK, Palestinianness is an idea, so that's why you, middle class, can claim a Palestinian belonging?," I provoked, somewhat clumsily. Abu Majid retained his composure: "Gustavo, class divisions weren't strong among rural communities in Palestine because people used to work on their own land. Class divisions were stronger in the cities.[. . .] Palestine saw the creation of the first Communist Party in this region. Even when we moved to al-Bass camp in Tyre when I was twelve, we saw no reason for any embarrassment because we were originally a *fallāḥ* family." I still tried to hold on to my own purified and reified understanding of class divisions: "But if you had money, why did you move to al-Bass camp?" Abu Majid tried to broaden my comprehension of "class": "My father wanted to own his house instead of renting. And, I suspect, he also wanted to be among his own people. You know, for someone of Lebanese origin, he was quite nationalistic and quite Palestinian actually. And, by then, the Lebanese authority had collapsed, so we simply built a house on a plot that belonged to the government." He joked: "You see, there's a good side to the lack of government." He added that there was no strict separation between al-Bass camp and Tyre back then: "Until 1982, people used the streets inside the camp to get to Tyre. We kept those of our friends, including Lebanese, [who were] living outside the camp. Al-Bass, remember, is in the middle of Tyre."

Abu Majid's parents sent him for military training with the Ashbāl (Cubs)[14] because they wanted to toughen him up: "As a child, I often fell sick; I had lots of health issues. And if people shouted at me, I'd easily cry. My parents didn't want me to be so fragile, so they sent me to the Ashbāl. I was eleven by then." He laughed:

And then they regretted it! Because sometimes they had no idea where I was. Whenever there was a problem, I'd go after it. I'd run after danger. If there was an explosion in the Rashidiyya camp, off there I went. If there was a fight in Ain-Hilweh [camp], there I was. By twelve, I already had a gun! And soon after, as I became a trainer for other boys and had to keep the weapons myself, I used to carry eighteen guns! It is true that I never shot anyone, but I was prepared to do so. Having a gun became a kind of ID for us. You know our ID is different from the ID of the Lebanese. So often we're treated as people with no identity. The gun became our identity.

In 1976, already an adult working with the Palestinian factions, Abu Majid left al-Bass. He then lived in Shatila for the first time: "I was

14. See note 10 in this chapter.

studying at the Beirut Arab University, and my father, whose financial situation changed dramatically with my siblings and me enrolling at the university, lacked the means to finance a house for me outside the camp." In 1978, he moved out of Shatila and shared a place with other students in al-Tariq al-Jadida/Fakhani in the immediate vicinity of the camp: "But, here again, Gustavo, try to understand that this whole area was part of the Sabra and Shatila complex." In 1979, already a PFLP member, he moved back to Shatila, working with the youth organizations. The following year, having obtained a scholarship, he left Lebanon for Romania to study journalism for four years.

He described the time spent in Romania as very rich, both intellectually and politically: "I met people from all over. I benefited a lot from that.[. . .] Because I was a member of the PFLP, I also got to work with people from Gaza and the West Bank. I met people from 1948 [i.e., from areas belonging to historic Palestine but annexed to Israel after 1948]. As far as the struggle is concerned, I learned a lot. And that's precisely what my father taught me: if I wanted to fight Zionism, I had to be an educated man. Because of that, I've never been a *fidā'ī* only. First, I was a *fidā'ī* and a student and then a *fidā'ī* and a journalist."

After graduating, he was unable to return immediately to Lebanon: "I couldn't go on living in Romania and yet couldn't come back to Lebanon. After '82 and the Israeli invasion, the Lebanese government was controlled by right-wing Christians, so we couldn't renew our travel documents. That's why I moved to Syria instead. There, I lived in the Yarmouk camp for four years, until 1988. Yarmouk isn't actually a camp: more accurately speaking, it's a suburb, with proper buildings and infrastructure and wide streets. Camps in Syria aren't as poor as [camps] in Lebanon.[15] [. . .] Palestinians, as Arab citizens, can work in Syria and lead a better life than here."

Abu Majid switched from Fatah to the leftist PFLP in 1977. He met some Communist members of Fatah, and they inspired him to turn left: "I was a student, and I was independent in my thinking; I always chose

---

15. I interviewed Abu Majid prior to the current civil war in Syria.

what I wanted. I liked the level of culture of PFLP members. There, one could talk, discuss, argue. They read; they knew. They were intellectuals. I liked that." In 1988, a position became available at the Sawt al-Shaab Radio Station, controlled by the Lebanese Communist Party, which had good relations with the PFLP, and that was how Abu Majid found his way back to Beirut.

Being a seasoned interviewer, Abu Majid made me feel comfortable enough to ask him the questions about killing people and having sexual relations with women fighters I had not dared pose to other *fidā'iyyīn*. "What's it like to kill someone?," I ventured. Abu Majid's answer assuaged the fear I had of facing a moral dilemma in my views of the *fidā'iyyīn*: "Oh, I never had to shoot. I was prepared for that, but by chance I never had to shoot. Remember, I wasn't on the field all the time; most of my time I spent in the offices. But I did take part in operations and went to the front line. We were in the middle of a war, and whether one wants it or not, one is part of one's community. I had this friend, a sheikh, who would come, change into military gear, and head off with me to the front line."

"And how was it, I mean, with the girls, on the front line?," I ventured again. Abu Majid gave me a generous smile:

In '82, we had four women fighters with us.[16] I had someone with me who was like my girlfriend; we were always together. We didn't make love because that was impossible in the war situation. But we protected each other. I saw her as a fighter; she was a fighter like myself. I took care of her, and she also took care of me. Now, outside of the battlefield, of course, there were relations. I met girls who made love with all the men they knew. You see, this period, mid-1970s, beginning of the '80s, was a period of blowing up traditions. Before and afterward, traditions worked, but not during that period. The girls with us in the Lebanese Communist Party weren't virgins, and they lost their virginity because they wanted to. And some of those girls were from the camps. Sometimes I wonder why this tiny membrane, the hymen, has such importance. But

16. Even though Abu Majid had left Lebanon to study in Romania in 1980, he returned to take part in the battles in 1982.

then again, those were exceptional years, and they affected the condition of women. The '70s weren't years of military revolution only; they were years of social revolution, too. In Lebanon, women from big cities already worked and were used to being outside their homes. The situation was different in the camps because they [the camps] were surrounded, so the older traditions persisted. But at the beginning the camps in particular were the basis for the revolution, and people started coming in from all over, from Africa, Europe, and South America, and shared their lives with Palestinians. So the camps started to be exposed to all these ideas, such as the communist principles of equality between men and women, and the Communists weighed in on this part of the world. Women, including those from the camps, began breaking out of the shells of tradition. So relations happened outside of wedlock. In the PFLP and DFLP [Democratic Front for the Liberation of Palestine], boys and girls were the same. But it wasn't like that with Fatah: the position of women depended on the impact of leftist ideas on the organization one belonged to. After 1982, with the defeat of the PLO in Lebanon, this social revolution, the ideas of that period—all that was gone. People went back to traditions and religion. Today, there's still a *thawra*, but it isn't my revolution anymore; it's another revolution. I was in a total revolution; it wasn't only about using guns; it was about changing everything. Now it isn't about changing everything anymore; it's only about fighting Israel. So it isn't actually a revolution today; it's a fight. In our era, it was a fight, and it was a revolution as well. We changed concepts!

At the time of the interview, Abu Majid worked for a leading Lebanese newspaper and managed to find time to volunteer in a Palestinian NGO, even though he was generally very critical of such organizations because of the dependence they created among their clients. And he continued to think of himself as a *fidā'ī*:

Being a *fidā'ī* isn't only about military operations. Military operations are the most idealistic thing, but one can be a *fidā'ī* in other forms. I go on being a *fidā'ī* because I don't think the conflict is a military one only; maybe it shouldn't even be military at a certain level now. I still work for the cause, through what I write, for example.[. . .] I think my life was worth it. Life is not like all or nothing. We did something.

Because we did what we did, we moved something. We made mistakes, true, but this wasn't about the Palestinian cause only: it was the Cold War, conflict worldwide, and we were part of it. We tried our best, but our enemies were very strong too. We did good things. And bad things. [. . .] [But] we've put Palestine on the political map. Even though we have been defeated so many times, politically we exist now.

On a political level, Abu Majid defined himself as an independent. Nonetheless, I still tried to label him one last time. When I asked him, "But you're still a Communist at heart, aren't you, Abu Majid?," he responded, "At heart, no, Gustavo. In the mind."

A civilian and yet military, a Palestinian and yet middle class and of Lebanese origin, a Palestinian refugee from Lebanon but with experience of having lived in Syria, Abu Majid defies my scientifically trained tendency to label and challenges my reified and purified categories. After all, how can pigeonholes, categorizations, and overarching abstractions—"patriarchy," "hegemonic masculinity"—be used to make sense of complexity?

Marcia Inhorn enumerates the clichés that characterize what she critically names "hegemonic masculinity, Middle-Eastern style":

In the Middle East, the hegemonically masculine man is said to be a *family patriarch.* He is socialized into patriarchy during boyhood, where he learns to dominate his sisters and even his mother, although he is still subordinated by the senior males of the family. Eventually, he achieves patriarchal control over his own family when he reaches adulthood, marries and produces offspring, especially sons who are necessary for the perpetuation of his lineage. Because he is a patriarch, he may exert power and authority over the women, junior males and children in his family through coercion and even force. This is especially true if *family honor* is threatened. . . . Marriage is not characterized by love, because it is *arranged* by families, often for the purposes of familial and tribal alliance. . . . In this context of fragile marital bonds, hegemonically masculine men enjoy their rights to *polygyny.* Muslim men may marry up to four wives simultaneously, as long as they promise to treat them equally.

Equal treatment demands *hypervirility*. . . . Furthermore, the Islamic mandate to reproduce an Islamic "multitude" encourages pronatalism within polygynous marriage, with some men producing their own small tribes of children from multiple spouses. *Tribalism* itself requires large families, not only for the purposes of nomadic pastoral labor but also for tribal raiding and defense. Hence, men's tendencies towards *violence* and *militarism* are perpetuated, indeed encouraged, through tribal structures, as well as through Islamic *jihad*, or the mandate to defend religion when it is threatened by outside forces. (2012, 49–50, original emphasis)

Under such a guise, hegemonic masculinity and patriarchy are notoriously orientalizing actualizations of the "theoretical metonyms" (Abu-Lughod 1989, 279)—tribes, the harem, and Islam— often adopted by a previous generation of anthropologists working in the Middle East. Such tropes—linking masculinity, violence, and militarism—also fuel other agendas within and beyond academia. The feminist writer Joane Nagel (1998), for instance, establishes a connection between manhood and nationhood as well as between masculinity and nationalism through a series of hastily proposed parallelisms. She takes pains to give a certain depth to both nationalism and masculinity, but at a definitional level only. In defining masculinity, for instance, she sets off by resorting to David Gilmore's controversial classic *Manhood in the Making* (1980), where "Man-the-Impregnator-Protector-Provider" (223) is a ubiquitous figure. According to Nagel, a current set of masculine standards can be defined as hegemonic, which also constitutes a core of modern "isms": (territorial) nationalism, colonialism, militarism. For her, there is something inescapably and structurally masculine, in both a cultural and a social sense, found in institutions such as crime, violence, and politics.

Nagel persistently ignores the notes of analytical caution conveyed by R. W. Connell and Mark Gerzon, notwithstanding her citations of both authors in her text. Connell (1995) rightly observes that men do not actually behave according to a "John Wayne model" of manhood, and Gerzon shows how hegemonic masculinity, always well beyond reach, remains an ever-impossible achievement: "In comparing themselves to the dashing figure riding off into the setting sun or racing across the goal line, ordinary men in ordinary life cannot help but feel overshadowed." In private, "men no longer feel like heroes" (1982, 5). Against the demanding requirements of an ideal–typical hegemonic masculinity, actual men—within their class, ethnicity, and/or sexuality—are pushed into eternal and mandatory crises by heuristic fiat. So, too, are the *shabāb* in Shatila, with their unspectacular rather quotidian masculinities.

In turn, Joseph Massad uses recent archival data on Palestinian nationalism to provide some historical scaffolding to a thesis not unlike Nagel's. He draws extensively on the Palestinian National Charter and the Palestinian Nationalist Charter, the first two documents issued by the PLO defining Palestinian political goals and rights, as well as on communiqués by the Unified Leadership of the Uprising (UNLU) during the First Intifada (1987–92) and, finally, on some remarks by Arafat to put forward the argument that Palestinian nationalist agency has a masculine basis: "Palestinian is always already conceived in the masculine," states Massad (1995, 483). The introduction to the Nationalist Charter characterizes the Zionist conquest of Palestine as rape, as a result of which the motherland can no longer be trusted to produce legitimate Palestinian children. Although residence in Palestine was enough to define someone as Palestinian until 1947, after that date "Palestinianness" became the monopoly of those born to Palestinian fathers only: in Massad's words, "territory was replaced by paternity" (1995, 472). The UNLU communiqués portray Palestinian mothers, sisters, and daughters as *manābit* (plant nurseries) or the soil where "manhood, respect and dignity" grow (quoted in Massad 1995, 474). Liisa Malkki (1992) observes that "botanical metaphors" deployed in nationalist discourses are commonly gendered. Massad also highlights that in some of the UNLU's calls and Arafat's utterances the Palestinian nationalist agent appears not only as a man but also as a bourgeois in the making, virile and able-bodied: *he* is working hard in the Gulf to help out *his* family; *he* is protecting *his* parents; *he* is raising *his* children; and *he* is paying for *his* siblings' education. The Palestinian people as a whole are seen as a body, a man's body, which "has *erected* itself and will not *bow*" (Massad 1995, 479, original emphasis).

Scholars have explored how gendered bodies become metaphors for the nation and how gendered subjectivities correspond to nationalist agendas (Bracewell 2000; Hemmings, Gedalof, and Bland 2006; Lambevski 1999; Puri 1999).[17] Healthy heterosexual bodies, duly idealized, stand for the nation and affect how intimate relationships are shaped. In the case of the *thawra*, the idealized bodies are the *fidā'iyyīn*'s: strong and scarred, they have survived torture. Abu Fawzi, the former wrestler, and Abu Naji proudly exhibited the bodily marks of their wounds to me. Moreover, the *fidā'iyyīn*'s bodies forcibly exude virility, as so often depicted in Palestinian imagery from the era and evinced on the cover photo of Rosemary Sayigh's classic study of the Palestinian saga in Lebanon, *Palestinians: From Peasants to Revolutionaries* (1979). Women who have transgressed the gendered limits of the *fidā'iyyīn* universe pay a price: Abu Fawzi's sister, who nursed the *fidā'iyyīn*, has remained single; forced into a marriage, Umm Latifah, the former fighter we met at the beginning of this chapter, stated that she did not feel her femininity. The *fidā'iyyīn*'s bodies indeed played a pivotal role in their own performance as daring commandos during the *thawra*—a performance that, as Samar Kanafani (2005, 2008) shows, allowed them to overcome, at least on a discursive level, their prior effeminized status as passive refugees.

The chroniclers of the Palestinian saga in Lebanon (Khalili 2007a, 2007b, 2008; Peteet 1991, 2005; R. Sayigh 1979, 1993) suggest that the camps, Shatila prominently among them, functioned as moral spaces during the *thawra*, providing a hospitable environment for refugees to recover a certain sense of pride. Jason Hart (2000, 2008), based on fieldwork among refugees in Amman, Jordan, goes one step further and argues that it is through a positively valued display of gender by their young male residents as intrepid and stubborn *mukhayyamjīn* (camp residents) and their female dwellers as modest persons that camps become differentiated from

---

17. The specialized literature under the influence of feminist studies has been remarkably prolific in researching Palestinian women's lives in light of the relation between gendered subjectivities and nationalism: see, for example, Abdallah 2006; Abdo 1999; Faier 1997, 2002; Jean-Klein 2000, 2001, 2002; Kanaaneh 2002; Peteet 1991, 1997; R. Sayigh 1987, 1998. Surprisingly, however, studies on the relation between Palestinian men and nationalism constitute an exception, amounting to a handful only: Hart 2008; Jean-Klein 1997; Kanaaneh 2003, 2005; Kanafani 2005, 2008; Peteet 1994; Pichter 1998.

the rest of Amman, where some 70 percent of the population is of Palestinian origin. In a similar vein, it can be argued that during the *thawra* and possibly afterward, too, gender display by the *fidāʾiyyīn* through the narration of their deeds, often with an aura of macho bravado, marked off the camps, especially Shatila, as a Palestinian moral space. In this sense, the *fidāʾiyyīn*'s quest is even more demanding than the one faced by Michael Herzfeld's Glendiotis (1985): in addition to displaying that they are good at being men, the *fidāʾiyyīn* have to show that they are good men. Nonetheless, their moral pursuit differs from that of their sons.

The discourse sustaining this imagined community—Palestine— is highly gendered. Through resistance, a new man was created. If the expulsion from their land and the defeats of 1948 and 1967 were blights on Palestinian honor (Humphries and Khalili 2007), restoring that honor through battle became for the *fidāʾiyyīn* a way of reclaiming their manhood. The *thawra* made heroes out of young men (and only rarely out of women) and brought them to the threshold of maturity: "Guns in hand," Sune Haugbolle writes, "boys become men" (2012, 120). Posters produced by the Palestinian factions during this period capture particularly well this image of the confident *fidāʾī*, bravely advancing over the crests of hills to make incursions deep into Palestine, *bunduqiyya* (machine gun) in hand and the black-and-white striped Arab headdress, the *kuffiyya*, covering his head (figure 7). Against such a background, in which a version of hegemonic hypermasculinity is valorized, the Shatila *shabāb* of today appear forcibly effeminized, their masculinity on the verge of crisis. But, in fact, it is not.

"Undoing Gender": The *Shabāb*'s Burden

In a manner quite similar to what I attempt in this study,[18] Nawaf, whose love stories opened this chapter, chose to use his paintings to portray trivial details of daily life in Shatila: the elements depicted by his pictures fit

---

18. I borrow from Judith Butler's book *Undoing Gender* (2004) for the title of this section.

well into what Lila Abu-Lughod describes as "ethnographies of the particular" (1991, 138). Although reserving due space for the ubiquitous symbols of Palestinian nationalism adorning the camp—including the flags; the murals with the Dome of the Rock in Jerusalem; the photos of Arafat, the *fidā'iyyīn*, and the *shuhadā'* (martyrs)—his art is in no sense confined to these themes as a source of inspiration. In one of his attempts to frame himself for the ethnographer, Nawaf stated: "As an artist, I need to look at the camp deeply and also at myself, my mind, the shadows, the movements of people. An artist needs to be a patriotic fighter, a dreamer, a poet, a passionate person, a horse rider."

As in Nawaf's paintings, the trivial details of the Shatila *shabāb*'s daily lives portrayed in the following pages contrast sharply with the *fidā'iyyīn*'s narrations of their deeds. Yet Nawaf and other *shabāb* have not been emasculated: rather, the content and boundaries of what count as masculinities (and femininities) are fluid and shift in space and time. Indeed, there are men beyond hegemonic masculinity, just as there is nationalism beyond territory, and (nonbare) life and citizens—including in Shatila—beyond sovereignty, the latter being precisely the theme that occupies the concluding paragraphs of this study.

○ ○ ○

With his first European activist girlfriend gone, Nawaf finally found his girl.

The European's departure had an awakening effect for Nawaf. He knew the European woman was not for him: "When I was with her, I was out of the camp all the time, going to bars, sleeping with her. After living like this for eight months, I had the feeling I wasn't myself anymore. I was out of focus all the time, often drunk.[. . .] In the beginning, I thought it was a nice life: dancing all night long, drinking, having sex, and smoking hashish. I was ignoring my university, my family. I was never home and didn't know my mother's, brother's, and sisters' needs. When the European woman traveled, I woke up." He warned the other *shabāb* against following the same path: "Most of the *shabāb* live in an illusion, not in reality. We, as *shabāb*, are poor refugees in the camp. This is our life. We shouldn't be ashamed of this. But the *shabāb*, because they meet foreigners and go to Hamra [a bohemian, middle-class district of Beirut], think they are someone else; they think they are different. In their subconscious, they start thinking they aren't refugees: they're class.[. . .] Because of this illusion, they start thinking they aren't related to camp society, and they want to marry a foreigner and live abroad."

Through his job at a Palestinian NGO, where he benefited from an attractive employment package—formal contract, paid vacation, paid sick leave, and relatively flexible working hours—Nawaf opened his horizons:

> Before, my world was the camp. When I went outside, it was to visit relatives in the South. But through my work I started relating to foreigners, Lebanese, and Palestinians from different areas. This is good, not to be closed in your own society.[. . .] Interaction with different people [. . .] enriches your mind and experience. But, *ya'nī* [that is to say or I mean], in the end I'm related to my society. I'm from the camp, I'm a refugee. If I want to marry, I have to marry a woman from my society. Living outside—Europe, the Gulf—would turn me into a fish out of water. Even if life is easier abroad, I don't know. I know everything here: my life, my family, my work is here. My wife should be from here, from my camp, even if she isn't Palestinian.

An attempt was made to marry Nawaf to a cousin, his father's *bint 'amm* (father's brother's daughter, until recently the preferred marriage partner for a man in the region),[19] who lived in Saudi Arabia. But he stuck

---

19. Reputed as ideal by previous generations for a series of reasons—such as maintaining wealth within the family, facilitating prewedding negotiations and reducing dowries, and potentially promoting more harmony between the two families (previously known to each other)—marriages with the father's brother's daughter are nonetheless on the decline in the region (Gunaid, Hummad, and Tamim 2004; Inhorn 2012; Shah 2004). Lebanon has one of the lowest rates of consanguineous marriages within the Middle East, though there has been a recent upsurge, one of the presumed reasons being the deep fractioning of Lebanese society during the Civil War (1975–90) (Inhorn 2012). In Shatila, though I have not investigated the matter comprehensively, I came across a number of marriages between men and their fathers' brothers' daughters among the members of the Nakba generation and also among the *thawra* generation, although less so. This pattern of

to his logic: "I don't want to go to Saudi Arabia; it'd be like taking a fish out of water: it's a closed society there. And my *bint 'amm* wouldn't be happy here either: her room there is bigger than my whole house in the camp.[. . .] Her parents also want a large amount in *muqaddam* [bride price], which I can't afford." Some of the lectures he was helping organize as part of a reproductive-health project at his NGO also affected his decisions: "We talk about marriage with relatives in this project. They say that marriage with a close relative causes lots of diseases. I also asked a *sheikha* about it, and she confirmed that there is a hadith [sayings attributed to the Prophet and sources of norms for Islamic schools of jurisprudence] suggesting that close relatives should not marry.[. . .] And I had a dream in which I bore an alien child. So I combined all this—hadith, dream, and reproductive-health program—and decided not to let the relation with my *bint 'amm* go ahead." He tried to repudiate her by breaking her heart: "I lied to her, saying that I knew lots of girls, smoked hashish, drank, and went to night clubs. But she loved me more.[. . .] By now, she and her family probably know I have kind of become engaged, and they probably also know that my girlfriend's family hasn't accepted me entirely."

With the European girl's departure, Nawaf decided the time had come to take his life seriously: "That life I had with the European wasn't stable. After she left, I started thinking I should get engaged, build a house, and have children.[. . .] I started looking for a girl who has the same life as me, the same conditions, including [the same] economic [status], same camp, same religion, so that she can understand and encourage me."

One day he crossed paths with Jamila in one of Shatila's alleys. He smiled; she smiled back: "I thought: she is the one! I asked a colleague and one of my sister's friends about her. I was thinking about how to approach her. You know how camp society is. Out of respect, I can't talk to her directly. I don't want to embarrass her or myself. Another time that I

marriage is, however, normally frowned upon by the *shabāb*. In the reproductive-health program conducted by a local NGO, discussed in chapter 5, consanguineous marriages were one of the topics young men and women wished to discuss, an indication that this pattern of marriage functioned as a source of anxiety among them.

passed by her, I just moved my lips, saying, "Ṣabāḥ al-khayr [Good morning]." She replied the same way. So I sent a colleague to her place to give her my phone number."

Jamila refused to call back, telling Nawaf's messenger that he had to talk to her father first if he wanted to meet her. Nawaf sent his colleague again to overcome her resistance. She finally conceded: "Over the phone, I told her I wanted to get engaged, but I had to finish my university [course] first. I suggested she ask the sheikh about me." The sheikh was an old friend. He had already offered psychological support to Nawaf during adolescence, when the latter thought he was being persecuted by *jinn* (spirits mentioned in the Qur'an) after the traumatic death of his father following a long illness.[20] Once again, the sheikh came to Nawaf's aid: he told Jamila he would marry his own daughter to him. She agreed to meet Nawaf.

Their first encounter happened in a juice shop. Nawaf recalls: "The first time we met, she seemed like a village girl to me. Her hands weren't soft; she worked a lot at her home. And she didn't have a proper education. I encouraged her to get back to school.[. . .] In my previous relationship, I had felt alone. But not in this one, even though we can't meet often enough."

Sensing his hesitation and aware of how much was at stake for a camp girl like her, Jamila forced Nawaf's encounter with her father: "Beforehand I was worried because I didn't know what they would ask for me to become engaged to Jamila. They aren't Palestinian, and we aren't completely familiar with their customs. As it turns out, their customs aren't so different from ours. We found out that in the case of Jamila's sisters they had asked for $10,000 in *muqaddam*. So we were worried they would ask for the same in my case, and that's a lot of money for me."

It was not the *muqaddam*, however, that came between Nawaf and Jamila. Nawaf reported how the much-feared meeting with her father went:

I was trying to decide whom I should take with me to meet him because my father died several years ago. In situations like this, the *wajih* [literally

20. Celia Rothenberg (2004) similarly reports how through relationships to *jinn* Palestinians from Artas in Palestine try to tackle the complexities of life.

"face," here meaning "leader"] of both families should meet. If my father were alive, the role would be his. I brought my elder brother, my aunt's husband, who works for the UN, my sister, my mother, and the sheikh. I was advised to talk as little as possible, not to make any mistakes, so I only answered what Jamila's father asked me. The sheikh introduced us, saying that I was like a son to him. The father asked whether I was able to provide for her, and he was informed that I hadn't finished university yet. He adjourned the meeting and suggested to my brother that we reconvene in a week, so he would have time to check Jamila's reaction. At first, it seemed he would agree.

To Nawaf's disappointment, however, the meeting one week later did not go smoothly. It started promisingly: "The father said he had been able to check on me and that it was OK for me to get engaged with Jamila. As *muqaddam*, they asked for $2,000 in gold and another $2,000 to get her ready for the wedding, less than what we were expecting, and $10,000 in *mu'akhkhar* [the amount to be paid in case of divorce]. But, then, when they reached the issue of the house. . . ."

Jamila's father agreed to a one-year engagement, at the end of which Nawaf was expected to have purchased a house for the newly wedded couple to live in. The future groom's brother counterargued that Nawaf needed at least two years to graduate from university. An agreement could not be reached. As a result, Nawaf now had two priorities in his life: "I need to graduate, and I need to build a house. My brother who lives in Denmark promised he would help me."

When I returned to Lebanon one and a half years after I completed my fieldwork, I discovered that Nawaf had graduated. Nonetheless, he had not yet married Jamila, and, according to some friends we have in common, he was becoming increasingly religious.[21]

21. Throughout my field research, I collected evidence of *shabāb*'s higher propensity to become religious, especially compared to their fathers: in addition to the story of Nawaf, see the stories of Adnan, Hilal, and Ghalib in this chapter. In contrast, the *fidā'iyyīn* were heavily influenced by the secular views of some ideologies, such as Marxism, from which they drew inspiration for the fight to reconquer Palestine. Nevertheless,

o o o

Being shot at by the Israelis in 2000 brought Adnan to the threshold of adulthood.

When the Israeli Defense Forces withdrew from southern Lebanon in 2000, several of the *shabāb*, Adnan among them, nineteen years old back then, traveled to the border. They wanted to see and touch Palestinian land:

> I was very excited when I saw Palestine. I wanted to enter, to touch the land. They [the Israeli soldiers] told us to get back, but we tried to force our way in: you know, there were only ten meters [thirty-three feet] separating us from Palestine. And then they shot at us. In my case, at my leg. Before that, I didn't think of Palestine.[. . .] But after that, the love for Palestine loomed large in my heart. Love for the land is more important and implies more responsibility than the love of women. A woman may not love you back, and even if and when she does, it becomes routine over time.

Because of the shooting, with "forbidden dumdum bullets,"[22] Adnan spent several days in the hospital, received twelve infusions of blood, and was faced with a life-changing threat: according to the doctors, he might never be able to walk properly again. At that point, he started exercising seriously so that he could recover his leg movements. At the time I met him, when he was twenty-eight years old, he went to the gym every day and tried to remain on what he considered the right track.

After the incident at the border in 2000, his life changed: "Between fifteen and nineteen, I was a bad person. I took drugs, especially benzhexol. I was often involved in fights because I had nothing to do.[. . .] When I was thirteen, I got lots of tattoos on my body. I'd be a man, I thought, if I

---

this increased religiosity was not consistently shared by all the young men with whom I worked, as evidenced by Mansur's story, told later in this chapter.

22. The use of dumdum bullets, which expand upon impact and thus cause more serious and potentially more lethal wounds, is forbidden by the Hague Declaration of 1899.

had tattoos and smoked. I see how those are childish thoughts and regret that now."

Aware of the frequency with which he used to get into trouble, Adnan was now cautious to avoid past mistakes: "After being shot by the Israelis, I began thinking about my future. I went to a professional center and learned how to operate a camera.[. . .] Now, if someone is fighting, I don't interfere unless they're fighting with me, but then that's another story altogether.[. . .] Today, I always wake up late. I think that's better than wandering in the camp's streets. Staying in bed keeps me away from problems. I have a lot of empty time on my hands. I use some of that time to pray. I prefer that."

After his late start to the day, Adnan gave his father a hand in the family shop, went to the gym, and finished the day with a visit to a camp-based internet café, where he spent several hours cyberchatting: "I prefer to chat about politics. I love politics. All Palestinians have politics in their souls. The *thawra* and the *fidā'iyyīn* brought no benefits for those of us [Palestinians] living outside [i.e., outside Palestine]. Actually, the *thawra* made the problem worse.[. . .] I'm against using guns outside Palestine. The only way to liberate our country is by bearing arms, but inside Palestine."

In his evaluation, his life was better now than before. But he told me that he needed to find work: "My only problem is to find a regular job. I want a regular job; I need a regular job. After all, a man is considered according to his achievements."

Some two years after this interview took place, and just when I was about to leave Lebanon again, I met Adnan by chance. He was sitting on a plastic chair in front of his gym, recuperating from his workout. He was even stronger: "I keep on exercising. I prefer it like this. You know how I am."

In the case of Hilal, also twenty-eight, it was the experience of being taken to prison that brought him to the threshold of adulthood.[23] Before being

23. Note the difference between Hilal's experience and the experiences of the *shabāb* in Palestine during the First Intifada reported by Julie Peteet (1994). There, being arrested

arrested, he told me, his teen years were tough: "I had very difficult years as a teenager.[. . .] I drew apart from my family; I met bad people. That was between the ages of sixteen and twenty or twenty-one. I stopped studying; I was doing nothing. I worked a little bit here and there as an electrician, but that wasn't what I wanted. Back then, I didn't find a way to continue with my education.[. . .] There were fights; lots of bad things. Everything came to me: sex, drugs. But between me and myself, I knew that wasn't the way to live. It's difficult to get the respect of your own society if you're bad: no one trusts you."

He attributed his problems to the influence of *jinn*, spirits mentioned in the Qur'an:

> It's hard to understand the experience with *jinn*. We believe in the Qur'an; we believe in magic [*siḥr*]. Some people can hurt you through magic; they don't hurt you physically. I felt, saw, and dreamed with *jinn* back then. It hurt. My life stopped. I still feel them.[. . .] If you have a pain in your stomach, it's easy: you go to a doctor. But not with the *jinn*. I went to a sheikh; he said there was nothing wrong with me. In the end, I managed to overcome the problem, but for a while the *jinn* were after me. Everything is written in the Qur'an. *Jinn* exist; humans too; both with different abilities.[. . .] This is another world; you feel that there are things conspiring against you. If you want to work or get an education, you're unable. Your life stops. The *jinn* live inside your body and control you.

In his view, a proper *shāb* or *rajul* (man) needs to control himself: "That way, he can be responsible toward himself and others.[. . .] That's why I had to get rid of the *jinn*. There are treatments for this."

Hilal classified being arrested as a "strange" experience: "I was in prison for some two months. It was a Lebanese prison. It was strange to

---

also brought the *shabāb* to the threshold of adulthood, but more in the sense that they became full political agents of their groups. The political dimension—at least in the sense of politics as resistance—is conspicuously absent from Hilal's discourse. His quest was a personal one.

be there. Inside, it was another life, completely different from the camp. I saw things you can't even imagine. One loses one's respect inside, one's humanity.[. . .] The fact that you're in prison doesn't mean you're a criminal. I was bad but not a criminal. So you have your choice: either you start establishing good relations, or you become a criminal. I found myself. I started thinking about my future."

Having been expelled from an UNRWA school, Hilal opted to finish high school at a private institution. Before that, he worked for two years as an electrician, a tailor, and a painter, often enduring daily work shifts that lasted sixteen hours so he could save money for the school fees. A relative living abroad also provided some financial help, and he finally graduated from a technical institute (ma'had) in computer engineering and business administration. When I met him, he had recently been accepted at the Beirut Arab University, a private university in al-Tariq al-Jadida, neighboring Shatila, to continue with his studies in business administration. He was trying to find ways to pay for the tuition.

Because of his academic ambitions, Hilal had postponed marriage plans: "Before, I thought a lot about getting married. But when I got to know more about life and met people from different cultures, my ideas started to change. I have a different view of marriage now. I think now about my education, I have my ambitions. Marriage is important, but I don't think of getting married now.[. . .] After all these years, I need to control my own life.[. . .] The guys here want to get married quickly. I was like that, but not anymore."

Marriage might not have been occupying Hilal's thoughts often, but migration was: "I love life in Lebanon, but only if there's something for Palestinians here. If I get work here, I'll never think of leaving Lebanon. If I get a regular job here, I'll stay. I grew up here; I'm used to it here. I know this country; my family and friends are here. It isn't easy to think of leaving; it's another life.[. . .] But I want to travel, get an education, a job, and be able to save money. Here you can work for several years and save nothing.[. . .] I don't think being abroad will be easy, but at least I should try. Maybe I'll get my chance."

Upon my return to Lebanon some two years after I interviewed Hilal, I found out that he had succeeded in migrating to the United Kingdom.

He was waiting to get the necessary papers to start looking for a job. He had dropped out of university and had yet to marry. In the secular United Kingdom, the *jinn* finally left Hilal in peace.

For Ghalib, twenty-four, several spells in jail had not had any major transformative effect. He had been arrested five times, twice doing time for the long period of a year and a half. As in Hilal's experience, prison did not make a national political agent out of Ghalib, either: "The Lebanese think we're Jews. Even in prison, we're treated worse. There are lots of Palestinians in jail. The food is awful: even dogs wouldn't eat it."

When he was still young, his life was thrown into disarray by the death of his father. He left school, started working as a carpenter, and held a handful of short-lived jobs. Soon he found his way to Sabra, the bustling market leading to Shatila: "I started taking drugs: coke, heroine, and hashish. And I also started stealing and cutting myself. I had these tattoos made. People think I'm a bad boy [*az'ar*] because of these tattoos. People with tattoos have a bad reputation [*ṣīt wusikh*]; others think tattooed people take drugs and fight. But in my case they have a point, no?"

Because of his reputation, the family of the girl he loves refused him: "I think of marriage all the time. But I'm poor and have a past. I think that's why her family didn't accept me, because they worry for her future. Nothing works for me. I think of one thing and always get something else."

He sees his mother's past as a *fidā'iyya* (female freedom fighter) as glorious, but that past is not available to him: "*Thawra* in the past was good, but not today. Today, the *tanẓimāt* [political factions], if they see someone dying, they do nothing; they even make it worse. If they see someone taking drugs, they take him by force and hand him over to the Lebanese. They are the reason for a person going to jail and for all his suffering [*'azābū*]."

Often using expressions drawn directly from Beiruti street language, immediately followed by a word from the Qur'anic vocabulary, Ghalib faced a dilemma. Although he was attracted to the risks and pleasures of the street, his was a moral and religious quest. Upon his latest release from prison, he tried to put his life back on track: he found two jobs, as a sales assistant in a CD shop in Sabra and as a construction worker on the project to recuperate the Shatila pipeline. Between his two salaries, he was making some $600 per month: "Enough for me as a *shāb* but not enough to build a house and get married."

Still single, he told me that he was at the end of adolescence (*murāhaqa*): "That's because a *murāhiq* [adolescent] doesn't think of anything else but girls and drinks. The life of a *murāhiq* is about [...] getting into problems. But, now, *al-ḥamdulillah* [thanks to God], I have become wiser [*ana w'īt*], and I have *'aql* [the capacity for reasoning]." As was so often the case with the Shatila *shabāb*, he complained about not having an older figure on whom he could count for guidance: "My father died, and I don't have an older brother. It would have been nice to have an older brother to give me advice on what to do."

Ghalib stopped going to the mosque and praying: "I used to, but not anymore. Why did I stop, you ask? It isn't permissible to go to the mosque and after to go drinking and commit *zinā* [a Qura'nic—and biblical— word for extramarital sex]. After drinks and *zinā*, I shouldn't even step on the *muṣallā* [rug used for praying]."

He does not believe in a bright future and thinks that his life would have been different were he living in Palestine: "The future? Well, when it happens, we talk about it.[...] I'd like to migrate, but I can't because I'm wanted [by the police] [*maṭlūb*].[...] Palestine is my country. If I were there, I wouldn't be in such a situation.[...] Even if I get another nationality, inside [*dākhil*] I'll always be Palestinian."

Although I intended to talk with both Ghalib and his mother, a former fighter, together, as I was attempting to do with all the pairs of parents and offspring I interviewed, the new encounter never materialized. When I tried to fix a date for meeting the two, I was informed that Ghalib was in prison yet again.

At a very young age, Halim, twenty-seven, a sales assistant at a minimarket, came to realize the consequences that sect and class differences would have on his life.

In his recollection, his was a happy childhood. After the destruction of the Tal al-Zaatar Palestinian refugee camp in 1976, his family, along with several others, moved to Raouche, a district of West Beirut by the sea, previously popular among tourists. Together with other Palestinians and Lebanese, the Abu Halim family installed themselves in an abandoned hotel. With just one functioning bathroom for all residents and with school located several kilometers away, Halim's life was certainly not immune to difficulties. Yet he remembered those years with the patina of nostalgia: "With the sea just 200 meters [218 yards] from us, I could go to the beach every day. I played football and ate loads of fish."

This tranquility came to an end when the family, having no option but to cede to the pressure of the Rafik Hariri government, moved to Shatila. Premier Hariri wanted to revamp the pleasant seaside districts of West Beirut and so pressed for the expulsion of the Lebanese Civil War–era occupiers from the area's hotels. To leave their former "home" "voluntarily," the Abu Halim family was offered the choice of either $5,000 or a place in Shatila. They opted for Shatila. Halim was then twelve.

Halim had an aunt (khāla, mother's sister) who was better off than his own nuclear family. Married to the owner of a taxi company, she lived outside the camp. As a child, Halim regularly inherited the clothes of his richer cousin. He never liked it:

> I didn't understand why I couldn't have new clothes. And my cousin had a basket full of toys. I had none. My aunt used to say things like: "How can your mother send you to me dirty like this?" I didn't understand the meaning of that back then, but I felt something inside, to the point that I remember this even today.[. . .] I felt lonely. I knew there was something different between them and me, but I didn't know what it was. The last time I saw her here in Shatila was four years ago. We don't visit them; they don't visit us. They're educated; we aren't. They have money; we don't. Of course, there are social differences among Palestinians. Money sometimes is everything, Gustavo.

Soon after his family moved to Shatila, Halim dropped out of school and started working at a blacksmith's workshop in the Shia-majority district Dahiya, which borders the camp. The salaries of his father and mother, as a car mechanic and a cleaner, respectively, were not enough to provide for the eight-member family: "We were really, really poor,

Gustavo. We had no money whatsoever. I didn't have a bag to take to school. And I never, not even for one single day in my life, enjoyed calm at home to study. Or electricity. So I told myself I'd better stop studying to begin working."

The beginning of Halim's work life was burdensome. His coworkers used to beat him: "I didn't know anything about being Sunni or Shia back then. But they didn't like Sunni there. And they made jokes that I was black because of the work with iron. Then I started to understand that some people don't like Palestinians or Sunni simply because we are Palestinians or Sunni. I understood I didn't belong to the same sect as them."

He quit the workshop and got a job at a restaurant in the camp owned by a Palestinian, so "at least there was respect." He worked up to twelve hours daily for very little money, $11 per day. Subsequently he managed to find a position at another restaurant, with a better salary, but the owner migrated to Canada. After Halim spent a couple of months in short-lived jobs, fixing electricity supplies and repairing elevators, his career at minimarkets started. He secured a job in an establishment outside the camp: "The job was fine. I started making some money and thinking of having my own minimarket.[. . .] Maybe that's when my life really began. I started thinking of what I need for a good life: to buy a house, get married, buy a car." He was twenty-three.

He started making some money—$700 per month—and building a house on the roof of the place where his family has an apartment and had only half-finished it when I talked to him. Nonetheless, he verbalized a deep distaste for camp life and wanted to leave: "To be honest with you, I would have preferred to have a house outside. And you'll ask: 'Why did you build in the camp, then?' Well, here I've spent $8,000 so far on this house; outside, I'd need $50,000 at least [for a house]. And I'd need a license from the government, which I'd never get. But I hate life in the camp *ktīr* [a lot]. Camp life isn't life—no electricity, no sun, no clean streets, no proper school, no proper sleep."

That is why he started seriously considering migration. And there was a girl.

He first tried to purchase a fake visa for the Schengen countries for $2,500. It did not work out, so he started contemplating alternatives:

I really wanted to leave. There is something deeply wrong here. My father, for instance, almost seventy, worked for his whole life. He is still working. He is tired and sick but can't stop working. And I don't want my children to lead the life that I've had. I want to move to any country where I can have a life, my children can study and go to university [. . .], a country where I can grow old and have some kind of protection.[. . .] So I thought and thought and thought a lot. What can I do? I thought of marrying a Sunni lady from abroad, German or European, Lebanese or Palestinian in origin. Lots of guys here in Shatila think of this. It seemed like the perfect solution.[. . .] I had some connections to people with relatives outside. So I started asking. It isn't easy to do that, you know, to look for a candidate for marriage like that. Psychologically speaking, it isn't easy. Some people I asked even made jokes about me and laughed at me. That destroyed me.

He was finally introduced to a Palestinian living in Germany and with German nationality. She was twenty and spoke very limited Arabic. She came to Saida, a city south of Beirut, and an eager Halim rushed there to meet his prospective bride. The outcome was not what he expected: "When I saw the girl, I felt nothing. She wasn't beautiful; I didn't like her; she wasn't the right girl for me. True, I wanted to travel, to have a good life outside, with my kids attending school. But that wasn't the way."

He asked her family to allow him a week to consider the subject. It was a difficult week for him: "Part of me said: get married. Maybe this marriage will work. And even if it doesn't, you can get a divorce and go on living in Germany. But another part of me said: you know you didn't like her. It isn't fair to her. If you divorce, she'll feel bad for a long time. She may even come to like you: ḥarām [a shame]!" So a week later he called her and apologized for not going ahead with the marriage plans. Retrospectively, he felt good about his decision: "I knew I wouldn't like her with time. All I'd get was the nationality. I'm happy I acted the way I did."

He told me that he had not given up on his plans to migrate but that for the time being he was trying to settle down in Lebanon. I attempted to push him a little further to understand what precisely "settling down" implied:

ME: *Ya'nī* [that means], you want Lebanese nationality?

HALIM: If I'm offered it, yes.

ME: But isn't that *tawṭīn* [naturalization]?

HALIM: [After a moment of hesitation] Gustavo, with *jinsiyya* [nationality], I can work legally, I can own property, I can receive social security. Having a *jinsiyya* is important.[...] Gustavo, before being Palestinian, I'm human; I look at life as a human being.[...] All the world is my country, not only Palestine. I'd go anywhere now where I can have a better life.

ME: [Pushing, insensitively] That means you don't think of *ḥaqq al-'awda* [right of return]?

HALIM: Gustavo, I'm Palestinian. I love Palestine and stuff [*wa kida*], but I also want to have a nice life. My heart is Palestinian; I can live anywhere, and this won't change.[...] But I don't have time in my life now to think about Palestine. I have more urgent matters calling for my attention. Palestine is distant from me.[...] True, I love Palestine, and sometimes I feel like leaving everything and fighting against Israel.[...] But I live in such tough conditions that I first have to worry about food, electricity, money.[...] There's no such thing as the return.[24] I won't go back. Maybe I think about this question just once

24. Halim's blunt remark on the impossibility of return creates a moral quandary for researchers like me, who identify with what we take to be the Palestinian cause. Nevertheless, although aware that what I write may have unanticipated consequences, never for a moment have I contemplated editing out Halim's comments because that would mean not only falsifying my data but also not abiding by the informal ethical contract that researchers establish with informants. Indeed, Halim's disillusionment with the possibility of the return speaks of nothing but a realpolitik understanding of the nonexistent peace talks with Israel. There is a subtle difference here that needs to be taken into consideration: thinking that the return will not happen—as Halim clearly did—does not automatically equate with giving up the right to return, as enshrined in the UN General Assembly Resolutions 194 (December 11, 1948) and 3236 (November 22, 1974) and UN Security Council Resolution 242 (November 22, 1967) (the latter calling for a just settlement of the refugee issue). I feel deeply and ethically committed to publicizing Halim's views and his perception of the price he pays for the maintenance of a certain discourse on the right to return, precisely because views like his are very much marginalized by mainstream Palestinian nationalism. For a similar discussion on the moral quandaries when dealing with this issue, see Allan 2007, 2014b.

or twice a year. I don't have time for it. Not even these organizations that keep talking about the return really believe in it. They keep talking about it because that's their job.

All of Halim's girlfriends were Sunni. He told me that there was no special reason behind the fact. Being Sunni and poor, he usually got to know others who were Sunni and poor, too:

I have [sexual] relations with *banāt wa niswān* [both younger and older women].[25] I don't have money to buy nice clothes. I don't have money to buy a house either, so finding women to marry or to date isn't straightforward.[. . .] I don't always think of sex; I also think of love.[. . .] But I'm not looking for a wife now. There are many conditions I need to meet to get married.[. . .] I don't want my kids to lead the life I've had. I don't want them to go to an UNRWA school or to live in the camp. If my child is sick, I want to be able to afford a hospital.

He was not convinced that life in the past was less difficult:

People say that life in the past was easier. There was money, there was *thawra*, there was Abu Ammar [Yasser Arafat], there was one clear enemy. But I don't know: if there was war, how could life have been better? My father was a *fidā'ī*, and he was always poor.[. . .] But I don't have enough information about the *thawra*; my father speaks very little about it. Today there is conflict between Hamas, Fatah, Jihad, Democratic Front. Before we were one, and there was one military force.[. . .] If there is *thawra* today, it is very weak. If it still exists, it's because of the Palestinian people. Every Palestinian has *thawra* inside himself.

In response to my standard question about playing any sports, Halim answered that he boxes, which served as a prompt for him to talk about not having any violence within himself and feeling weak and hopeless:

25. *Bint*, plural *banāt*, usually refers to a younger woman who is expected not to have had sexual relationships, as distinct from *niswān*, referring to usually older and sexually experienced women.

I like sports. I like boxing. Every day I practice a little bit here at home. Even though I smoke, you know me. There's no violence in boxing, you know.[. . .] It's a strong sport, but it isn't violent.[. . .] I have no violence inside me whatsoever. I've never had any and wish I had. It's important to have violence inside; my problem is precisely that I haven't. Life is hard. If you're kind, people eat you; they think you're weak.[. . .] I don't know if I'm really strong. I don't know for how much longer I'll bear this situation. One or two years ago, I felt stronger, but now it isn't the same. Life is becoming hard; I'm becoming weaker. Before I used to think: I'm young, I can work, marry, travel. But time is passing; chances are getting fewer.[. . .] I remember when I was eighteen, I had so much hope.[. . .] I had hope that I'd marry and make my parents and friends proud of me. But I couldn't achieve that. I'm weak at this moment, and I don't know if I have hope anymore.[. . .] Life is sad, Gustavo. You just need to be human to feel sad. Inside, I feel a lot of *zulum* [injustice].

In addition to boxing, Halim liked surfing the internet. He spent hours navigating Google Earth, making virtual visits to countries he knew would be very difficult for him to reach.

Some two years after this interview, I chatted to Halim over the internet. He was in a detention center for refugees in a European country. For $7,000, he had purchased a package that included air tickets and a fake visa. On disembarking in Europe, he claimed asylum status. At the detention center, where he shared a room with five other asylum seekers, he complained that life was extremely tough: he had no privacy and constantly felt scared. It took him almost a year to have his asylum claim approved. Once he got his papers, he moved to Germany. The last time we talked, he was extremely cash strapped but sounded hopeful.

Very little in Mansur's life happened the way he wanted. Twenty-nine years old and an accounting graduate, Mansur often saw his biography dramatically invaded by the events of history: "I've seen the Israeli invasion of 1982. My grandfather died in the Sabra and Shatila massacre. Between '85 and '87, I saw the War of the Camps. During the war, we lived under the earth [in subterranean shelters], all cramped, like sardines in a tin. No room for anyone. Everyone slept together in the shelter: old, young, men, women, with bombs and bullets all around.[. . .] It was a life without dignity [*karāma*]."

At the end of the War of the Camps, one event changed Mansur's biography forever: "A bomb exploded near us, and the debris hit my father. He fainted, revived, opened his eyes for a couple of seconds, cried, and closed his eyes again. Forever. I was only eight." Since then, Mansur has been looking for compensation for his loss, a replacement. As for other *shabāb*, his is a story of a missing father: "Maybe my life would have been different if I had a father or someone older to pass on his experience [*tajruba*] and wisdom [*ḥikma*] to me."

Mansur attributed his interest in medicine to his father's premature death. He spent his high school years reading medical books and hoped to become a doctor: "I think my interest was provoked by the loss of my father. I was attempting to defeat death. Is death really the end?" He was never accepted into medical school.

As a child he found some comfort at a Palestinian NGO, Beit Atfal al-Sumud (House of the Children of Steadfastness).[26] His mother became an employee there, and he started going to Beit Atfal al-Sumud, through which he was "adopted" by a British Malay,[27] who started sending money to the organization to cover some of Mansur's needs. Sometimes, instead of using the whole amount to pay for essentials, Beit Atfal al-Sumud would hand over a portion of the money directly to Mansur: "It was a negligible amount, around $30, just enough to buy a pair of shoes or trousers. But it was nice to think that someone was thinking of us. It offered us some

26. Originally set up in 1976, catering to orphans from the Tal al-Zaatar massacre, Beit Atfal al-Sumud continues to operate in the camps in Lebanon. In Shatila, it provides a variety of services, ranging from education to dental care. More information on the organization can be obtained on its website at http://www.socialcare.org.

27. Beit Atfal al-Sumud runs a sponsorship program through which donors can "adopt" a Palestinian child by making financial contributions that help to foster him or her. More information is available at http://www.socialcare.org/portal/child-in-a-family-sponsorship/9/.

kind of emotional compensation. We were compensated for not having a father."

Beit Atfal al-Sumud also had a library, which lured the young Mansur. He would rush there from school and borrow two or three books at a time: "As you know, Gustavo, in Shatila we don't have the basics for life: electricity, clean water, silent spaces. I really wanted and want to leave Shatila. I want to see the world. So I started traveling—through books. And without a father or an elder to help me understand the world, I needed guidance. Books started filling that role. And, you know, in Shatila and when you're Palestinian, you don't have wide horizons. Books opened those horizons for me. The journey of reading and writing started."

By spending a large amount of time reading, Mansur believed he had become different from other Shatila *shabāb*: "Until then I was just like any other Shatila guy, but I may have become different since then. By virtue of books, my dreams and desires, I may have created a different personality. I isolated and differentiated myself. This happened at the same time as I gained consciousness of what it means to be Palestinian and deprived of rights."

On failing to enter medical school, Mansur studied accounting at the private Beirut Arab University. That was not his first career choice, and it took him seven years to graduate: "Accounting was like prison for me. I didn't like the university, but I liked my university years because I started meeting people from all walks of life and making friends with them. We talked about everything: sex, love, freedom, religion, Marxism. I became a member of the Communist Party. I read about history, dialectics, materialism. Everything but accounting."

He failed his exams for three consecutive years, feeling increasingly embarrassed around his mother, who was helping him make ends meet. He also started reading philosophy at the public Lebanese University but never managed to graduate: "My life is like this. I wanted to become a doctor but didn't succeed. I like philosophy and started studying it but never managed to graduate. Instead, my major is in something I never liked. And I graduated in 2006, two weeks before the outbreak of the war between Hezbollah and Israel, which made finding a job almost impossible."

Mansur could have migrated to Abu Dhabi, where his ʿamm (father's brother) had been living for more than twenty-five years, but he never seriously contemplated it: "Some of my classmates from university traveled to the Gulf, and I know how they live there. True, there's money, but I can't bear how they live, sharing a room with five people they don't even know. I like to have my privacy. I prefer to stay here; I like Lebanon, but of course I don't want to be a second-class citizen. Here, there are books. In other places, there's surveillance. And I don't like the sulṭa [sovereign power].[28] In Lebanon, there's freedom. You can believe in whatever you want. I like the ethnic and religious diversity of Lebanon."

It was not only the lack of appropriate financial means that led Mansur to shelve his plans to get married, at that time at least: "No, I'm not thinking of marriage now. I don't like regimes, routines. I always think of living by myself in a small place, outside the camp. If I have money, I'll leave Shatila.[. . .] I think of having someone, but someone who thinks like me. Here, you don't marry a woman only; you marry her entire family. There are visits, obligations, burdens: it curbs your freedom. That I can't stand."

He could not stand the prospect of having children, either, and yet again the reason was not just the lack of financial means: "Why does one want to have kids? Why would I let my children grow up in an environment like Shatila, with [. . .] no infrastructure? How do you put bits of yourself into a place like this? One has moral responsibilities [masʾūliyyāt ʾakhlāqiyya] toward one's children." In this respect, a gift Mansur once gave me is very telling: a book entitled The Trouble of Being Born by E. M. Cioran ([1976] 1998), a collection of pessimistic aphorisms about existence being meaningless. There one can read: "Not to be born is the best plan of all. Unfortunately it is within no one's reach" (223).

In Ismail, an old philosopher living in Shatila, Mansur found much needed guidance. Born in Haifa in 1948, Ismail arrived in the camp as an infant. Leaving school at a very young age, he was self-taught. In 1971, he was imprisoned for political reasons and spent twenty-one years behind

28. On sulṭa, see note 12 in this chapter.

bars. In jail, he read philosophy, history, and psychology. In him, Mansur finally found an interlocutor: "I've always longed for a father. And with Ismail, I could talk about everything: life, death, sex, love. I started consulting him about every issue in my life, about my plans for the future and my classes. There was an exchange between us and reciprocity [*tabādul*]." Ismail was very sick, suffering from diabetes and high cholesterol, and because of gangrene had to have a foot amputated: "I'd like to be able to help him—by buying him his medicine, for instance." Even that, however, Mansur could not afford.

Mansur did not believe in the redemption of the return: "Talking about the *ḥaqq al-ʿawda* [right of return (to Palestine)] as something present is silly.[29] There's Israel; there's no Palestine. There is, if you wish, the Palestinian *sulṭa* [authority] in Gaza and the West Bank. We won't be given the right to return. *Khalaṣ* [Enough]! You can talk about the *ḥaqq al-ʿawda*, but you can't achieve it, except by force. But is there any Arab country ready to fight Israel? I don't believe so. They have the money and could have the weapons to defeat Israel, but they don't have the will. And the Palestinian *sulṭa* doesn't have the strength. It has speeches only."

Exposed to European secular philosophy, Mansur did not think of himself as religious: "I don't classify myself as a Muslim. I don't pray; I don't fast; I don't read the Qur'an; and I'm not interested in any of these. [. . .] And I don't differentiate people according to their religion; I differentiate people according to their morals. On those grounds, do we all deserve to be called humans? Do we all have the ethics and the morality?" I was surprised, therefore, when he volunteered that he believed in God, but only to add a moment later the following pessimistic note: "I also believe that we have been deserted and abandoned."

I still ventured one last question: "You have no hope [*ʾamal*]?" In response, he could only say, "I'm tired, Gustavo."

In November 2012, when the UN General Assembly upgraded Palestine's status within the organization to "nonmember state," I posted a

---

29. On the meaning of such remarks concerning the impossibility of the return to Palestine, see note 24 in this chapter.

number of celebratory comments on my Facebook page. Mansur's reaction came as fast and incisive as ever via a message on Facebook, too: "What does it really mean, Gustavo, a Palestinian state?"

In the time since our interview took place, he had succeeded in securing a job as an Arabic teacher but received a low salary.[30] Ismail died from his multiple diseases.

All of these "ethnographies of the particular" (Abu-Lughod 1991, 138) depict Shatila *shabāb* not only "making mistakes, . . . enduring tragedies and personal losses, . . . and finding moments of happiness" but also "trying to make themselves look good" (Abu-Lughod 1991, 158). Theirs is a moral quest—sometimes but not necessarily admitting nationalistic or religious overtones[31]—to be good men, even if and when it may be impos-

30. One of the anonymous reviewers of this book rightly commented that although *The Best of Hard Times* portrays the Shatila *shabāb*'s aspirations for an education, a job, a home, marriage, and a family, it offers no "success stories." There is good reason for this: there are no "success cases" to be told because what I depict here is a very specific moment in *shabāb*'s lives, a moment in which they aspire to (and often become frustrated by) a future that has not yet happened and in which they feel considerable anxiety about being unable to buy and furnish a house, find a proper job, and start a family. I should add nonetheless that I did follow the *shabāb*'s trajectories beyond my period in Shatila, much more as a friend than as a researcher. Both ethically and analytically, I do not think that I could or should add to what is already included in the book, for in this postfieldwork period I was not collecting data consistently or in my capacity as a researcher. In any case, I do have the feeling that, given the lack of better options and compared to the dreams and aspirations that they nurtured when I was living in the camp, the *shabāb* generally have had to settle for a much less ambitious understanding of what perhaps cannot even be properly described as "success."

31. In an "Islamic-informed" version of Simone de Beauvoir's famous dictum, Lahoucine Ouzgane argues that men are also not born but made and, moreover, made within specific social and historical contexts. He coins the term *Islamic masculinity* when extending his invitation to scholars working in a social-constructionist perspective to render "Muslim men visible as gendered subjects" (2006, 1). When I prompted research participants to tell me whether there were different phases in the life of a man and, if so,

sible to be good at being men (Herzfeld 1985) within the parameters of previous understandings of what that meant. Nevertheless, the anxiety generated by the possibility of failing to meet certain expectations placed on them is not in any sense indicative of a "crisis of masculinity." Rather, as I now look to demonstrate, it suggests the need to promote another crisis, one of an epistemological nature: the crisis of gender and hegemonic-masculinity discourses.

Nawaf's dilemma between finishing his university studies and making money quickly to afford marriage with Jamila; Adnan's fears of doing wrong; Hilal's experiences with persecution by *jinn*; Ghalib's attraction to the pleasures and risks of the street and his repeated imprisonments; Halim's admission of weakness, refusal of the temptation of a "visa marriage" that would help him migrate, and distress over his self-admitted nonviolent nature; and Mansur's rejection of the idea of becoming a father because of the "trouble with being born"—all bear testimony to the difficult of fulfilling certain ideals, including gender ideals. Whereas the *fidā'iyyīn*'s recollections contribute to the ideology of hegemonic masculinity, the Shatila *shabāb* expose the difference between the latter ideology and their own practices (of gender or other). If, as Samar Kanafani (2005, 2008) indicates, the *fidā'iyyīn*'s reminiscences reserve no place for the feminine, hegemonic-masculinity discourses also operate through omissions. Within such discourses, the current experiences of the *shabāb* disappear from purview: they come across as not worth considering. On an epistemological level, the

---

what these phases were and what markers indicated passage from one to another, several of them directed me to a specific hadith. In the hadith, Ali Ibn Abi Talib, Prophet Mohammed's cousin and son-in-law, prevented the stoning of an insane woman accused of adultery. He explained the reason for the Prophet's action. According to Abi Talib, Prophet Mohammed taught that three kinds of people should not be held accountable: the lunatic until restored to reason; the sleeping until awake; and *boys before reaching puberty* (*bulūgh*). In the different versions of the hadith that my informants shared with me or that I found, the idea of reaching puberty is sometimes replaced by growing up (*yakbar*) or achieving the faculty of understanding and wisdom (*'aql* or *wa'ī*) (on this subject, also see notes 7 and 9 in this chapter).

result is to be expected: nonhomosexual men with limited access to power have no place in hegemonic-masculinity discourses. For an ethnographic analysis, however, this absence remains unjustifiable.

Marcia Inhorn contends that in studies of the Middle East—and, I would add, in US media portrayals—"we need to rethink whether patriarchy," or, as she puts it elsewhere, "hegemonic masculinity, Middle-Eastern style," "should remain the dominant theoretical trope" (2012, 15). By nuancing our patriarchal polemics and opening them up to more closely reflect ethnographic findings, she anticipates that men in the Middle East will not necessarily show up as always "patriarchal, hypervirile, brutal and religiously fanatical" (54). Although ideals of manhood may reveal a certain obstinate persistence, the way manhood is lived in practice changes from place to place and time to time as the social contexts vary—when men age, for example—or from one generation to the other.[32] The eventual gap between ideal and practice does not necessarily entail a "crisis of masculinity."

"Crisis of masculinity" discourses are required for the functioning of certain gender theories and the frameworks of "hegemonic masculinity" and patriarchy. If men, for whatever reason, cannot fulfill the expectations placed on them, their masculinity needs to be in crisis, at least discursively. Rather than tuning their analyses to changes in the practices of manhood in varying times and spaces, "crisis of masculinity" scholars proceed to an epistemic freezing of the ideal: theirs is an ideological, politically loaded, and politically motivated discussion of masculine values, considered to be either in decline because real men are not in a position to live by them (Bly 1991; Campbell 1991; Faludi 1999; Gibbs and Merighi

---

32. Recent research from different ethnographic settings has registered similar tendencies for young men willing neither to follow the steps of their fathers—sometimes experimenting with ideas of conjugality and sexuality in the process—nor to attend to the expectations and demands of normative masculinity: for the Dominican Republic, see Mark Padilla's work (2007); for Mexico, Matthew Gutmann's (2003, 2007) and Jennifer Hirsch's (2003); and for Japan, Emma Cook's (2012, 2013), Romit Dasgupta's (2012), and Mark McLelland and Romit Dasgupta's (2005).

1996) or intrinsically pathological because there is something wrong with them (Campbell 1993; Clare 2001; Horrocks 1996).

James Heartfield harshly critiques such lines of reasoning: there is no crisis of masculinity, he contends, because "masculinity" is an ideological and methodologically suspect concept. He writes: "In posing the analysis of the condition of men in terms of masculinity the theories tend to make a fetish of sexual difference. . . . [O]nce the differences [in the division of labor] are relocated into the theory of 'masculinity,' they become mystified as psychological and cultural figures that defy empirical substantiation. . . . Considered as a crisis of masculinity, the transformation of the sexual division of labor is conceived of with the two genders related to each other only externally, and in opposition" (2002).

The popularity of "crisis of masculinity" discourses stems from the fact that they seem to capture an ongoing loss of power by men. At the same time, however, we are not in the presence of a zero-sum "war of the sexes" game in which men's losses necessarily translate into women's gains. Based on data from the United Kingdom, Heartfield shows that the transformation of capitalism in the past few decades has forced a reorganization of both the production and the reproduction spheres, with women entering the workforce in underpaid and part-time jobs. True, in terms of capital, working-class men have lost out. Working-class women, however, have lost, too: dual-income families allow for twice the surplus labor without twice the cost, as Marx has taught us. Overall, families have paid the price, with even this most rudimentary form of solidarity being incessantly assaulted by capital's rule. The real crisis, Heartfield concludes, is not of masculinity but of the working class.

The fact that "crisis of masculinity" discourses constitute a fetish does not mean that they do not produce effects in practice—"toxic" ones at that, especially in the Western media industry. The idea that men in (very) specific parts of the world are in crisis or cannot live up to the demands of an atavistic, misogynist, and hypersexual masculinity, as in pseudoanthropological and psychological-behavioralist approaches, feeds terrorology industries in the service of the neocolonial enterprise of empire (Amar 2011). As such, the idea serves epistemologically to contain emergent social forces in the Middle East while in the process racializing, moralistically depoliticizing, and misrecognizing them (Amar 2011). Seen—or, more properly speaking, not actually being seen—against such a background, (some) actual men and their biographies become forever silenced: epistemically invisible, they cannot speak on their own terms. Rather, they are ever-present problems to be solved.

As Jasbir Puar argues, the terrorist is taken to be a failed man. By framing terrorism as issuing from masculinities in crisis and thus often helping to promote the figure of the "stateless-monster-terrorist-fag" (2007, 100), a number of authors (Kimmel 2002; Morgan 1989; Tiger 2001, 2002) depoliticize the phenomenon and remain oblivious to the critique of political economies often expressed by the terrorists themselves. Here, rather than further faggotizing alleged terrorists, I aim to "queer" power, a point I further develop in the concluding remarks of this book.

In the case of the *shabāb* from Shatila encountered in this chapter, neither is their masculinity threatened by their predicaments, nor are they "terrorists in the making" as a result of the difficulties in their lives. If the concept of culture risks a (further) exoticization of the Other (Abu-Lughod 1991), I should here insist that Nawaf's problems in concretizing the marriage with the partner he loves, Hilal's commitment for several years to a job he does not particularly like in order to save for tuition, and Halim's feeling of weakness vis-à-vis the obstacles he has to tackle echo situations that other friends of mine from other latitudes and I also deal with.

In a sense, the "stateless-monster-terrorist-fag" and the nonhomosexual Muslim man with limited access to power constitute the abject Other of liberal feminism and LGBTIQ movements, and this is precisely why they are "retraditionalized" and their masculinity stigmatized (Ewing 2008): mythologies of traditional Muslim men, who in practice may not be as traditional as the prejudices and expectations of liberal feminism and LGBTIQ movements want them to be, feed social fantasies, fears, and anxieties about differences and the "Other."

In a two-moment episode of events followed from close up, Sylvain Perdigon (2012) reports how a newborn infant, found soaking in blood in an alley of a Palestinian refugee camp in southern Lebanon, was rushed to the hospital, followed by his young, single mother. Her father, whom Perdigon names "Abu Ahmed," was distraught, and a whole group—including local leaders, a doctor, relatives, and state security agents—intervened to break the news of his daughter's pregnancy, of which he had been unaware. Six months later, Perdigon meets the same Abu Ahmed, who, while holding his grandson on his lap, elaborated on how he managed to control the impulse to murder his own daughter. This forced the researcher to investigate the "dense and mobile terrains of ethical [and] affective . . . life that one [finds] . . . in the Palestinian communities of Southern Lebanon, in lieu of the fantasy of a script of honor that would make the performance of violence a clear and binding obligation upon a man confronted with public whispers concerning the deviance of one of his female relatives" (2012). As Perdigon argues, the archetypal image of the hot-blooded Arab and Muslim man as ruthless in the protection of his honor and defense of his male pride fails to pay proper attention to the fact that there is a wound that bleeds in cases like Abu Ahmed's. There is an epistemological reason why such a wound needs to remain invisible: it entails a move that is masculinizing and effeminizing at the same time, "as though he can't really be that much of a man, he whom a woman can wound so easily" (2012). In Perdigon's understanding, this invisibility is owing to a liberal, secular, and modernist rejection of the possibility that vulnerability to others is a legitimate way of living relationships and being in the world.

The faggotization and/or hypermasculinization of the Muslim and/or Arab Other are required because their "connective selves" (Joseph 1993a, 1994, 1999b) expose the limits of one of the ideals most cherished by political modernity, liberal feminism, and certain LGBTIQ movements: freedom from norms. This is precisely why freedom from norms—"liberal humanism's authorization of the fully possessed speaking subject, untethered by hegemony or false consciousness . . . and rationally choosing modern individualism over the ensnaring bonds of family" (Puar 2007, 22–23)—ends up being regulatory. The "being in the world" of Nawaf and other *shabāb* has thus become an epistemic impossibility. Yet they insist on existing and on inviting us, "the Victorians," to reconsider some of our epistemological convictions.

We, the Victorians (and Some Arabic)

We, the Victorians, don't talk *sexe*.[33]

As Stella Sandford (2011) argues, the Anglo-Saxon term *sex* does not capture what the French mean by *sexe*—and, I further contend, it does not translate well into the Arabic term *jins* either. Sandford's point is that sex has increasingly come to be conceived in terms of its distinction to gender since the latter's inception in the 1950s through the work of the American psychologist Robert Stoller. In the following decades, such a tendency became all the more pronounced after the feminist movement seized upon both concepts. One of the unanticipated side effects of sex being defined in reference to its difference to gender is that it is hijacked by gender and hardly receives any adequate theoretical attention. We, the Victorians, have never felt completely at ease with these *sexe* talks. As Geneviève Fraisse puns, gender is a "cache-*sexe*" (quoted in Sandford 2011, 25).

The feminist thought produced in France makes the case that the concept "gender" still produces a deficit in terms of meaning, despite its value in political struggles and wonders in fine theoretical thinking (Sandford 2011). Thus, the distinction between a biological sex and a socially constructed gender does not open a comfortable space for thinking of *sexualité* on the fantasmatic level of drives, or what the French call *pulsions*. Yet because both power and the lack thereof are realized through the most intimate, intersubjective relations (Foucault 1985, 1986, [1978] 1998; Hemmings, Gedalof, and Bland 2006), *sexe*/sex talk is not only a problem of translation. There is an ideological reason for the persistence of "sex"—and, I would add, of "gender"—as a concept, despite all its inadequacies, Sandford states.

At a clinical level, scientists again and again come up with evidence that the physical distinction between male and female—or what Anglo-Saxons would normally label *sex*—does not function to describe the

---

33. The title of this section is a modified version of the title of the chapter "We 'Other Victorians'" in *The Will to Knowledge*, volume 1 of Foucault's *The History of Sexuality* ([1978] 1998).

multiplicity of sexed forms that bodies have or can assume. The distinction's descriptive shortcomings notwithstanding, the illusion of a binary division between male and female still informs medical practice to the point that those bodies that happen not to fit into one or other of these categories are forced to conform, often through invasive and painful surgical intervention. This renders all the more evident the fact that sex has no heuristic value in terms of description: its surprising persistence comes from its ideological strength as a prescriptive notion.

Thus, sex is an illusion, Sandford claims. It is a certain pervasive misreading in the Anglo-Saxon world of Simone de Beauvoir's ([2009] 2012) idea, originally formulated in 1949, whereby one is not born a woman but becomes one, which has led to a certain naturalization of sex—as if it really exists. Nonetheless, de Beauvoir is read differently by her own compatriots: sex itself is created. If we Victorians encounter difficulties in thinking of sex, it is precisely because we tend to reduce it to biology. By not opening the concept up to proper theoretical inquiry and analytical thought, we tend to lose track of the fact that sex—the distinction between male and female—is a modern "natural-biological" invention.

The fact that sex is a modern illusion, though, does not mean that it does not produce effects in practice. The naturalization of sex, precisely because it reifies a distinction that has no purely descriptive value, serves as an ideological justification for oppression. Christine Delphy (1991) effectively reminds us that sex, rather than a natural given, is a social relation, the reification of which as nature functions as powerful leverage for the justification of what otherwise shows its true nature as dire exploitation.

Such reification, which hides the inescapable epistemological contradiction of sex as both a naturalized bicategorization and a denaturalized social-historical relation, is all the more bewildering in view of its endurance over time—the empirical evidence pointing to the limited applicability of the concept to practice notwithstanding. Sandford (2011) resorts to Kant in trying to make sense of the persistence of the concept "sex." In Kant's philosophy, reason has no other way to think but through giving objective forms to ideas. This leads to hypostatization: in the case of sex, although it is an abstract idea, it appears as material, attached to anatomical difference, notably genitalia. Sandford goes one step further and claims that sex is not only a case of hypostatization but also one of sub-reption: that is, it conceals facts in order to sustain a misrepresentation. In Gregory Bateson's ([1958] 2003) vocabulary, with which I started this study, we are in the presence of a case of misplaced concreteness. Again, this does not mean that the idea of sex does not produce serious effects in practice. Yet we can investigate these effects only when we understand—and accept—that, appearances notwithstanding, sex is not a natural but a social phenomenon and thus open to changes through time (and space). A critical concept of sex, namely one that makes room to reflect political struggles, cannot remain alien to history: sex must be historicized.

Now, what happens to gender? Whereas sex tends to naturalize a dif-ferentiation between male and female that has no foundation in reality without remainder, gender presents such a differentiation as an opposition and, in addition, one of a hierarchical kind. Gender implies and necessi-tates men and women holding differential access to power. I do not suggest that gender provides yet another example of Kant's transcendental illu-sion, yet the case can be made that gender also needs to be historicized and "culturalized." Especially when accompanied by the pretension of univer-sal and timeless validity, gender becomes the illusion of Euro-American societies or of some liberational and academic movements within them at the very least.

Heterosexual men with limited access to power, such as the Shatila *shabāb*, find no comfortable space within gender discourses. They con-stitute matter out of place, noise in the stream of communication, and it comes as no surprise that they have become virtually invisible within the specialized and engaged literature on gender, prominently so in the literature on Middle Eastern societies. Although not intending to invite an overculturalist interpretation of sex and gender, I still consider it useful to recall what Clifford Geertz writes in *Negara*: "Impressed by command, we see little else" (1980, 121). Once we remove the (sometimes disempower-ing) blinkers of command and power, though, there is much more to see.

I have no intention, either, of reducing the socioeconomic-political-cultural complex of sex/gender to its linguistic dimension, but like the less than perfect match between Anglophones' *sex* and the French *sexe*, the Arabic term *jins* simultaneously and paradoxically means more and less than the Anglo-Saxon term *sex*.[34] As the English teacher from the Mar Elias camp told us at a certain point in this chapter, if *jins* can be translated as both "sex" and "gender," then it exhibits sufficient flexibility as a concept to accommodate both meanings. On this front, *jins* retains a similitude to what Fraisse argues for "*différence des sexes*," defined by her as a "philosopheme," which "implies the empirical recognition of the sexes without leading to any definition of content" (quoted in Sandford 2011, 24). Nonetheless, although "*différence des sexes*" obviously entails difference—a difference that in the case of "sex" has been upgraded to an opposition and implies a hierarchy when it comes to "gender"—in Arabic this semantic universe is organized differently. *Jins* sets in relief what members of the same category have in common rather than what differentiates them from members of another category. At first glance, the Arabic term *jins*—admitting renditions into English as "sex," "gender," "race," "class" and "nation"[35]—makes transparent what gender theorists have been taking pains to argue for quite some time under the label *intersectionality*: that "sex" and "gender" are raced, "classed," and nationalized. At a second and more careful take, however, the term *jins* does more and also calls attention to what is lost in much of what has been written under the label *gender theories* in the past few decades: its emphasis is on the similarities and belonging-together among those pertaining to the same kind rather than on the opposition between those and others or on the eventual hierarchy established among them.

34. Afsaneh Najmabadi (2013) engages in a similar exercise, mapping out the reconfigurations during the late nineteenth and twentieth centuries of the biomedical knowledge and marital practices through which in Persian *jins* came to mean "sex."

35. Albeit increasingly less often, *gender* also originally had the sense of "type" in several European languages, keeping its meaning closer to its Latin roots. In the case of modern Arabic, it should be remarked for the sake of the fairness of the argument that "race" is increasingly referred to by native speakers as *'unṣur*, "class" as *ṭabaqa*, and "nation" as *waṭan* (although "nationality," *jinsiyya*, as well as "nationalization" or "political categorization," *tajnīs*, retain the relation to *jins*). It remains the case, however, that *jins* is used indistinguishably for "sex" and "gender," the latter admitting no obvious rendition into Arabic, a point further explored in chapter 5.

The root of the word *jins, j, n, s,* is used for the construction of verbs, which allows for various translations into English, depending on the form (*wazin*)[36] adopted—all of them, however, emphasizing similitude. According to *The Hans Wehr Dictionary,* the verb *jannasa* means in form 2 "to make alike, to assimilate, to naturalize, to class, to classify, to categorize"; in form 3, "to be akin, related, similar and of the same kind or nature, or to resemble"; in form 5, "to acquire citizenship or to be naturalized"; and finally in form 6, "to be akin or homogenous." Other derivatives of the same root, *j, n, s,* are also telling because of the same emphasis on what is similar: *tajnīs* means "naturalization"; *mujānasa,* "relatedness," "kinship," "affinity," "likeness," and "resemblance"; *tajānus,* "homogeneity"; and *'istijnās,* "homosexuality."

If *jins* can indeed work as a philosopheme, without any prior and mandatory definition of content, as I argue here, this does not mean just that the sex–gender complex needs to be raced and "classed." Open to resignification in space and time, *jins* also needs to be "culturalized" and historicized, which implies and mandates both an ethnography and a history. As Ahmad, the accountant we met earlier, once confided to me when reflecting somewhat nostalgically on how his own life was different from that led by the *fidā'iyyīn*: "I remember the *fidā'iyyīn* so clearly. They were all-powerful, walking in the alleys of the camp with their guns. We so much wanted to be like them. They were like Conan [the Barbarian]." Times are in flux and have shifted, however, so the moment may have come to change the beat.

---

36. From a root normally composed of three letters, Arabic derives—through the root's transformation by the apposition of prefixes, the intercalation of long vowels, or the utilization of different diacritics—up to ten different verbal forms, with changes in meaning. A good example—because it is faulty in just one form, normally referred to as form 9—is provided by the verb *qaṭaʿa,* "to cut" in form 1, which when transformed through the recourse to prefixes, long vowels, or diacritics can come to mean "to chop up" (*qaṭṭaʿa,* form 2); "to cut off" (*qāṭaʿa,* form 3); "to divide up" (land, for example) (*'aqṭaʿa,* form 4); "to be chopped up" (*taqaṭṭaʿa,* form 5); "to intersect" (*taqāṭaʿa,* form 6); "to be cut off" (*'inqaṭaʿa,* form 7); "to take a cut of" (*'iqtaṭaʿa,* form 8); and "to deduct" (*'istaqṭaʿa,* form 10).

4

Pororoca, Thinking through Music

Fidā'iyyīn and *Shabāb* Talk
(Sometimes) Past Each Other

Pororoca

The natural phenomenon known as "pororoca" has always interested and amazed me. Meaning "a loud roar" in Tupi, a language formerly spoken by indigenous communities in my native Brazil, "pororoca" is the name given to the tidal bore that occurs when very high sea tides rush up the Amazon River. It can last for up to an hour and a half and advance fifty kilometers (thirty-one miles) upstream, at a speed of thirty kilometers (nineteen miles) per hour, sometimes even inverting the river current and creating waves four meters (thirteen feet) high. Its violence uproots trees along the riverbanks, but that does not deter a handful of intrepid surfers, who have learned not to struggle against the water's movements, from surfing the pororoca. The pororoca eventually subsides, and the river regains its normal flow, but, depending on the time of the year, when the sea tide rises again in a twelve-hour interval, the phenomenon recurs.

To what extent can the pororoca function as a "meta for" (M. Bateson 1987)[1] to bring intelligibility to the interactions of challenge and acceptance between the Shatila *shabāb* and their forebears, the *fidā'iyyīn*? Can the fast curves made by those few brave surfers, who have mastered

---

1. On the concept, borrowed from Gregory Bateson, that the "syllogisms of metaphor" enable insight through analogy, see the introduction.

8. Palestinian rhapsody: searching for freedom under constraint. The members of the rap band Katibe 5. Photograph by and reproduced with permission by Laura Boushnak.

enough understanding of the pororoca to be able to navigate it, work as a "meta for" for my own journey in and through Shatila?

Here I use ethnographic evidence from workshops held with Palestinians from different generations to investigate how *shabāb* and *fidā'iyyīn* talk to each other—and sometimes *past* each other. During the workshops, participants were invited to listen to two songs—a nationalist piece of music from the 1980s and a recent rap song by a Palestinian band—and express their views about each. What emerged from the workshops show the different ways *shabāb* and *fidā'iyyīn* not only relate to Palestine but also frame their gendered subjectivities. Whereas the *fidā'iyyīn* preserve the ideology of the return and claim a place for themselves as men in the fight to reconquer the motherland, the *shabāb* opt for a more subtle relation to Palestine as a cause combined with another preoccupation: the need to cope with the dire conditions of life in Lebanon, where they cannot own property and have limited access to the labor market. Through rap, I sustain, the *shabāb* find a medium to speak about what is otherwise silenced: namely, the fact that the enduring demands for the return have to be combined with more immediate urgencies in Lebanon. Therefore, rap songs are not infrapolitical: they point to other ways of being political.

Some Music

I had barely finished playing Katibe 5's rap "Ahlān fīk bil-mukhayyamāt" (Welcome to the Camps) to a group of men ages thirty and older on a sunny afternoon of October 2009 in al-Bass camp, southern Lebanon, when the criticisms came ricocheting in.

"What kind of mind game are you attempting with us here? First [when I played the song "Romana" by Samih Shokair from the 1980s], you make us feel all nostalgic, only then to take us along a completely different path and make us feel awful with this new song. You took us to paradise and then pushed us into hell! This new music makes me feel frustrated. The lyrics are wrong and unrealistic," a forty-year-old al-Bass resident admonished.

A fifty-year-old Palestinian from the Rashidiyya camp, also in southern Lebanon, concurred: "This music ["Ahlān fīk bil-mukhayyamāt"] is exaggerated and false. The singers are taking advantage of people's suffering. They take us away from the right of return, from liberation, and from the new Palestinian state. We accept that we live in the camps so as to strengthen the right to return."

A neighbor of the latter, age forty-four, was even more vehement: "This can only be the work of the Israeli Mossad. Pay attention to the words, listen to the rhythm: this music is Zionist all over. It insults us and our people and bears no relation to the reality of the camps. The *thawra* [revolution] will remain until the last Palestinian generation, even after a thousand years have passed. The Palestinian cause [*al-qaḍiyya al-filasṭīniyya*] is handed down from one generation to the next. This song doesn't call for the revolution and transforms our leadership into pirates."

The previous session held that morning, during which another group of Palestinian refugees was proposed exactly the same activity, had not prepared me for such a strong reaction. The morning meeting went much more smoothly, and participants did not attack the rap as pointless,

Zionist, or, even more seriously, Mossad inspired. The "methodological bliss" I had experienced when organizing the workshops ultimately proved ephemeral.

While setting up the workshop, I faced obstacles from the very outset. To begin with, I thought of organizing the activity through an NGO with a branch in Shatila. The director of this branch, after listening carefully to what I had in mind—inviting Palestinian refugees divided into two distinct groups, one composed of people up to twenty-nine years old and the other of people ages thirty and older, to listen to a song from the *thawra* period and a present-day rap and then to express their views on both—suggested I speak to the president of the organization. For his part, the president also paid thorough attention to what I was proposing and yet was not precisely forthcoming: "Why Palestinian rap? You could very well play Zamzam, which is also contemporary and won't invite too strong a reaction." Zamzam is a singer from the Burj al-Barajneh camp, near Shatila, who reworks old Palestinian songs and presents them in a new guise. I attended one of his shows in Shatila: he was accompanied by a group of young dancers, the girls dressed in traditional gowns (*'athwāb*) and the boys performing vigorous *dabka*, a folk dance from the Levant. But I turned down the NGO president's suggestion: in fact, it was precisely the strong reaction that I was after.

With my hopes of effectively conducting the workshop increasingly dashed, I shared my frustration with some of my Shatila *shabāb* friends. They volunteered to step in. I confess I had to overcome my initial suspicion regarding their organizational skills. In the end, though, co-organizing the workshop with Shatila *shabāb* was the "best methodological decision ever happened"—if I am allowed to make my own an expression that they so often used in deliberately broken English. As if aware of my initial doubts, they suggested that we hold pilot sessions with participants from the camps in southern Lebanon prior to the one scheduled in Shatila. We all rapidly settled on Katibe 5's "Ahlān fīk bil-mukhayyamāt" as the rap song we would use. The song depicts the lives Palestinians lead in the camps today, with all their predicaments: unhealthy living conditions; the dearth of social services; skyrocketing unemployment; and frequent migration attempts. It took us some time to track down Shokair's song

"Romana" (Grenade). Shokair's marchlike composition portrays Palestinian efforts to resist the Israeli invasion of Lebanon in 1982 and subsequent
siege of West Beirut, which culminated in the departure of Arafat and the
fidā'iyyīn from the country. After some discussion, we all decided to "go
for it"—again to make use of an expression that the *shabāb* like.

They provided me the lyrics of both songs, and we worked on their
respective translations into English. I did some editing, and here is the
result of our combined efforts:

Romana (Grenade)   رمانة

Romana . . . romana on my waist[2]   رمانة . . . رمانة ع خصري
And a Kalashnikov in my hand   وكلاشينكوف بإيدي
And the world is on fire (2)   ودنيي شعلانة (2)
Their planes bring tons of death   وطياراتن ترمي الموت
Upon us, and we weren't rescued (2)   أطنانه علينا ترمي والعون ما جانا (2)

We fought back as much as we could   ردينا يللي بينردّ
We fought tanks with guns   وقابلنا المدفع بالفرد
Oh Beirut, witness that . . .   اشهدي يا بيروت علينا

If you asked the south[3]   لو تسأل الجنوب
How many fighters it saw   شو شاف طوابير وعسكر
If you asked Shakif[4]   لو تسأل الشقيف
How many attacks and air raids tried to   كم هجمة وغارة تتكسر (2)
    destroy it (2)
Ask Saida and Tyre and Khaldeh[5]   واسأل صيدا وصور وخلدة
If they remember the defying   بتذكر وقفات التحدي (2)
    challenges (2)
We called, and no one replied   وصوت ينادي وما في حد

2. In the lyrics of "Romana" and "Ahlān fīk bil-mukhayyamāt," ellipses indicate
pauses rather than omissions of text. The number (2) inserted in "Romana" indicates that
the line is repeated twice.

3. South: south of Lebanon.

4. Shakif: a historical castle in Saida, a city south of Beirut.

5. Saida, Tyre, and Khaldeh: Lebanese cities south of Beirut.

So we fought with knives and hands
Oh Beirut, witness that . . .

نقاتل بالخنجر واليد
اشهدي يا بيروت علينا

We were besieged in Beirut
The fear became bigger, but we were
    stronger than death,
While everything around us was
    exploding (2)
And when we left Beirut by sea,
Your tears, Beirut, covered us (2)
We said good-bye to Beirut
And promised to return the favor
Oh Beirut, witness that . . .

تحاصرنا ببيروت
كبر الهم وكنّا أكبر
من عصفات الموت
وكل شي حولينا يتفجر (2)
ولما طلعنا بالسفينة
دموعك بيروت تغطينا (2)
ودعناكي وقلنا عهد
نردّ جميلك هذا وعد
اشهدي يا بيروت علينا

Welcome to the Camps

أهلا فيك بالمخيمات

For the lads who have had enough of
    life and of filling in emptiness
For a wall stands still in the camp
    holding memories
When the last cent comes in, it'll be
    stolen by NGOs
They transformed their offices into
    political organizations
To the point of witnessing the
    destruction of everything in
    which we believe
The leader's photo remains standing
    alone . . .
The meat is given only to those who
    carry slogans
Officials keep lying to us

لشباب زهقوا الحياة عمال بيعبوا فراغات،
لحيط صامد بالمخيم هادا للذكريات،
واخر قرش بيجي بتسرقوا الجمعيات،
غيروا المكاتب، بس عشكل التنظيمات،
لوقت منشوف كل شي عم يدمر منحارب عشانو،
صورة الزعيم بتضلها صامدة لحالا . . .
واللحمة ما تتوزع إلا للعم يحملوا لافتات،
وبعدن عم يضحكوا علينا صحاب البدلات،

Enough with the nationalist songs,
    khalas, let's play the beat
Souls and ghosts of the dead remain in
    the air

خلصت الأغاني الوطنية خلص دقوا البيت،
أشباح وأرواح الميتين بعدن فلتانين،

Some people have already forgotten,
and some people still remember
في ناس خلص نسيوا، وناس بعدن متذكرين،

Some martyrs' photos are erased, but
more are coming on their way
في صور شهدا انمحت وفي صور تاني جايين،

While all the militants have slept, the
Kalashnikovs remain
كل المناضلين ناموا، بقيوا الكلشنات،

Poems written on the wall and the
remains of bullets
شعر عالحيطان وبقايا رصاصات،

For the lads who have had enough of
visiting the embassies
لشباب كتير ملّت من الروحة عالسفارات،

For the homes built on slopes
لبيوت كتير زهقت من كتر الإنحدارات،

Tomorrow a new overpass will be built,
and before it [plenty of] buildings
بكرا يبينوا جسر، وقبلا عمارات،

Behind all the ugly clouds, the leader's
photo will remain standing alone . . .
ورا كل الغيم البشع صورة الزعيم بتضلها
صامدة لحالا . . .

Welcome, bro, to the camps (welcome)
أهلا فيك أخوي بالمخيمات (أهلا)

Welcome, bro, to the camps (welcome)
أهلا فيك أخوي بالمخيمات (أهلا)

We saw the roofs in the camp, we saw
them devout
شفنا سطوح المخيم، شفناها إنو خاشعة،

Because my country's flags fly above
them
لأنو أعلام بلادي عم بترفرف فوق عليها،

The soul of the biggest cause resides in
the smallest alley
نفس أكبر قضية بأصغر زاروبة فيها،

The small boy calls the pigeon flying in
the sky
حمام بالسما وطفل عمال يناديها،

People in the camps are deprived by God
أكتر ناسها بالحرمان الله باليها،

A man fights with his wife and then
makes it up to her
رجل يتعارك مع مرتو بعدين يراضيها،

Moms curse their children but still
make sacrifices for them
أمهات تدعي على أبنائها أرواحها تعطيها،

A student studies hard to please his mom

طالب يدرس عشان إمو يحاول يرضيها،

A painter draws the map of his country
and its lands

فنان يرسم خريطة بلادو وأراضيها،

A girl and her beloved are hiding amid
the destruction

بنت وعشيقها بالخراب يقوم يخفيها،

A guy turns up the music

شاب لآخر حد بيعلي الموسيقى،

And turns it off during the prayers, our
youth are lost

وعند الآذان يطفيها، شباب ضايع،

They fight if people curse their country

اذا شُتم وطنهم قلبوا عاليها واطيها،

An old man telling stories of his
country to his grandchild

عجوز يروي لحفيدو بلادو بحكاييها،

He smiles at the good memories, and
then a tear follows the smile

يضحك لذكرى شقية والدمعة تتليها،

Beautiful houses with no colors
covering them

بيوت جميلة بلا ألوان تغطيها،

One warm sun, and Palestine remains
it all

شمس دافئة واحدة، وفلسطين تبقيها

Welcome, bro, to the camps (welcome)

أهلا فيك أخوي بالمخيمات (أهلا)

Welcome, bro, to the camps (welcome)

أهلا فيك أخوي بالمخيمات (أهلا)

A dwelling with no roof, going backward

مسكن بلا سقف، تقدم إلى الخلف،

Walls of adverts, War of the Camps

حيطان إعلانات، حرب المخيمات،

Buildings have been destroyed by many
bullets

بنايات مهدومة من كتر الطلقات،

Roads are like mazes full of insects

طرقاتها متاهات مليانة حشرات،

The sky is like heaven

سماها جنة، مجموعة بالكشات،

All dead bodies are gathered in one
cemetery

بمقبرة وحدة إحتشدت الوفيات،

God bless their souls	برحمتك الله إرحم الأموات،
They hang onto the UN, OK, then collect their aid	متمسكين باليو- أن، طب إجمع الإعاشات،
No one can hear their screams inside	ما حدا سامع بالداخل صرخات،
In the hospital, wait for death in death's hall	بالمستشفى انتظر الموت بقاعة الأموات،
So decide between the people of beards and the people of slogans	إختار بين جماعة اللحي أو الشعارات،
From now until the time of return . . .	من هلأ لموعد العودة عقبال الآذان . . .

Welcome, bro, to the camps (welcome)	أهلا فيك أخوي بالمخيمات (أهلا)
Welcome, bro, to the camps (welcome)	أهلا فيك أخوي بالمخيمات (أهلا)

Look, the camp I'm living in is still resisting alone	ليك، بالمخيم الأنا في بعدو صامد لحالو،
Its form has changed, but its struggle is the same	إتغيرت أشكالو بس باقي نضالو،
On the wall there are obituaries of ordinary people	عالحيطان في ورق نعوة لناس عاديين،
The memory of Palestine, the remains of militants	ذكرى فلسطين، بقايا مناضلين،
Look at the sky, and you'll see the electricity wires	إطّلع عالسما شرطان كهرابا،
If you didn't steal from them, how could you see? How?!	اذا ما سرقت خط، كيف بدك تشوفو؟ كيف؟!

Ceilings are going to fall on the heads of their owners	عروس صحابا، رح توقع السقوفي،
Water, stop flooding from underground	يا ميّ من تحت الأرض ما عاش إطوفي،

Lads are drowning in unemployment	الشباب غرقانين بالبطالة بالعطالة،

There's no work, there's no money, children are without education	فش شغل، فش مصاري، الولاد بلا دراسة،
God bless UNRWA, we vote for it for presidency	الله يخليلنا الأونروا عالرئاسة،
They solve our problems with Panadol from their clinics	بيحلّو مشاكلنا بحبة بانادول من العيادة . . .
Welcome, bro, to the camps (welcome)	أهلا فيك أخوي بالمخيمات (أهلا)
Welcome, bro, to the camps (welcome)	أهلا فيك أخوي بالمخيمات (أهلا)

Equipped with the music, we discussed the format of the workshop, and the *shabāb* agreed with my proposal to divide participants into two age groups: younger than thirty, thirty and older. Each group would be invited to listen to "Romana" and "Ahlān fīk" and then have an initial discussion among its members, with the groups still separated, and then finally the two groups would be brought together for a joint discussion. We used the *shabāb*'s networks and my own to find venues for the workshop in the al-Bass camp in southern Lebanon and in Shatila. As far as attendance was concerned, their networks were of course infinitely superior to mine. Moreover, we decided that they conduct the activity and take notes. When the day of the workshop in al-Bass finally arrived, after I introduced myself and my research to the participants, it was obvious there was no other major role for me to play. I just sat on the margins and observed. Never for a second did I anticipate that being on the margins and undertaking *nonparticipant* observation could be so rewarding.

The session on that pleasant October morning in al-Bass was lively. The twenty-three participants of the two groups—men and women between sixteen and seventy years old—engaged with the proposed activity. The younger cohort admitted to being unmoved by "Romana": a sixteen-year-old girl from al-Bass even confessed that she had previously thought "Romana" was the name of a village in Palestine. Several acknowledged the lack of information about events of the revolutionary past, and a young woman age twenty-seven stated that she did not understand what conflict really meant until the July War of 2006. Some admired the sense of pride (*fakhr*) that, together with rage (*ghaḍab*), they identified in the song, different from more recent lyrics, which, the same twenty-seven-year-old woman commented, were all about imploring and begging (*'istijdā'*). Having remarked on the political unity characteristic of times gone by, they deplored current Palestinian schisms. "Ahlān fīk," however, immediately engaged this younger audience. "It expresses the lives we lead," one of the members commented, to which another added, "The beat captivates me. And we need space to breath."

As might have been anticipated, it was "Romana" that enthralled the older group, nostalgic about what they defined as the "the enthusiasm of the struggle." They regretted the failure to pass on the "meaning of the fighting" to their offspring, who "are too busy, trying to move on with their lives under the extreme conditions of the camps today." A fifty-four-year-old man sighed: "Oh, all these memories. I feel like putting on my uniform again." This sentiment was seconded by the forty-two-year-old man seated next to him, who asserted, "We loved the struggle, unlike the present generation."

In contrast, "Ahlān fīk" sparked controversy among older participants. Their frustration centered on what they described as the song's lack of revolutionary content and supposed "chilling" effect. They blamed themselves for having failed to properly transfer the *thawra* heritage to the youngsters. Nevertheless, some common ground existed between the two age groups, with the elders opting to turn a deaf ear to some of the remarks made by the younger participants, saying that they simply cannot be moved by "Romana," like their parents, who "lived the Palestinian cause [*al-qaḍiyya al-filasṭīniyya*] and the resistance [*al-muqāwama*] in all their intensity," while today's youth have been reduced to "lives of refugees in overcrowded camps, with no electricity and increasing unemployment." Gradually, the older age set adopted a patronizing attitude toward the younger: as a fifty-five-year-old said, "We need to solve the problems challenging the youth today."

In the momentous afternoon session, however, I detected no sign of self-assigned responsibility or deaf ears to the remarks of the youngsters or patronizing attitudes. Instead, the clash between the two age sets assumed full gear.[6] An outspoken twenty-two-year-old from Rashidiyya took the floor after listening attentively to "Romana": "We're all singing for the revolution like those people who sing for the past and long-dead poets.[. . .] We need to start looking forward instead of commemorating forever the victories of the past." He was seconded by a nineteen-year-old, also from Rashidiyya: "How can we continue to have faith in the cause when they [the *fidā'iyyīn*] left Lebanon?" A twenty-year-old from Burj al-Shemali, another camp in southern Lebanon, added: "This song only talks about weapons. What we need now are new ideas for the *thawra* to move forward."

The lyrics of "Ahlān fīk" just deepened their convictions. A twenty-four-year-old from al-Bass set the tone for the discussion: "You see, what this music shows are the outcomes of the *thawra*'s failures. Up to now, we pay the costs for the previous generation's mistakes. What they've left us with, in the end, is suffering, deprivation of civil rights, humiliation [*khunū'*], and subjection [*khuḍū'*]." The remarks by the same twenty-year-old from Burj al-Shemali quoted in the previous paragraph were almost pitiless: "Let's just face it; the *thawra* has come to an end in the camps in Lebanon."

Thus, it should not have come as a surprise that the later discussion involving both age sets verged on open confrontation, forcing the Shatila *shabāb* to exercise their diplomatic skills. This is a sample of how the debate went:

AL-BASS RESIDENT, FORTY-EIGHT: Rap came out of the gangs in America. The youth of today, they're rapping to make fun of our heritage.[. . .] Rap is stupid; it's for beggars. I'd kill my son if he listened to that in my house.

6. Two differences distinguished the afternoon gathering from the one held in the morning. First, among the twenty-two participants, eight were from Rashidiyya, and in the morning there was only one participant who traveled the several kilometers separating Rashidiyya—farther to the south, closer to Palestine, and historically a PLO/Fatah stronghold—from al-Bass. Word-of-mouth notice about the workshop, I gather, quickly reached Rashidiyya: this explains the high turnout of Rashidiyya residents in the afternoon. Second, all of the participants in the afternoon were male.

AL-BASS RESIDENT, TWENTY-FOUR: Life isn't static. Things change, so the styles used to express oneself also change. Of course, the reality we live affects the style in which we express ourselves.

AL-BASS RESIDENT, TWENTY-TWO: We aren't canceling out the traditions [*turāth*] through rap. We're simply trying to express our current economic and social problems [. . .] through a modern style.

AL-BASS RESIDENT, TWENTY-FOUR: [. . .] And let me ask, What has the Palestinian *thawra* given us?[. . .]

AL-BASS RESIDENT, FORTY-EIGHT: The *thawra* gave a lot to us Palestinian people.[. . .] The *thawra* has turned us from scattered populations into a people with representation. We are even represented in the United Nations, and there has been some delineation of borders in the West Bank and Gaza. If we're here, it's because of the *thawra*. We have a sense of identity in spite of what the world wants. The youth should complete what we achieved before them.

AL-BASS RESIDENT, FORTY: [Addressing himself to the younger cohort] You should read the lyrics of "Romana" and try to understand the history of the revolution. The fact that the *fidā'iyyīn* left [Lebanon] was an honor and not a defeat. There are several reasons why we left Beirut. The youth doesn't know the history of the Palestinian revolution.

RASHIDIYYA RESIDENT, THIRTY-NINE: [Also addressing the younger cohort] You're an extension of the revolution.

RASHIDIYYA RESIDENT, FORTY-ONE: The PLO gave us a sense of identity. That's why the Palestinian cause [*al-qaḍiyya al-filasṭīniyya*] is very much alive.

BURJ AL-SHEMALI RESIDENT, TWENTY: (Ironically) Which great Palestinian cause [*qaḍiyya filasṭīniyya*] are you talking about? I can't even get an education![. . .]

AL-BASS RESIDENT, TWENTY-FOUR: [Addressing the older cohort] [. . .] I ask you back: Which party has given us the chance to do or say anything?

AL-BASS RESIDENT, FORTY-EIGHT: [Addressing the younger cohort] Please, do not kill the revolution and the martyrs [*al-shuhadā'*] twice. We have a cause [*qaḍiyya*], so don't defend rap and tell me it's a natural evolution. Please, don't kill our heritage![. . .]

AL-BASS RESIDENT, FORTY: What now, music is for dancing?! Young people [. . .] don't understand the revolution.

RASHIDIYYA RESIDENT, FORTY-ONE: And yet they [the youth] have a role to play, which is to maintain the struggle and our heritage and to preserve our identity.

In comparison, the session we held in Shatila some two weeks later—with ten participants, all male,[7] their ages ranging between fourteen and eighty—was almost anticlimactic. Indeed, politics does not live on dissent only. The younger cohort expressed a certain sense of pride (*fakhr*) in "Romana": "It encourages us to remain steadfast [*ṣāmidīn*] and to go on with the struggle [*al-niḍāl*]," one twenty-two-year-old volunteered, though adding immediately: "We simply cannot compare the past to today. 'Romana' even displays some sweetness because of the sense of pride we felt back then. But today it's as though we are subservient [*dhalīl*]." A seventeen-year-old concurred: "The very thinking about the struggle has changed because of the sorrow [*'asaf*] we feel." And an eighteen-year-old spoke thus: "In the past, there was the struggle and power [*quwwa*], while today people need to go after foreign aid. We forgot the right of return." "Ahlān fīk" confirmed their convictions, as the words of a seventeen-year-old capture: "You see, that's what we mean. We forgot the cause [*al-qaḍiyya*] because everyone wants the support [provided by NGOs]." He continued: "We're going backwards, aren't we? Yesterday, we could still do something, and today we simply can't."

"Romana" put our older cohort in a nostalgic mood, and yet this did not imperil the dialogue with the younger set scheduled immediately after the two groups met separately. A sixty-two-year-old triggered the discussion: "Together with the Kalashnikov, the *romana* [grenade] was the symbol of the *thawra*. I guess our community here today cannot even understand the words in this song.[. . .] The real problem is that we don't

7. I can only speculate as to why, contrary to my aims, women did not show up for the session in Shatila. One reason may have been that the workshop was organized by Shatila *shabāb*: among us, the organizers, there was just one half-Palestinian woman, but not a resident of Shatila. Another possible reason was the fact that I decided *not* to hold the workshop through the local NGO that I had initially approached for the purpose. The NGO may have discouraged participation among its own constituency, mainly female.

actually like each other in this camp. The Palestinian schism is every-where: [. . .] here in Shatila we have three different popular committees. Even within the camp, we're separated, and it wasn't like that in the past." A thirty-three-year-old echoed that opinion: "It was the Palestinian par-ties who destroyed Shatila.[. . .] The war on us today involves a different tactic: they try to starve us so that we need to seek bread and medicine. In the meantime, al-Aqsa [the mosque in Jerusalem] remains under siege, and we in the camp are asleep."

The analysis of "Ahlān fīk" by the older group translated a degree of disapproval toward the younger cohort, and yet, once again, this did not jeopardize the exchange between the two age sets in Shatila. The same sixty-two-year-old man initiated the debate: "I just wish that those guys who are singing would implement what they're saying. You see, they talk about steadfastness [ṣumūd], but they're the first ones queuing up at the embassy gates. They criticize the organizations, but they're members of them." A forty-five-year-old considered the depiction of the camps in the rap song to be accurate: "The issues mentioned portray the reality in the camps. But they have been like this for a while.[. . .] The Palestin-ian parties, through their popular committees, brought the mafias into the camp."

Once the two groups were brought together, the information flow between them continued and did not lead to a clash. This is how the debate proceeded:

SEVENTEEN-YEAR-OLD: If they [the older cohort] object to the rap song because it isn't pragmatic, I'd agree that's true. But we have to shed light on the problems of the camp and the level of corruption before we can do something about it.

TWENTY-TWO-YEAR-OLD: You see, these days you find thousands of parties—Hamas, Fatah, Jihad—and nongovernmental organizations. But we can ask: What do they really do [. . .] to find solutions to our problems?

TWENTY-TWO-YEAR-OLD: Some people from the previous generation try to [. . .] marginalize us. They never allow us to play any role.

FORTY-FIVE-YEAR-OLD: It is true that some older people from Sha-tila disregard the needs and contributions of the youth. We back the reform called for in the rap song. So young people should impose themselves on the parties.

With the stature of his eighty years, the eldest of our participants finally spoke. It was his only intervention, but enough to put an end to the debate: "Some corrupt people gained control of the camp. And we call upon the youth to participate in the camp's reform. Some elders mock the younger. But in reality we're tired and need the younger to participate in the reform of Shatila. We want Shatila to become better with the young of this camp. We want the young to intervene and promote change."

If the caesurae of certain regimes of authority may require the death of a father, commonly intertwined with the figure of the leader (Borneman 2004, 2007; Hammoudi 1997; Sawaf 2013), in Shatila—local leaders and NGO presidents patently excluded—there seems to be little will to resuscitate him, particularly among several of the *shabāb*.

Appalled by the systematic neglect with which gender studies have traditionally treated age—as if what is known as patriarchy were only about the relation between men and women and seldom about that between seniors and juniors[8]—I seriously engage with the latter in subsequent sections. Just as I have demonstrated in the previous chapter that "gender" falls short as a heuristic tool to make sense of today's *shabāb* biographies, here I look to show that neither "youth" nor "generation" leads us onto firmer analytical ground. Indeed, the *fidā'iyyīn* constituted a "generation"—because

---

8. Although recognizing that patriarchy is indeed also about relations between seniors and juniors (sometimes of the same sex) and thus not just about those between men and women, one of the main scholars of kinship and families in Lebanon, Suad Joseph, focuses most of her ethnographic investigation on hierarchical connective relations between the sexes—husbands and wives (Joseph 1993a, 2004), brothers and sisters (Joseph 1993b, 1994), and mothers and sons (Joseph 1999b)—rather than on same-sex relations. In this chapter, I focus mostly—though by no means solely—on relations between fathers and sons.

they shared the "drama of their youth" (Manheim 1952, 301)—and were immortalized in it by a hundred accounts, ethnographic and otherwise (Chesnot and Lama 1998; Kanafani 2005, 2008; R. Sayigh 1979). The Shatila *shabāb*, for their part, do not fit comfortably into either category: "youth" or "generation." Their lives expose not only the frail foundations of the all-too-facile clichés about the "clash of generations" but also invite us to catch a glimpse of the heuristic limits of the increasingly popular category "youth." I take up the task of developing such an argument by first showing how and why nationalistic songs have ceased to "capture"—in the multiple senses of "to record," "to catch," and "to control"—the *shabāb*'s political imaginations.

Lords of the Palestinian Marches

Upon listening to the first lines of "Romana," fifty-five-year-old Abu Hassan shared a generous smile: "Even in the worst misery, one should seek for ways to continue with one's life. This song stirred in us the desire to continue fighting.[. . .] This song reminds me of my war and my enemy, who wants to distance me from my roots.[. . .] Revolutionary songs gave us the strength to survive and stay firm."[9]

His son, twenty-one-year-old Hassan, concurred: "This song talks about the departure of the *thawra* from Lebanon in '82. All these revolutionary songs give you the power to stay put, the motivation for the battlefield." He searched for a more recent context to illustrate his thoughts: "The same happens in Gaza today. Different from here, there the *thawra* goes on."

This father and son spoke in a Palestinian dialect. They were originally from the Nahr al-Barid camp, whose inhabitants spoke a version of Arabic closer to the one used in Palestine because the camp was more isolated than others in Lebanon. In 2007, following the destruction of Nahr

9. I name this section after Michael Gilsenan's book *Lords of the Lebanese Marches* (1996).

al-Barid by the Lebanese army fighting a group of Fatah al-Islam militants who had infiltrated the camp, Abu Hassan and Hassan moved to Shatila. They described the event as a new *nakba* (catastrophe).

The first notes of "Ahlān fīk bil-mukhayyamāt" precipitated yet another smile: this time Hassan's. He immediately identified the music: "I know this one. It's by Katibe 5, right? I have other songs like this one on my mobile."

Abu Hassan did not condemn his son's musical tastes: "These kinds of songs, they tell about what's going on with us now. It isn't only about fighting the enemy anymore; it's also about an inner fight. This music criticizes those responsible for the situation we find ourselves in now. [. . .] We need responsible leaders [*qāda*], ready to sacrifice [*bitdaḥḥī*] and give [*ta'ṭī*] and who care [*tahtamm*]. You know what? I'm with these guys [the rappers]."

This conversation happened when I interviewed father and son together. Previously, I had spoken with each separately. These interviews were one of the research activities I conducted. Including Abu Hassan and Hassan, I interviewed sixteen pairs of parent and child to collect their life stories and views on certain events and concepts based on a list of words proposed to them: twelve father–son pairs, one father–daughter pair, two mother–son pairs, and one set of a mother and two daughters. All of the parents were former fighters. All were Shatila residents, with three exceptions: two pairs were middle-class Palestinians living outside the camp, and one pair lived at the Gaza Hospital in the immediate vicinity of Shatila. When I paired parent and child, I prompted them to express their views on "Romana" and "Ahlān fīk bil-mukhayyamāt" as well as on the following names, words, and phrases: "Nakba" (Catastrophe); "Filasṭīn" (Palestine); "'Isrā'īl" (Israel); "Lubnān" (Lebanon); *al-mukhayyamāt al-filasṭīniyya* (the Palestinian camps); "Shātīlā" (Shatila); *fallāḥīn* (peasants); *fidā'iyyīn* (freedom fighters); *'ayyām al-thawra* (days of the revolution); "Ḥarb al-Mukhayyamāt" (War of the Camps); *zawāj* (marriage); *ta'līm* (education); *shughul* (work); *hijra* (migration); *dīn* (religion); *al-kabar ka-zalamī* (growing up as a man); *al-kabar ka-marā* (growing up as a woman); *'ummahāt* (mothers); *'ikhwāt* (sisters); *banāt* (daughters); *bayyāt* (fathers); *'ikhwa* (brothers); *'awlād* (sons); *al-'ajyāl al-mādiya* (past generations) and *jīl al-yawm* (the present generation). My initial worries about a certain "artificiality" in prodding participants with these words proved short-lived: on several occasions, the words set off a lively dialogue between father or mother and son or daughter that frequently moved in unexpected directions, with the researcher merely observing the interaction and contributing only when necessary to keep the conversation going. Again, *nonparticipant* observation proved epistemologically rewarding and experientially gratifying.

o o o

Studying what Jean-Jacques Nattiez calls the "total musical fact" (2004, 55, my translation) implies a semantics. Indeed, as appropriated by members of the group being researched, songs not only point to the syntax of relations between elements of musical nature but also expose the enveloping context. If songs acquire meanings in this way, there needs to be a reason, nonetheless, why people opt to say certain things by singing them.

In the case of the "Palestinian marches," Joseph Massad (2003) shows how their lyrics responded closely to the evolving exigencies of the nationalist struggle. Thus, the confidence that Arab unity—especially as expressed in the Nassirist revolution and in Abd al-Wahhab's martial hymns—would carry on the struggle for the Palestinian right of return in the 1950s was later replaced by despair with the defeat of 1967, which would set the tone for the often lachrymose laments by the Rahbani brothers and Fayrouz for the land beyond reach and then again by the renewed hope aroused by the *fidā'iyyīn*'s actions inside and outside Lebanon from the 1970s on. While Fayrouz nostalgically sings of migrating birds that can fly back to Palestine in "Sanarjiʿu yawman" (We Will Return One Day),[10] songs celebrating the Palestinian militia's deeds assume a more defiant tone. As a rule and as was evident in Egypt and Lebanon, only songs not deemed to be too threatening to a regime's interests would be

---

10. The Shatila *shabāb* of today, rather than simply lamenting their lack of freedom compared to the kind enjoyed by birds, play with the latter—and, I would add, also partake in some measure in the birds' freedom. This is one of the subjects of the next chapter.

broadcast by national TV and radio stations, showing the respective state's (qualified) support for the Palestinian cause. If the PLO allowed more leeway for composers, it also ensured that lyrics remained faithful to certain canons and a certain ideology. After its expulsion from Jordan in 1971 and relocation to Lebanon, the PLO established its own radio station: Sawt Filastin Sawt al-Thawra al-Filastiniyya (Palestinian Voice, Voice of the Palestinian Revolution). A group associated with Fatah and created in 1969, al-Firqah al-Markaziyyah (the Central Band), produced a true crop of martial hymns, sung with Palestinian rural accents. Illustrative of this crop is "Al-Fiddaya" (The Fighters' Movement):[11]

> Our revolution strengthens and intensifies
> As the hearts and arms of the masses
> Fight the popular war[...][12]
> Revolution against the occupier
> Without the cannon, there is no solution
> To restore the Arab land[...]
> We are the people who are right
> *Fiddaya, fiddaya*[...]
> We dictate our will on the usurper
> With our bullets, our blood, our revolution[...]
> *Fiddaya, fiddaya,*
> A popular revolution
> One blood, one path,
> No one stops our revolution.

Yet today's Shatila *shabāb* do not see an obvious revolution with their eyes. Despite what "Al-Fiddaya" preaches, it simply is not true—or not anymore—that Palestinians have "one blood, one path." The "Voice of the Palestinian Revolution" has ceased to be the "voice of Palestinians" (at least as far as the Shatila *shabāb* are concerned), and the "liberating

---

11. This song is not to be confused with the song of a similar title, "Fidā'ī," that became the Palestinian anthem.

12. In these lyrics, ellipses in brackets indicate omission of text.

songs" used as the very title of Massad's article (2003) have ceased to be liberating. As Abu Hassan aptly remarked, the fight itself has changed: it is no longer about the Palestinian struggle but rather about the struggles plural by Palestinians plural. The struggles include those rather unspectacular ones conducted on a daily basis by the *shabāb*—searching for a job or giving up hope of ever finding one, working physically demanding and almost unbearably long shifts for a low salary, searching for a bride or giving up hope of finding one, worrying about not having the means to start an independent household. These struggles do not bear the glamorous mark of the liberation.

○ ○ ○

"I'd like to be like my father." This was the very first sentence uttered by Hassan when I met him alone for an interview prior to pairing him with his father for yet another interview some two months later. In Hassan, Abu Hassan finds a loquacious admirer: "I wish I was with the *fidā'iyyīn* and had the chance to fight with my father. Palestine without a gun is nothing. The revolution is getting stronger in Palestine, but here it no longer exists. I wish I were there to give my support, by any means."

Abu Hassan taught his five children politics—"so they know what to say and when"—but he did not want his two sons to join the *fidā'iyyīn*. To his mind, the logic of the struggle has changed: "In the past, I fought with guns, to defend us, but today I fight with my mind. It may be because I'm getting old. You know, my age is like the easing of the tornado. It's like childhood [*ṭufūla*] but with knowledge [*'ilim*]. Today, I can talk to everyone in the camp, as my father used to when he was my age. Every age has its beauty and its own truth [*ḥaqq*]."

Being a bookish man (whenever I stopped by for a visit, he was reading about herbal medicine), Abu Hassan very much wanted his children to study, but they all dropped out of school. He was forgiving toward them: "You know, with the situation we have in Lebanon, it's difficult to get an education. Even if one studies, ultimately it's impossible to find a job in the area in which one specialized." He instead made sure his children—including the girls—had the capacities to stand on their own feet. Only one daughter did not obtain any kind of training because she married at a very early age. As for the other two, the first was trained as a hairdresser and the second as a secretary. In the case of his two sons, he managed to pass on his craft—candy making—to them.

Abu Hassan owned a large candy shop in Nahr al-Barid. It took him more than a decade of hard work, mainly as a construction worker, to put enough money aside to set up the shop. At eighteen, Abu Hassan had left Lebanon for Libya, where he had stayed for three years as a construction worker, "working in the middle of the desert, under very high temperatures." With the outbreak of the Civil War in Lebanon, he returned but did not stay for long. He got engaged to Umm Hassan, whose family was from the same village in Palestine as his own, and flew back to Libya to work under the unrelenting sun yet again, saving money for the marriage. He stayed in Libya for an additional year, then once back in Lebanon paid 2,000 Lebanese pounds in *muqqaddam* (bride price)—"a lot of money, back then"—and finally married Umm Hassan. He put away enough money to purchase a house and to renovate his parents' dwelling. A leg injury suffered in battle, however, forced him to cut short his years as a construction worker and to contemplate alternatives. He started working in a candy shop, while Umm Hassan, a talented tailor, began working from home to help the family make ends meet. He used to take his sons to the shop to initiate them into the art of candy making. Some twelve years of hard work and careful family budgeting left Abu Hassan with enough money to open his own candy shop in Nahr al-Barid: "It was a nice shop. Our clients were from all over, Palestinians, Syrians, and Lebanese. I had a big party when we opened it. We had a comfortable life. And then with the destruction of Nahr al-Barid [in 2007], all that was gone. Several years of work gone like that, in a month."

Abu Hassan tried to stay in Nahr al-Barid for as long as safety permitted, trying to defend his property, but at a certain point he was forced to leave. The family fled to Shatila, where his married daughter was living. Abu and Umm Hassan were living in a one-room dwelling when I met them. He spent his days reading his books on herbal medicine, hoping that in the future he might be able to help heal the sick, while Umm Hassan was back to sewing from home to raise some money, providing the family with at least enough for basic expenses. Hassan, for his part, was painfully aware that his father's past golden days would be extremely difficult for Hassan himself to replicate: "You know, once I was in love, but *al-ḥamdulillah* [thank God] it didn't work out. Marriage is expensive. One needs some $20,000 to get married, and how can I have that kind of money? I'm paid $600 a month. To marry, I need to have all the power [*quwwa*]; I need to be respected as a man; I need to have a house and a future. I often think of the future. I'd like it to be like the past. I'd like to have what I used to have in Nahr al-Barid: a good house and a good job. And I want to get married and have children. And to raise my children in a proper way."

In a similar vein, Abu Hassan's golden days in Nahr al-Barid are—and may have always been—beyond the reach of Shatila fathers. Abu Hassan was wise to retire from his military career and regain his productive life, which included even being able to instruct his sons in his craft. He speaks with pride about Hassan and Hassan's brother: "My sons are the light of my eyes [*nūr ʿuyūnī*]. When they were born, I felt they were me. I want them to be stronger than me. They're my descendants [*dhurriyatī*]; they're my heirs. They'll keep my name forever."

Comparatively, the lot of Shatila fathers seems much gloomier. They have little to pass on to their children, apart from the memories of the glorious *'ayyām al-thawra.*

In her study of village history books written by Palestinians, Rochelle Davis (2011) shows how memory is gendered—and, I would add, aged. The majority of the authors of the village books were elderly men, enacting what is framed as their responsibility: documenting village stories and passing them on to enable present-day and diasporic Palestinians to maintain a land-based national identity. Such histories are celebrated by subaltern studies as examples of alternative sources that bring to light stories by and of marginalized populations that do not normally find their way into official records. Yet these histories also bear the mark of those authoring them. In this sense, although village history books are indeed revealing as narratives of those who in the struggle for Palestine have been marginalized within the global state system, they do not reflect the perspectives of the entire Palestinian society: often enough, they are still the work of an elite, with specific interests and views, in terms of both gender and age. To support her argument, Davis carefully observes how the main texts of village history books completely gloss over the fact that women held and traded property, even though the books do abundantly make this clear in their annexes. Moreover, women are seldom depicted as working the land prior to 1948, a feature patently at odds with reality: the books are thus more telling of the class sensibilities of their upwardly and increasingly urbanized authors, whose economic conditions allowed them to spare their wives and daughters from engaging in labor. Making the "real" true requires certain abilities (White 1980), compelling scholars to question "why certain narratives dominate at certain times despite the existence of other sources, counterarguments, and other narratives" (Davis 2011, 17).

Davis writes of how Palestinians entwine past and present through village books. Accordingly, the books serve as bases for a reconfiguration of present-day expressions of Palestinian identity, scaffolding specific forms of national identification into the future. Yet for the retiring *fidā'iyyīn* interviewed by Christian Chesnot and Josephine Lama, who used to live under the motto "to combat is to exist," the present has an "acid taste," forcing them to temper their "past ardors" (1998, 7, 15). Indeed, one may justifiably ask what happens when the past looks increasingly idyllic and irreplicable, as it does for Shatilans. Although the past is continuously recalled with nostalgia, it has undoubtedly ceased to serve as a foundation for hope because the future has also stopped being imaginable. What happens, then, when there are no more reasons to continue singing the Palestinian marches?

John Borneman (2007) diagnoses the recent lack of fine-grained ethnography with political relevance on relations among men in the Arabic-speaking world. He rightly points out that anthropologists in particular and for a couple of decades now have been attempting to compensate for the traditional neglect of studies on relations among women in the region. As a result, there has been a true blossoming of research on the lives of women in the so-called Middle East.[13] Men, however, have not as yet been the object of the same kind of analytical attention. Setting out to remedy this situation by investigating the relations between fathers and sons in Aleppo, northern Syria, Borneman nonetheless faced an unanticipated obstacle: fathers were not exactly forthcoming in response to the anthropologist's advances. This is how he explains their relative silence: "I suspect that fathers were reticent to explain themselves at length because the conditions of paternal authority in Syria have been severely compromised— in terms of an inability to procure jobs for their sons and daughters; an inability to reverse a trend in contemporary representation to reduce Arab men to terrorists, Islamic extremists, and ineffectual victims of Israeli politics; and an inability to assert any influence over the political sphere in their own country" (2007, xiv). If "in the Middle East the father never dies," as a professor friend remarked to Borneman (11), both the Aleppo and the Shatila *shabāb* have had to learn how to make do without a father.

In such a scenario, what happens to "lineal masculinity"—the "perceived ontological essence that flows to and through men across the generations" (King and Stone 2010, 323)—which is pervasive in the region and serves for the transmission of identity, status, and wealth from fathers to sons? What if there is little—or no—wealth or status to be passed on? In a series of skillful demarches, Diane King and Linda Stone manage to bring "gender" and "age" together as "mutually constituted domains." They can do so because, as they argue, "crucial dimensions of gender are transmitted through structures of kinship" across generations (2010, 324).

Their argument proceeds as follows: David Schneider's (1984) censure of kinship as being flawed by Western notions of reproduction as well as Jane Collier and Sylvia Yanagisako's (1987) similar critique of gender led research to a position of radical relativism. Both kinship and gender were considered, at most, emic concepts and as such demanded investigation into each society separately, thus providing very fragile leverage for comparative analytical exercises. Yet King and Stone believe that analyses

13. To name just a few of those studies: Abu-Lughod 1993; Delaney 1991; Friedl 1989; Joseph 1983; Kapchan 1996; and Mernissi 1988.

can allow both proper consideration of local constructions of kinship and cross-cultural comparison.

Here they summon the help of one of the most ambitious comparative analysts in the history of anthropology: Jack Goody. According to Goody, in the Eurasian context as opposed to sub-Saharan Africa sons normally inherited land, while daughters inherited movable property. In Eurasia, the dowry played an essential role in enabling parents to "match" brides and grooms—or, more properly speaking, the dowries of the former and the inheritance prospects of the latter. In Eurasia, the dowry thus functioned as a form of class maintenance. Although Goody did not thoroughly investigate the implication of such a system for gender patterns, he remarked that it was telling that the more propertied a woman was, the less freedom to choose a partner she would enjoy—at least as far as marriage arrangements were concerned. Inappropriate relationships were further tabooed through the valorization of women's premarital virginity and the "honor complex." Even so, it is surprising that Goody and especially later writers inspired by his work have had so little to say about how class-stratified patriliny also affects men.

At this juncture in their reasoning, King and Stone resort to the work of one of the most productive writers on patriliny: Meyer Fortes. On the concept of *naam* among the Mole-Dagmane-speaking groups from West Africa, they quote from one of Fortes's papers: "*Naam*, fluid-like, is all pervasive; it comes from the hero founders from the Mamprussi stock and body politic who first created it. By the lineal principle, all the patrilineal descendants, recognized or putative, of the hero founders, wherever they may have wandered, have a stake in it" (quoted in King and Stone 2010, 327). Hence, for patriliny to work as what King and Stone call a "mascu-line" (327), not only is the idyllic past of the heroic founders at stake, but so is the present, where descendants are expected to build on their received lineal masculinity, projecting it into the future. Regarding the region covered by my study, Fuad Khuri (1975) had already showed how men's deeds kept alive in collective memory among Lebanese families assured identity along agnatic descent lines. Ideally—and here King and Stone's findings correspond with those of Michael Herzfeld (1985), R. W. Connell (1987, 1995), and R. W. Connell and James Messerschmidt (2005)—a man needs to be good at being a man and show performative excellence, thus crystallizing hegemonic expressions of masculinity. In this way, not only is his "mascu-line" eternalized into the future, but he can also sometimes even establish his own patriliny by exceeding his forebears and surpassing their endeavors: indeed, there is no other "ability more potentially hegemonic than that of putting one's stamp of identity on the next generation and multiple generations into the future" (King and Stone 2010, 330).

Not merely oriented toward the present, lineal masculinity takes the past as its referent and points into the future. Yet once again my customary "heuristic troublemakers," the Shatila shabāb, with their predilection for giving people (especially researchers) a hard time, expose the (false) idealism built into such a principle. Indeed, the analyst should not lose sight of the fact that both features brought together by lineal masculinity, kinship and gender, are ideas—imaginary systems—and as such necessarily admit all kinds of adaptation when put into practice (Bourdieu 1977). So what happens to lineal masculinity, kinship, and gender when in practice the past looks simultaneously bright and unrepeatable, the present increasingly dark, and the future no longer conceivable? What happens when the father—of sons (Borneman 2004, 2007) and of nations (Borneman 2004; Özyürek 2006; Sawaf 2013)—dies, and there is no will or reason to revive him?

The sons whom John Borneman met during his fieldwork in Aleppo still aspired to patrilineal prerogatives: "I would rather have children than fly," one of them retorted to the anthropologist (2007, 13). In contrast to their Syrian counterparts, the Shatila shabāb are apparently left with little alternative but to fly.[14]

Fermata

A fermata—represented in musical notation by a cyclops eye or bird's eye placed over the note—indicates that the note should be sustained for longer than usual. It is left to the conductor or the performer to decide how

---

14. Borneman provides only anecdotal data about class belonging among the Aleppo sons. I suspect that starting a family was less of an issue for them because they were less destitute than the Shatila shabāb.

much longer. Should the performer sustain it for too long, however, she or he runs the risk of losing track of the musical tempo. Can the fermata thus work as yet another "meta for," musical this time, for those *fidā'iyyīn* who, too attached to the memories of bygone battles, nourish them perhaps for a little too long—to the point of ignoring the struggles of their own sons?

○ ○ ○

It took me quite some time to pay off the debt that I incurred while setting up the interview with Abu Kamal. Although he did not ask for it directly, he let me know through Malik, the friend who had arranged our meeting, that he was looking for a complete set of Brazilian jerseys for the soccer team of the cultural club in Shatila where he was the president. I did grab the first chance to have the shirts brought from Brazil when my mother decided to pay me a visit in Lebanon. Abu Kamal's request became a family affair, with my mother counting on the help of her own sister to visit sports shops in Rio that would sell the entire set of team jerseys for a reasonable price. On the flight to Beirut, the set of eleven shirts took up half of my mother's suitcase. Once the gift was in my hands, and not wishing to make Abu Kamal uncomfortable in any way, I decided to use the same channel of communication he had selected: I asked for Malik's good offices to take the jerseys to Abu Kamal. I waited a couple of weeks for Malik to tell me about Abu Kamal's reaction. Malik did not bring up the matter, though, so I pressed him one day. An embarrassed Malik told me, "I knew it was hopeless, Gustavo. No matter how hard I tried to avoid the subject, I knew you would raise it with me. Yes, I took the shirts to Abu Kamal. He complained that eleven shirts aren't enough because the whole set also needs to include uniforms for the players sitting on the bench on standby."

At fifty-four and a civil engineer, Abu Kamal was a proud man. His public persona inspired respect. He assumed a professorial tone when talking to me and lectured for several minutes on the eventful saga of the Palestinian diaspora in Lebanon since the Nakba before I was able to make clear that I was also after his personal biography. Abu Kamal held all the credentials for the authority he exuded: a former Fatah member, imprisoned and tortured between 1982 and 1984—a period he described as a "huge experience" (*tajriba*)—he came from a family of *fidā'iyyīn*. Four of his brothers were *fidā'iyyīn* and died in battle. His father was also a fighter. After the failure of his first marriage to a Lebanese Shia, with the Palestinian–Shia conflict of the 1980s having played a role in the couple drifting apart, he wed Umm Kamal, a Palestinian and a *fidā'iyya*, "though she never held a gun as her task was to bring ammunition and provisions to the camp." All this allowed Abu Kamal to claim a potent belonging to a deep-rooted chain of uninterrupted struggle, a chain that culminated in his own history and that was at odds with present-day trends:

> From the moment that the first Zionist Congress took place in Basel in 1897, the *thawra* started. This means fifty years of struggle rarely mentioned by the books. And from 1947, we had only two alternatives before us: *thawra* or slavery ['*ubūdiyya*]. That's why I left Tyre to [go to] Saida in '85 and from there [moved] on to Shatila. Their intention was to destroy Shatila, and my brothers ['*ikhwatī*, meaning "brothers-in-arms"] came here to defend the camp and our people's dignity [*karāma*].[. . .] And today, what are they [the enemy] after? They want us to spend our lives smoking hashish and watching porn movies so that we lose our heads and forget the real question. They want to kill off any hope of return on the horizon. Fighters today, they aren't true *fidā'iyyīn*. They're after a salary [*ma'āsh*]; they hold their guns while watching TV and smoking. [. . .] They have an empty life.

In Abu Kamal's remarks, the struggle for return not only assumes a moral tone but also admits a religious rendition: "We're Muslims. Our reference is the Qur'an. In the Qur'an, there's the promise that we'll return to Palestine, whatever the violence is and no matter how far Israelis have progressed. We'll return to our homeland [*waṭan*], and this is a promise from God in the Qur'an. We're believers and have no doubt. If not me, my son. If not him, my grandson.[. . .] Thoughts never change. Principles [*mabādi'*] never change. You may miss the purpose at certain points, but what's important is to reawaken."

At eighteen, Kamal was trying his best to live up to his father's expectations. He studied computer maintenance at an institute but was unable to find a job in his area of specialization. Employed at a firm that produces steel for air-conditioning units, he worked without a contract and without medical insurance. He talked to me about his memories of a nice and peaceful childhood. The July War of 2006 was the first war he witnessed. Kamal defined himself as a *shāb*. In his opinion, a *shāb* is "someone who has a good way of thinking [*tafkīr salīm*] about his country [*baladū*], his religion, and his people [*'ahlū*]." He had not yet been given any opportunity to prove his bravery, yet he dreamed of being a *fidā'ī*:

> KAMAL: If there's the chance, I so much wished to be a *fidā'ī*. Today, there are still *fidā'iyyīn*, but they don't openly appear. In the past, everybody was fighting for Palestine. But now even the camp is no longer Palestinian, if we can say that, because there are lots of nationalities, all different groups [*fi'āt*] in Shatila. In the days of Abu Ammar [Yasser Arafat], it wasn't like that. There were weapons [*silāḥ*], and there was *thawra*.
>
> ME: Does *thawra* exist today?
>
> KAMAL: No.
>
> ME: Why not?
>
> KAMAL: Because today no one embraces ['*ahhal*] *thawra*.
>
> ME: What do you mean?
>
> KAMAL: Take my father's situation, for example. I feel sorry because no one mentions him, despite everything that he's given to the *thawra* and to the struggle [*al-niḍāl*].

When I met father and son together, Abu Kamal assumed a professorial attitude toward both Kamal and me. Maybe for lack of any other option, both of us, Kamal and I, surrendered. The following dialogue includes examples of how our conversation went:

> ME: What can you tell me about the Nakba?
>
> ABU KAMAL: It triggered all the wars. For us, it means diaspora [*shatāt*] and losing all the essentials of civil life. It made revolutionaries [*thuwwār*] out of us.
>
> KAMAL: It means diaspora.
>
> ME: How about Palestine?
>
> KAMAL: It's the mother [*al-umm*].
>
> ABU KAMAL: [Addressing me] He means that the mother is Palestine, and Palestine is the mother. [Asking Kamal] What does Palestine mean to you?

KAMAL: It means so much to me.

ABU KAMAL: [To Kamal] So tell Gustavo.

KAMAL: It means history. Past, present, and future.[. . .]

ME: How about the Palestinian camps? What can you tell me about them?

ABU KAMAL: Camps are the fuel [*wuqūd*] of *thawra*. They're a transitory station and not a replacement [*badīl*]. They're transitory stations toward Palestine, now and in the future.

KAMAL: They're roads toward Palestine.

I tried to encourage Kamal to speak first:

ME: And the *fallāḥīn* [peasants]? What would you say about them, Kamal?

KAMAL: Peasants . . . I don't know what to say. The word has a lot of meanings.

ABU KAMAL: But what does the word mean to you?

KAMAL: The *fallāḥīn* are symbols [*rumūz*] of strength [*quwwa*].

ABU KAMAL: Yes. Symbols of strength, patience [*ṣabr*], endurance [*taḥammul*], and hard work. Normally, peasants are described in books as full of vigor [*'unfuwān*][15] and strength [*quwwa*]. [To Kamal] Is that right? At the same time, they're generous [*kuramā'*], brave [*shuj'ān*], and have a bond to the earth. He [the peasant] eats from the earth and defends it.

Also with my next word—*fidā'iyyīn*—I addressed Kamal first. He was a bit more loquacious this time but still spoke under his father's monitoring eyes (and ears):

KAMAL: The *fidā'iyyīn* are the revolutionaries, who see the cause [*al-qaḍiyya*] and defend it.

ABU KAMAL: The *fidā'iyyīn* are planets in the sky and generous stones toward the ultimate goal [*al-hadaf al-aqsā*], which is freeing land and human beings.

---

15. The term *'unfuwān* is probably better translated as "zeal." In the Beiruti version of Arabic, at least, the word often has nationalistic, almost militaristic, connotations.

ME: And what about the *thawra*? Anything you want to tell me about the *thawra*?

ABU KAMAL: The *thawra* is the past and present. It didn't stop. It still is and will continue despite all the twists [*mun'aṭafāt*] that have happened. The *thawra* is the torch [*shu'la*] for all the free spirits of the world. It's a torch that never becomes extinguished.

KAMAL: The *thawra* is not only about Palestinians but also for all the free spirits of the world.

The son kept following his father closely, irrespective of which words I proposed:

ME: What do you want to say about the War of the Camps?

ABU KAMAL: It's a bitter event forced upon us. We aren't addicted to war and siege. But we erected the banner [*shi'ār*] of the *thawra* to live with dignity [*karāma*].

KAMAL: This war was forced upon us.

I deliberately compelled Kamal to speak first when we came to the word *bayyāt*, "fathers":

KAMAL: He [the father] is the one who shows the road in life. He directs us. He makes us conscious [*ywa''ī*][16] about life.[. . .]

ME: What would you say about your father's generation?

KAMAL: It set an example for the future. My own generation is empty. The older generation was more conscious.

Once the moment arrived for us to discuss religion and for father and son to comment on the two songs "Romana" and "Ahlān fīk bil-mukhayyamāt," Abu Kamal increasingly took control of the interview, alienating Kamal and me from the activity:

16. As we have seen in the previous chapter, achieving wisdom and conscience (*'aql* or *wa'ī*) is a requirement for a man to come of age. It is telling here that Kamal transfers to his father that capacity of making him, Kamal, conscious. See notes 7, 9, and 31 of chapter 3.

KAMAL: Religion is the straight way [al-ṣirāṭ al-mustaqīm].

ABU KAMAL: [To Kamal] Be free in your answer. Gustavo didn't ask for an explanation about Islam.[. . .] [R]eligion, what does it mean to you in general? The question is clear. Give a suitable explanation without getting deep into details and differences about religions. Religion is a dogma ['aqīda] and a principle [mabda'], my son.[. . .] Do all Muslims follow Islamic instructions [ta'ālīm]? No.

KAMAL: Religion is a principle and a dogma.[. . .]

[After listening to "Romana," Abu Kamal proposed a love song for us to listen to, Sheikh Iman's "Ya filasṭīniyya."]

ABU KAMAL: [Asking his son] What does this song mean to you? In life, one needs to combine commitment ['iltizām][17] and personal affairs. To combine, for example, sentimental songs and songs like "Romana."

KAMAL: This song ["Romana"] talks about the life of the Palestinian people under injustice [ẓulum] and oppression ['iḍṭihād]. It sings for the land and for steadfastness [ṣumūd]. It's a song about the misery [ta'āsa] of the Palestinian people. It also talks about the right to return [ḥaqq al-'awda].

As might be anticipated, Katibe 5's song "Ahlān fīk" stirred Abu Kamal's indignation. Once more, his son scarcely had any chance to talk: "First of all," Abu Kamal said, "this song is alien [gharība] to our society [mujtama'nā]. This song doesn't belong to our heritage [turāthnā]. Its lyrics are sharp, scornful ['istihzā'], negative, and an offensive criticism without proof. I'm suspicious about the people who wrote this song.[. . .] I mean that this song, instead of changing something, only criticizes. It doesn't offer new solutions." Cornered, Kamal had to concede: "I don't like this song. It doesn't depict the reality." But not completely: "Actually, some verses do."

As we reached the end of the interview, Abu Kamal took over the conversation one more time and commented on my research, framing it in a way I would hardly recognize as my own: "Your research is very important.

17. Samuli Schielke dedicates a chapter of his book *Egypt in the Future Tense* (2015) to the concept of *'iltizām* among young Egyptian men.

The data or information that you're collecting from father and grandfather is true and transparent because they were peasants and simple [*basīṭīn*]. They always tried to stick to their land [*'arḍhum*].[. . .] No one sold his land. I'm telling you honestly. Those who sold land to the Jews were actually Lebanese, Syrian, and Egyptian landowners.[. . .] Palestinians stuck to their land as much as they could."

It may be the case, as Abu Kamal stated, that principles do not change. Despite Kamal's loyalty, however, thoughts do. What other Shatila *shabāb* sing is not music to everyone's ears.

Palestinian Rhapsody

Simultaneously intriguing and revealing, the various definitions I have found for the term *rhapsody* invariably emphasize the idea of freedom, which increasingly informs my study from here on. Featuring free-flowing structures, rhapsodies harbor contrasting moods and tonalities, preserving unscathed a certain sense of improvisation. In this sense, they function well as "meta for" for how *shabāb* of a more challenging nature than Kamal relate to their forebears (figure 8). Indeed, it is worth investigating what happens when the *fidā'iyyīn*'s narratives cease to inspire respect and admiration and trigger reaction instead.

Ibrahim did not sound seventeen. Having dropped out of school in grade 6, he had already been working for a couple of years: first at a mechanic shop run by some of his relatives, then as a car painter, a job he both enjoyed and excelled at, and finally at a sweet shop in the immediate vicinity of the camp. He endured a very long shift at work, from 8:00 a.m. to midnight, and made less than $10 a day. As yet, he did not define himself as a young man (*shāb*) but dreamed of reaching that threshold.

> IBRAHIM: I'm a *walad* [boy] because a *shāb* has enough money to build a house and look for a girl to marry.[18] I don't think of marriage. What's the point? I need money for that.[. . .]

18. Among my Shatila acquaintances, perceptions of age gradations have changed from one period to the other. Shatilans report that whereas in the past there was a smooth

ME: Do you have hope? Or dreams?

IBRAHIM: Hope to return, you mean? No, I have no hope to return to Palestine.[19] Again, what's the point? But, yes, I have the dream of leaving the camp, marrying, and living in my own home.

Ibrahim censured his father for failing to live up to a number of responsibilities. The relationship between the two, according to him, was not good: "My father makes no money. He doesn't work. He depends on his sons for everything. When he wants to buy something, he needs to borrow." He even denied that his father had been a *fidā'ī*. And yet Abu Ibrahim, forty-three, indeed claimed to have been a fighter from 1982 to 1987.

Only for a very brief moment during our encounter did Abu Ibrahim allow himself to feel nostalgic. Although never setting foot in Palestine, he saw it once from the Fatima Gate on the southern border of Lebanon: "I saw some relatives. But from a distance." He added, smiling: "And I could see the olive trees as well."

During the rest of our meeting, I found Abu Ibrahim to be embittered by the events that marked his life. The Israeli invasion of 1982 and the massacres at Sabra and Shatila forced a still young Abu Ibrahim, sixteen then, to join the ranks of the *fidā'iyyīn* because of a lack of alternatives: "It was either fight or die. During the War of the Camps, we thought we would end up dying. So we defended ourselves." With the War of the Camps over and already a married man, he tried to return to his civil life. Following in his father's footsteps, he opened a bakery. He did not have the same talent for the business, however, and soon closed the shop doors. Going back into military service was not an option: "When the PLO was here, there was money coming in. But after Abu Ammar [Yasser Arafat] left, there was no money. The *fidā'iyyīn* started being paid some $200 per month. And that isn't enough when you have a family. Your life changes

movement from being a *ṭifl* (baby) to being a *walad* (boy), a *shāb* (lad), a *rajul* (a man), and, finally, a *khiṭiār* (elderly man), today camp dwellers have no childhood (*ṭufūla*), and the *shabāb* remain so forever, never acquiring the *'aql* necessary to become a *rajul*.

19. On the meaning of remarks about the impossibility of the return, see note 24 in chapter 3.

when you get married; you become responsible for a family." For a while, his family even endured living in what was (and, to a certain extent, still is) Shatila's poorest neighborhood, the *stablāt* (stables).[20] At the time of the interview, his household depended entirely on his son Ibrahim's meager salary, which was hardly enough for them to make ends meet. While reflecting on his predicaments, Abu Ibrahim extended his sense of disillusion to the whole of his people: "In a situation like this, how can we even think of fighting to win back our land? We're trying to survive, that's all. We, Arabs, are *mahzūmīn* [defeated]."

When I brought father and son together, dissent often marked the interaction between the two, even if it did not lead to an open clash. A self-confident Ibrahim often felt comfortable enough to talk ahead of his father:

> ME: What could you tell me about the Nakba?
>
> IBRAHIM: I don't know anything about it.
>
> ABU IBRAHIM: Palestine is my country. I can't say I don't want to go back.
>
> IBRAHIM: Palestine is my country, yes, but I don't think about the return. I can't return anyway.[...]
>
> ME: And is there anything you want to say about the *fidā'iyyīn*?
>
> IBRAHIM: They defended the camp and protected it during the war.
>
> ABU IBRAHIM: *Fidā'iyyīn* came because of the Israeli occupation. Every Palestinian is a *fidā'ī*.
>
> IBRAHIM: My father wasn't a *fidā'ī*.
>
> ABU IBRAHIM: I'm not a *fidā'ī* now because I'm trying to find a way to live.[...]
>
> ABU IBRAHIM: [While listening to Katibe 5's song "Ahlān fīk bil-mukhayyamāt" on my iPhone] I don't like this music. Never. I don't want to go on listening to it. These singers are silly people [*tāfihīn*]. They're Lebanese, not Palestinians.

---

20. According to research participants, the *stablāt* were stables previously used for horse rearing. I heard that the animals went astray during the Civil War, and people moved in. The area is still used for housing today.

ME: [In an unwarranted moment of overdirecting my interviewees] They're Palestinians. From Burj [al-Barajneh, a Palestinian camp in southern Beirut].

IBRAHIM: And this is a very nice song. Why don't you send it to me right away via Bluetooth?

For better or worse, the Bluetooth of my mobile never worked properly.

The humor characterizing the relationship between Umm Rafik, forty, and Rafik, twenty, did not preclude a deep respect between mother and son.[21] There was a telling absence in their interaction, however: Abu Rafik. Abu Ibrahim did not display the same stature as Abu Kamal as far as paternal authority goes, and in the case of the Abu Rafik family we have moved one step more: the father is missing, almost completely so.

In Umm Rafik's matter-of-fact recollection of her life, violence was such a daily affair as to sound banal:

This is what I saw in my childhood. People in the street being slaughtered all the time. The War of the Camps beginning. Our home was on the border of the camp, and Hezbollah and Harakat Amal [Shia parties cum militias] fought Palestinians then. After that came the Six-Month War. We helped the fighters [*muqātilīn*]. We baked bread for them. But the oven was very far. Life was very harsh. Amal attacked the camp. My aunt [*khālatī*, mother's sister] was pregnant and preparing food. Out of nowhere, a projectile killed her. We took her to the Palestinian Red Cross; there she died. '*Ammatī* [my father's sister] was also injured. People passed by, greeted us, and then [later] we heard that they had died or been injured. The six months passed. My husband[22] was having

21. Relations between mothers and sons in the Arab world certainly deserve more ethnographic attention than has been the case up to now. On the subject, see Joseph 1999b and Rugh 1984.

22. This was the only time Abu Rafik was mentioned voluntarily during my meeting with the Abu Rafik family. On other occasions, Abu Rafik came up only when I explicitly prompted mother and son to talk about him.

lunch one day; a projectile hit him and left him handicapped in his leg. Life was very difficult. Then there was the war inside the camps between Palestinians. It was very difficult because it was Palestinians against each other: Palestinians with Syria and Palestinians with Abu Ammar [Yasser Arafat]. My brother was killed during this time, and 'ammī [my father's brother] too. We escaped from the camp to the Gaza [Hospital] building.[23] Back then, the Gaza building was empty. Before, it had been better than the American Hospital of Beirut. The building had nothing to offer us in terms of survival. But I continued to live here. And I did my best to give my children what I myself didn't have as a child. Then the Aoun War took place.[24] Several projectiles were launched against us. All my life it has been war after war.

Challenged by such an eventful biography, Umm Rafik developed her own coping techniques, which she was proud to have transferred to her children: "I have the habit that when I hear fire exchange, I keep cool. It gives me a strange feeling of calmness, almost happiness, because that's familiar to me: I've gone through wars. My children don't know the meaning of war. But in July 2006 [when Israel attacked Lebanon], they learned its meaning. I had experience from before, so I tried to support them. Now they know the difference between fire exchange and fireworks. During the

23. The Gaza building, located in Sabra and close to Shatila, used to be a hospital, an exemplary one for health services according to my informants' recollections. It was invaded by Amal during the War of the Camps, and several patients were killed. It ceased functioning as a hospital after the attack. After its closure, several homeless refugee families moved in. Today a vertical shantytown, it is still used as housing. On the early history of the Gaza building, see R. Sayigh 1979.

24. Also known as the War of Liberation, the Aoun War happened during the final phase of the Lebanese Civil War, between 1989 and 1990. The part of the Lebanese army that was loyal to General and Prime Minister Michel Aoun, appointed by the previous president, Amine Gemayel, fought another part of the Lebanese army that was loyal to President Elias Hrawi and to Prime Minister Selim Hoss, newly appointed by the Taef Agreement, as well as to the Syrian Armed Forces. In October 1990, the Syrian army stormed Aoun's strongholds and ousted him, resulting in the death of hundreds of soldiers and civilians and bringing the Lebanese Civil War to an end.

July War, they went up to the roof here on the Gaza building to look at the
Israeli airplanes attacking [nearby] Dahiya."

Umm Rafik also prided herself in having been a *fidā'iyya*, even though
her career as a fighter was cut short and replaced by the less dramatic job
of tailor:

> UMM RAFIK: I was a Flower [Zahra, from a term meaning "flower"
> but here meaning something like "Girl Scout"] among the flowers
> [Zahrāt].[25] I left school because of the war. And I became a *fidā'iyya*,
> the only girl in my family to have done so, and received military
> training. In our society, boys and girls should have military training.
> But I never took part in real operations, just the training. There were
> women planning operations but not taking part in them. Women
> conducted activities to trick [*takhda'*] the enemy. Though some
> women conducted operations, too. Dalal Moughrabi, for example,
> took part in military operations without her family knowing. And
> there was also Leila Khaled, who hijacked airplanes.[. . .] There was a
> salary [*ma'āsh*], you know, for the *fidā'iyyīn*, but I don't consider it to
> be work [*shughul*].
>
> ME: And how did your husband react to the fact that you were a *fidā'iyya*?
>
> UMM RAFIK: He was a *fidā'ī*, too, but he left when he was injured and
> went to Syria to work as a taxi driver there. And I left the *fidā'iyyīn*
> when I was fourteen because of pressure from my brother. He didn't
> think it was the right thing for a teenage girl. So I learned tailoring.
> That is our culture. But the *thawra* still exists, and I swear, swear, and
> swear: if I were in Palestine, I'd take part in military operations.

In contrast to the nostalgic and romantic mood of his mother in rec-
ollecting her *fidā'iyya* years, Rafik had no option but to be very down to
earth. He had a heavy shift working as a cook from 5:00 p.m. to 1:00 a.m.,
without a contract or insurance and with only one day off per week. On
three occasions, he had problems with the police after ridiculing them and

---

25. The Zahrāt (Flowers) was roughly the female counterpart to the Mu'askar
al-'Ashbāl (Cubs' Camp). See note 10 in chapter 3.

with the intelligence services after fighting with one of their informants. As a result, he ended up in prison twice, the first time for three months and the second time for four. When I asked him, he described his relationship with his father as *hayk* (so-so): he thought it was a mistake for his parents to have had children. He gave me a rather austere description of his routine and plans for the future:

> As a Palestinian in Lebanon, I can't ensure my life like everyone else does. Everyone wants to work and live. But in Lebanon, I can't. I want stability ['*istiqrār*].[. . .] I'm not thinking of marriage now. I need some $10,000 for that. Here in the Gaza building, people buy an apartment and divide it up so that several families can live in it.[26] And the wedding party alone costs some $4,000.[. . .] My mother was a *fidā'iyya*, and I would have no problem with marrying a *fidā'iyya*. I like the *fidā'iyyīn*. And a *thawra* is necessary when you have an enemy. Now, I don't approve of women working, but sometimes this is a necessity because life is very difficult. If women work, it should be in their field of education, as a secretary or an accountant. If she isn't educated, she should work with embroidery.[. . .] No, I don't think about the return to Palestine. And I don't think about obtaining Lebanese nationality either.[. . .] I'm tired here. I think of migrating to Europe.

For a brief moment, Rafik smiled when talking about what he did to escape from his routine: "I sing. I really like singing. Normally, I don't like international songs, but I like Katibe 5. I sing at home. And also at Sumud.[27] At Sumud, we sing traditional songs and some international ones. But I can't sing Katibe 5 over there!" He continued smiling when describing his relationship with his mother: "She is like a friend to me. But in serious situations I respect her: she's my mom, after all."

---

26. In Shatila, prospective grooms often build a new household on the roof of their parents' house. Such initiatives are partially the reason for the camp's rapid verticalization. Of course, this option does not exist in the case of the Gaza building.

27. Beit Atfal al-Sumud is a Palestinian NGO that has a branch in Shatila. Also see note 26 in chapter 3.

When I sat down with mother and son together, the rapid ricochet of questions and answers and humorous provocations between them provided me with one of the most pleasant afternoons I had during fieldwork:

ME: What can you tell me about Palestine?

UMM RAFIK: Palestine for me is everything. It is sacred for Arabs. And also for Christians. It's a pure land [*'arḍ ṭāhira*]. And rich in everything. That's why the Jews occupied it. All the prophets were born in Palestine. Palestine is everything to me.

RAFIK: [To his mother] Have you ever been to Palestine to say that it's rich?

UMM RAFIK: It's got all the resources [*khayrāt*]. It's everything to me.

RAFIK: Sabra is full of *khayrāt*, too.

UMM RAFIK: Oh, yes? And where are you from?

RAFIK: I'm from Syria.[28]

UMM RAFIK: What do you say? No, you're from Yafa [a town in Palestine]. [. . .]

UMM RAFIK: [Answering my question about the War of the Camps] During that period, no one could enter Shatila.

RAFIK: Harakat Amal [the Shia party cum militia] could.

UMM RAFIK: How can you say that? Your uncle [*khālak*, mother's brother] was hurt by Harakat Amal.

RAFIK: But he was creating problems, wasn't he?[. . .]

ME: If I say the word *fallāḥīn* [peasants], what does that bring to your mind?

UMM RAFIK: Well, I'm a *fallāḥa*.

RAFI: And I'm a *madanī* [urbanite]. OK, if my mother says that, she's a *fallāḥa*. What can I say? She tells me that the *fallāḥ* plants and gives food to the *madanī*. But I think they use chemicals on their crops. [. . .]

ME: OK, the word I have now is *fidā'iyyīn*.

RAFIK: I don't know what to say.

28. Rafik probably answered "Syria" just to provoke his mother. It is relevant, though, to note that Abu Rafik, although Palestinian, was working at the time as a taxi driver in Syria.

UMM RAFIK: My son doesn't know anything about the *fidā'iyyīn*. We lived under very difficult conditions. Other countries conspired [*ta'āmar*] against us and took our weapons. They slaughtered us. The *fidā'ī* protects his land [*'arḍū*], his family [*'ā'ilatū*], and his neighbors.[. . .]

ME: And how about the *thawra*: what can you tell me about it?

RAFIK: Think of a balloon, Gustavo. What happens if you keep squeezing it? It explodes, right? It's the same thing in a *thawra*: if you keep putting pressure on people, they explode in a revolution. Not only in Palestine but all over. Now, the results of a *thawra* aren't always positive. In reality, there are more negative aspects to it.

UMM RAFIK: *Thawra* until victory [*naṣr*].

RAFIK: Mom, now it's *thawra* until the end of the month [i.e., when the militiamen get paid].

UMM RAFIK: But one should protect one's land [*'arḍū*]. I told you that *thawra* is to protect the land.

RAFIK: Oh, Mom, being a victim is stupid.[. . .]

ME: Now, if I say *zawāj* [marriage], what would you tell me?

RAFIK: [Laughing] Yes, it's all very nice. Settling down ['*istiqrār*], caring more about one's children and wife than oneself. But I advise you to be as free as a bird and fly from one place to another. And I also advise you not to ask my mother this question.

UMM RAFIK: No one can say everything.

RAFIK: But my mother is like Reuters.

UMM RAFIK: I advise everyone not to get married because life is difficult. "You who trust men are like water in a sieve [Yā m'ammin bil-rijāl zay al-may bil-ghirbāl]."[29] Thanks to God for having sent me good children. But I need to have patience with them.[. . .]

ME: My next word is *umm* [mother].

RAFIK: "A mother is a school."[30] But mine is also Reuters.

UMM RAFIK: I talk to you so that you know how life is.[. . .]

UMM RAFIK: [Upon listening to "Romana"] I like revolutionary songs. It gives you motivation [*dāfi'*] and enthusiasm [*ḥamās*] and doesn't

---

29. This proverb means that men are not to be trusted.

30. Perhaps not precisely a proverb, this saying was often repeated by various research participants.

let you be afraid. During the war, I liked listening to these songs. Even today, whenever I listen to them, I feel like joining the resistance [*muqāwama*].

RAFIK: I like songs like these, but I don't listen to them all the time.

UMM RAFIK: [Upon listening to "Ahlān fīk bil-mukhayyamāt"] The singers are talking about Palestine. We're said to be terrorists, but Palestine is our country.[31]

RAFIK: Mom, they aren't talking about Palestine in this song. They're talking about NGOs.

UMM RAFIK: Ah, OK, but there are other songs talking about the terror issue.

RAFIK: Those songs are in Palestine. This one here is about NGOs.

UMM RAFIK: I don't like listening to these songs. With music like "Romana," you feel like grabbing Palestine with your hands. But this song ["Ahlān fīk"] is just talk.

RAFIK: I have songs by Palestinian rappers talking about Israel. But here, in "Ahlān fīk," they talk about the internal situation here.

UMM RAFIK: Yes, the singers are talking about the internal situation. About Hamas and Fatah. They're talking about the fact that they hate each other.

RAFIK: Reuters again. . . .

A couple of reasons can be advanced to explain why rap is increasingly popular among the Shatila *shabāb*.[32] Basically consisting of words spoken to a rhythmic beat, rap has always had a "hands-on" quality (Bennett 2001), meaning that the rapper, although undeniably needing to show musical talent, does not need to have spent long years at a conservatory

---

31. "Ahlān fīk" probably made Umm Rafik think of another rap song from 2001, "Mīn 'irhābī?" (Who's the Terrorist?) by the Palestine-based group DAM.

32. Writing in 2007, Nicolas Puig reports a limited acceptance of rap among Palestinians in Lebanon. According to my own findings, in Shatila at least the level of acceptance of rap is linked to age: whereas older-generation Shatilans were divided in terms of whether they liked or even knew "Ahlān fīk," virtually all the *shabāb* I got to know were familiar with the song, and the vast majority liked it.

to master an instrument and learn musical theory. In addition, rappers exhibit many of the features of what Claude Lévi-Strauss (1962) describes as *bricoleurs*, collecting musical elements and beats from different sources and mixing them up. In the words of one student of the style, "This license to move across musical boundaries untangles fixed cultural artifacts and liberates rappers from the hegemonic into the hybrid world. . . . This is the process of constructing, transforming, borrowing, taking it all in, and releasing new meaning back into the center" (Nassar 2011b, 362). The formal and lyrical freedom thereby achieved enables rappers—and *shabāb*— to say, or rather to sing, through rap what has hitherto remained mute.

It should come as little surprise that rap music and hip-hop culture, displaying such a potential, rapidly expanded from their origins in New York's South Bronx, where since their beginnings in the early 1970s they provided a powerful and critical commentary on everyday life and ethnic tensions in the US inner-city ghettos (Bennett 2001; Lipsitz 1994). As a technique, rapping is older than that, though, and its features can be found in early rural music and religious songs in the United States. From the mid–twentieth century on, that is, from bebop to hip-hop, so-called Black music played a role in the "transmission and distribution of counter-hegemonic narratives" (Neal 1998, 5), closely reflecting the vicissitudes faced by the Black community in America. Tellingly, it also provided the space for the articulation of a "counter-public" even within the community itself (Neal 1998), exposing some of the chasms characterizing it as mass migration from the South continued to raise the anxiety of the liberal bourgeois Black elite. The Harlem and Detroit riots of the 1940s revealed the distance between Black youth and the mainstream Black middle class, with the leadership unable to address mounting stratification within the community. This stratification curtailed the prospects for Black youth, ever more marginalized in public life. Capturing the ensuing discontent, rap in the 1970s gained more consistency and became a genre, serving to express dissatisfaction with the dim socioeconomic prospects for the young people of inner-city ghettos in New York. Eventually, from the 1980s on, the style became mainstream, used to vent youth frustration at the scant socioeconomic opportunities, police surveillance, urban-renewal projects, and neglect by the cultural industry in diffuse settings all over the world.

Soon enough, rap was deployed to express discontent by those marginalized in other latitudes (Bennett 1999; Condry 1999; Filippa 1996; Jamoulle 2005; Maxwell 1994; Tony Mitchell 1996; Sharma 1996). In Lebanon, it is the adaptability of hip-hop, both as music and as lyrics, that allows young people to use it as a means to imagine and project other desired realities (Nassar 2011a, 2011b). In this sense, contrary to the widespread image of the Lebanese postwar generation as escapist, submerged in a culture of consumption, spectacle, and kitsch, hip-hop indicates that "pockets of resistance to the usual politics of the social order" (Nassar 2011a, 95) exist in the country. Among the Shatila *shabāb*, I propose, rap also serves as a way of expressing discontent with the present (and perhaps with the past as well) and of imagining what may be defined as local and nonsovereign political futures (Arendt 1963; Jennings 2011; see also chapter 2 in this volume).

Drawing upon Barbara Hampton and Cynthia Schmidt's fluvial metaphor, Julien Mallet praises the heuristic value of what he labels the "musical confluence" of the analytical category *jeunes musiques*, "young songs" (2003–4, 483, my translation),[33] emphasizing how they, like pidgin language, allow us to interrogate concepts such as identity, tradition, and belonging and to contemplate ideas such as acculturation, syncretism, and miscegenation. Such is possible, too, for Palestinians in a country like Lebanon, which has known a "rehabilitation of ethnicity" (Picard 1994, 50, my translation) over recent decades owing to the all-encompassing and ever-present frame of explanation: the Civil War of 1975–90. Hip-hoppers and rappers search for a way out: "In Lebanon's cultural politics of music,

33. I suggest that rap can be included in such a category. Julien Mallet (2003–4) makes the point that *jeune musique* (young music) is not to be confused with *musiques de jeunes* (music of the young). This is not a matter of age, and even an aging researcher such as myself can enjoy the "nonstabilized state, in movement" as well as the "multiple concordance" of the "refusal of overexclusive belongings" (Mallet 2003–4, 486, my translation) of a *jeune musique* such as Palestinian rap.

hip-hop emerges as an instrument for contesting inherited forms of meaning. It socializes alternative discourse—with its own ideological terms, creative yearnings and lexicon of ideas—into the public sphere. . . . It is about testing the limits and pushing the boundaries of what is considered acceptable. Hip-hop in Lebanon emerges as a space of possibility" (Nassar 2011b, 360). Indeed, the time may have arrived for us to finally move on.

Malleable, Palestinian rap, rather than asserting itself as the guardian of a nationalist identity frozen in time, constitutes a discourse of the contemporary (Puig 2007). Neither nostalgic nor romantic, it does not celebrate a bucolic Palestine, eternalized by the so-called patrimonial music of the past with its pleasant rurality, its olive trees, and its tiny villages. Palestinian rap is not purely nationalistic: rather, it conveys an image of a nation that is not bound to a territory. Instead of glorifying the battles of the past, it concentrates on the everyday as the site of resistance as well. Not every resistance needs to lead to a revolution, the phantasms and fantasies of the 1960s and 1970s notwithstanding. Owing to its attention to the everyday as an arena of struggles and its unrestrained exposition of the deficiencies of life in the camps, rap is characterized by Nicolas Puig (2007) as infrapolitical. In fact, I contend, it is political to the full. It may even be suggested that, actually, it is the music of the past—with its obsessive celebration of a pastoral Palestine and its litany-like exaltation of battles gone by—that is ironically not political enough. Rather than opting to expose the contemporary challenges facing Palestinians—such as proper access to the labor market, housing, education, and health care—the music of the past adopts a conciliatory tone toward policies implemented by Arab regimes (Puig 2006), including the Palestinian authorities. Yet it is in the present that urban Palestinian youth from Lebanon are understandably in anger.

While in "Ahlān fīk bil-mukhayyamāt" Katibe 5 exposes the hurdles of camp life, in "Jam'iyyāt" (NGOs) the band identifies—literally so, by naming them—one of the culprits in causing the problems: NGOs. Sarcastically and didactically, the singers instruct how to start an organization of this kind:

How to found your NGO to support you in life:
First: Read about human rights and memorize some terms

Second: Evaluate miserable situations and list their reasons
Third: Throw yourself in front of funders and activate communications
Fourth: Accept offers without reading the goals
Fifth: Kill your humanity, kill your consciousness, and of course you
    get the aid
And tell us: Volunteer
And the sixth step is to attract the means
Seventh: Pretend that you are sociable and attend lectures
Eighth: Fill your NGO with foreigners like you fill your car with gas
And, last, enjoy betraying the martyrs of the cause.

These instructions nonetheless come with a warning:

People are hungry
And the worst thing is when you manipulate people's hunger.

In "Ḥatta 'ish'ār 'ākhar" (Until Another Announcement), the rappers of Katibe 5—after urging listeners not to "capitulate to their peace" and lamenting the fact that "our blood became commercial"—resort once more to a didactic tone, this time telling the audience—from "Africa, Arabs, Asia"—how to make a Molotov cocktail:

With a bottle of glass
A piece of cloth
And some benzene
Say no to their democracy
And scream: "Viva Iraq, Viva Palestine!"
Fill the bottom of the bottle
Burn the cloth like a fuse
Stand back and throw it at your goal
Start the fight
Burn a fire
Spread destruction and ruin, kill the enemy, burn a fire
Molotov, Molotov, Molotov.

A song by another Palestinian rap group from southern Lebanon, Hawiyya Zarqā (Blue ID, like the cards identifying Palestinians in Lebanon), poignantly sums up the challenges faced by refugees. The song—with the same name as the group, "Hawiyya zarqā"—ends with a call for listeners to free Jerusalem and fight for the return, but independently of the sleepy state governments:

> Blue identity card, I'm called a refugee
> I grew up in discrimination and racism
> We've been chased, we've been defeated
> And we lived in camps
> I'm no terrorist, no sweetheart, no passionate [lover]
> I look for work and I'm asked for my identity
> What's your identity?[34] I'm Palestinian.[. . .][35]
> A Palestinian forbidden to express [himself]
> A Palestinian forbidden to strike
> We can't buy a shop or a house
> We can't talk or write on walls[. . .]
> I'll never cease to change the past into the present[. . .]
> Everyday plots against us
> We have fallen into oblivion[. . .]
> Governors have no other interest save for their cigars and drinks
> They're interested in money and dignity is crushed[. . .]
> And all over the world our Arab nation is ignored[. . .]
> We don't want to stay asleep like our Arab governors
> We want to stand up before we get the disease
> Our governors don't give a fuck, and we try to do something[. . .]
> To liberate al-Aqsa, we want no other but Palestine as a country[. . .]
> Keep the trust, al-Aqsa lives in us[. . .]
> We raised our right hand and swore to God, the master of the worlds
> No to naturalization [tawṭīn], no to migration, but the return to
> Palestine.

In this song, Hawiyya Zarqā insists on the traditional themes forever present in the Palestinian political agenda (the refusal of nationalization,

---

34. As in English, the term *hawiyya* (identity) in Arabic has multiple meanings. Thus, it refers both to identification papers and to social belonging.

35. In the lyrics to this song, ellipses in brackets indicate omission of text.

the right of return, the liberation of Jerusalem), intermingling them, none-theless, with the demand for rights here and now in Lebanon—the rights to free expression, to strike, and to have access to the job and housing markets. Katibe 5, for its part, also speaks of the need for freedom. In the highly poetic and sometimes cryptic song "Ṣilat raḥim" (Womb Link), an ode to the mother, the iconic figure so often present in Palestinian litera-ture and song, the rappers establish a distance between their generation and that of their parents:

> She [the mother] needed memories
> We needed freedom

Accordingly, the song ends with birds—the other image so often present in Palestinian text and music—in a touching call to turn over the page:

> A place [referring to the camps] filled with emptiness
> But with the first sunrays the birds returned
> And the smell of death began to die
> And what happened [in the past] kept on living but as memory.

Rapper Yaseen from Burj al-Barajneh camp describes his hybrid hip-hop as "ta-rap" (Nassar 2011a, 362). Here, he likens his music to an almost immemorial Arab tradition according to which songs are intended to induce an ecstatic emotional state, or *ṭarab*, in the listener, while claiming a distance from it. Puig (2006, 2007) recalls how older Palestinian music—revolutionary songs included—observed what he identifies as the formula of the three Ts: *turāth* (patrimony), *turāb* (soil),[36] and *ṭarab*.[37] Along with other, more directly politically motivated reasons, it is precisely the fear of a loss of identity in exile that, Puig argues, explains the older genera-tion's overinvestment in the three Ts formula. By comparison, Palestinian

36. *Turāb* denotes the concrete and material sense of "soil" and is thus relevant to the *fallāḥīn* (peasants).

37. In the Arabic alphabet, the *t* in *ṭarab* is emphatic and different, therefore, from the *t*'s in *turāth* and *turāb*.

rap, undisciplined by the institutionalization derived from party affilia-
tion and not domesticated by the commercial drive of the leisure industry, enjoys freedom, functioning as a channel to express the subjectivities
of young camp dwellers. "Palestinianness" and attachment to the "cause"
(*al-qaḍiyya*), still forcefully present, are nonetheless more nuanced and
less direct. Puig has described this approach as follows:

> A planetary musical form, rap is simultaneously a channel for subjecti-
> vation and a tribune for denouncing everyday problems and promoting
> the "cause." As far as this latter point is concerned, there is continuity
> between rap and the important current of nationalist and political song.
> But weaving the political in an indirect way, rather than entertaining
> large political mobilizations, rap individualizes the cause and exposes
> itself to the criticism by members of various organizations concerned
> with the respect toward the classical modes of engagement. Similarly, by
> conveying an ethics of social transformation, it runs the risk of offend-
> ing the existing consensus about the rhetoric of the struggle, addressing
> less-universal and encompassing questions through the recitation, with
> no revolutionary flourishing or romanticism, of the everyday, its dif-
> ficulties and its routines. (2007, 147, my translation)

Thus, for an older generation rap can appear devoid of merits, whether
artistic or political (or sometimes religious).[38] Censured for being supposedly counterrevolutionary and inauthentic, rap appears simultaneously
alien and alienating.[39] Here the relevant point is the characterization of

---

38. Islam has always had a complex relationship to music (Gazzah 2011; Landau
2011).

39. Likewise, Mauro Van Aken (2007) reports that in Jordan the incorporation of
new movements into the traditional *dabka*—which then came to be known as *al-jakson*
after the American singer—was met with resistance by older Palestinians. As in Shatila,
in Jordan there is also a gender and generational dynamic in play. Van Aken (2006) writes
of a party in which older men—enjoying the fact that the music was being played by
an increasingly rare *yarghul* (a kind of double clarinet) musician—seized control of the
dance floor with their harsher, less varied, and more disciplined way of dancing *dabka*.

what precisely counts as authentic. Investment in certain identity markers—such as those of the land-bound *fallāḥīn*[40]—by an older generation of refugees has an almost therapeutic role for those who have lost nearly everything. Yet with technological advances in recording methods, place has become increasingly separate from space (Schade-Poulsen 2004): music can follow migrants and refugees wherever they go and sometimes even travel independently of them. Music that forever celebrates origins in monochord fashion may end up contributing to cultural stagnation (Baily and Collyer 2006). Indeed, why should songs by Palestinian *shabāb*, commenting on their daily lives, the challenges they face, and the hopes they nonetheless nurture, be taken as any less authentic than songs by their parents and grandparents?

Furthermore, it is revealing how older songs freeze understandings of "resistance." Such understandings, as Marc Schade-Poulsen convincingly shows, obscure analysis about the social meaning of *raï*, an Algerian folk song, for young men from the Oran area in the northwestern part of the country. Overemphasis on the sexual tropes sometimes present in *raï* songs contributes to the genre being pictured by some scholars and media pundits as "a deliberate transgression of established powers" (2004, 191). Such framing—although remaining blind to the ethnographic evidence that the Oran *shabāb* were upholding a certain moral code when listening to the earlier, lust-celebrating "dirty" *raï outside* of the home, preferring the later, domesticated versions of the music whenever in the company of

---

They also resisted giving up the position of *lawih* (leader of the *dabka* line) to one of the *shabāb* present. The *shabāb*, bored by a *dabka* too monotonous for their own taste, left the floor one by one and eventually abandoned the party altogether.

40. Shatila is home to a museum: the Memories Museum. It celebrates the *fallāḥīn* saga, with a collection composed of chopping, weeding, harvesting, and cooking utensils; lamps; cutlery; clothing; cosmetic objects; waterpipes; pieces of currency; photos; house keys; a radio; and land-tenure documents, among other items. Visiting the museum was no easy affair. It took me a while to find out who held the museum key and to organize an appointment. Hardly any of the *shabāb* I knew had ever visited the museum, and several did not know where it was located.

family members—also helps consolidate the vision, not at all politically naive, that outside of *raï* or the freedoms of sex Algerians are the "depersonalized victims of a monolithic fundamentalism" (191).

Indeed, the relevant question is: How is resistance to be understood today? Why should Shatila *shabāb* (and scholars) forever pay respect to the way resistance was conceived by the older generation of Shatila *fidā'iyyīn* (and by the scholars who write about them)? Why is the demand for access to the labor and housing markets as well as to health and education services so forcefully depicted in Palestinian rap any less political or less resistant than the calls for the return eternalized in older songs? Why are the little camp stories of students studying hard, mothers reprimanding their children, and lovemaking in the debris, all so movingly described in "Ahlān fīk," less authentic than the images of the olive trees and cactuses of Palestine and the *fidā'iyyīn* in the older music? As the rappers of Katibe 5 sing, "Enough with the revolutionary songs, *khalaṣ*, we play the beat."

"We Play the Beat" (and Some Palestinian Arabic)

The differences in the ways in which the *fidā'iyyīn* and *shabāb* evaluate each other's music betray the sense in which "youth" is in fact a contested category. From a certain standpoint, indeed, it may be argued that "youth" in and by itself does not actually or necessarily exist or even that it has never always necessarily existed. Historians contend, even if quite controversially, that childhood in its present form—and presumably youth as well—is a recent invention: prior to the modern period, one moved straight from miniature adulthood to adulthood (Ariès 1962). Paradigmatically, Pierre Bourdieu (1993) stated on one occasion that *youth* is just a word, thus setting in relief how its deployment might actually serve to render opaque all kinds of class distinctions glossed over by this overarching category. Words nonetheless produce effects in the real world, as we know from the previous chapter on gender.

Contested and not taken for granted, age, as proposed by Zina Sawaf (2013), should be submitted to a Schneiderian revolution. David Schneider (1984) exposed the ethnocentric basis of kinship stemming from its anchoring in sexual relations, a Eurocentric bias. This exposure has offered the leverage for the later development of the much more flexible category "relatedness" (Carsten 1995, 2000) and has given further impulse to the analytic disconnection of "biological sex" from "social gender." Similarly, Sawaf recommends severing "biological age" from "social age." Here, she aligns herself with an older tradition: in what is perhaps the only sociological study dealing with age deserving to be ranked as a classic, Karl Manheim distinguishes "generation units," which simply congregate people of around the same age, from "generation unities," or people who have lived together the "drama of their youth" (1952, 301). It is precisely in this sense that John Collins (2004) claims that the *shabāb* of the First Intifada constituted a real generation because they shared a drama that became the object of nostalgic narratives later, when the unity of yore was challenged by the "politics as usual" set in motion by the Palestinian Authority once it acquired autonomy over the Occupied Territories through the Oslo Agreements. The drama of *shabāb* youth, as portrayed by Collins, is eminently a political one, and it is here that I wish to take Sawaf's suggestion one step further and offer a revolution of "age," but one not strictly within the Schneiderian frame. Indeed, the time has come to put politics back into youth studies, as Phillip Mizen (2002) advises.

Age and youth function as tools of governmentality. Mizen (2002) convincingly demonstrates how governments make use of age either to justify access to public benefits—as during Keynesianism, when it was an advantage to be young in the United Kingdom—or to bar such access—as during monetarism, when it became pernicious to be identified in such a category. Also at the international institutional level, during an age that Jean Comaroff and John Comaroff call "futilitarianism" (2005, 29), youth and in particular youth employment function to justify the implementation of certain policies. Thus, although the neoliberal agenda may have come under increasing criticism, multilateral bodies such as the United Nations, the International Labor Organization, and, prominently so, the World Bank have offered a new guise to the same old procedures, as Mayssoun Sukarieh and Stuart Tannock (2008, 2015) argue: shrinking public expenditure, reducing government employment, and downgrading labor protection are now presented as leverage for enhancing youth employment. In the specific case of the Middle East, a crude Malthusian rhetoric is used to scaffold the defense of such an agenda. Thus, Middle East experts and think tanks specializing in the area rather prodigiously deploy the language of "youth bulges," which are said to be forcing new generations of Arabs to live in "waithood" (Dhillon and Yousef 2009).[41] The ultimate rationale for following this credo is alarmist: in an age of apocalyptic fears, unemployed youth are depicted as ticking time bombs. Palestinian refugees are often subject to such unflattering depictions (see, e.g., International Crisis Group 2009).

The image of youth as a "crisis in the making" has not always been so omnipresent (Swedenburg 2007). Imagined as the civilizing vanguard and the future of the nation, youths were celebrated by their states during periods of political optimism, as in Kemalist Turkey in the 1920s and 1930s, Egypt after the independence in 1952, Iran after the revolution in 1979, and, relevant here, Lebanon during the *thawra*. Comaroff and Comaroff describe the quandaries of present-day youth:

> It is on the back of those situated in the liminal space between childhood innocence and adult responsibility that modernist socio-moral anxieties have tended to be borne. For another thing, it is crucial, if we are to make any real sense of the contemporary predicament of youth, of its neomodern construction as a category in and for itself, that we stress its intrinsic bipolarity, its doubling. Youth is not *only* a signifier of exclusion, of impossibility, of emasculation, denigration, and futility. Nor, by all accounts, is it experienced as such. While they may not, for the most part, have captured the mainstream—and may, indeed, constitute an infinitely exploitable market, an inexhaustible reservoir of consumers, an eternal font of surplus value to be extracted—the young remain a constant source of creativity, ingenuity, possibility, empowerment, a source of alternative, yet-to-be-imagined futures. (2005, 229, original emphasis)

41. For a different interpretation of the "youth bulge" in the Arab world and specifically of the phenomenon of "waithood" in Egypt, see Courbage 2011 and Singerman 2011, respectively.

I would add political and yet nonsovereign futures as well.

Here, the Shatila *shabāb* are particularly well placed to contemplate such futures. For although they are definitely young, they are not necessarily "youth." With limited financial means, they do not fit well into the category of consumers; school dropouts and often unemployed, they may even be a source of surplus value to be extracted, though not without protest and definitely not an eternal one. Moreover, the Shatila *shabāb* do not constitute a generation either. In the same vein that I indicated how "gender" is a pertinent heuristic tool to make sense of the *fidā'iyyīn* biographies but not those of their offspring, here I want to propose that the same is true of "generation." Romantically eternized in their youth, the *fidā'iyyīn* were a generation, for they shared what Manheim calls the "drama of their youth" (1952, 301): the *thawra*. The *shabāb*'s dramas, however, are too daily, too vulgar, and too un-epic for them to merge as a unity. If "generations" signal moments of history, the *shabāb* appear to be outside of (nationalistic) history, their biographies crystallizing, on more than one level, the defeat. This is nicely and acutely captured in Palestinian parlance, in which past generations are always referenced in relation to a historical frame, as in *jīl al-Nakba*, "generation of the Catastrophe"; *jīl al-thawra*, "generation of the revolution"; and *jīl al-'intifāḍa*, "generation of the intifada." Today's *shabāb*, by contrast, are simply that: *shabāb*.

5
Reemerging
Noncockfights

A Workshop on *"al-Gender"*

"I hate having to do it, Gustavo."

My good friend Jihad, twenty-eight, was complaining about yet another workshop on "gender" that he had to facilitate. Jihad was a social worker at a local Palestinian NGO, which was hosting a series of lectures on reproductive health for young Shatila residents, both boys and girls, in cooperation with its Italian counterpart. The Italian NGO financing the exercise provided the social workers with supporting material—a DVD and a guidebook in both Arabic and English—that set out the procedures for the workshop. Jihad thought it best to make some adaptations to the general guidelines in order to render them more culturally appropriate: "I tell the participants that one of Prophet Mohammed's wives was his boss and that it's not a problem to have women in leading positions. The local director of our center here in Shatila is a woman. But it's true that it's taken even me forever to understand what 'gender' is."

Jihad also used another strategy to help participants grasp the elusive concept of "gender." He wrote the word in English on a whiteboard, Arabicizing it by placing the article *"al-"* (equivalent to *the*) in front of it: *al-gender*. He then invited the participants to share with others what they understood by the concept: "People come up with the most unbelievable definitions. During one workshop, a participant said that 'gender' is a terminal disease."

236

9. Freedom over Shatila. Photograph by Hisham Ghuzlan and Gustavo Barbosa.

I regretted not having taken part in Jihad's activity: as happened all too often during my period in Shatila, it seemed I had missed yet another golden opportunity. So I did what an ethnographer has gotta do: I invited myself to the next workshop on "gender" that Jihad was due to facilitate in a couple of months.

This chapter is written from the premise that the participant in Jihad's workshop who defined "gender" as a terminal disease may have had a point, even if the remark was probably unintentional. Although the notion of "gender" may correspond to the power relations known by the older male refugees, who acted as *fidā'iyyīn* during the *'ayyām al-thawra*, as suggested in chapter 3, its utilization is less appropriate when dealing with their offspring, the *shabāb* of today, with their very limited access to power. In this chapter, I make use of the workshop conducted by Jihad, the one I eventually attended, as illustrative of the highly stereotyped and moralized views that NGOs hold of so-called gender systems in settings considered conservative, such as Shatila. I then present an arena of sociality where the Shatila *shabāb* displayed sex roles until recently: the raising and hunting of pigeons. I explore the differences between this "noncockfight"—pigeon raising among the *shabāb*—and the Balinese cockfights (Geertz 2000): though both involve men and birds, they diverge profoundly, among other reasons because Shatila today houses several anti-state trends, whereas Bali is very much a "state machine." Thus, I ask what happens when a state is not present to "organize" a "sex–gender system" at the local level and suggest that more studies are needed to clarify the exact relation between "gender" and "state machines."

"Gender Troubles"

In contrast to what happened in Jihad's previous workshop, no dramatic definitions were offered when he wrote *al-gender* on the whiteboard during the workshop I attended.[1] The guidebook prepared by the Italian NGO did anticipate that participants may not be sufficiently acquainted with the concept and reported that in pilot sessions some guessed that "gender" was a telephone model, a name, a law, a provocation, and a competition—though, again, in the latter three cases I suspect that the participants may not have been entirely wrong. Jihad confided to me that his own organization's contribution to the workshop was half-hearted at most. His boss, a Shatila resident too, once expressed to him her frustration with the topic: "Oh, these Europeans! They should give us their lives so that we can implement their agenda. We lead lives very different from theirs!"

Some twenty camp residents took part in the workshop, both boys and girls, some of the latter wearing head scarves, ranging in age from fifteen to twenty-four. The boys clustered at the two ends of the table, with the girls in between; a female facilitator, Rola, worked with Jihad to direct the discussions. Only one of the participants, a boy, volunteered that *al-gender* was about roles (*al-'adwār*), which Jihad diligently wrote on the

---

1. The title of this section is inspired by Judith Butler's book *Gender Trouble* (1990).

whiteboard. The others were somewhat more candid, stating that they simply did not know what it was, that it was the first time they were hearing the term, and that *al-gender* was the same as *al-jins* (sex).

Sticking to the manual, Jihad divided the whiteboard into two columns identified with the headers "Male" (*Dhakar*) and "Female" (*'Unthā*) and challenged the participants to enumerate characteristics of each. The participants suggested the following qualities for "male": facial hair, huge muscles, Adam's apple, fertilizing capacity (*'amaliyyat al-talqīḥ*), hard work (*al-'amal al-shāq*), going out of the house, masturbation (*al-'āda al-sirriyya*, literally "the secret habit"), not shy (*mā 'indū khajal*), and harshness (*khushūna*). Meanwhile, for "female" they ascribed: the head scarf (*al-ḥijāb*), breasts, work, pregnancy, the ability to give birth (*al-qudra 'alā al-'injāb*), cleaning the house, not leaving the house, child rearing (*tarbiyat al-'awlād*), menstruation (*al-dawra al-shahriyya*, literally "the monthly cycle"), the womb, shyness (*khajal*), and softness (*al-nu'ūma*). Using markers of different colors, Jihad differentiated features that were bodily traits (*al-ṣifāt al-jasadiyya*)—thus "sex" (*al-jins*), he explained—from those that were "roles" (*al-'adwār*) or a social type (*al-naw' al-'ijtimā'ī*)—thus "gender" (*al-jindir*). He continued: "Gender changes from society to society." One of the young men thought it relevant to remark: "Yes, one needs to take religion into consideration."

The next activity of the workshop, also prescribed by the manual and slightly adapted by Jihad, was designed to consolidate the participants' understanding of "gender" as different from "sex." The whiteboard was once again divided into two halves, identified by a girl's name and a boy's name, "Hala" and "Jad." Jihad invited the participants to list what they would give Hala and Jad as presents on their fourth, tenth, and eighteenth birthdays. For their fourth birthdays, Hala would receive a Barbie, pink pajamas, boots, and earrings, and Jad a bicycle, a Spider-Man toy, black boots, and a football. Hala's tenth-birthday gift would be a dress and a golden necklace,[2] whereas Jad's would be a scooter and yet again a football.

---

2. Golden accessories are normally associated with marriage for women, and for girls nine is the canonical age for marriage.

Hala would receive a second golden necklace and other golden accessories, makeup, a car, a book, and a computer for her eighteenth birthday; Jad, in turn, would receive a motorcycle, a car, a book, a computer, a PlayStation, and a silver bracelet.[3] Jihad remarked that the lists contained both common items and distinct ones because some objects were considered appropriate for a girl, others for a boy, and a handful for both. Somewhat theatrically, Jihad then asked his audience: "What is gender [Shū huwa al-jindir]?" The participants understood his point completely; nevertheless, one of the girls responded that "boys always want more things than us," which triggered a wave of laughter.

For my present analytic purposes, it is the workshop's third activity that is particularly relevant. Jihad and Rola distributed blue and green cards to the participants, irrespective of sex. He explained: "Those with the blue cards can't do anything except remain seated. Those with the green cards can do whatever they feel like." A green-card holder turned on some loud music on his mobile; some others rushed out of the center to stretch their legs and smoke much-needed cigarettes because the workshop was already into its second hour. Another male green-card holder opted to tease an unlucky girl holding a blue card. "Now, you'll swap your cards," Rola instructed. It was the girl's turn to take her revenge.

Once the activity was over, Jihad prompted the participants to share with others how they felt when in possession of the differently colored cards. Faithfully observing the manual's guidelines, Jihad once more divided the whiteboard into two columns, labeled "No Power" (*Ḍa'īf*, literally meaning "weak") and "Power" (*Quwwa*). Participants stated that while in the *quwwa* position they felt special (*mumayyazīn*), gained their rights, and were able to express themselves. Under the "Power" column, they suggested the inclusion of the words *al-ḥurriyya* (freedom), *al-ḥaraka* (mobility), and *al-'amān* (safety). The content under the heading "No Power" was considerably more dramatic. When holding the blue cards,

3. One of the research participants told me that although silver for a man was not a problem, gold was frowned upon because it was considered to take away his sexual potency. The hadith, sayings and deeds attributed to the Prophet, condemn the use of gold by men.

the Shatila boys and girls reported that they experienced *al-malal* (bore-dom), *al-dhill* (humiliation), *al-quyūd* (restrictions), *al-'infi'āl* (emotional stress), *al-ghaḍab* (rage), *al-'iḥtiqān* (frustration), and *al-ṣamt* ([enforced] silence). In the end, Jihad and Rola had conducted the activity precisely as intended, and the Italian NGO's objective had been attained. Indeed, the manual reads: "Make the point that gender relations are power relations and that subordination (power-over) should be replaced by cooperation (power-with) and empowerment (power-to)."

On my way out of the center, I bumped into another friend, Omar, a twenty-eight-year-old greengrocer, in the alleys of Shatila. He had grown up hearing about workshops similar to Jihad's and asked where I had spent the morning.

> M E : I've attended a workshop at an NGO.
> O M A R : Oh, what was the workshop about?
> M E : *Al-gender.*
> O M A R : And what's that?
> M E : [Under the influence of Jihad's workshop, replying with an expres-sion probably even more bizarre in Arabic than it is in English] It's the "social sex" [*al-jins al-'ijtimā'ī*].
> O M A R : [In English] Ah, that bullshit.

Difference does not necessarily lead to the establishment of hierarchy, and even when it does, the ranking of superiority may contradict the out-sider's expectations and change over time and context, even within the same community. Shatilans do not require a workshop to teach what is tautological to them: that men and women are different, both physically and socially, whether they have a word for the latter or not. Rather, it may be the case that some of us need a workshop to understand how Shatilans conceptualize and practice that difference.

During a previous meeting I attended at Jihad's NGO, a group of Norwegian photography students came to make their first acquaintance with camp residents before wandering around Shatila taking shots for an exhibition back home. After making us wait for a couple of hours, the stu-dents, some fifteen boys and girls, finally arrived: to general bewilderment, almost embarrassment, all of the Norwegian girls were veiled, while barely half of their female Palestinian hosts were dressed the same way. Awad, in his mid-twenties, could not resist the obvious joke and whispered to me: "I didn't know that Norway is a Muslim country!" At a certain point, a female organizer discreetly encouraged one of the Norwegian girls to remove the *ḥijāb*: all the others followed, revealing a fiesta of different haircuts and colors—including pink—much to the amusement of the Shatilans.

For its part, the workshop on sex/gender described earlier is indicative of some of the international NGOs' expectations concerning sex/gender systems. First, the workshop was part of a series on "reproductive health": it medicalized sexuality in a setting considered conservative, such as Shatila. Second, all the activities of the workshop followed a strict dichotomizing logic—sex/gender, Jad/Hala, power/no power—as if difference necessarily entails an opposition and the creation of a hierarchy. Last, the utilization of the colored cards introduced the idea of gender as a disparity in terms of access to power. This is a hasty transposition of a notion of gender informed by important albeit geographically circumscribed political struggles in Euro-America. The automatic transplantation of the notion into settings such as Shatila, where both women *and men* today have very limited access to power, raises serious issues. Indeed, not all fights are about cock.

Noncockfights

The image depicted in figure 9 is not infrequent in Shatila today. Every warm afternoon the sky over the camp swarms with flocks of pigeons. That the breeders of the birds are Shatila *shabāb*, however, has become unusual. The practice of raising pigeons was common among the *shabāb* until some twenty years ago. Since then, it has largely been discontinued.

> I was really sad and angry when the guy from the camp Security Committee, together with my brother, killed Hanun.[4] Hanun was my favorite

---

4. The name "Hanun," which I have Anglicized to facilitate reading, should have been transliterated as "Ḥanūn" following the *IJMES* system. The word *ḥanūn* admits

pigeon, with his red feathers. He hatched at our place here in Shatila and was the leader of my bunch. He used to come to me whenever I called, perch on my knees, and eat straight from my hand. Hanun was just like a dog.

This was my friend Ahmad, whose biography is given in chapters 1 and 2, telling me about the tragic end to his years as a pigeon raiser. His father did not anticipate the annoyance it would cause for himself and his neighbors when he brought the teenage Ahmad a female pigeon one day. After a while, Ahmad remarked to his father that he was worried the pigeon was feeling too lonely and might die if not provided with a partner. His father was always willing to comply with his studious son's requests. After all, education, often referred to as a weapon (*silāḥ*), was a matter of pride for an older generation of refugees, and Ahmad deserved to be rewarded for always scoring among the top students at the local UNRWA school. So his father bought him a male pigeon. A very talented handyman, the father also constructed a coop (*al-qunn*) on the roof of the house to accommodate the newly formed couple. It should have come as no surprise to Ahmad when a few weeks later he opened the gate of the *qunn* to feed the pigeons and found newly laid eggs. He celebrated his pet's fertility: "The female was like a machine, man. She was very fat; she couldn't even fly. But every three months, she laid two eggs."

After a while, Ahmad had six pigeons, and the flock was further enlarged by yet another two given to him by a friend who, saddened by the death of one of his birds, lost interest in pigeon raising. Very soon Ahmad was raising, breeding, buying, and selling pigeons. He developed his own expertise in the activity. He was delighted to try to initiate me into the art of differentiating the various kinds of pigeons: Chefar, named after the name "Chevrolet" for being big; Buaz, after the name given to a species of falcon because they are very tall; Caracandiat, possibly after the word *caracand*, "lobster," in spite of the absence, at least to my eyes, of any

---

several renditions into English, invariably with positive meanings: "affectionate," "compassionate," "motherly," and "tenderhearted."

apparent similitude between the two animals; and, finally, the Yahūdiyyat (Jews) because, Ahmad clarified, "those pigeons come from Palestine." Within a year, the *qunn* was running the risk of overpopulation: at its peak, Ahmad's flock numbered thirty-seven birds, which ate through—in corn, wheat, and penicillin when needed—$50 of the family's relatively limited budget. "All very loyal to me," Ahmad rejoiced. "They never flew away." By then, he had begun to fly his pigeons.

And then the problems started.

"It's just like in life," Ahmad told me, exploding into laughter. "The male always goes after the female." He was explaining to me how to fly the pigeons. First, the birds are set free. Always following a leading male, they take off. But they tend to come back too quickly, so the raiser, to keep them airborne, throws stones at them and whistles, which is what soon began to generate protests from Ahmad's neighbors. Once it is time to get the flock down, the raiser waves the female of the leading male to attract him back. The flock comes down in circles, and once on the ground the birds start cooing.

What attracted the Shatila *shabāb* to the practice was not only flying the birds. While in the sky, pigeons from different flocks sometimes mixed. And then there was the hunt (*al-ṣayd*). If one pigeon raiser's bird joined someone else's flock, the former person would try to attract the latter person's birds the next time the respective bands were in the sky simultaneously. This led to all kinds of problems and accusations of theft among the *shabāb*.

To avoid the escalation of tensions, one of the pigeon raisers, a married man, came up with a timetable for the various breeders to fly their flocks. For quite some time, a year perhaps, the system worked wonderfully. The source of the new difficulties, when they arose, was precisely Ahmad's household.

His younger brother, Abbas, kept flying the birds outside the time slot allocated to Ahmad. The other owners became very angry and sent a menacing message to Ahmad: "We're in a hunt." This effectively meant that they would not restrict themselves to the timetable and would try to catch Ahmad's birds. As a good *'ibn al-mukhayyam* (son of the camp) and Shatila *shāb*, Ahmad, of course, would not step back in the face of the threat:

"A war started among us. We all were flying our pigeons at the same time and trying to catch each other's birds. But my pigeons were very loyal to me, and normally I was the one who caught the other owners' birds. This is like theft; it's ḥarām [forbidden].[. . .] I caught three birds belonging to one of my neighbors. They promised revenge, but I was young and stubborn, and retreat was simply not an option."

The settling of scores between the rivals happened soon thereafter. One day Ahmad went up onto the roof and found the *qunn* (coop) gate wide open, one pigeon killed, and ten missing. Suspicion lay on Ahmad's neighbors. Originally confined to the skies, the dispute soon enough landed, leading to a direct confrontation among the *shabāb*. When Ahmad's older brother asked him how he would react, he replied: "I'll do what needs to be done." The brother accompanied him to the neighbor's house. The neighbor was challenged to go outside. A fierce fight followed, which left the neighbor with a broken leg.

By then, the camp Security Committee had come to the conclusion that the situation was no longer acceptable and decided to step in. The Security Committee knew people were overly attached to their birds, however, so it came up with a lie, as Ahmad explained. The lie concerned an accident that supposedly almost happened at the not so far-off Beirut International Airport. As the story goes, a pigeon was sucked into the propeller of a jet, and the plane almost crashed as a result. The Security Committee, Ahmad reported, claimed that the Lebanese government had decided to imprison anyone who insisted on continuing to raise pigeons. So breeders had to stop flying their birds, and the birds had to be culled or at least have their wing feathers carefully trimmed to stop them from flying.

But this order was not enough to make people change their habits, so guards of the Security Committee started visiting homes and killing the birds they found. Ahmad's household was no exception. A guard came by, accompanied by Ahmad's older brother. To set an example to the neighbors, the guard selected three pigeons to be sacrificed. Hanun was one of them. Filled with sadness, Ahmad recalled: "I was so angry, so completely out of control, that afterward I cut the throat of all the remaining pigeons. And I yelled at my brother, saying that we weren't siblings anymore. My mother cleaned the pigeons, and for a month they took up almost all of our refrigerator[. . .]. But after a month, she had to throw the pigeons away because none of us would take a bite."

It took Ahmad a couple of years to recover from the trauma. He made another attempt to raise birds, a falcon this time. He took care of the bird, which had been shot by a Syrian guard. He fed the falcon hot-dog sausages beyond their expiration date that a nearby shopkeeper was about to throw away. When the falcon grew big, the same older brother sold it for $50. Ahmad gave up: "*Khalaṣ*! That's the end of it: that's my story about pigeons, my falcon, and my brother."

Nasir, thirty-nine, a housepainter, still has six pigeons on his roof, but he no longer thinks of himself as a breeder. He was one of the largest pigeon raisers in Shatila, and at a certain point his flock, which he had started assembling some twenty-five years ago, totaled fifty-one birds. He used the strategic advantage of his roof being higher to successfully hunt other *shabāb*'s birds, so he became the "king of capture" and gained control of the sky. Yet, save for just one occasion, he did not have disputes with the other breeders. He kept a good-neighbor policy: whenever one of his birds was "stolen" in a hunt, he paid a visit to his rival, sat down, and drank tea. Conversely, sometimes when he caught someone else's bird, he did not mind giving the pigeon back to its original owner. Nasir managed to keep his birds despite the restrictions imposed by the Security Committee. He was rather evasive as to why a year earlier he had gone to Saida, a pleasant seaside town some forty kilometers (twenty-five miles) south of Beirut, and sold all of his flock to a local breeder. "I had some problems" was all that Nasir volunteered. I knew that in several cases wives, feeling neglected, would censure their husband's pigeon-breeding activities: Nasir was married and had a ten-year-old daughter. I was intrigued by the presence of the six pigeons on his roof:

ME: You told me you sold all your birds.
NASIR: But the ones sleeping over our heads right now are actually some of the birds that I sold in Saida. They've flown back here.
ME: They've found their way back here all the way from Saida?!
NASIR: Yes. A pigeon always comes back to his prison ['alā ḥabsā].

The presence of the six pigeons triggered new ideas in Nasir's mind: "I'll start again with pigeon raising. I can't give it up. I don't have any other hobby. Pigeon raising is a *sūsa* [literally 'a pest,' but here probably meaning 'a vice']."

Moreover, it is a vice difficult to give up. Ahmad told me Saqr's story. Saqr, some fifteen years older than Ahmad, was taken to prison because of pigeons—in Germany. He had also been among the biggest breeders in Shatila. At a certain point in his life, the opportunity arose for him to migrate, a dream cherished by several of the *shabāb*. Once in Germany, Saqr was puzzled to discover that pigeons do not belong to anyone in Europe. He gathered a bunch from the street and took them to his house. After a while, he was flying them, unencumbered by any competing hunters. His German neighbors, however, were even less understanding of a *shāb*'s needs than his neighbors back home. In response to the stone throwing and constant whistling needed to fly a flock, they called the police. Saqr ended up behind bars.

About five years after his departure from Lebanon, by now with German nationality, a wife, and children, Saqr paid a visit to Shatila. Unsurprisingly—and in a poignant commentary on *al-ghurba*, the longing for a place left behind—one of his first actions in the camp was to climb onto his family's household roof and fly some pigeons, now at a safe distance from the apparently more treacherous German skies.

Antistate, Nonpower, and Card Games

Paraphrasing Clifford Geertz (2000), it may very well be the case that the Shatila *shabāb*'s identification with their *noncocks*, the pigeons, is unmistakable—and the double entendre here is probably more radical than it is for the Balinese of Geertz's classic text. Actually, it is remarkable that the word for "pigeon" in Arabic, *ḥamāma*, has a sexual connotation, too, but different from the one normally implied by the English term *cock*. The Arabic term *ḥamāma* corresponds more closely to what Anglophones would call a "willy."

A dramatization of local anxieties related to social prestige, Geertz's Balinese cockfights are an affaire d'honneur. "Joining pride to selfhood,

selfhood to cocks, and cocks to destruction" (2000, 444), the Balinese strive through cockfights to protect their esteem, honor, and dignity: in brief, their social standing. In Bali, nevertheless, only those entitled to prestige and honor can take part in serious cockfighting. It is not an activity for social outcasts: women, subordinates, or youths. The situation there could not be more different from the one in Shatila. The majority of my interlocutors named in this chapter are refugees, young, and poor. In Shatila, noncockfighting is not a privilege of those with prestige. If the Shatila *shabāb* insist on keeping their flocks airborne, it is because they also have their pride and dignity to protect.

There may indeed be tension between the "asociality" of the *shabāb* in their efforts to express themselves through bird hunting and the disciplinary measures of a statelike institution such as the Security Committee, which violently asserted its authority regarding the pigeons. Yet the Security Committee can be characterized as consolidating a "statelike" environment in Shatila only up to a very limited point. Shatilans have learned how to live without counting on statelike institutions. Here, it is telling that, well beyond any clearly defined source of state authority, it was the *shabāb* themselves—and a married man among them—who tried to organize pigeon flying in such a way as to avoid disputes. Upon marriage, a man is considered to have finally achieved *'aql*, the eminent social faculty of judiciousness and prudence, and to have come of age.

Geertz (2000) also presents the Balinese cockfight as a means of expression: through the medium of feathers, he writes, social passions are displayed. The same happens, I believe, with the noncockfight in Shatila: it is a means of displaying the *shabāb*'s sex roles. True, pigeon raising is a male affair: women are expected to be kept at bay in such matters. Yet it is not about performing gender. In order to perform, one necessarily needs to display, but the contrary is not always the case. Performance theory sometimes betrays a certain voluntarism, and it is not everywhere that people can do, redo, and undo their "genders." In most settings, people need to display proper observance of adequate sex roles, however, and the inability to do so comfortably, as our *shabāb* know all too well, leads to genuine anxiety. In this sense, it is revealing that Shatila *shabāb* chose pigeon raising as a pastime and that they selected birds, among all animals, as the objects of their affection. Immersed in the social immobility dictated by utter poverty, without the means to travel despite constantly queuing up in embassies in Beirut, only to have their visa applications turned down by foreign service officers, and with their capacity to dream of a future overshadowed by the political-economic complexities of the refugee situation in Lebanon, the *shabāb* have understandably come to think of pigeons, with their unencumbered freedom to fly, as irresistibly appealing.

In another aspect, Balinese cockfighting and Shatilan noncockfighting are opposites. In Bali, an umpire is called upon to ensure that the "civic certainty of the law" is strictly observed throughout, notwithstanding the passions aroused by the fight. Cockfighting in Bali is ultimately a state affair, a matter of men with political prestige:

[W]hen there were no bureaucrats around to improve popular morality, the staging of a cockfight was an explicitly societal matter. Bringing a cock to an important fight was, for an adult male, a compulsory duty of citizenship; taxation of fights, which were usually held on market day, was a major source of public revenue; patronage of the art was a stated responsibility of princes; and the cock ring, or *wantilan*, stood in the center of the village near those other monuments of Balinese civility— the council house, the origin temple, the market place, the signal tower, and the banyan tree. (Geertz 2000, 424–25)

In Shatila, where some NGOs house bureaucrats to align local morality with "modernizing" discourses on "gender," the umpire, the council house, and all other statelike figures are either obsolete or simply nonexistent.

Shatila nowadays lives in a postrevolutionary and postutopic nonstate order, where sometimes very dated ideologies and various "isms"—socialism, nationalism, feminism—have for the most part and rather depressingly all but vanished, notwithstanding isolated brave spots of resistance. Politics has to be dramatically redefined in such a setting, and, indeed, there may be something deeply and unashamedly political about insisting on the simple display of adequate sex roles. Because this is what today's *shabāb* strive for: to find a bride, to construct a house, and, rather than simply perform a gender, to actually do and make sex.

One may wonder what "agency" in such a context has come to mean. In social life, whether in Shatila or Bali, a person needs to "play the game" even when not in possession of all the cards. In *Un Captif amoureux* (*Prisoner of Love*, [1986] 2004), Jean Genet writes about the period he spent with young Palestinian commandos in Jordan during the war in 1970. One of Genet's stories goes like this: the commanders gave strict orders that subordinates should not play poker, this "bourgeois game for bourgeois people" (45, my translation). Yet what Genet witnessed was the young men rejoicing precisely in the forbidden game with "scandalously realistic movements" (47, my translation). Through their hands, though, no kings, queens, or jacks—all the figures symbolizing power—passed: the commandos were playing poker, yes, but with no cards.

6

Resurfacing

The Antilove of Empire

"Welcome to Shatila, Maddafakazzzz!"

The short movie runs for barely two and a half minutes. The director, Raad Raad, counted on the help of other Shatila *shabāb* to complete *Ahlān wa sahlān fī Shatila* (Welcome to Shatila, 2006) on time and present it as the final piece of work for a filmmaking course he was taking. StudioCamps, an art collective whose goal is to foster artistic projects among Palestinian refugees, has made the movie available on YouTube.[1] Raad remained impervious to my persistent requests for him to explain his movie, so what I offer here is merely my own interpretation. *Welcome to Shatila* shows numerous anonymous feet, maybe what certain trends in feminism would label as "bodies." Faceless, mindless, displaying no specific markers, these "bodies" could easily be lumped together in some kind of overarching category, such as "refugees" or "Palestinian." Yet multiplicity forces its way in. There are the feet of an old lady: we can tell by the dress she is wearing and by the fact that she has placed her cane next to a shopping bag. Maybe she stopped for a breath before heading back home? Then there are the feet of a young girl, framed by nice-looking clogs: Maybe she is

---

1. See *Welcome to Shatila* at http://www.youtube.com/watch?v=Uvu-hrtc4LE. A collection of other short movies by young Palestinian refugees is available on StudioCamps' YouTube webpage: https://www.youtube.com/channel/UCpqCyVc8gV3plddUz2yFBKQ. For a discussion of StudioCamps and the role of insurgency in art, consult Nakad 2016.

10. Looking back at the city, maddafakazzzz! Frame from the short film *Welcome to Shatila* (StudioCamps, 2006) by Raad Raad.

ready to visit a relative? And then in rapid sequence: The feet of a mother and her child, still in their pajamas—maybe they overslept? The feet of a *shāb*, sitting next to an electric heater (Shatila is freezing during winter, and there seems to be electricity for a change), and the feet of what is probably an older man, fingering a *masbaḥa* (the string of beads that help Muslims keep track of their prayers) and sitting on the steps leading to a shop: rather than praying, he seems to be allowing time to pass. The feet of a teenager, sitting on a motorbike while smoking, letting time pass as well. The feet of several friends, also smoking, but this time a *narguileh*: Maybe resting after a hard day at work or just chatting to others and lamenting several months of unemployment? The feet of the mandatory young man in military gear, holding a rifle, and the feet of the hairdresser in his salon, his sandals surrounded by copious quantities of hair. And so on.

Welcome to Shatila ends with a scene of the feet of a man, putting on a pair of well-worn shoes (figure 10). After scrutinizing the feetfull but headless and mindless bodies in the camp, the film viewers are invited to *invert* their gaze. In calm and almost elegant moves, the man, standing on the roof of a taller building (Shatila is increasingly becoming a vertical shantytown), puts on his shoes and from up above looks across the camp and beyond to the city. Can the spectator accept what to me looks like an invitation to put on those shoes, too, and at least try to see what the camp and, beyond, the city look like *from there*? The credits of the movie finally display its title, first in Arabic, *Ahlān wa sahlān fī Shatila*, and then in English, *Welcome to Shatila*. After the English rendition, however, so as to ensure that spectators are not allowed the option (and the luxury) of misinterpreting this hospitality, the following word is added after a couple of seconds: *maddafakazzzz*, "motherfuckers" in plain English.

Indeed, what happens when we, the *maddafakazzzz*—journalists, NGO workers, activists, sympathizers of the cause, researchers, and an ethnographer from Brazil—look at the camp? What do we see, or, more appropriately, what are we willing to allow ourselves to see? How do the city (and citizenship, one might add); diverse "grand narratives" (El-Mahdi 2011; Sawaf 2013), including nationalism, socialism, Marxism, and feminism; and "master words" (Gayatri Chakravorty Spivak, quoted in Olson and Worsham 2003, 181), including *woman, youth, working class*, and *refugee*, look when gazed upon from Shatila? How willing are the *maddafakazzzz* to let go of those grand narratives in order to engage in an anthropological exercise that truly functions as a two-way bridge (Clastres 1968) or to accept that the master words—*gender, youth*, and *generations*—will necessarily emerge from this encounter transformed? This study has attempted to seriously engage such a platform.

As explored in chapter 3, does "gender" have a very specific grounding in the history of Euro-America and thus serve as leverage for the exercise of empire when automatically transplanted to other latitudes? Is *woman* one of these "master words" claiming to represent a group, when "out there" we find no "woman," just women? There seems thus to be a space open for an academic-political platform of deconstruction (Derrida 1976) and a decentering and "provincialization" of Europe (Chakrabarty 2000) as well as of America through the "reversing, displacing, and seizing [of] the apparatus of value-coding" (Spivak 1990, 228). The Shatila *shabāb* have suggested to me a tactic (de Certeau 1984) for sustaining such a platform on both the analytic and the political fronts. The older questions ("Within the Lebanese legal framework, what constitutes a 'refugee,' and what are his or her entitlements?," in chapter 2; "What is the average salary of Shatila dwellers, and what is the unemployment level in the camp?," also in chapter 2; and "How can a man come of age and act as a patriarch in the absence of material means?," in chapter 3) of my disciplines (statistics, gender studies, Marxism) were disavowed for being incommensurable with my observations "from the field." I began with numbers, surveys, pieces of legislation, revolutionaries, and military-political power and ended with flying pigeons (chapter 5). Life itself as well as the ordinary and daily desires and disappointments of trying to find a partner, secure a job, save for a house, and engage in a hunt (*al-ṣayd*) with one's birds became wholly political (Bayat 2010).

Impurity and Danger

The attempt at conversion of Indians to Christianity in May 1817 under the shade of a tree grove outside Delhi, as registered by Homi Bhabha (1985), did not have a good ending (though, depending on one's perspective, that in itself was actually good).[2] The audience did not refuse conversion on religious grounds—that would have been accepting the very terms of the debate—but rather because the attempt was being conducted by a meat eater. The "colonial discourse" was disavowed for being incommensurable, and the subjects—never truly completely subjected—retained, creatively so, their capacity to act through a certain ironic mimicry of the catechist's discourse. Chapter 3 posed the question about the extent to which gender—as a binary understanding, informed by power—is a neocatechism. Along with certain trends in "human rights," "gender" can serve as a tool of empire, providing justification for war machines: we kill, but we kill softly because we have the good intention of saving children

---

2. To name this section, I have purposely corrupted the title of Mary Douglas's book *Purity and Danger* (1991).

and women and gays and lesbians, the perennial victims of the supposedly patriarchal regimes overseas.

Confronted by the immense power of empire, the weak lose if they follow the rules of the game. Thus, they "creatively play different, more flexible and constantly changing games" (Bayat 2010, 24), so that the logic of the ordinary may appear in representation. As seen in chapter 5, the Shatila *shabāb* set their birds free not because they want either to resist or to affirm power. There certainly are a poetics of manhood and maybe even a performance of masculinity at play here; however, the aim is not to consolidate hegemonies (that would be a rather innocuous exercise, were it the goal) but to have fun or, more ambitiously and perhaps ironically, to flirt with freedom (even within severe constraints). Irony, we learn from the deconstructionist literary critic Paul de Man, functions for the "sustained interruption from a source relating 'otherwise' to the continuous unfolding of the main system of meaning" (quoted in Spivak 1999, 430). As such, it never puts the ethics of alterity at the service of a politics of identity—a lesson for the struggle, Gayatri Chakravorty Spivak proposes (1999, x).

The purity of categories—necessary for identity politics and cherished by scholars, statisticians, and policy makers alike—implies dangers for what is left out, teaches Mary Douglas (1991). Indeed, as a "dispositive" for governmentality, the purity of categories and associated notions of hygiene have played a role in struggles over the meanings of the city, scaffolding binary divisions such as inside/outside and enclosure/exclusion and orienting "purification impulses" (Sennett 2008). Nonetheless, what is left out also endangers the purity of categories, forcing their transformation.

As men with very limited power and sometimes none, the Shatila *shabāb* act as "space invaders" (Puwar 2004), disturbing the neatness necessary for the consolidation of purified categories and certain discourses, including those of gender as a binary opposition, as seen in chapter 3. I take the notion of hybridity from Bhabha's (2004) reading of Frantz Fanon. Whereas Fanon (1970) has shown how the phobic image of the Negro— the abject Other—is deeply woven into the psychic pattern of the West, producing the Manichaean delirium that characterizes the colonial space of consciousness and society, Bhabha opts to cut the Manichaeism short.

Rather than arguing along the lines of self and other, he shows the otherness of self and how self and other are tethered to each other: assemblages of pigeons and *shabāb* (chapter 5); fathers and sons (chapter 4); *shabāb* and researcher (chapter 1). Perhaps we can even call these assemblages "colonies," no longer in the sense given to the word by political economy but, more appropriately, corrupted by how biology understands the concept, as congregates of two or more individuals, cohabiting—and tethered one to the other—mostly for mutual benefit. Also in this sense, colonies—and, in the case of Palestinian refugees, there is often no *post-* to be attached to the word—produce new habits of the heart (Stoler 2002).

A Beating Heart and the Ethics of Cohabitation

It is a heart, with its new habits, that keeps beating, somewhat surprisingly and defiantly, even when challenged by trials such as those engendered by the arrival in Lebanon, including the Palestinian camps, of Syrian and Palestinian refugees from Syria since the outbreak of the uprisings and the eruption of the civil war there in 2011 and 2012.[3] In the recent Syrian saga in Lebanon, one hears all over echoes of the Palestinian experience in the country (International Crisis Group 2013; Knudsen 2018).

Home to a dwindling infrastructure and yet hosting the largest number of refugees per capita in the world (Mencütek 2015; Nassar and Stel 2019), Lebanon has received an estimated 1.5 million Syrians (UN High Commissioner for Refugees 2020) and 29,145 Palestinians from Syria (UNRWA 2019) since the start of the Syrian Civil War. The Lebanese government has attempted to handle the arrival of these newcomers—many of whom were actually *not* new to the country at all, having for a couple of decades already worked there as seasonal labor in agriculture and construction (Chalcraft 2009)—by adopting, first, what came to be described as a "no-policy policy" and then in 2014 and 2015 a "formalization of informality" (Nassar and Stel 2019).

---

3. I name this section after Judith Butler's essay "Precarious Life, Vulnerability, and the Ethics of Cohabitation" (2012).

Aware of how much was at stake—with Lebanon, having survived the brutal Pax Syriana (1976–2005), still deeply polarized between pro- and anti-Assad forces—and interested in avoiding the spillover of the Syrian turmoil into Lebanese territory, although such spillover was in reality inevitable, the government in Beirut initially attempted to dissociate itself from the crisis developing next door (International Crisis Group 2013; Mencütek 2015). The "no-policy policy" *not* adopted was structured around two "no's": *no* refugees and *no* camps. As a repercussion of the scarred history of Palestinians in Lebanon, discussed in the introduction and chapter 1, Beirut opted not to recognize the arriving Syrians as refugees, labeling them as "displaced" (*nāziḥīn*) people instead (Janmyr 2016; Knudsen 2018), and not to allow the establishment of new refugee camps (Knudsen 2017), fearing that they would become permanent, politicized, and eventually militarized. Through the active promotion of invisibility—of refugees, even though Syrians met the international definition for refugees (Mencütek 2015), and of camps, despite the rapid multiplication of tented gatherings throughout the territory—this no-policy policy very deliberately attended the purpose of enabling the government in Beirut to avoid assuming responsibility for the newcomers: if knowledge is power, *not* knowing, even if feigned, is power as well.

Toward the end of 2014, the Lebanese government dramatically changed gear, introducing a new set of policies on the entry, registration, and permanence of Syrians in the country. The Kafkaesque maze of legislation that ensued was very stringent and for the refugees very costly and burdensome, replicating in some aspects the evolution of the legislation impinging on Palestinian refugees depicted in chapter 2. In practice, the new legislation made room for discretionary implementation and pushed Syrians and Palestinians from Syria into informality, when not into unequivocal illegality (Janmyr 2016). Several had already "settled"—even though that is definitely not the appropriate word—in Palestinian camps, where they had family or friendship ties; others arrived later, hoping that, with the Lebanese authorities avoiding these spaces, they would be afforded some protection. The so-called spaces of exception (the limits of which are exposed in chapter 2) actually became "spaces of refuge."

In the camps and beyond, these newcomers, even when they were not new at all, were met, according to some scholars, with what Jacques Derrida would have described as "hostipitality," a dizzying combination of hospitality and hostility (Carpi 2016). Hostility is to be expected: after all, Syrian refugees and Palestinians from Syria compete with poor Lebanese and Palestinians from Lebanon for jobs, resources, and lodging, and there are several reports of spikes in rental-market prices and labor exploitation of the "newcomers" (Carpi and Şenoğuz 2019; Chatty 2017a, 2017b; Mackreath 2014). What may seem perplexing, though, is the persistence of hospitality (Fiddian-Qasmiyeh 2016; Mackreath 2014), often described by analysts as "ambivalent" or "ambiguous" (Christophersen, Thorleifsson, and Tiltnes 2013; Mencütek 2015; Thorleifsson 2014).

On this front, Estella Carpi's ethnography (Carpi and Şenoğuz 2019) from Akkar in northern Lebanon is illuminating. With a porous border separating northern Lebanon from Syria, Syrian nationals have historically traveled to Akkar for seasonal labor, leaving their families behind. With the escalation of the conflict in Syria, though, they also brought their wives and children. There were traditional kin or friendship ties and thus ensuing obligations between the two communities. With the arrival of the Syrian families, the humanitarian apparatus, aiming at involving the host community in the reception of the Syrian guests, started paying Lebanese families to provide shelter to the "newcomers." As a result, what before existed as an obligation imbued in kinship or friendship idioms became commercialized. In the process, the Lebanese were reinvented as hosts and the Syrians as guests and "others." Even the border, once completely permeable, was in this way reconceptualized as a "proper" frontier.

This "neoliberalization" and "humanitarianization" of the dynamics of receiving Syrian refugees in Akkar should prompt analysts to consider whether "ontologies of hospitality" (Carpi 2016) do actually capture what was originally at play. I wish to propose that this process of "othering" serves much more to appease analysts' obsessions with purified categories, such as "Syrians," "Palestinians" (chapter 2), "refugees" (chapter 2), "men" and "women" (chapter 3), and "youth" (chapter 4). In the specific case of Palestinian camps, the arrival of Syrians and Palestinians from Syria indicated how the so-called spaces of exception may indeed function not only as "spaces of refuge" but also and perhaps mostly as "spaces of recognition" (Carpi 2016), enabling empathy—at this juncture not merely a discipline anymore, as was proposed in the introduction—between hosts and guests, self and other, to the point that even an Italian ethnographer cum footballer could be accepted into a local soccer team.

The Italian ethnographer cum footballer, Stefano Fogliata, tells the story of how he joined a Palestinian soccer team in the Burj al-Barajneh camp near Shatila (Fogliata 2015–16). The coach celebrated the arrival of the new players from Syria, Lebanon, and Italy: in his words, on the pitch no one can tell the difference. Fogliata remarks that in Italian, as is also the case in my native Portuguese, the pitch is *campo*; the field (of research) is *campo*; the camp, Palestinian or otherwise, is *campo*: one can probably still tell the difference between them, but there seems to be room to navigate, more or less smoothly, between the three. If, as we say in Brazil, the national squad is the homeland in sneakers, and if indeed popular sports can at times encapsulate the nation (Rommel 2014), the Palestine whose presence we are in here is not the one torn by internal conflicts and insurmountable schisms (as portrayed in the introduction) or the all-encompassing one of the monochordic nationalist discourse that admits no dissent. It is the "Palestine [that] remains it all," as Katibe 5 puts in it the rap "Welcome to the Camps": an *accommodating, embracing* Palestine, which welcomes into itself Syrians, Palestinians from Syria, the Italian and the Brazilian ethnographers (despite the latter's absolute lack of talent for sports), as well as other *maddafakazzzz*. It is a Palestine that tethers host to guest, self to other, but without ever taming difference.

It is indeed time to make our way back to two of the Palestinian camps in Beirut: Burj al-Barajneh and Shatila. In Burj al-Barajneh, Fogliata reports, the team coach asked Syrian children attending a training session who among them did not know how to go back home. "Home" is obviously a loaded expression for both Syrian and Palestinian refugees: in the Palestinian monochordic nationalist discourse, "home" would necessarily be compelled to mean the Palestinian Territories (Allan 2014b). One of the readings of the coach's question might indeed be the hypervalorization of the disparity between Syrian and Palestinian refugees with their different homes. As it happens, though, another preoccupation altogether informed the coach's remark: he wanted to make sure that the Syrian children, newly arrived in Burj al-Barajneh, could safely find their way back "home," the place where they currently lived, through the camp's dimly lit alleys. There is a practice of care here—and care provided by men, as was the case in chapter 1 toward me—that is not completely captured by mere "ontologies of hospitality." I propose, therefore, that we are much better served by thinking along the lines of an "ethics of cohabitation" (Butler 2012), which makes the disparity between here and there, hosts and guests, researcher and *shabāb*, self and other eventually and perhaps ultimately irrelevant.

On returning to Shatila in 2014, after having lived there during her fieldwork in the 2000s, Diana Allan confesses her bewilderment over what she describes as a "dialectics of unity and disunity" (2014a). Syrians and Palestinians from Syria were already living in the camp by then, increasing its population to an estimated 35,000, rivaling the density of Gaza City (Allan 2014a). Palestinians from Shatila were now the hosts—or, perhaps more appropriately, the distinction between hosts and refugees became blurred (Fiddian-Qasmiyeh 2016). Wounds from the War of the Camps were reopened, and the original dwellers of Shatila used everything—child rearing, behavior during Ramadan, domestic cleanliness, and personal hygiene—to emphasize the disparity between themselves and the newcomers. And yet during daily demonstrations against the war then ravaging Gaza, they all were brought together, for "Palestine remains it all."

When I was finishing this book, I got in touch through WhatsApp with Mohammed, who liked to describe me as his "buddy." I told him my manuscript was under contract.

MOHAMMED: That's a wonderful title, Gustavo. Those were indeed the best of hard times, even though we didn't realize it back then. We all were young. The situation in Shatila is so different now.

ME: Yes, so I hear. Is it because of the Syrians and Palestinians from Syria?

MOHAMMED: No, Gustavo, they're most welcome. They're like us. Different but the same: we're in the same position. It's because of the drug mafias, which control the camp now.

In the absence of *campo*—proper field research—I cannot comment on the latter. But I think I can comment on the former: that one can be different from and still the same as the other by sharing the same position. In this sense, perhaps even Suad Joseph's (1993a, 1994, 1999b) concept of "connectivity" can admit a political-economic reading in addition to its role in the constitution of the psychological self. Indeed, a political connectivity can tether host and guest, self and other, thus establishing the foundation for the otherness of the self: this is the result of an ethical solicitation (Butler 2012).

Queering Power

When an essentialized and individualized subject-agent ceases to be obvious, what happens to agency? Here the Foucauldian paradigm reaches its limits because it is constructed for the most part around what Lois McNay describes as "a primarily negative paradigm of identity formation—of subjectification as subjection" (2000, 2; see also McNay 1991). If an original situation of constraint is at the basis of subject formation, the purchase of agency within such a framework is limited. Bodies become either docile—the (mindless) feet in Raad's movie are then bound to an uncreative replication of the same acts again and again—or bravely defiant in the face of domination, and then common everyday actions or attitudes that actively pursue submission (Mahmood 2001, 2005) are not regarded as agential in any sense. In his later works, Foucault (1988) attempts a correction through the proposition of the notion of "technologies of the self" (the pigeon stories of chapter 5 can indeed be read along such lines): through an "aesthetics of existence," some space is opened for gestures pointing to autonomy and creativity. And yet Foucault only asserts such a possibility rather than explains how it works. His reasoning ultimately vacillates between voluntarism and determinism.

Talal Asad (2000) is not convinced that endeavors to solve the philosophical problem generated by the clash between free will and constraint constitute a productive course of investigation for anthropologists. He shows how "agency," typically considered as "resistance to power," is dependent on a teleological notion of history that nurtures the goal of promoting universal emancipation from suffering and an ethnographically specific psychology according to which empowerment, understood as both having the power to act and giving that power to someone, is indispensable to human subjectivity (even though increasing self-empowerment, as Asad astutely remarks, does not tend to the practical requirements of social life). Agency thus forms part of what Asad describes as the paradox of representation: the figure represented is both absent and present. Is the person who represents and re-presents acting in her own capacity or in someone else's? Hannah Arendt (1963) and Ronald Jennings (2011) (as discussed in chapters 2 and 4) show how by accepting the seminal distinction between constituent and constituted power, we have ceased being able to imagine nonsovereign political futures (see chapter 2). Spivak (1988), in turn, cogently accuses all of us—scholars included—of complicity with constituted powers, wherein we end up consolidating the supposed legitimacy of *Vertretung* (representation, as in politics) in our efforts at *Darstellung* (re-presentation, as in art or philosophy). Then, as Marx taught, small peasant proprietors "cannot represent themselves, they must be represented. Their representative must at the same time appear as their master, as an authority over them, an unlimited governmental power which protects them from other classes and sends them rain and sunshine from above" (Karl Marx, quoted in Spivak 1988, 276–77). In this study, I have tried not to succumb to such a collusion.

If the constituted power has become increasingly estranged from the constituent power in Western political philosophy and tradition, plunging us right into the paradox of representation, it is because agency is forever taken to be external and resistant to power, the latter often conceived as repressive of the agent (Asad 2000). Nonetheless, this Western philosophy and tradition may contrast with other traditions and political philosophies, as Asad argues: "Assuming, then, that agency need not be conceptualized in terms of individual self-empowerment, or universal historicity, how should it be understood? One might begin by looking at usages of the term (or what we take to be its equivalents) in different historical contexts. This would indicate not merely that agency is not a natural category, but that successive conceptions of agency as a discursive category have opened up or closed very different possibilities for acting or being" (2000, 33).

Interested in opening up other possibilities for acting and being, I have sought usages and understandings of the term *agency* in the ethnographic setting of this study, engaging in an exercise similar to the one I conducted with *jins* (sex/gender) and *jīl* (generation) in chapters 3 and 4, respectively. In this ethnographic setting, agency is not necessarily understood as external and resistant to power but rather, per Asad's suggestion, as saturated with it. In one move, this understanding saves us from the complicated distinctions between constituted and constituent powers and from the paradox of representation depicted earlier. When I asked friends of mine—native Arabic-speaking anthropologists and Shatila *shabāb*— they all told me that the term *agency* has no obvious translation into Arabic, which is probably why NGO documents and personnel prefer to use the word in English (in the case of NGO staff, on the rare occasions that they speak Arabic at all and can think of alternatives to *agency* in local idioms). We all agreed that *wikāla* is inappropriate: too material, it serves to indicate an office (as in the CIA, a friend remarked), not an action. I suggested *qudra*, which, following *The Hans Wehr Dictionary*, means "to possess strength, power, and ability," and convinced an anthropologist friend, who nevertheless preferred to add a second word to fully grasp the sense of agency: '*irāda* (will). Nadim, a *shāb* from the surroundings of Shatila, provided the most intriguing definition, as so often happened throughout my period in Lebanon: "That's a difficult one, Gustavo. Maybe '*abbada* is what you're looking for." '*Abbada* is form 2 of the verb '*abada*, the religious overtones of which are captured by *The Hans Wehr Dictionary*: "to serve, worship, adore, venerate, idolize, deify." Form 2 in Arabic is often a causative version of the original verb, so that '*abbada*, standing for "to make serve, to make worship, to make idolize," is defined by *The Hans Wehr Dictionary* as not only "to improve, develop, make serviceable" but also "to enslave, enthrall, subjugate, subject." Thus, agency, in this rendition at least, is not heroically opposed to power but conspires with it.

That is precisely why I adopted the methodology the *shabāb* suggested: when one has limited power or none, better to *queer* it. Both on an epistemological and methodological level, queering is *not* the most recent incarnation of gay and lesbian studies, nor does it have homosexuality as its sole object of interest (Amar and El Shakry 2013). Rather, it designates a movement *against* appropriation by mainstreaming LGBTIQ and feminist movements, both of which provide, unwittingly or not, ideological scaffolding for the mantra of a neocolonial "civilizing mission," a bare disguise for intervention and war (Jacob 2013).[4] Queering refuses the all-too-facile freezing of purified identities, forces analysts to interrogate their categories ("woman," "refugee," "Palestinian"), and rejects exclusionary binaries that can serve to pathologize the categorically nonnormative (such as heterosexual men with limited or no power, as discussed in chapter 3).

Anti-identitarian and antiprogrammatic, queering is disruptive: it liquefies frozen identities and renders bare not life but structures of power—academic or otherwise. It exposes genealogies of the invisible within dominant histories (Sedgwick 1991), such as *shabāb* with limited power or none. Through constant intervention to avoid identitarian paralysis, it places movement before position (Massumi 2002; Puar 2007) and is forever a verb: *to queer*. Anticategorical, it does not allow domestication through submission to *one* nationality, *one* legal status, *one* race, *one* sex, *one* sect, *one* gender, which so easily nurtures the statistical hunger for grids (as shown in chapter 2). More exactly, it proliferates nationalities, legal statuses, sexes, sects, genders, races: a thousand tiny sexes (Grosz 1993; Deleuze and Guattari [1987] 2004), a thousand tiny races (Saldanha 2006), a thousand plateaus (Deleuze and Guattari [1987] 2004), a thousand feet, as in Raad's film *Welcome to Shatila*. Instead of the reproduction of the same, queering envisages the regeneration of the multiple (Puar 2007). "Against purity" (Gedalof 1999), queering allows the contemplation of open-ended horizons; nonsovereign political futures; other modes of living, engaging, and relating; alternative modalities of belonging and connectivity; new communities, colonies, and politics based on "affective confusion" (Amit Rai, quoted in Puar 2007, 208).

---

4. Based on such a framework, it is as if Afghanistan needs to be invaded so that its women can be liberated, and Israel needs to continue its settler policies so that Middle Eastern gays and lesbians can have a safe haven in an otherwise supposedly homophobic region (Puar 2007, 2013).

Sex and the Citizen

By queering sex and gender in chapter 3, I opened up space for contemplating new possibilities of manhood. I have not treated "men" as an internally coherent category and have used age and historical experience to fracture it and then to map out alternative masculinities: the *shabāb* may have limited or no economic, political, or military power, but they are not emasculated. I have avoided succumbing to the binarisms that serve to scaffold "battle-of-sex" dystopias (Eltahawy 2012). Chapter 4, in turn, attempts to queer youth. It shows how youth works as a tool for a neocolonial governmentality: "remove your barriers to free trade, reduce labor-protection standards, trim down state controls so that youth can blossom," preaches the neoliberal agenda.

Following in the footsteps about to be taken by the shoes in the last scene of Raad's movie, chapter 5 seeks to queer citizenship. Citizenship normally rests on oversimplifying categorizations, reducing variation so as to fit into grids (as in chapter 2). Difference, though, is often intransigent (Mikdashi 2013). Chapter 5 invites the reader to gaze at and set free citizenships of the otherwise (Povinelli 2006, 2011). The exploits by the pigeon raisers and noncockfighters from Shatila illustrate how Foucault's "care of the self" has ethical-political dimensions. The "care of the self" is an art—an "art of presence" (Bayat 2010)—and is used to describe those who, having ascetically gained possession and control of themselves (Shatilans would say, those who have acquired *'aql*, as we saw in chapter 3), submit to no other and can thus take their rightful place in the community (Foucault 1988; Gaonkar 1999). In this sense, the "care of the self" is a practice of freedom. But here I want to take the concept one step further and suggest that it is also an "act of [queered] citizenship." Instead of being an entitlement, "acts of citizenship" designate those moments in which subjects constitute themselves as citizens (Isin 2008).

It is at this point that Hannah Arendt comes to Shatila. By distinguishing political power and sovereignty, Arendt (1963, 1973), in an anti-Hobbesian move, shows that there is a politics beyond the sovereign (see also Jennings 2011). Hobbes assumes that the sovereign and the tyrant are one and the same. The whole of the revolutionary tradition tries to come to terms with the fact that the constituent power of the people is forever gone the moment sovereignty is instituted. Sovereignty is thus nothing but the constituted power over which we, the people, have ceased to have claims. Arendt does not pay homage to the philosophical fiction at the origin of this edifice, according to which men in the state of nature have agreed to give up their power and submit to Leviathan. Arendt prefers history to fiction and brings examples—such as the commune in Paris in 1871, the Soviets in Russia in 1917, and the workers' council in Hungary in 1956— that give proof that when states collapse, people are not pushed back into a "war of all against all" and may actually govern themselves. This is so because the constituent and constituted power have never been external to one another, and there is no pristine moment, other than in philosophical fiction, of brutalized wolfmen giving up their power to become equal under Leviathan. That is why in the polis, as described and envisaged by Arendt, each person lives up to her political role: there is no anarchy, and there is freedom, with freedom understood not simply as liberation from oppression. Over Shatila, the pigeons can fly.

If camps have traditionally worked as laboratories for political experiments, allowing for the containment and imprisonment of those considered dangerous, suspicious, and abject, first in the colonies but eventually also in Europe (Panourgiá 2009; Petti 2013), chapter 5 considers the possibility that they may also work as sites for political invention, enabling the contemplation of nonsovereign political futures. If there is no clear functioning source of political authority in Shatila, no state that is one (De Cesari 2010), and no Leviathan to keep us all in awe (we are not easily terrorized or amazed), Shatilans have learned how to do without. They used to manage to keep their birds airborne, and here their experiments meet those of other Palestinians in the Dehesha refugee camp in Bethlehem. There, the refugee community has appropriated a site—which once functioned consecutively as a military compound for the British army, the Jordanian army, and the Israeli army and was to become a prison under the Palestinian Authority—and has effectively put an end to the disciplinary history of the place (Petti 2013). The community instead uses the site today as a culture center and has named it, quite evocatively, "al-Finīq"

(Phoenix), after the mythological bird that rises from the ashes of its predecessor. Al-Finīq is a multifunctional facility and hosts weddings, a library (dedicated to Edward Said), a gym, a guesthouse, and the Campus in Camps, a university in exile, which brings together participants from various places to "explore and produce new forms of representation of camps and refugees," in the words of one participant.[5] Campus in Camps not only produces new forms of representation of camps and refugees but also, according to the acting director, Alessandro Petti, "aims at transgressing, without eliminating, the distinction between camp and city, refugee and citizen, center and periphery, theory and practice" (2013).

In her effort to dissolve sovereignty and to separate the nation from its supposedly mandatory founding on a territory, Arendt believes in "modes of belonging" and polities that are not reduced to the concept of the nation-state (Butler 2007)—the latter a stratagem that has consistently produced enormous numbers of stateless people. When chastised by Gershom Scholem for showing "no love of Jewish people," Arendt responded that being a woman and being a Jew are indisputable facts of her life. She continued: "There is a basic gratitude for everything that is as it is, for what has been *given and not made*; for what is *physei* and not *nomo*" (quoted in Butler 2007, original emphasis). Yet, as argued in chapter 3, there is always a making of what is supposedly given—a "woman"—and thus the distinction between *physei* and *nomo* is never completely clear-cut. Indisputably a Jew, Arendt still takes a political stand that would not conform to what a Jew should say according to Scholem's binary "with us or against us" logic. Here is her answer to Scholem:

> You are quite right—I am not moved by any "love" of this sort, and for two reasons. I have never in my life "loved" any people or collective—neither the German people, nor the French, nor the American, nor the working class or anything of that sort. I indeed love "only" my friends and the only kind of love I know of and believe in is the love of persons. Secondly, this "love of the Jews" would appear to me, since I

---

5. For more on Campus in Camps, see http://www.campusincamps.ps/en/about/.

am myself Jewish, as something rather suspect. I cannot love myself or anything which I know is part and parcel of my own person. (quoted in Butler 2007)

Hence, for Arendt, there is love beyond Narcissus. A love of difference is possible and serves as a basis for politics.

The Antilove of Empire

I would like to conclude this study in a manner similar to the way I started it.[6] I invite my reader to find our way back to downtown Beirut. There, once again, we can admire another installation by Nada Sehnaoui, *Light at the End of the Tunnel*. The installation was exhibited from September 12 to October 14, 2012, at Zaytouna Square, a promenade of restaurants and fashionable shops bordering the Mediterranean, not far from the space where Sehnaoui exposed the six hundred toilets in her work *Haven't 15 Years of Hiding in Toilettes Been Enough?* some four years earlier (see chapter 1). This time Sehnaoui created mazelike structures by piling or lining up 360 wooden parallelepipeds painted bright red. Once again, the artist's intention was to provoke passersby. The hollow structures spoke of the obstacles of navigating the labyrinthine conflicts in Lebanon (Taylor 2012). Once inside the red maze, one could see through it and realize that there was a way out despite the difficulties of maneuvering, or one could let oneself become entrapped by the vicious structure. Moreover, onlookers could simply grab one of the parallelepipeds and put it in a new position, helping reshape the labyrinth. The artist explained: "The way out can be horizontal, vertical, that isn't important. It is necessary always to try to find it. No doubt the enclosure is at the level of the city, but also at that of our thoughts" (quoted in Khalaf 2012).

In today's tragic times of disenchantment, when the intellectual and political certainties of the 1970s are bygone and missed, we—other researchers and I, the Shatila *shabāb* and other *shabāb*—are searching for a

---

6. This section is named after Elizabeth Povinelli's book *The Empire of Love* (2006).

way out. Here, I propose putting on the shoes offered by Raad, the film-maker, to imagine an alternative musing. Instead of paying homage to structuralism's highly sophisticated abstractions (Lévi-Strauss 1986), I wish to suggest a move from metaphor back to metonym. Challenging though metonyms may be to think with, at least within certain canons, they are good to act with politically. The logics of belonging explored in this study do not depend on exclusionary, precise, or purified categories: the antilove of empire—academic or otherwise—may bring us all, including *shabāb*, researcher, and reader, metonymically together in what Jean Genet ([1986] 2004) would call "love." For, ultimately, I have challenged the immemorial wisdom of the Arab proverb "Man ʿāshara qawmān, raḥala ʿanhum aw ṣāra minhum": "He who lives with a people either leaves them or becomes one of them." I have left and yet sustain the hope and fantasy of remaining "one of them." When I shared with Ahmad, whose story I told in chapters 1 and 2, the difficulties I was facing to renew my visa to return to the United Kingdom to finish my doctoral work, he commented: "Oh, Gustavo, you lived for too long among us. Now you know not only how difficult it is to live here. You also know how difficult it is to leave Lebanon and Shatila behind." Indeed.

Glossary
of Levantine
Arabic Terms

References

Index

Glossary of Levantine Arabic Terms

This glossary was elaborated with the nonspeaker of Arabic in mind. I often removed the article *al-*, "the" in English, from the front of the words, even when the latter appear with the article in the text. In the glossary, I kept the article in a few cases only, when mandated because of grammar or meaning. In arranging the words alphabetically, I also ignored the article *al-*, when present, as well as the differences between ayn and hamza and between emphatic and nonemphatic letters.

'abada: To serve, worship, adore, venerate, idolize, and deify
'abbada: To make serve, to make worship, to make idolize, to improve, to develop, to make serviceable, to enslave, to enthral, to subjugate, to subject
abu, pl. *bayyāt*: Father
al-'āda al-sirriyya: Secret habit; i.e., masturbation
'ādī: Normal, ordinary
'adwār: Roles
afham: To understand, to gain consciousness
'ahhal: To embrace
"Ahlān fīk bil-mukhayyamāt": "Welcome to the Camps," song by the rap group Katibe 5
'ahlū: His people
'ahzāb: Political parties
'ā'ila: Extended family
'ā'ilatū: His family
al-'ajyāl al-mādiya: Past generations
'akh, pl. *'ikhwa*: Brother
"'Akl al-rijāl 'alā qad 'af'ālahā": "A man eats what he does."
'alā habsā: To prison

273

'*alāma*: Trousseau, normally consisting of clothes, makeup, and perfume for the
     bride
'*amm*: Uncle (father's brother)
'*amal*: Hope
al-'amal al-shāq: Hard work
'*amaliyyat al-talqīḥ*: Fertilizing capacity
'*amān*: Safety
'*ammatī*: My aunt (father's sister)
'*ammī*: My uncle (father's brother)
"**Ana w'īt**": "I got wiser." See also *wa'ī*.
'*aqīda*: Dogma
'*aql*: Capacity for reasoning
'*aqṭa'a*: To divide up (land, for instance)
'*arḍ*: Honor
'*arḍ*: Land
'*arḍhum*: Their land
'*arḍ ṭāhira*: A pure land
'*arḍū*: His or one's land
'*asaf*: Sorrow
'*ashbāl*: Cubs
'*athwāb*: Traditional Middle Eastern gowns
'*ayyām al-thawra*: The days of the revolution from 1967 to 1982, the heyday of the
     Palestinian resistance in its military form in Lebanon and other diasporas
'*azābū*: His suffering
az'ar: Bad boy
badīl: Replacement
baladū: His country
basīṭīn (pl.): Simple
bazziq wa lazziq: "Glued with saliva," meaning work not properly executed
bi-hudū': Quietly
bil-bayt: In the house; a woman *bil-bayt* is a housewife.
bint, pl. *banāt*: Girl, woman assumed to be a virgin, daughter
bint 'amm: Father's brother's daughter
bitḍaḥḥī: To sacrifice
bulūgh: Puberty, maturity
bunduqiyya: Machine gun
bunya: (Strong) build

chauffage: Heating

dabka: Folk dance from the Levant

dāfiʿ: Motivation

ḍāʾiʿa: Lost

ḍaʿīf: Weak, no power

dākhil: Inside

darak: Police

al-dawra al-shahriyya: Monthly cycle; i.e., menstruation

dhakar: Male

dhalīl: Subservient

dhill: Humiliation

dhurriyatī: My descendants

dīn: Religion

fakhr: Pride

fallāḥ, pl. *fallāḥīn*: Peasant

fallāḥa: Female peasant

faltānīn (pl.): Loose

farāgh: Emptiness

faṣīla, pl. *faṣāʾil*: Faction

fiʾāt: Groups

fidāʾī, pl. *fidāʾiyyīn*: Male freedom fighter, willing to sacrifice himself in the fight
    for the liberation of his homeland

fidāʾiyya, pl. *fidāʾiyyāt*: Female freedom fighter; feminine of *fidāʾī*

fidāya: Fighters' movement

Filasṭīn: Palestine

finīq: Phoenix

ghaḍab: Rage

gharīb, fem. *gharība*: Stranger, alien, foreign

ghurba: Homesickness, longing for a place left behind

ḥabībatī: My girlfriend

al-hadaf al-aqṣā: The ultimate goal

ḥall: Solution

ḥamāma: Pigeon; willy (penis)

ḥamās: Enthusiasm

"Al-ḥamdulillah": "Thanks to God."

ḥanūn: Affectionate, compassionate, motherly, tenderhearted

ḥaqq: Right, truth

ḥaqq al-'awda: Right of return (to Palestine)
ḥaraka: Mobility
ḥarām: Forbidden; sometimes "what a shame"
Ḥarb al-Mukhayyamāt: War of the Camps
"Ḥatta 'ish'ār 'ākhar": "Until Another Announcement," song by the rap group
    Katibe 5
hawiyya: Identity
hawiyya zarqā: Blue ID card (e.g., that identifies Palestinians in Lebanon)
"Hawiyya zarqā": "Blue ID Card," song by the group Hawiyya Zarqā
ḥayāt karīma: A decent life
hayk hayk: So-so
ḥijāb: Head scarf
hijra: Migration
ḥikma: Wisdom
ḥiqd: Hatred
ḥirik: Active
hudū': Tranquility
ḥukūma: Government
ḥurriyya: Freedom
'ibn al-balad: Literally a "son of the country," meaning a national
'ibn al-mukhayyam: Son of the camp
'idhlāl: Humiliation
'iḍṭihād: Oppression
'iḥtiqān: Frustration
'ikht, pl. *'ikhwāt*: Sister
'ikhwatī: My brothers (in the context of this book, meaning brothers-in-arms)
'ilim: Knowledge, colloquial version of *'ilm* (see below)
"Illī byākul al-'iṣī mish mitil illī bi'iddā": "He who's being whipped is not like
    he who's counting the blows."
"'Illī jāyī": "What will come."
'ilm: Science, sometimes education
'iltizām: Commitment
'infi'āl: Emotional stress
'inqaṭa'a: To be cut off
'inshiqāq: Division
'iqtaṭa'a: To take a cut of
'irāda: Will

'Isrā'īl: Israel

'istaqṭa'a: To deduct

'istihzā': The fact of being scornful

'istijdā': To beg

'istijnās: Homosexuality

'istiqrār: Stability, settling down

jaha: A committee composed of respected members within the community, often elderly men, who conduct processes of reconciliation in situations of dispute; see also ṣulḥa and muṣālaḥa

jam'iyya, pl. jam'iyyāt: Joint pooling of resources by different households, to be used by those taking part in the arrangement when and if the need arises; also used to refer to an NGO

"Jam'iyyāt": "NGOs," song by the rap group Katibe 5

jannasa: Various meanings, depending on the form: form 2, to make alike, to assimilate, to naturalize, to class, to classify, to categorize; form 3, to be akin, related, similar, and of the same kind or nature or to resemble; form 5, to acquire citizenship or to be naturalized; and form 6, to be akin or homogenous

jīl: Generation

jīl al-'intifāḍa: Generation of the intifada

jīl al-Nakba: Generation of the Nakba, or Catastrophe

jīl al-thawra: Generation of the revolution

jīl al-yawm: Present generation

al-jindir: The gender

jinn: Genie; a magical creature with free will, mentioned in the Qur'an

jins: Sex and, according to some, gender

al-jins al-'ijtimā'ī: The social sex

jinsiyya, pl. jinsiyyāt: Nationality

al-kabar ka-marā: Growing up as a woman

al-kabar ka-zalamī: Growing up as a man

karāma: Dignity

khajal: Shyness

khāl: Uncle (mother's brother)

khāla: Aunt (mother's sister)

khālak: Your uncle (mother's brother)

khalaṣ: Over, enough, the end of it

khālatī: My aunt (mother's sister)

khayrāt: Resources

khitiār: Elderly man

khuḍū': Subjection

khunū': Humiliation

khushūna: Harshness

khuṭūba: Engagement, which normally requires that the groom buy an engagement ring and sometimes also pay the first part of the bride price, the *muqaddam*

kifāḥ: Struggle

ktīr: A lot

kuffiyya, pl. *kuffiyyāt*: Arab headdress

"Kul hadhā 'ādī": "All this is normal."

kuramā': Generous

"Lā 'ilāha 'illā Allāh, wa Muḥammad rasūl Allāh": "There is no god but God, and Mohammed is his messenger." This is the *shahāda*, or testimony, a single but sincere enunciation of which several schools consider sufficient for conversion to Islam.

la 'uyūnak: Literally, "for your eyes," meaning "you're welcome"

lawih: Leader of a *dabka* dance line

Lubnān: Lebanon

al-lubnānī: Lebanese man

ma'ārif: Acquaintances

ma'āsh: Salary

mabda', pl. *mabādi'*: Principle

madanī: Urbanite

maftūḥ: Open

ma'had: Educational institute

mahr: Bride price

mahzūmīn (pl.): Defeated

mā 'indū khajal: Not shy

malal: Boredom

mamnū': Forbidden

manābit: Plant nurseries

"Man 'āshara qawmān, raḥala 'anhum aw ṣāra minhum": "He who lives with a people either leaves them or becomes one of them."

maraḍ nafsī: The psychological condition of *mal d'âme*, soul sickness

masbaḥa: String of beads that helps Muslims keep track of their prayers

māshī ṣaḥ: Walking the right line

mashkaljī: Troublemaker
mas'ūliyya: Responsibility
mas'ūliyyāt 'akhlāqiyya: Moral responsibilities
maṭlūb: Wanted (by the police)
min al-dākhil: Deep inside
"Mīn 'irhābī?": "Who's the Terrorist?," song by the Palestine-based group DAM
mu'akhkhar: Second part of the bride price, negotiated prior to the wedding and
    paid in case the husband asks for a divorce
mū'amman: Secure
Mu'askar al-'Ashbāl: Cubs' Camp, an organization similar to the Boy Scouts that
    trained young Palestinian men during the *thawra*
muḥtaram: Respectable
muḥtashima: Modest
mujaddara: Dish made of rice, lentils, and caramelized onions
mujānasa: Relatedness, kinship, affinity, likeness, and resemblance
mujtama'nā: Our society
mukhābir: Intelligence agent
al-mukhayyamāt al-filasṭīniyya: The Palestinian camps
mukhayyamjīn: Camp residents
mumayyazīn (pl.): Special
mun'aṭafāt: Twists
muqaddam: First part of the bride price, *mahr*, paid by the groom to the bride at
    the marriage ceremony or immediately prior to or after it
muqaddarīn (pl.): Appreciated
muqātilīn: Fighters
muqāwama: Resistance
murāhaqa: Adolescence
murāhiq: Adolescent
Al-Murāqaba wa al-mu'āqaba (1990): Arabic translation of *Discipline and Pun-
    ish* ([1977] 1995) by Michel Foucault
muṣālaḥa, pl. *muṣālaḥāt*: Reconciliation
muṣallā: Rug used for praying
mushkila: Problem
Nakba: Catastrophe
naṣr: Victory
al-naw' al-'ijtimā'ī: Social type or grouping
nāzihīn (pl.): Displaced

niḍāl: Struggle

niswān: Older women, normally sexually experienced

niẓām: System

nūr ʿuyūnī: Light of my eyes

nuʿūma: Softness

qāda: Leaders

qaḍiyya: Cause, case, question

al-qaḍiyya al-filasṭīniyya: The Palestinian cause

qaraf: Disgust

qāṭaʿa: To cut off

qaṭaʿa: To cut

qaṭṭaʿa: To chop up

qudra: To possess strength, power, and ability

al-qudra ʿalā al-ʾinjāb: The ability to give birth

qunn: Coop

quwwa: Power, strength

quyūd : Restrictions

rābiṭa: Association

rajul: Man

"Al-rijjāl mā biʿībū ʾillā jībū": "Only his pocket shames a man."

ruʿb: Terror

rummāna: Pomegranate, grenade

rumūz: Symbols

"Ṣabāḥ al-khayr": "Good morning."

ṣabr, ṣabir: Patience

safar: Migrating

"Ṣallā Allāhu ʿalayhi wa-sallam": "May God honor him [Prophet Mohammed] and grant him peace." Muslims often say this to praise Prophet Mohammed whenever they mention his name.

ṣāmidīn **(pl.)**: Steadfast

ṣamt: Silence

ṣayd: Hunt

shāb, **pl.** *shabāb*: Lad, young man (normally still single)

shahāda: Testimony

shahīd, **pl.** *shuhadāʾ*: Martyr

sharaf: Honor

shatāt: Diaspora

Shātīlā: Shatila
shiʿār: Banner
"Shū chauffage?": "What is heating?"
shūf: Have a look
shughul: Work
"Shū huwa al-jindir?": "What is gender?"
shujʿān **(pl.):** Brave
shuʿla: Torch
al-ṣifāt al-jasadiyya: Bodily traits
siḥr: Magic
silāḥ: Weapon
"Ṣilat raḥim": "Womb Link," song by the rap group Katibe 5
al-ṣirāṭ al-mustaqīm: The straight way
ṣīt wusikh: Bad reputation
stablāt: Stables
ṣubbār: Cactus
ṣulḥa: Reconciliation
sulṭa: Sovereign power
ṣumūd: Steadfastness
sūsa: Pest
taʿālīm: Instructions
taʾāmar: To conspire
taʿāsa: Misery
tabādul: Reciprocity
ṭabaqa: Class
tāfihīn **(pl.):** Silly
tafkīr salīm: A good way of thinking
taḥāluf: Alliance
taḥammul: Endurance
tahtamm: To care
tajānus: Homogeneity
tajnīs: Nationalization or political categorization
tajriba **or** *tajruba:* Experience
takhdaʿ: To trick
takhdimnī: "[She] serves me."
taʿlīm: Education
ṭammāʿīn **(pl.):** Greedy

tanẓīm, **pl.** *tanẓīmat*: Organization, in this text sometimes meaning "political faction"

taqāṭaʿa: To intersect

taqaṭṭaʿa: To be chopped up

ṭarab: Ecstatic emotional state induced by music

tarbiya madaniyya: Civil education

tarbiyat al-ʾawlād: Child rearing

taʿṭī: To give

tawṭīn: Naturalization (for instance of Palestinian refugees in Lebanon)

thawra: Revolution

thuwwār: Revolutionaries

ṭifl: Baby, child, little boy

ṭufūla: Childhood

ṭumūḥ: Ambition

turāb: Soil

turāth: Traditions, heritage, patrimony

turāthnā: Our heritage

ʿubūdiyya: Slavery

umm, **pl.** *ʾummahāt*: Mother

ʿunfuwān: Zeal, vigor

ʿunṣur: Race

ʾunthā: Female

ʾunūthatī: My femininity

ʾusra jayyida: Nice, good family

ʾuṭlub al-ʿilm: Seek knowledge

waḥsh, **pl.** *wuḥūsh*: Monster

waʿī: To understand, to gain consciousness

wājib: Duty

wajih: Literally "face" but sometimes meaning "leader"

wa kida: And stuff

walad, **pl.** *ʾawlād*: Boy, son

wāsṭa: Means, often referring to the connections and network of influences one needs to expedite procedures or enhance chances of success when, for example, getting a job or a promotion, having documents issued, or securing a bed in a hospital

waṭan: Nation, homeland

wazin: Form

wikāla: Agency (as in Central Intelligence Agency)
wuqūd: Fuel
yā 'akhī: My brother, my bro
yahūdiyyat (fem., pl.): Jews
yakbar: [He] grows up.
"Yā m'ammin bil-rijāl zay al-may bil-ghirbāl": "You who trust men are like water in a sieve."
ya'nī: "That is to say" or "I mean"
yarghul: A kind of double clarinet
yataḥakkam: [He] controls.
yiṭayyaz: "[He] shows his ass [to somebody]," meaning sometimes to ignore (something, somebody)
zahra, pl. *zahrāt* (pl): Literally "flower" but also used to name gatherings, Zahrāt, to which, during the *'ayyām al-thawra*, young Palestinian girls were sent, where the young girls sang nationalistic songs or read and wrote nationalistic poetry but were provided no military training—different, therefore, from what happened in the Mu'askar al-'Ashbāl, normally reserved for the boys
zalamī: Man
zawāj: Marriage
zinā: A Qura'nic and biblical word for extramarital sex
ẓulum: Injustice

References

Aasheim, Petter. 2000. "The Palestinian Refugees and the Right to Work in Lebanon." Graduate thesis, Univ. of Lund.

Abbas, Mahmoud, Hussein Shaaban, Bassem Sirham, and Ali Hassan. 1997. "The Socio-economic Conditions of Palestinians in Lebanon." *Journal of Refugee Studies* 10, no. 3: 378–96.

Abdallah, Stéphanie. 2006. *Femmes réfugiées palestiniennes.* Paris: Presses universitaires de France.

Abdo, Nahla. 1999. "Gender and Politics under the Palestinian Authority." *Journal of Palestine Studies* 28, no. 2: 38–51.

Abélès, Marc. 2005. *Anthropologie de l'état.* Paris: Payot.

Abu-Lughod, Lila. 1989. "Zones of Theory in the Anthropology of the Arab World." *Annual Review of Anthropology* 18:267–306.

———. 1991. "Writing against Culture." In *Recapturing Anthropology: Working in the Present,* edited by Richard Fox, 137–54. Santa Fe, NM: School of American Research Press.

———. 1993. *Writing Women's Worlds: Bedouin Stories.* Berkeley: Univ. of California Press.

Agamben, Giorgio. 1998. *Homo Sacer: Sovereign Power and Bare Life.* Translated by Daniel Heller-Roazen. Stanford, CA: Stanford Univ. Press.

———. 2005. *State of Exception.* Translated by Kevin Attell. Chicago: Univ. of Chicago Press.

Agier, Michel. 1999. *L'Invention de la ville: Banlieues, townships, invasions et favelas.* Paris: Archives contemporaines.

———. 2010. *Esquisses d'une anthropologie de la ville: Lieux, situations, mouvements.* Louvain-la-Neuve, Belgium: Academia Bruylant.

Ahmed, Leila. 1992. *Women and Gender in Islam.* New Haven, CT: Yale Univ. Press.

Allan, Diana. 2007. "Eating Their God: The Contingencies of Nationalism and Survival in Shatila Camp." PhD diss., Harvard Univ.

————. 2014a. "Boom: A Photo Essay: Construction and Destruction in Shatila and Gaza." Stanford Univ. Press blog, July 31. At https://stanfordpress.type pad.com/blog/2014/07/boom-a-photo-essay.html.

————. 2014b. *Refugees of the Revolution: Experiences of Exile in Lebanon.* Stanford, CA: Stanford Univ. Press.

Altorki, Soraya. 1986. *Women in Saudi Arabia: Ideology and Behavior among the Elite.* New York: Columbia Univ. Press.

Amar, Paul. 2011. "Middle East Masculinity Studies: Discourses of 'Men in Crisis,' Industries of Gender in Revolution." *Journal of Middle East Women's Studies* 7, no. 3: 36–70.

Amar, Paul, and Omnia El Shakry. 2013. "Introduction: Curiosities of Middle East Studies in Queer Times." In "Queer Affects," special issue of *International Journal of Middle East Studies* 45, no. 2: 331–35.

American Anthropological Association. 1998. "Code of Ethics of the American Anthropological Association." Ethics Code Collection. At https://ethics.iit .edu/ecodes/node/3163.

————. 2009. "Code of Ethics of the American Anthropological Association." Ethics Code Collection. At https://ethics.iit.edu/ecodes/node/4861.

————. 2012. "Principles of Professional Responsibility." AAA Ethics Forum. At http://ethics.americananthro.org/ethics-statement-0-preamble/.

Anand, Nikhil. 2010. "Pressure: The Politechnics of Water Supply in Mumbai." Paper presented at "Workshop on Waterscapes, Labor, and Uncertainty." Department of Anthropology, London School of Economics and Political Science.

Arendt, Hannah. 1963. *On Revolution.* New York: Viking Press.

————. 1973. *The Origins of Totalitarianism.* New York: Harcourt Brace Jovanovich.

Ariès, Philippe. 1962. *Centuries of Childhood: A Social History of Family Life.* Translated by Robert Baldick. New York: Knopf.

Asad, Talal. 1993. "The Concept of Cultural Translation in British Social Anthropology." In *Genealogies of Religion: Discipline and Reasons of Power in Christianity and Islam,* 171–99. Baltimore: Johns Hopkins Univ. Press.

————. 2000. "Agency and Pain: An Exploration." *Culture and Religion* 1, no. 1: 29–60.

————. 2008. "Where Are the Margins of the State?" In *Anthropology in the Margins of the State,* edited by Veena Das and Deborah Poole, 279–88. Santa Fe, NM: School of American Research Press.

Baily, John, and Michael Collyer. 2006. "Introduction: Music and Migration." In "Music and Migration," special issue of *Journal of Ethnic and Migration Studies* 32, no. 2: 167–82.

Barbosa, Gustavo. 2004. "A Socialidade contra o Estado: A Antropologia de Pierre Clastres." *Revista de Antropologia* 47, no. 2: 529–76.

Bateson, Gregory. [1979] 1980a. *Mind and Nature: A Necessary Unit.* New York: Bantham Books.

———. [1972] 1980b. *Steps to an Ecology of Mind.* New York: Ballantine Books.

———. [1958] 2003. *Naven: A Survey of the Problems Suggested by a Composite Picture of the Culture of a New Guinea Tribe Drawn from Three Points of View.* Stanford, CA: Stanford Univ. Press.

Bateson, Mary Catherine. 1987. "So What's a Meta For?" In Gregory Bateson and Mary Catherine Bateson, *Angels Fear: Towards an Epistemology of the Sacred*, 183–200. New York: Macmillan.

Bauman, Zygmunt. 2000. *Liquid Modernity.* Cambridge: Polity Press.

Bayat, Asef. 2010. *Life as Politics: How Ordinary People Change the Middle East.* Stanford, CA: Stanford Univ. Press.

Bennett, Andy. 1999. "Hip Hop am Maim: The Localisation of Rap Music and Hip Hop Culture." *Media, Culture, and Society* 21, no. 1: 77–91.

———. 2001. *Cultures of Popular Music.* Berkshire, UK: Open Univ. Press.

Bhabha, Homi. 1985. "Signs Taken for Wonders: Questions of Ambivalence and Authority under a Tree outside Delhi, May 1817." *Critical Inquiry* 12, no. 1: 144–65.

———. 2004. *The Location of Culture.* London: Routledge.

Bianchi, Sergio. 2011. "Vers un nouvel imaginaire national? Transformation de l'action associative au sein de la Communauté Palestinienne au Liban." In *Le Développement, une affair d'ONG? Associations, états et bailleurs dans le monde Arabe*, edited by Caroline Aub-Sada and Benoît Challand, 95–124. Paris: IREMAN and IFPO.

Bly, Robert. 1991. *Iron John: A Book about Men.* Dorset, UK: Element Books.

Bocchi, Giovanni. 2007. "The Production of Difference: Sociality, Work, and Mobility in a Community of Syrian Dom between Lebanon and Syria." PhD diss., London School of Economics and Political Science.

Borneman, John. 2004. *Death of the Father: An Anthropology of the End in Political Authority.* New York: Berghahn Books.

———. 2007. *Syrian Episodes: Sons, Fathers, and an Anthropologist in Aleppo.* Princeton, NJ: Princeton Univ. Press.

Bourdieu, Pierre. 1977. *Outline of a Theory of Practice*. Translated by Richard Nice. Cambridge: Cambridge Univ. Press.

———. 1993. *Sociology in Question*. Translated by Richard Nice. London: Sage.

Bracewell, Wendy. 2000. "Rape in Kosovo: Masculinity and Serbian Nationalism." *Nations and Nationalism* 6, no. 4: 562–90.

Butler, Judith. 1990. *Gender Trouble: Feminism and the Subversion of Identity*. London: Routledge.

———. 1993. *Bodies That Matter: On the Discursive Limits of Sex*. London: Routledge.

———. 2004. *Undoing Gender*. London: Routledge.

———. 2007. "I Merely Belong to Them." *London Review of Books* 29, no. 9. At https://www.lrb.co.uk/the-paper/v29/n09/judith-butler/i-merely-belong-to -them.

———. 2012. "Precarious Life, Vulnerability, and the Ethics of Cohabitation." *Journal of Speculative Philosophy* 26, no. 2: 134–51.

Campbell, Beatrix. 1991. "Kings of the Road." *Marxism Today*, final issue: 20–23.

———. 1993. *Goliath: Britain's Dangerous Places*. London: Methuen.

Carpi, Estella. 2016. "Against Ontologies of Hospitality: About Syrian Refugehood in Northern Lebanon." Middle East Institute. At https://www.research gate.net/publication/309479780_Against_Ontologies_of_Hospitality_About _Syrian_Refugeehood_in_Northern_Lebanon.

Carpi, Estella, and Hatice Şenoğuz. 2019. "Refugee Hospitality in Lebanon and Turkey: On Making 'the Other.'" *International Migration* 57, no. 2: 126–42.

Carsten, Janet. 1995. "The Substance of Kinship and the Heat of the Hearth: Feeding, Personhood, and Relatedness among the Malay in Pulau Langkwai." *American Ethnologist* 22, no. 2: 223–41.

———. 2000. *Cultures of Relatedness: New Approaches to the Study of Kinship*. Cambridge: Cambridge Univ. Press.

Caton, Steven. 1985. "The Poetic Construction of the Self." *Anthropological Quarterly* 58, no. 4: 141–51.

Chakrabarty, Dipesh. 2000. *Provincializing Europe: Postcolonial Thought and Historical Difference*. Princeton, NJ: Princeton Univ. Press.

Chalcraft, John. 2009. *The Invisible Cage: Syrian Migrant Workers in Lebanon*. Stanford, CA: Stanford Univ. Press.

Charrad, Mounira. 2001. *States and Women's Rights: The Making of Postcolonial Tunisia, Algeria, and Morocco*. Berkeley: Univ. of California Press.

Chatty, Dawn. 2017a. "An Anthropological Approach to Understanding Percep-tions, Aspirations, and Behavior of Refugees, Practioners, and Host Com-munity Members in Jordan, Lebanon, and Turkey." *Middle East Journal of Refugee Studies* 2, no. 1: 35–49.

———. 2017b. "The Syrian Humanitarian Disaster: Understanding Perceptions and Aspirations in Jordan, Lebanon, and Turkey." *Global Policy* 8, no. 1: 25–32.

Chesnot, Christian, and Josephine Lama. 1998. *Palestiniens 1948–1998, généra-tions fedayin: De la lutte armée à l'autonomie.* Paris: Autrement.

Christophersen, Mona, Catherine Moe Thorleifsson, and Åge A. Tiltnes. 2013. *Ambivalent Hospitality: Coping Strategies and Local Responses to Syrian Ref-ugees.* Oslo, Norway: Fafo Foundation.

Cioran, E. M. [1976] 1998. *The Trouble with Being Born.* Translated by Richard Howard. New York: Arcade.

Clare, Anthony. 2001. *On Men: Masculinity in Crisis.* London: Arrow.

Clastres, Pierre. 1968. "Entre silence et dialogue." *L'Arc* 26:76–78.

———. 1987. *Society against the State: Essays in Political Anthropology.* Trans-lated by Robert Hurley in collaboration with Abe Stein. New York: Zone Books.

Collier, Jane, and Sylvia Yanagisako. 1987. "Towards a Unified Analysis of Gen-der and Kinship." In *Gender and Kinship: Essays Towards a Unified Analysis,* edited by Jane Collier and Sylvia Yanagisako, 14–50. Stanford, CA: Stanford Univ. Press.

Collins, John. 2004. *Occupied by Memory: The Intifada Generation and the Pales-tinian State of Emergency.* New York: New York Univ. Press.

Comaroff, Jean, and John Comaroff. 2005. "Reflections on Youth from the Past to the Postcolony." In *Makers & Breakers: Children & Youth in Postcolonial Af-rica,* edited by Alcinda Honwana and Filip de Boeck, 19–30. Oxford: James Currey.

Condry, Ian. 1999. "The Social Production of Difference: Imitation and Authen-ticity in Japanese Rap Music." In *Transactions, Transgressions, Transfor-mation: American Culture in Western Europe and Japan,* edited by Heide Fehrenbach and Uta Poiger, 166–84. New York: Berghahn Books.

Connell, R. W. 1985. "Theorising Gender." *Sociology* 19, no. 2: 260–72.

———. 1987. *Gender and Power.* Sydney: Allen & Unwin.

———. 1995. *Masculinities.* Cambridge: Polity Press.

———. 2002. *Gender.* Cambridge: Polity Press.

Connell, R. W., and James Messerschmidt. 2005. "Hegemonic Masculinity: Re-thinking the Concept." *Gender and Society* 19, no. 6: 829–59.

Consultation and Research Institute. 2007. *Mapping of Studies on the Employability of Palestinians in Lebanon.* Beirut: Consultation and Research Institute.

Cook, Emma. 2012. "Still a Child? Liminality and the Construction of Youthful Masculinities in Japan." In *Super Girls, Gangstas, and Xenomaniacs: Gender and Modernity in Global Youth Cultures,* edited by Susan Dewey and Karen Brison, 58–84. Syracuse, NY: Syracuse Univ. Press.

———. 2013. "Expectations of Failure: Maturity and Masculinity for Freeters in Contemporary Japan." *Social Science Japan Journal* 16, no. 1: 29–43.

Courbage, Youssef. 2011. "The Demographic Youth Bulge and Social Rupture." In *Arab Youth: Social Mobilisation in Times of Risk,* edited by Samir Khalaf and Roseanne Khalaf, 79–88. London: Saqi.

Crapanzano, Vincent. 1980. *Tuhami: Portrait of a Moroccan.* Chicago: Univ. of Chicago Press.

Cushman, Thomas. 2004. "A Conversation with Veena Das on Religion and Violence, Suffering and Language." *Hedgehog Review* 6, no. 1. At https://hedgehogreview.com/issues/religion-and-violence/articles/a-conversation-on-religion-and-violence-with-veena-das.

Daily Star (Beirut). 2009. "IMF Report Proposes Adding Remittances to Lebanon's GDP." Sept. 30. At https://www.dailystar.com.lb//Business/Lebanon/2009/Sep-30/55628-imf-report-proposes-adding-remittances-to-lebanons-gdp.ashx.

Das, Veena, and Deborah Poole, eds. 2008. *Anthropology in the Margins of the State.* Santa Fe, NM: School of American Research Press.

Dasgupta, Romit. 2012. *Re-reading the Salaryman in Japan: Crafting Masculinities.* London: Routledge.

Davis, Rochelle. 2011. *Palestinian Village Histories: Geographies of the Displaced.* Stanford, CA: Stanford Univ. Press.

De Beauvoir, Simone. [2009] 2012. *The Second Sex.* Translated by Constance Borde and Sheila Malovani-Chevallier. New York: Vintage.

De Certeau, Michel. 1984. *The Practice of Everyday Life.* Translated by Steven Rendall. Berkeley: Univ. of California Press.

De Cesari, Chiara. 2010. "Creative Heritage: Palestinian Heritage NGOs and Defiant Arts of Government." *American Anthropologist* 112, no. 4: 625–37.

Delaney, Carol. 1991. *The Seed and the Soil: Gender and Cosmology in Turkish Village Society.* Berkeley: Univ. of California Press.

Deleuze, Gilles, and Félix Guattari. [1987] 2004. *A Thousand Plateaus: Capitalism and Schizophrenia*. Translated by Brian Massumi. London: Continuum.

Delphy, Christine. 1991. "Penser le genre: Quels problèmes?" In *Sexe et genre: De la hiérarchie entre les sexes*, edited by Marie-Claude Hurtig, Michèle Kail, and Hélène Rouch, 89–101. Paris: Centre national de la recherche scientifique.

Derrida, Jacques. 1976. *Of Grammatology*. Translated by Gayatri Chakravorty Spivak. Baltimore: Johns Hopkins Univ. Press.

Dhillon, Navtej, and Tarik Yousef. 2009. *Generation in Waiting: The Unfulfilled Promise of Young People in the Middle East*. Washington, DC: Brookings Institution Press.

Dias, Amanda. 2009. "Du Moukhayyam à la favela: Une Étude comparative entre un camp de réfugiés palestiniens au Liban et une favela carioca." PhD diss., École des hautes études en sciences sociales and Universidade do Estado do Rio de Janeiro.

Douglas, Mary. 1991. *Purity and Danger: An Analysis of the Concepts of Pollution and Taboo*. London: Routledge.

Egset, Willy. 2003. "The Labour Market." In *Socio-economic Conditions of Palestinian Refugee Camps in Jordan, Lebanon, Syria, the West Bank, and Gaza Strip*, vol. 1 of *Finding Means: UNRWA'S Financial Crisis and Refugee Living Conditions*, edited by Laurie Jacobsen, 110–43. Oslo, Norway: Fafo Foundation.

Eltahawy, Mona. 2012. "Why Do They Hate Us? The Real War on Women Is in the Middle East." *Foreign Policy*, May–June. At https://foreignpolicy.com /2012/04/23/why-do-they-hate-us/.

Escobar, Arturo. 2001. "Culture Sits in Places: Reflections on Globalism and Subaltern Strategies of Localization." *Political Geography* 20, no. 2: 139–74.

Ewing, Katherine. 2008. *Stolen Honor: Stigmatizing Muslim Men in Berlin*. Stanford, CA: Stanford Univ. Press.

Faier, Elizabeth. 1997. "Looking In/Acting Out: Gender, Modernity, and the (Re) Production of the Palestinian Family." *Political and Legal Anthropology Review* 20, no. 2: 1–15.

———. 2002. "Domestic Matters: Feminism and Activism among Palestinian Women in Israel." In *Ethnography in Unstable Places: Everyday Lives in Contexts of Dramatic Political Change*, edited by Carol Greenhouse, Elizabeth Mertz, and Kay Warren, 178–209. Durham, NC: Duke Univ. Press.

Faludi, Susan. 1999. *Stiffed: The Betrayal of the Modern Man*. London: Chatto and Windus.

Fanon, Frantz. 1970. *Black Skin, White Masks*. Translated by Charles Markmann. London: Paladin.

Ferme, Mariane. 2008. "Deterritorialized Citizenship and the Resonances of the Sierra Leonean State." In *Anthropology in the Margins of the State*, edited by Veena Das and Deborah Poole, 81–115. Santa Fe, NM: School of American Research Press.

Fiddian-Qasmiyeh, Elena. 2016. "Local Communities: First and Last Providers of Protection." *Forced Migraton Review* 53. At https://jliflc.com/wp-content/uploads/2018/08/fiddianqasmiyeh.pdf.

Filippa, Marcella. 1996. "Popular Song and Musical Cultures." In *Italian Cultural Studies: An Introduction*, edited by David Forgacs and Robert Lumley, 327–43. Oxford: Oxford Univ. Press.

Financial Times. 2010. "Palestinians Seek More Rights to Work in Lebanon." Aug. 23. At https://www.ft.com/content/25752a4e-aec6-11df-9f31-00144feabdc0.

Fogliata, Stefano. 2015–16. "'Who Does Not Know How to Go Back Home?': Overlapping Spatio-temporalities of Exile in Lebanon's Palestinian Camps." PhD diss., Univ. of Bergamo.

Foucault, Michel. 1985. *The Use of Pleasure*. Vol. 2 of *The History of Sexuality*. Translated by Robert Hurley. London: Penguin.

———. 1986. *The Care of the Self*. Vol. 3 of *The History of Sexuality*. Translated by Robert Hurley. New York: Pantheon.

———. 1988. *The Final Foucault*. Cambridge, MA: MIT Press.

———. 1990. *Al-Murāqaba wa al-muaʿaqaba*. Translated by Ali Muqalid. Beirut: Markaz al-Inmāʿ al-Qawmiyy.

———. 1991. "Governmentality." In *The Foucault Effect: Studies in Governmentality*, edited by Graham Burchell, Colin Gordon, and Peter Miller, 87–104. Chicago: Univ. of Chicago Press.

———. [1977] 1995. *Discipline and Punish: The Birth of the Prison*. Translated by Alan Sheridan. New York: Random House.

———. [1978] 1998. *The Will to Knowledge*. Vol. 1 of *The History of Sexuality*. Translated by Robert Hurley. London: Penguin.

———. [1970] 2010. *The Order of Things: An Archeology of the Human Sciences*. London: Routledge.

Freud, Sigmund. 1964. "Femininity." In *New Introductory Lectures on Psychoanalysis*, translated by James Strachey, 112–35. New York: Norton.

———. 1991. "Female Sexuality." In *On Sexuality: Three Essays on the Theory of Sexuality and Other Works*, translated by James Strachey, edited by Angela Richards, 367–92. Harmondsworth, UK: Penguin.

Friedl, Erika. 1989. *Women of Deh Koh: Lives in an Iranian Village*. Washington, DC: Smithsonian Institution Press.

Gaonkar, Dilip. 1999. "On Alternative Modernities." *Public Culture* 11, no. 1: 1–18.

Gazzah, Miriam. 2011. "European Muslim Youth: Towards a Cool Islam?" In *Arab Youth: Social Mobilisation in Times of Risk*, edited by Samir Khalaf and Roseanne Khalaf, 319–36. London: Saqi.

Gedalof, Irene. 1999. *Against Purity: Rethinking Identity with Indian Feminisms*. London: Routledge.

Geertz, Clifford. 1980. *Negara: The Theatre State in Nineteenth-Century Bali*. Princeton, NJ: Princeton Univ. Press.

———. 2000. *The Interpretation of Cultures: Selected Essays*. New York: Basic Books.

Genet, Jean. [1986] 2004. *Un Captif amoureux*. Paris: Gallimard.

Genet, Jean, Layla Barrada, and Rudiger Wischenbart. 1987. "Affirmation of Existence through Rebellion." *Journal of Palestine Studies* 16, no. 2: 64–84.

Gerzon, Mark. 1982. *A Choice of Heroes: The Changing Faces of American Manhood*. Boston: Houghton Mifflin.

Ghannam, Farha. 2013. *Live and Die Like a Man: Gender Dynamics in Urban Egypt*. Stanford, CA: Stanford Univ. Press.

Giannou, Chris. 1991. *Besieged: A Doctor's Story of Life and Death in Beirut*. London: Bloomsbury.

Gibbs, Jewelle, and Joseph Merighi. 1996. "Young Black Males: Marginality, Masculinity, and Criminality." In *Just Boys Doing Business? Men, Masculinities, and Crime*, edited by Tim Newburn and Elizabeth Stanko, 64–80. London: Routledge.

Gilmore, David. 1980. *Manhood in the Making: Cultural Concepts of Masculinity*. New Haven, CT: Yale Univ. Press.

Gilsenan, Michael. 1996. *Lords of the Lebanese Marches: Violence and Narrative in Arab Society*. London: I. B. Tauris.

Granqvist, Hilma. 1931. *Marriage Conditions in a Palestinian Village*. Helsinki, Finland: Akademische.

———. 1947. *Birth and Childhood among the Arabs: Studies in a Muhammadan Village in Palestine*. Helsinki, Finland: Söderström.

Green, Sarah. 2005. *Notes from the Balkans: Locating Marginality and Ambiguity on the Greek–Albanian Border.* Princeton, NJ: Princeton Univ. Press.

Grosz, Elizabeth. 1993. "A Thousand Tiny Sexes: Feminism and Rhizomatics." *Topoi* 12, no. 2: 167–79.

Gruenbaum, Ellen. 2000. *The Female Circumcision Controversy: An Anthropological Perspective.* Philadelphia: Univ. of Pennsylvannia Press.

Gunaid, Abdullah, Nuria Hummad, and Khaled Tamim. 2004. "Consanguineous Marriage in the Capital City San'a', Yemen." *Journal of Biosocial Science* 36, no. 1: 111–21.

Gutmann, Matthew C. 1997. "'Trafficking in Men': The Anthropology of Masculinity." *Annual Review of Anthropology* 26:385–409.

———. 2003. *Changing Men and Masculinities in Latin America.* Durham, NC: Duke Univ. Press.

———. 2007. *Fixing Men: Sex, Birth Control, and AIDS in Mexico.* Berkeley: Univ. of California Press.

Halberstam, Judith/Jack. 1998. *Female Masculinity.* Durham, NC: Duke Univ. Press.

———. 2002. "An Introduction to Female Masculinity: Masculinity without Men." In *The Masculinity Studies Reader,* edited by Rachel Adams and David Savran, 355–74. Malden, MA: Blackwell.

Hammoudi, Abdellah. 1997. *Master and Disciple: The Cultural Foundations of Moroccan Authoritarianism.* Chicago: Univ. of Chicago Press.

Hanafi, Sari. 2007. *Employability of Palestinian Professionals in Lebanon.* Oslo, Norway: Fafo Institute for Applied Studies.

———. 2008a. "Palestinian Refugee Camps as a Space of Exception." *Revue Asylon(s)* 5. At https://www.reseau-terra.eu/article798.html.

———. 2008b. "Palestinian Refugee Camps in Lebanon: Laboratories of State-in-the-Making, Discipline, and Islamist Radicalism." In *Thinking Palestine,* edited by Ronit Lentin, 82–100. London: Zed Books.

———. 2010. "Palestinian Refugee Camps in Lebanon: Laboratory of Indocile Identity Formation." In *Manifestations of Identity: The Lived Reality of Palestinian Refugees in Lebanon,* edited by Muhammad Ali Khalidi, 45–74. Beirut: IFPO/IPS.

Hanafi, Sari, and Taylor Long. 2010. "Governance, Governmentalities, and the State of Exception in the Palestinian Refugee Camps in Lebanon." *Journal of Refugee Studies* 23, no. 2: 134–58.

Haraway, Donna. 1985. "A Manifesto for Cyborgs: Science, Technology, and Socialist Feminism in the 1980s." *Socialist Review* 80:65–108.

Hart, Jason. 2000. "Contested Belonging: Children and Childhood in a Palestinian Refugee Camp in Jordan." PhD diss., Univ. of London.

———. 2008. "Dislocated Masculinity: Adolescence and the Palestinian Nation-in-Exile." *Journal of Refugee Studies* 21, no. 1: 64–81.

Hatem, Mervat. 1986. "The Enduring Alliance of Nationalism and Patriarchy in Muslim Personal Status Law: The Case of Modern Egypt." *Feminist Issues* 6:19–43.

Haugbolle, Sune. 2012. "The (Little) Militia Man: Memory and Militarized Masculinity in Lebanon." *Journal of Middle East Women's Studies* 8, no. 1: 115–39.

Heartfield, James. 2002. "There Is No Masculinity Crisis." *Genders* 35. At https://www.colorado.edu/gendersarchive1998-2013/2002/01/25/there-no -masculinity-crisis.

Hemmings, Clare, Irene Gedalof, and Lucy Bland. 2006. "Sexual Moralities." In "Sexual Moralities," special issue of *Feminist Review* 83, no. 1: 1–3.

Hermez, Sami. 2017. *War Is Coming: Between Past and Future Violence in Lebanon.* Philadelphia: Univ. of Pennsylvania Press.

Herzfeld, Michael. 1985. *The Poetics of Manhood: Contest and Identity in a Cretan Mountain Village.* Princeton, NJ: Princeton Univ. Press.

Hirsch, Jennifer. 2003. *A Courtship after Marriage: Sexuality and Love in Mexican Transnational Families.* Berkeley: Univ. of California Press.

Hirst, David. 2010. *Beware of Small States: Lebanon, Battleground of the Middle East.* London: Faber and Faber.

Hobbes, Thomas. [1651] 2008. *Leviathan.* Oxford: Oxford Univ. Press.

Hoodfar, Homa. 1997. *Between Marriage and the Market.* Berkeley: Univ. of California Press.

Horrocks, Roger. 1996. *Masculinity in Crisis.* London: Palgrave Macmillan.

Humphries, Isabelle, and Laleh Khalili. 2007. "Gender of Nakba Memory." In *Nakba: Palestine, 1948, and the Claims of Memory,* edited by Ahmad Sa'di and Lila Abu-Lughod, 207–28. New York: Columbia Univ. Press.

Inhorn, Marcia. 2012. *The New Arab Man: Emergent Masculinities, Technologies, and Islam in the Middle East.* Princeton, NJ: Princeton Univ. Press.

International Crisis Group. 2009. *Nurturing Instability: Lebanon's Palestinian Camps.* Beirut: International Crisis Group. At https://d2071andvip0wj.cloud

front.net/84-nurturing-instability-lebanon-s-palestinian-refugee-camps .pdf.

———. 2013. *Too Close for Comfort: Syrians in Lebanon*. Beirut: International Crisis Group. At https://d2071andvip0wj.cloudfront.net/too-close-for-comfort -syrians-in-lebanon.pdf.

International Labor Organization (ILO). 2010. *Employment and Unemployment*. Geneva: ILO. At http://www.ilo.org/global/What_we_do/Statistics/topics /Employment/lang--en/index.htm.

———. 2019. *Quick Guide on Interpreting the Unemployment Rate*. Geneva: ILO. At https://www.ilo.org/wcmsp5/groups/public/---dgreports/---stat/documents /publication/wcms_675155.pdf.

International Labor Organization (ILO), Committee for the Employment of Palestinan Refugees in Lebanon (CEP). 2011. *Labour Force Survey among Palestinian Refugees Living in Camps and Gatherings in Lebanon*. Beirut: ILO, CEP.

———. 2012. *Palestinian Employment in Lebanon: Facts and Challenges. Labour Force Survey among Palestinian Refugees Living in Camps and Gatherings in Lebanon*. Beirut: ILO, CEP. At https://www.ilo.org/wcmsp5/groups/public /---arabstates/---ro-beirut/documents/publication/wcms_236502.pdf.

Isin, Engin. 2008. "Theorizing Acts of Citizenship." In *Acts of Citizenship*, edited by Engin Isin and Greg Nielsen, 15–43. London: Zed Books.

Jabbour, Elias. 1996. *Sulha: Palestinian Traditional Peacemaking Process*. Montreal: House of Hope.

Jacob, Wilson. 2013. "The Middle East: Global, Postcolonial, Regional, and Queer." In "Queer Affects," special issue of *International Journal of Middle East Studies* 45, no. 2: 347–49.

Jacobsen, Laurie. 2003. "Education and Human Capital." In *Socio-economic Conditions of Palestinian Refugee Camps in Jordan, Lebanon, Syria, the West Bank, and Gaza Strip*, vol. 1 of *Finding Means: UNRWA'S Financial Crisis and Refugee Living Conditions*, edited by Laurie Jacobsen, 79–109. Oslo, Norway: Fafo Foundation.

———. 2004. *Educated Housewives: Living Conditions among Palestinian Refugee Women*. Oslo, Norway: Fafo Foundation.

Jacobsen, Laurie Blome, and Aziza Khalidi. 2003. "Housing and Environment." In *Difficult Past, Uncertain Future: Living Conditions among Palestinian Refugees in Camps and Gatherings in Lebanon*, edited by Ole Fr. Ugland, 183–208. Oslo, Norway: Fafo Foundation.

Jamoulle, Pascale. 2005. *Des Hommes sur le fil: La Construction de l'identité masculine aux milieux précaires*. Paris: La Découverte.

Janmyr, Maja. 2016. "Precarity in Exile: The Legal Status of Syrian Refugees in Lebanon." *Refugee Quarterly Survey* 35, no. 4: 58–78.

Jayawardena, Lal. 1995. Foreword to *Mistrusting Refugees*, edited by E. Valentine Daniel and John Knudsen, vii–ix. Berkeley: Univ. of California Press.

Jean-Klein, Iris. 1997. "Palestinian Militancy, Martyrdom, and Nationalist Communities in the West Bank Occupied Territories during the Intifada." In *Martyrdom and Political Resistance: Essays from Asia and Europe*, edited by Joyce Pettigrew, 85–110. Amsterdam, Netherlands: Centre for Asian Studies.

———. 2000. "Mothercraft, Statecraft, and Subjectivity in the Palestinian Intifada." *American Ethnologist* 27, no. 1: 100–127.

———. 2001. "Nationalism and Resistance: The Two Faces of Everyday Activism in Palestine during the Intifada." *Cultural Anthropology* 16, no. 1: 83–126.

———. 2002. "Alternative Modernities, or Accountable Modernities? The Palestinian Movement(s) and Political (Audit) Tourism during the First Intifada." *Cultural Anthropology* 16, no. 1: 83–126.

Jeganathan, Pradeep. 2008. "Checkpoint: Anthropology, Identity, and the State." In *Anthropology in the Margins of the State*, edited by Veena Das and Deborah Poole, 67–80. Santa Fe, NM: School of American Research Press.

Jennings, Ronald. 2011. "Sovereignty and Political Modernity: A Genealogy of Agamben's Critique of Sovereignty." *Anthropological Theory* 11, no. 1: 23–61.

Joseph, Suad. 1983. "Working-Class Women's Networks in a Sectarian State: A Political Paradox." *American Ethnologist* 10, no. 1: 1–22.

———. 1993a. "Connectivity and Patriarchy among Urban Working-Class Arab Families in Lebanon." *Ethos* 21:452–84.

———. 1993b. "Gender and Relationality among Arab Families in Lebanon." *Feminist Studies* 19, no. 3: 465–86.

———. 1994. "Brother/Sister Relationships: Connectivity, Love, and Power in the Reproduction of Patriarchy in Lebanon." *American Ethnologist* 21:50–73.

———, ed. 1999a. *Intimate Selving in Arab Families: Gender, Self, and Identity*. Syracuse, NY: Syracuse Univ. Press.

———. 1999b. "My Son/Myself, My Mother/Myself." In *Intimate Selving in Arab Families: Gender, Self, and Identity*, edited by Suad Joseph, 174–90. Syracuse, NY: Syracuse Univ. Press.

———, ed. 2000. *Gender and Citizenship in the Middle East*. Syracuse, NY: Syracuse Univ. Press.

———. 2004. "Conceiving Family Relationships in Post-war Lebanon." *Journal of Comparative Family Studies* 35:271–93.

Kanaaneh, Rhoda. 2002. *Birthing the Nation: Strategies of Palestinian Women in Israel.* Berkeley: Univ. of California Press.

———. 2003. "Embattled Identities: Palestinian Soldiers in the Israeli Army." *Journal of Palestine Studies* 32, no. 3: 5–20.

———. 2005. "Boys or Men? Duped or 'Made'? Palestinian Soldiers in the Israeli Army." *American Ethnologist* 32, no. 2: 260–75.

Kanafani, Samar. 2005. "When We Were Men: Fidāʾiyyn Re-collecting." Master's thesis, American Univ. of Beirut.

———. 2008. "Leaving Mother-land: The Anti-feminine in *Fidaʾi* Narratives." *Identities* 15, no. 3: 297–316.

Kandiyoti, Deniz. 1991. *Women, Islam, and the State.* Philadelphia: Temple Univ. Press.

———. 1994. "Bargaining with Patriarchy." *Gender and Society* 2:274–90.

———. 1996. *Gendering the Middle East.* Syracuse, NY: Syracuse Univ. Press.

Kapchan, Deborah. 1996. *Gender on the Market: Moroccan Women and the Re-voicing of Tradition.* Philadelphia: Univ. of Pennsylvania Press.

Kelly, Tobias. 2008. "Attractions of Accountancy: Living an Ordinary Life during the Second Palestinian Intifada." *Ethnography* 9, no. 3: 351–76.

Khalaf, Colette. 2012. "Nada Sehnaoui parle avec la ville." *L'Orient le jour*, Sept. 14.

Khalili, Laleh. 2007a. *Heroes and Martyrs of Palestine: The Politics of National Commemoration.* Cambridge: Cambridge Univ. Press.

———. 2007b. "Heroic and Tragic Pasts: Mnemonic Narratives in the Palestinian Camps." *Critical Sociology* 33, no. 4: 731–59.

———. 2008. "Commemorating Battle and Massacres in the Palestinian Refugee Camps of Lebanon." *American Behavioral Scientist* 51, no. 11: 1562–74.

Khawaja, Marwan, and Laurie Jacobsen. 2003. "Familial Relations and Labour Market Outcomes: The Palestinian Refugees in Lebanon." *Social Science Research* 32, no. 4: 579–602.

Khayyat, Munira. 2012. "Battlefield Pastoral." *Third Text* 26, no. 4: 475–77.

———. 2013. "A Landscape of War: On the Nature of Conflict in South Lebanon." PhD diss., Columbia Univ.

Khuri, Fuad. 1975. *From Village to Suburb: Order and Change in Greater Beirut.* Chicago: Univ. of Chicago Press.

Kimmel, Michael. 2002. "Gender, Class, and Terrorism." *Chronicle of Higher Education*, Feb. 8. At http://www.xyonline.net/content/gender-class-and -terrorism.

King, Diane, and Linda Stone. 2010. "Lineal Masculinity: Gendered Memory within Patriliny." *American Ethnologist* 37, no. 2: 323–36.

Knudsen, Are. 2017. "Syria's Refugees in Lebanon: Brothers, Burden, and Bone of Contention." In *Lebanon Facing the Arab Uprisings: Constraints and Adaptations*, edited by Rosita di Peri and Daniel Meier, 135–54. London: Palgrave Macmillan.

———. 2018. "The Great Escape? Converging Refugee Crises in Tyre, Lebanon." *Refugee Survey Quarterly* 37, no. 1: 96–115.

Kooy, Michelle, and Karen Bakker. 2008. "Splintered Networks: The Colonial and Contemporary Water of Jakarta." *Geoforum* 39, no. 6: 1843–58.

Kortam, Manal. 2010. "Politics, Patronage, and Popular Committees in the Shatila Refugee Camp, Lebanon." In *Identity, Space, and Place in the Levant*, edited by Are Knudsen and Sari Hanafi, 193–204. London: Routledge.

Kovats-Bernat, J. Christopher. 2002. "Negotiating Dangerous Fields: Pragmatic Strategies for Fieldwork amid Violence and Terror." *American Anthropologist* 104, no. 1: 208–22.

Lamb, Franklin. 2010. "Chickenfeed for the Soul." *Counterpunch*, Aug. 18. At http://www.counterpunch.org/2010/08/18/chickenfeed-for-the-soul/.

Lambevski, Sasho. 1999. "Suck My Nation: Masculinity, Ethnicity, and the Politics of (Homo)Sex." *Sexualities* 2, no. 4: 397–419.

Landau, Carolyn. 2011. "Music Consumption and the Navigation of Identities: Transnational Moroccan Youth in Britain." In *Arab Youth: Social Mobilisation in Times of Risk*, edited by Samir Khalaf and Roseanne Khalaf, 337–57. London: Saqi.

Leacock, Eleanor. 1983. "Interpreting the Origins of Gender Inequality: Conceptual and Historical Problems." *Dialectical Anthropology* 7, no. 4: 263–84.

Lévi-Strauss, Claude. 1962. *La Pensée sauvage*. Paris: Plon.

———. 1986. *O Totemismo hoje*. Translated by José António Braga Fernandes Dias. Lisbon: Edições 70.

Lipset, David. 1980. *Gregory Bateson: The Legacy of a Scientist*. Englewood Cliffs, NJ: Prentice-Hall.

Lipsitz, George. 1994. *Dangerous Crossroads: Popular Music, Postmodernism, and the Poetics of Place*. London: Verso.

Mackreath, Helen. 2014. "The Role of Host Communities in North Lebanon." In "The Syria Crisis, Displacement, and Protection," special issue of *Forced Migration Review* 47. At https://www.fmreview.org/syria/mackreath.

MacLeod, Arlene 1993. *Accommodating Protest: Working Women, the New Veiling, and Change in Cairo*. New York: Columbia Univ. Press.

El-Mahdi, Rabab. 2011. "Orientalising the Egyptian Uprising." *Jadaliyya*, Apr. 11. At http://www.jadaliyya.com/pages/index/1214/.

Mahmood, Saba. 2001. "Feminist Theory, Embodiment, and the Docile Agent: Some Reflections on the Egyptian Islamic Revival." *Cultural Anthropology* 16, no. 2: 202–36.

———. 2005. *Politics of Piety: The Islamic Revival and the Feminist Subject*. Princeton, NJ: Princeton Univ. Press.

Malinowski, Bronislaw. 1992. *Argonauts of the Western Pacific: An Account of Native Enterprise and Adventure in the Archipelagoes of Melanesian New Guinea*. London: Routledge.

Malkki, Liisa. 1992. "*National Geographic*: The Rooting of Peoples and the Territorialization of National Identity among Scholars and Refugees." *Cultural Anthropology* 7, no. 1: 24–44.

———. 1995. *Purity and Exile: Violence, Memory, and National Cosmology among Hutu Refugees in Tanzania*. Chicago: Univ. of Chicago Press.

Mallet, Julien. 2003-4. "Ethnomusicologie des 'jeunes musiques.'" *L'Homme* 171-72:477–88.

Manheim, Karl. 1952. "The Problem of Generations." In *Essays on the Sociology of Knowledge*, 276–320. London: Routledge.

Marcus, George. 1985. "A Timely Rereading of *Naven*: Gregory Bateson as Oracular Essayist." *Representations* 12:66–82.

Massad, Joseph. 1995. "Conceiving the Masculine: Gender and Palestinian Nationalism." *Middle East Journal* 49, no. 3: 467–83.

———. 2003. "Liberating Songs: Palestine Put to Music." *Journal of Palestine Studies* 32, no. 3: 21–38.

Massumi, Brian. 2002. *Parables for the Virtual: Movement, Affect, Sensation*. Durham, NC: Duke Univ. Press.

Maxwell, Ian. 1994. "Discourses of Culture and Nationalism in Contemporary Sydney Hip Hop." *Perfect Beat* 2, no. 1: 1–19.

McLelland, Mark, and Romit Dasgupta. 2005. *Genders, Transgenders, and Sexualities in Japan*. London: Routledge.

McNay, Lois. 1991. "The Foucauldian Body and the Exclusion of Experience." *Hypatia* 6, no. 3: 125–39.

———. 2000. *Gender and Agency: Reconfiguring the Subject in Feminist and Social Theory.* Cambridge: Polity Press.

Mencütek, Zeynep. 2015. "The Impact of the Syrian Crisis in Lebanon." *Project in the Middle East and the Arab Spring* 10:1–10.

Mernissi, Fatima. 1987. *Beyond the Veil: Male–Female Dynamics in Modern Muslim Society.* London: Saqi.

———. 1988. *Doing Daily Battle: Interviews with Moroccan Women.* London: Women's Press.

———. 1991. *The Veil and the Male Elite: A Feminist Interpretation of Women's Rights in Islam.* New York: Basic Books.

Messer-Davidow, Ellen. 2002. *Disciplining Feminism: From Social Activism to Academic Discourse.* Durham, NC: Duke Univ. Press.

Meunier, Jacques. 2001. *Les Gamins de Bogotá.* Paris: Payot and Rivages.

Mikdashi, Maya. 2013. "Thinking Citizenship in a Revolutionary Arab World: The Intransigence of Difference." *Jadaliyya*, Apr. 26. At http://www.jadaliyya .com/pages/index/11402/thinking-citizenship-in-a-revolutionary-arab -world.

Mitchell, Timothy. 1991. *Colonising Egypt.* Berkeley: Univ. of California Press.

Mitchell, Tony. 1996. *Popular Music and Local Identity: Rock, Pop, and Rap in Europe and Oceania.* London: Leicester Univ. Press.

Mizen, Phillip. 2002. "Putting the Politics Back into Youth Studies: Keynesianism, Monetarism, and the Changing State of Youth." *Journal of Youth Studies* 5, no. 1: 5–20.

Moore, Henrietta. 1999. "Whatever Happened to Women and Men? Gender and Other Crises in Anthropology." In *Anthropological Theory Today*, edited by Henrietta Moore, 151–71. Cambridge: Polity Press.

Moors, Annelies. 1996. *Women, Property, and Islam: Palestinian Experiences, 1920–1990.* Cambridge: Cambridge Univ. Press.

Morgan, Robin. 1989. *The Demon Lover: On the Sexuality of Terrorism.* London: Methuen.

Mundus, Hani. 1974. *Al-ʿAmal wa al-ʿummāl fi al-mukhayyam al-Filisṭīnī: Baḥth maydānī ʿan mukhayyam tall al-Zaʿtar.* Beirut: Palestine Research Centre.

Nagel, Joane. 1998. "Masculinity and Nationalism: Gender and Sexuality in the Making of Nations." *Ethnic and Racial Studies* 21, no. 2: 242–69.

Naguib, Nefissa. 2015. *Nurturing Masculinities: Men, Food, and Family in Contemporary Egypt.* Austin: Univ. of Texas Press.

Najmabadi, Afsaneh. 2013. "Genus of Sex or the Sexing of *Jins.*" In "Queer Affects," special issue of *International Journal of Middle East Studies* 45, no. 2: 211–31.

Nakad, Rose. 2016. "InsUrgency in Community Arts." PhD diss., Univ. of Technology.

Nassar, Angie. 2011a. "Scratch That, This Is Our Soundtrack: Hip Hop in Lebanon." Master's thesis, American Univ. of Beirut.

———. 2011b. "Scratch the Past, This Is OUR Soundtrack: Hip-Hop in Lebanon." In *Arab Youth: Social Mobilisation in Times of Risk*, edited by Samir Khalaf and Roseanne Khalaf, 359–86. London: Saqi.

Nassar, Jessy, and Nora Stel. 2019. "Lebanon's Response to the Syrian Refugee Crisis: Institutional Ambiguity as a Governace Strategy." *Political Geography* 70:44–54.

Al-Natour, Souheil. 1993. *Les Palestiniens du Liban: La Situation sociale, économique et juridique.* Beirut: Al-Taqqadom al-Arabi.

Al-Natour, Souheil, and Dalal Yassine. 2007. *The Legal Status of the Palestine Refugees in Lebanon and the Demands of Adjustment.* Beirut: Human Development Center.

Nattiez, Jean-Jacques. 2004. "Ethnomusicologie et significations musicales." *L'Homme* 3, nos. 171–72: 53–81.

Neal, Mark. 1998. *What the Music Said: Black Popular Music and Black Public Culture.* London: Routledge.

Nuwayhed al-Hout, Bayan. 2004. *Sabra and Shatila: September 1982.* London: Pluto.

Olson, Gary, and Lynn Worsham. 2003. *Critical Intellectuals on Writing.* New York: State Univ. of New York Press.

Ortner, Sherry. 1974. "Is Female to Male as Nature Is to Culture?" In *Woman, Culture, and Society*, edited by Michelle Rosaldo and Louise Lamphere, 68–87. Stanford, CA: Stanford Univ. Press.

Ouzgane, Lahoucine. 2006. *Islamic Masculinities.* London: Zed.

Özyürek, Esra. 2006. *Nostalgia for the Modern: State Secularism and Everyday Politics in Turkey.* Durham, NC: Duke Univ. Press.

Padilla, Mark. 2007. *Caribbean Pleasure Industry: Tourism, Sexuality, and AIDS in the Dominican Republic.* Chicago: Univ. of Chicago Press.

Palestinian Human Rights Organization (PHRO). 2005. *Narrative Report: 2005.* Beirut: PHRO.

————. 2010. *Position Paper: Law Adopted by the Lebanese Parliament on 17th August 2010 Regarding Palestinian Refugees' Right to Work and Social Security*. Beirut: PHRO.

Panourgiá, Neni. 2009. *Dangerous Citizens: The Greek Left and the Terror of the State*. New York: Fordham Univ. Press.

Pely, Doron. 2008–9. "Resolving Clan-Based Disputes Using *Sulha*, the Traditional Dispute Resolution Process of the Middle East." *Dispute Resolution Journal* 63, no. 4: 80–88.

Perdigon, Sylvain. 2012. "'A Word Not Heard in Thirty Years': On Honor, Ordinary Ethics, and the Embodiment of Relatedness in the Palestinian Community of Tyre." Oral presentation, Department of Sociology, Anthropology and Media, American Univ. of Beirut.

Peteet, Julie. 1987. "Social-Political Integration and Conflict Resolution in the Palestinian Camps in Lebanon." *Journal of Palestinian Studies* 16, no. 2: 29–44.

————. 1991. *Gender in Crisis: Women and the Palestinian Resistance Movement*. New York: Columbia Univ. Press.

————. 1994. "Male Gender and Rituals of Resistance in the Palestinian Intifada: A Cultural Politics of Violence." *American Ethnologist* 21, no. 1: 31–49.

————. 1997. "Icons and Militants: Mothering in a Danger Zone." *Signs: Journal of Women in Culture and Society* 23, no. 1: 103–29.

————. 2005. *Landscape of Hope and Despair: Palestinian Refugee Camps*. Philadelphia: Univ. of Pennsylvania Press.

————. 2007. "Unsettling the Categories of Displacement." *Middle East Research and Information Project* 244 (Fall). At http://www.merip.org/mer/mer244/unsettling-categories-displacement.

Petti, Alessandro. 2013. "Beyond the State: The Refugee Camp as a Site of Political Invention." *Jadaliyya*, Mar. 26. At http://www.jadaliyya.com/pages/index/10813/beyond-the-state_the-refugee-camp-as-a-site-of-pol.

Picard, Elisabeth. 1994. "Les Habits neufs du communautarisme libanais." *Cultures et conflits, état et communautarisme* 15–16:49–70.

————. 1996. *Lebanon, a Shattered Country: Myths and Realities of the Wars in Lebanon*. New York: Holmes and Meier.

Pichter, Linda. 1998. "'The Divine Impatience': Ritual, Narrative, and Symbolization in the Practice of Martyrdom in Palestine." *Medical Anthropology Quarterly* 12, no. 1: 8–30.

Pirinolli, Christine. 2009. *Jeux et enjeux de mémoire à Gaza*. Lausanne, Switzerland: Antipodes.

Poole, Deborah. 2008. "Between Threat and Guarantee: Justice Community in the Margins of the Peruvian State." In *Anthropology in the Margins of the State*, edited by Veena Das and Deborah Poole, 35–65. Santa Fe, NM: School of American Research Press.

Povinelli, Elizabeth. 2006. *The Empire of Love: Toward a Theory of Intimacy, Genealogy, and Carnality*. Durham, NC: Duke Univ. Press.

———. 2011. "Routes/Worlds." *e-flux* 27 (Sept.). At http://www.e-flux.com/journal/routesworlds/.

Puar, Jasbir. 2007. *Terrorist Assemblages: Homonationalism in Queer Times*. Durham, NC: Duke Univ. Press.

———. 2013. "Rethinking Homonationalism." In "Queer Affects," special issue of *International Journal of Middle East Studies* 45, no. 2: 336–39.

Puig, Nicolas. 2006. "*Shi filastini*, quelque chose de Palestinien: Musiques et musiciens palestiniens au Liban: Territoires, scénographies et identités." *Tumultes* 27:110–34.

———. 2007. "'Bienvenue dans les camps!' L'Émergence d'un rap palestinien au Liban: Une Nouvelle chanson sociale et politique." In *Itinéraires esthétiques et scènes culturelles au Proche-Orient*, edited by Nicolas Puig and Franck Mermier, 147–71. Beirut: Presses de l'IFPO.

Puri, Jyoti. 1999. *Woman, Body, Desire in Post-colonial India: Narratives of Gender and Sexuality*. London: Routledge.

Puwar, Nirmal. 2004. *Space Invaders: Race, Gender, and Bodies Out of Place*. Oxford: Berg.

Qifa Nabki. 2010. "Talking to Nadim Shehadi: Palestinian Civil Rights in Lebanon" (interview). June 30. At http://qifanabki.com/2010/06/30/nadim-shehadi-palestinian-refugee-civil-rights/.

Rommel, Carl. 2014. "A Veritable Game of the Nation: On the Changing Status of Football within the Egyptian National Formation in the Wake of 2009 World Cup Qualifiers against Algeria." *Critical African Studies* 6, nos. 2–3: 157–75.

Rosaldo, Michelle, and Louise Lamphere, eds. 1974. *Woman, Culture, and Society*. Stanford, CA: Stanford Univ. Press.

Rosaldo, Renato. 1989. *Culture and Truth: The Remaking of Social Analysis*. Boston: Beacon Press.

Rothenberg, Celia. 2004. *Spirits of Palestine: Gender, Society, and Stories of the Jinn*. Lanham, MD: Lexington Books.

Rougier, Bernard. 2007. *Everyday Jihad: The Rise of Militant Islam among Palestinians in Lebanon*. Cambridge, MA: Harvard Univ. Press.

Rubin, Gayle. 1975. "The Traffic in Women: Notes on the 'Political Economy' of Sex." In *Toward an Anthropology of Women*, edited by Rayna Reiter, 157–210. New York: Monthly Review Press.

Rugh, Andrea. 1984. *Family in Contemporary Egypt*. Syracuse, NY: Syracuse Univ. Press.

Saadawi, Nawal. 1980. *The Hidden Face of Eve: Women in the Arab World*. London: Zed.

Sabbah, Fatna. 1984. *Women in the Muslim Unconscious*. New York: Pergamon.

Said, Wadie. 1999. "The Palestinians in Lebanon: The Rights of the Victims of the Palestinian–Israeli Peace Process." *Columbia Human Rights Law Review* 30, no. 2: 315–57.

Saldanha, Arun. 2006. "Reontologising Race: The Machinic Geography of Phenotype." *Environment and Planning: Society and Space* 24, no. 1: 9–24.

Salibi, Kamal. 2005. *A House of Many Mansions: The History of Lebanon Reconsidered*. New York: I. B. Tauris.

Sandford, Stella. 2011. "Sex: A Transdisciplinary Concept." *Radical Philosophy* 165:23–30.

Sawaf, Zina. 2013. "Youth and Revolution in Egypt: What Kinship Tells Us." *Contemporary Arab Affairs* 6, no. 1: 1–16.

Sayigh, Rosemary. 1979. *Palestinians: From Peasants to Revolutionaries. A People's History*. London: Zed Press.

———. 1987. "Femmes palestiniennes: Une Histoire en quête d'historien." *Revue d'études palestiniennes* 23:13–33.

———. 1993. *Too Many Enemies: The Palestinian Experience in Lebanon*. London: Zed Books.

———. 1995. "Palestinians in Lebanon: Harsh Present, Uncertain Future." *Journal of Palestinian Studies* 25, no. 1: 37–53.

———. 1998. "Palestinian Camp Women as Tellers of History." *Journal of Palestine Studies* 27, no. 2: 42–58.

Sayigh, Yezid. 1997. *Armed Struggle and the Search for State: The Palestinian National Movement, 1949–1993*. Oxford: Clarendon Press.

Sayigh, Yusif. 1952. "Economic Implications of UNRWA Operations in Jordan, Syria, and Lebanon." Master's thesis, American Univ. of Beirut.

Schade-Poulsen, Marc. 2004. *The Social Significance of Rai: Men and Popular Music in Algeria*. Austin: Univ. of Texas Press.

Scheper-Hughes, Nancy. 1992. *Death without Weeping: The Violence of Everyday Life in Brazil*. Berkeley: Univ. of California Press.

Schielke, Samuli. 2015. *Egypt in the Future Tense: Hope, Frustration, and Ambivalence before and after 2011*. Bloomington: Indiana Univ. Press.

Schiocchet, Leonardo. 2011. "Refugee Lives: Ritual and Belonging in Two Palestinian Refugee Camps in Lebanon." PhD diss., Boston Univ.

Schneider, David. 1968. *American Kinship: A Cultural Account*. Englewood Cliffs, NJ: Prentice-Hall.

———. 1984. *A Critique of the Study of Kinship*. Ann Arbor: Univ. of Michigan Press.

Scott, James. 1998. *Seeing Like a State: How Certain Schemes to Improve the Human Condition Have Failed*. New Haven, CT: Yale Univ. Press.

———. 2009. *The Art of Not Being Governed: An Anarchist History of Upland Southeast Asia*. New Haven, CT: Yale Univ. Press.

Sedghi, Hamideh. 2007. *Women and Politics in Iran: Veiling, Unveiling, and Reveiling*. Cambridge: Cambridge Univ. Press.

Sedgwick, Eve. 1991. *Epistemology of the Closet*. London: Harvester Wheatsheaf.

Sennett, Richard. 2008. *The Uses of Disorder: Personal Identity and City Life*. New York: Norton.

Sfeir, Jihane. 2008. *L'Exil palestinien au Liban: Le Temps des origines (1947–1952)*. Beirut: IFPO; Paris: Karthala.

Shah, Nasra. 2004. "Women's Socio-economic Characteristics and Marital Patterns in a Rapidly Developing Muslim Society, Kuwait." *Journal of Comparative Family Studies* 35, no. 2: 163–83.

Sharma, Sanjay. 1996. "Noisy Asians or 'Asian Noise'?" In *Dis-orienting Rhythms: The Politics of the New Asian Dance Music*, edited by Sanjar Sharma, John Hutnyk, and Ashwani Sharma, 32–57. London: Zed Books.

Singerman, Diane. 1995. *Avenues of Participation: Family, Politics, and Networks in Urban Quarters of Cairo*. Princeton, NJ: Princeton Univ. Press.

———. 2011. "The Negotiation of Waithood: The Political Economy of Delayed Marriage in Egypt." In *Arab Youth: Social Mobilisation in Times of Risk*, edited by Samir Khalaf and Roseanne Khalaf, 85–108. London: Saqi.

Smith, Linda. 1999. *Decolonizing Methodologies: Research and Indigenous Peoples*. London: Zed Books; Dunedin, New Zealand: Univ. of Otago Press.

Sørvig, Bendik. 2001. "Exile without Refuge: Experiences and Practices of Exile among Young Palestinian Camp Refugees in Beirut." Master's thesis, Univ. of Oslo.

Spivak, Gayatri Chakravorty. 1988. "Can the Subaltern Speak?" In *Marxism and the Interpretation of Culture*, edited by Cary Nelson and Lawrence Grossberg, 271–313. Urbana: Univ. of Illinois Press.

————. 1990. "Poststructuralism, Marginality, Postcoloniality, and Value." In *Literary Theory Today*, edited by Peter Collier and Helga Geyer-Ryan, 219–44. London: Polity Press.

————. 1999. *A Critique of Postcolonial Reason: Toward a History of the Vanishing Present*. Cambridge, MA: Harvard Univ. Press.

Stoler, Ann Laura. 2002. *Carnal Knowledge and Imperial Power: Race and the Intimate in Colonial Rule*. Berkeley: Univ. of California Press.

Strathern, Marilyn. 1988. *The Gender of the Gift: Problems with Women and Problems with Society in Melanesia*. Berkeley: Univ. of California Press.

Sukarieh, Mayssoun, and Stuart Tannock. 2008. "In the Best Interests of Youth or Neoliberalism? The World Bank and the New Global Youth Empowerment Project." *Journal of Youth Studies* 11, no. 3: 301–12.

————. 2013. "On the Problem of Over-researched Communities: The Case of the Shatila Palestinian Refugee Camp in Lebanon." *Sociology* 47, no. 3: 494–508.

————. 2015. *Youth Rising: The Politics of Youth in the New Global Economy*. London: Routledge.

Suleiman, Jaber. 1997. "Palestinians in Lebanon and the Role of Non-governmental Organizations." *Journal of Refugee Studies* 10, no. 3: 397–410.

————. 1999. "The Current Political, Organizational, and Security Situation in the Palestinian Refugee Camps of Lebanon." *Journal of Palestine Studies* 29, no. 1: 66–80.

Swedenburg, Ted. 2007. "Imagined Youths." *Middle East Report* 245:4–11.

Sykes, Karen. 2003. "My Aim Is True: Postnostalgic Reflections on the Future of Anthropological Science." *American Ethnologist* 30, no. 1: 156–68.

Taylor, Alex. 2012. "Geometry, Red Paint, and Politics." *Daily Star* (Beirut), Sept. 18. At https://www.dailystar.com.lb/Culture/Art/2012/Sep-18/188304-geometry-red-paint-and-politics.ashx.

Terre des Hommes. 2011. *The Dom People and Their Children*. Beirut: Terre des Hommes.

Thorleifsson, Catherine Moe. 2014. "Coping Strategies among Self-Settled Syrians in Lebanon." In "The Syria Crisis, Displacement, and Protection," special issue of *Forced Migration Review* 47. At https://www.fmreview.org/syria/thorleifsson.

Tiger, Lionel. 2001. "Rogue Males." *Guardian*, Oct. 2. At https://www.theguardian.com/world/2001/oct/02/gender.uk.

————. 2002. "Is Manliness Back in Favor? (Interview with Charlotte Hayes)." *Women's Quarterly* 12, no. 3: unpaginated.

Tiltnes, Åge. 2005. *Falling Behind: A Brief on the Living Conditions of Palestinian Refugees in Lebanon.* Oslo, Norway: Fafo Foundation.

———. 2007. "Characteristics of the Palestinian Labour Force in Lebanon." Presentation at a workshop organized by the Follow-Up Committee for Employment of Palestinian Refugees in Lebanon (FCEP), Beirut.

Trabulsi, Fawwaz. 2007. *A History of Modern Lebanon.* London: Pluto.

Tyldum, Guri, and Najla Bashour. 2003. "Education." In *Difficult Past, Uncertain Future: Living Conditions among Palestinian Refugees in Camps and Gatherings in Lebanon,* edited by Ole Fr. Ugland, 107–25. Oslo, Norway: Fafo Foundation.

Ugland, Ole Fr. 2003. "Putting the Pieces Together." In *Difficult Past, Uncertain Future: Living Conditions among Palestinian Refugees in Camps and Gatherings in Lebanon,* edited by Ole Fr. Ugland, 253–76. Oslo, Norway: Fafo Foundation.

United Nations High Commissioner for Refugees. 2020. "Global Focus: Lebanon." Dec. 29. At https://reporting.unhcr.org/sites/default/files/pdfsummaries /GA2021-Lebanon-eng.pdf.

United Nations Relief and Works Agency (UNRWA). 2007. *Mapping Palestinian Refugee Employment.* Beirut: Follow-Up Committee for Employability of Palestine Refugees in Lebanon.

———. 2019. "Palestine Refugees from Syria in Lebanon." At https://www .unrwa.org/palestine-refugees-syria-lebanon.

———. n.d. "Where We Work: Lebanon." At https://www.unrwa.org/where-we -work/lebanon. Accessed Sept. 26, 2021.

Van Aken, Mauro. 2006. "Dancing Belonging: Contesting *Dabka* in the Jordan Valley, Jordan." *Journal of Ethnic and Migration Studies* 32, no. 2: 203–22.

———. 2007. "La mémoire et l'oubli du rituel: Marginalité et dabkeh chez les palestiniens en zone rurale de Jordanie." In *Territoires palestiniens de mémoire,* edited by Nadine Picaudou, 313–40. Paris: Karthala/IFPO.

Von Schnitzler, Antina. 2010. "Gauging Politics: Water, Commensuration, and Citizenship in Post-apartheid South Africa." *Anthropology News* 51, no. 1: 7–9.

Weber, Max. 1978. *Economy and Society.* Translated by Ephraim Fischoff et al. Berkeley: Univ. of California Press.

White, Hayden. 1980. "The Value of Narrativity in the Representation of Reality." *Critical Inquiry* 7, no. 1: 5–27.

Wikan, Unni. 2008. *In Honor of Fadime: Murder and Shame.* Chicago: Univ. of Chicago Press.

Zetter, Roger. 1991. "Labelling Refugees: Forming and Transforming a Bureaucratic Identity." *Journal of Refugee Studies* 4, no. 1: 39–62.

Zureik, Elia. 2001. "Constructing Palestine through Surveillance Practices." *British Journal of Middle Eastern Studies* 28, no. 2: 205–27.

Index

Photos, figures, and tables are indicated by italicized page numbers.

180, 185; *shabāb* and, 70; women
carrying, 51
Burj al-Barajneh camp, 45n1, 70, 184,
217, 229, 259–60
Butler, Judith, 129n3, 148n18, 238n1,
256n3

cactus. *See ṣubbār*
Cairo Agreement (1969), *xxii–xxiii*, 57,
96, 124
Campus in Camps, 267
Camp Wars. *See* War of the Camps
capacity to reason. *See 'aql*
Carpi, Estella, 258
categories, 32–33, 144, 177, 255, 269;
"other" and, 258–59
Cedar Revolution, *xxiii*, 6–7
cemeteries, 188; Christian burials and,
53, 53n3; War of the Camps and,
53–54
Chamoun, Camille, 131, 131n5
childhood. *See ṭufūla*
Christians, 254; burials and, 53, 53n3;
of Lebanon, 46, 68, 113, 138, 141; as
Maronite, 4, 6, 48, 136; as Palestinian
martyrs, 53, 53n3; Palestinians on,
14–15, 61, 69, 138, 221; political statements and, 49, 141
citizenship: agency and, 32; antistate
and, 25–26, 255; Beirut margins and,
32; queering of, 265; Shatila and, 39;
tawṭīn and Palestinians with, 56;
water on, 29–30
class: divisions, 139, 160–61; gender and
sexuality as, 179, 179n35, 180n36;
"other" and, 88, 93–94, 117; working
class and, 173, 253, 267
Clastres, Pierre, 28–29, 63
cohabitation, 256–61

Collier, Jane, 205
Collins, John, 233
colonization: feminism and, 35–36; in
India, 254; masculinity and, 145
Comaroff, Jean, 233–34
Comaroff, John, 233–34
coming of age: age and, 214n18; *'aql*
as, 17, 17n11, 212, 212n16; before *jīl*
al-Nakba, 36; in masculinity and
fidā'iyyīn, 124; maturity and, 132–33,
132n7; *shabāb* and, 17, 17n11, 36–38,
154–56, 159
commitment. *See 'iltizām*
committee. *See jaha*
connecting patterns, 19, 22, 24–25
connections. *See wāsṭa*
Connell, R. W., 127, 145, 206–7
control. *See* social control
cooperatives. *See jam'iyyāt*
Crapanzano, Vincent, 62
Creatura, 20–21
crisis of masculinity, 126, 148, 171–74

Dahiya district, 7, 15, 51, 160, 218–19
daily life, 44, 76, 148–49; Jean-Klein on,
49–50; Lebanese Civil War photos
on, 51; politics and, 50; Shatila camp
and, 14–15, 17; during war violence,
49, 51
daughter. *See bint*
Davis, Rochelle, 115–16, 203–4
days of the revolution. *See 'ayyām
al-thawra*
Deleuze, Gilles, 2, 26–27, 32n19, 38, 41,
66n9, 264
Delphy, Christine, 177
de Man, Paul, 255
Democratic Front for the Liberation of
Palestine (DFLP), 143

homesickness. *See al-ghurba*
homosexuality, 61–62, 174–75
honor. *See sharaf*
hope: *fidāʾiyyīn* and, 199, 209; Palestinians and, 131, 134, 138, 204, 215, 231;
shabāb and, 18–19, 71–72, 83, 85, 102,
110, 164–66, 169, 201
hospitals: in Gaza, 198, 218; health care
and, 85n3, 119, 154, 174–75, 189,
218n23; violence on, 218, 218n23
housing: destruction of, 107; "gatherings" as, 107, 107n7; marriage requiring, 12, 16, 82, 121, 128, 153, 159,
161, 164, 170n30, 214, 220, 220n26;
as vertical, 6, 57, *74*, 116, 218n23,
220n26, 253
hunt. *See al-ṣayd*
hymen, 142

Iatmul culture, 20–21, 23
ʿilim (knowledge), 201
ILO. *See* International Labor
Organization
ʾiltizām (commitment): to family, 137,
213; to revolution, 133
imprisonment: of *fidāʾiyyīn*, 84, 130, 135,
208; mothers on, 50; of *shabāb*, 14,
155–59, 171, 219–20, 247
Inhorn, Marcia, 144, 172
institutional violence, 36–37
International Crisis Group, 117
International Labor Organization (ILO),
101–2, 101n5
internet, 60, 155, 165
intifada, 49–51, 146, 155n23, 233, 235
Israel, 266; on Arabs, 12, 15, 53; Cairo
Agreement on, *xxii–xxiii*, 57, 96, 124;
1948 war and, *xxi*, 89–90, 124, 141,
148; 1967 war by, *xxii*, 48, 148; 1978

war with, *xxii*, 133; 1982 war by, *xxii*,
5–6, 46, 53–54, 57–58, 141, 165, 185,
215; 1993 and, 28, 59; Palestinians
and, 50, 57, 84, 143, 154, 163, 169, 183,
205, 209, 216, 223; settler policies by,
264n4; Shatila and Sabra massacre
with, 53–54, 57, 96, 136–37, 215;
siege by, *xxii*, 96, 185–86, 195; South
Lebanon withdrawal by, *xxiii*; 2006
war by, *xiv*, 52, 54, 83, 167, 190–91,
210, 218–19

Jabra, Stavro, 51
Jacobsen, Laurie, 109
jaha (committee), 118
jamʿiyyāt (cooperatives), 39, 39n24,
111
Jean-Klein, Iris, 49–50
Jennings, Ronald, 120–21, 262
jihad, 117, 145, 164
jīl (generation), 198–99, 205, 207;
fidāʾiyyīn as, 134n10, 138, 182–83,
195–97, 223n32, 230, 232, 235; of
Nakba, 59–60, 79, 139, 150n19, 208,
210, 216, 235; of refugees, 231, 243;
shabāb and, 182, 191–92, 196–97,
212, 229, 235; youth and, 233
jīl al-Nakba (the Catastrophe), *xxi*;
Camp Wars and, 198; coming of age
before, 36; economies before and
after, 89; Lebanon and refugees of,
91; migration and, 131n4; people of,
59–60, 79, 139, 150n19, 208, 210, 216,
235; politics and, 115
jinn (spirits), 70–71, 152, 152n20, 156,
158, 171
jins (sex and gender), 126–27, 176, 178–
80, 179n34, 180n36, 239, 241, 263
Joseph, Suad, 196n8, 261

on methodologies, 38–39; queering
of, 174, 261, 263–64; *shabāb* and, 36,
38, 255; Shatila camp and, 19, 27, 65,
69; sovereignty and, 265–66
precarity, 18–19
principle of reciprocity, *xxi*, 94–95, 97
property ownership, 40, 89, 121; Law 296
on, *xxiii*, 80; power and domination
in, 34; vertical housing and, 6, 57,
74, 116, 218n23, 220n26, 253; women
and, 204
proverb on men, 222, 222nn29–30
psychoanalysis, 62, 127
psychological condition. *See maraḍ nafsī*
Puar, Jasbir, 174
Puig, Nicolas, 223n32, 226, 229–30

al-qaḍiyya al-filasṭīniyya (Palestinian
cause), 183, 191, 193–94, 211, 230
queering: of power, 174, 261, 263–64; of
sexuality, 264–65, 264n4

Rābiṭa ahl Majd al-Krum (Association of
the People of Majd al-Krum), 6, 119
raï (Algerian folk song), 231–32
rap music: age groups and gatherings on,
183–84, 190, 230nn38–39; Hawiyya
Zarqā and, 227–28; hip-hop culture
and, 224–26, 229; history of, 224–25;
in Lebanon, 225–26; NGOs and, 184,
223, 226–28; over-thirty opinion on,
192–93, 195–96, 198, 216; as Palestinian, 226, 229–30, 229nn36–37, 231;
politics and, 225–26, 228–30; by
shabāb, 40, *182*, 182–83, 214; under-
thirty opinion on, 193, 195, 223–24,
223n32; on youth, 188
real estate. *See* property ownership

reconciliation. *See muṣālaḥa*
refugees: disease for, 106–7; as feminine,
147; generation of, 231, 243; labels
and, 113–14; Lebanon and, 91–94,
256–57; movie on, 251–53, 251n1,
252, 265, 269; negative spiral for, 106,
116; Palestinians as stateless, 33, 36,
41, 94–95, 114; politics and, 31, 100;
social and economic inclusion of,
111–12; from Syria, 55, 58, 90, 99,
105–6, 257–60; UNRWA on numbers and, 100; as water or sewage,
29–32, 107
relatedness, 45, 180, 232–33
relatives, 61, 83, 150n19, 151
relief services: UNRWA for, 9–11, 59, 60,
70, 79, 91, 93, 106, 116; UNRWA for
hardship and, 58, 58n6
religions, 17; Lebanon politics and, 4;
maps representing, 48–49; *shabāb*
and, 153–55, 153n21, 159, 169; Shatila
friendships and, 15; *tawṭīn* and Palestinian Sunni, 56; towns and mixtures
of, 138
remittances, 79, 90, 96–97, 106, 109
resistance: agency as, 35, 261–62; *'ayyām
al-thawra* as, 57, 274; as changing,
232; music on, 231
responsibility, 154, 191–92, 203, 234,
249, 257; *mas'ūliyya* as, 18, 168; sisters as, 18, 113, 119–20, 144, 146,
149
revolutionary: commitment to, 133;
fidā'ī as, 71n12, 125, 132–33, 136,
143, 147, 200, 210–11, 235, 254, 266;
masculinity as, 19, 38, 71n12. *See also
'ayyām al-thawra*
right of return. *See ḥaqq al-'awda*
right to work, 6
romana (grenade), 194

Gustavo Barbosa is associate researcher at the Center for Middle Eastern Studies at Universidade Federal Fluminense in Rio de Janeiro, Brazil. He holds a PhD in anthropology from the London School of Economics and Political Science. He has published several articles in English and Portuguese on Palestinian refugees, masculinities, gender, and anthropological theory. His academic interests are political and medical anthropology, gender, refugees, masculinities, and new reproductive technologies. His homepage is at gustavo-barbosa.com.